WITHDRAWAL

Key Concepts for Understanding Curriculum

Key Concepts for Understanding Curriculum is an invaluable guide for all involved in curriculum matters. Now fully updated, this revised and enlarged fourth edition not only provides a solid grounding in the subject but also covers the latest trends and issues affecting the field. Written in Marsh's clear and accessible style, the book details the strengths, weaknesses and controversies around major concepts in curriculum, including

- curriculum planning and development
- curriculum management
- teaching perspectives
- collaborative involvement in curriculum
- curriculum ideology.

Now updated with new chapters on curriculum models, school-based curriculum development, learning studies, ICT developments in assessment, the new edition includes extra detail on standards and essential learning factors that have recently been introduced in a number of countries, including the UK, USA and Australia.

This up-to-date edition of a definitive text will be essential reading for anyone involved in curriculum planning or development. It will be especially useful to students training to be teachers, and practising teachers following professional development programmes.

Colin J. Marsh is Adjunct Professor at Curtin University, Western Australia. He has been involved in teaching at all levels, from primary school to university, over many years. He has written over thirty books on teaching and learning, including in the areas of curriculum planning, development and evaluation.

The Teacher's Library

Series Editor: Professor Ivor F. Goodson, Warner Graduate School, University of Rochester, USA and Applied Research in Education, University of East Anglia, Norwich, UK

The prime intention of The Teachers' Library is to provide impetus and support to analytical and research-oriented teaching practice. Each book in the series has been written to satisfy the needs of teachers wishing to study education and reflect upon their own practice.

Search and Re-search
What the inquiring teacher needs
to know
Rita S. Brause and John S. Mayher

Doing Qualitative Research
Circles within circles
*Margot Ely, Margaret Anzul, Teri Freidman,
Diane Garner and Ann McCormack*

Beginning Qualitative Research
P. Maykut and R. Morehouse

Becoming a Teacher
Gary Borich

Participatory Evaluation in Education
J. Bradley Cousins and Lorna M. Earl

Schooling for Change
*Andy Hargreaves and Lorna M. Earl
and J. Ryan*

Studying School Subjects
Ivor F. Goodson and Colin J. Marsh

On Writing Qualitative Research
Living by words
*Margot Ely, Ruth Vinz, Maryann Downing and
Margaret Anzul*

Subject Knowledge
Readings for the study of school subjects
*Ivor F. Goodson with
Christopher J. Anstead and
J. Marshall Mangan*

**Fundamentals of Education
Research, new edition**
Gary Anderson

Students as Researchers
Creating classrooms that matter
Shirley R. Steinberg and Joe L. Kinchloe

Teachers as Researchers
Qualitative inquiry as a path to
empowerment, 2nd edition
Joe L. Kincheloe

**Key Concepts for Understanding
Curriculum, 4th edition**
Colin J. Marsh

**Becoming a Scholar–Practitioner
Leader**
The critical empowerment of educators
Raymond Horn and Patrick Jenlink

Key Concepts for Understanding Curriculum

Fourth edition

Colin J. Marsh

Routledge
Taylor & Francis Group

LONDON AND NEW YORK

First published 2009
by Routledge
2 Park Square, Milton Park, Abingdon, Oxon OX14 4RN

Simultaneously published in the USA and Canada
by Routledge
270 Madison Ave, New York, NY 10016

Routledge is an imprint of the Taylor & Francis Group, an informa business

© 2009 Colin J. Marsh

Typeset in Times New Roman by
Taylor & Francis Books
Printed and bound in Great Britain by
CPI Antony Rowe, Chippenham, Wiltshire

British Library Cataloguing in Publication Data
A catalogue record for this book is available from the British Library

Library of Congress Cataloging in Publication Data
Marsh, Colin J.
  Key concepts for understanding curriculum / Colin J. Marsh. – 4th ed.
    p. cm.
  1. Education–Curricula. 2. Curriculum planning. 3. Education–Curricula–
  Philosophy. 4. Educational tests and measurements. I. Title.
  LB1570.M3668 2009
375'.001–dc22   2008023711

ISBN 978-0-415-46577-9 (hbk)
ISBN 978-0-415-46578-6 (pbk)

March 28, 2009

To Glen, for all her love and support

Contents

Illustrations

Figures

Tables

Boxes

Preface

Reynolds (2003) uses various metaphors to describe curriculum – lines of flight; a river runs through it – and to express images of inspiration, movement, continuity and integration.

Glatthorn and Jailall (2000) also use the metaphor of curriculum as several streams flowing through the system 'ebbing at times, then gathering strength and flowing together in a dynamic confluence' (p. 98).

By contrast, Wright (2000) describes curriculum in more chaotic but cutting-edge ways. He argues that it is problematic to categorize the field of curriculum – 'as difficult as attempting to nail Jell-O to a wall' (p. 12).

There continues to be much interest in curriculum matters – a range of very different theoretical discourses continue to be widely discussed. Major initiatives by governments and politicians to exert their respective stamps on what they consider to be essential learning and standards have appeared (and sometimes reappeared).

As we close out the final years of the first decade of the twenty-first century we should reflect on these heady days. There is an international interest in the OECD's Programme for International Student Assessment (PISA) rankings between countries. Ambitious, large-scale curriculum reforms have been initiated in a number of countries, especially the UK and the USA and also in Singapore and Hong Kong. The results to date have demonstrated some short-term successes but long-term issues still have to be resolved.

The players who are taking leading roles in policy formulation are changing, with increasing pressures coming from politicians and employer groups, as well as from community interest groups, parents, teachers and students. A number of these individuals and groups have very limited understanding of curriculum theories, principles and processes, even though they are prepared to commit enormous amounts of funds and energy to advance their preferred solutions to specific curriculum problems.

Key Concepts for Understanding the Curriculum is aimed at assisting various personnel concerned about and involved in curriculum decision-making. Of course, a major clientele are those pre-service teachers who will be commencing full-time careers in schools, namely students who are taking teacher education degrees (BA (Education), Bachelor of Education, Diploma of Education, Diploma of Teaching and PGCEs). Another major group who are likely to be very interested in the book include those practising teachers who are embarking upon professional development programmes. Parents and community members involved as school governors and members of school councils, boards and districts will obtain considerable assistance from the succinctly stated commentaries about major curriculum concepts.

The book provides details about twenty-one major concepts in curriculum. In such a small space each chapter cannot provide an exhaustive treatment of each concept, but every attempt has been made to highlight major features, controversies, strengths and weaknesses. In particular, the follow-up questions and web sources challenge the reader to reflect further upon specific issues relating to each concept and there is a listing of recent references at the end of the book.

I acknowledge various colleagues in curriculum, both within Australia and in the United Kingdom, the United States of America and Canada, who have helped me hone my ideas over the decades about curriculum. They include Michael Fullan, Gene Hall, Paul Klohr, Michael Huberman, Elliot Eisner, Bill Reid, Helen Simons, Kerry Kennedy, Eric Hoyle, Ray Bolam, Michal Connelly, Christine Deer, David Smith, Noel Gough, Chris Day, Ivor Goodson, Brian Caldwell, Paul Morris, David Tripp and John Elliott.

The fourth edition includes a number of new concepts which are having considerable impact during the twenty-first century.

For permission to reproduce figures and tables I am most grateful to Patricia Broadfoot, Brian Caldwell, Chris Day, Stephen Kemmis and Barry Fraser. A special word of thanks is due to Suzanne Stocker for her expert secretarial assistance in the preparation of the manuscript.

Part I

Introduction

Chapter 1

What is curriculum?

Introduction

Defining the word curriculum is no easy matter. Perhaps the most common definition derives from the word's Latin root, which means 'racecourse'. Indeed, for many students, the school curriculum is a race to be run, a series of obstacles or hurdles (subjects) to be passed. It is important to keep in mind that schools in Western civilization have been heavily influenced since the fourth century BC by the philosophies of Plato and Aristotle and that the word curriculum has been used historically to describe the subjects taught during the classical period of Greek civilization. The interpretation of the word curriculum broadened in the twentieth century to include subjects other than the classics. Today, school documents, newspaper articles, committee reports and many academic textbooks refer to any and all subjects offered or prescribed as 'the curriculum of the school'.

In the 1970s Pinar (1974) produced a different term, 'currere' – the Latin infinitive of curriculum, because he wanted to highlight the running (or lived experience). He has subsequently elaborated on this term (Pinar et al., 1995; Pinar, 2004) and has emphasized its value in self-study via an autobiographical method.

One useful starting point when studying what is curriculum is to consider three levels, namely the 'planned curriculum', the 'enacted curriculum' and the 'experienced curriculum' (Marsh and Willis, 2007).

The planned curriculum is all about what knowledge is of most worth – the important goals and objectives. Campbell (2006) refers to this as 'curricular authority' – the legitimacy of standardized curricular guidelines.

The enacted curriculum deals with professional judgements about the type of curriculum to be implemented and evaluated. Teachers have to judge the appropriate pedagogical knowledge to use. As noted by Campbell (2006), teachers' professional authority in enacting the curriculum may cause conflicts with the planned curriculum. Harris (2005) describes some of the contestation that can occur between a curriculum plan (for example a history syllabus) and how it is implemented (enacted).

The experienced curriculum refers to what actually happens in the classroom. As noted by Smith and Lovat (2003), lived experience defies complete description either before or after it happens – it is individual, ongoing and unpredictable (Marsh and Willis, 2007). Kennedy (2005) notes that curriculum experiences are no longer confined to the classroom. There is an increasing gap now between "'official' school knowledge and real-world knowledge to which students have access through information technology" (p. 37). He suggests that a major issue for school curriculum in the twenty-first century is how to 'create a sense of community and common values in a context where knowledge cannot be restricted in any way and where individual control is much more powerful' (p. 37).

McNeil (2003) concentrates upon the enacted curriculum but takes it further by highlighting the live curriculum rather than the inert, dead curriculum. He contends that the live curriculum is when teachers and students engage in classroom activities that are meaningful.

Much earlier, Whitehead (1929) used the metaphor of romance to characterize the rhythm of curriculum. As reported in Walker and Soltis (2004), he argued that 'we should begin an engagement with any subject in a romantic way, feeling excitement in its presence, being aroused by its attractiveness, and enjoying its company' (p. 44).

Tomlinson and Germundson (2007) elaborate on the rhythm of curriculum by comparing teaching to creating jazz. The enacted curriculum for these authors is characterized by a teacher blending musical sounds: 'blue notes for expressive purposes and syncopation and swing to surprise ... to create curriculum with the soul of jazz – curriculum that gets under the skin of young learners' (p. 27).

Some definitions of curriculum

Many writers advocate their own preferred definition of curriculum, which emphasizes other meanings or connotations, particularly those the term has taken on recently. According to Portelli (1987), more than 120 definitions of the term appear in the professional literature devoted to curriculum, presumably because authors are concerned about either delimiting what the term means or establishing new meanings that have become associated with it.

Hlebowitsh (1993) criticizes commentators in the curriculum field who focus 'only on certain facets of early curriculum thought while ignoring others' (p. 2).

We need to be watchful, therefore, about definitions that capture only a few of the various characteristics of curriculum (Toombs and Tierney, 1993), especially those that are partisan or biased.

Oliva (1997) also points out that definitions of curriculum can be conceived in narrow or broad ways. He suggests that differences in the substance of definitions of curriculum are largely due to whether the emphasis is upon:

- purposes of goals of the curriculum (for example a curriculum is to develop reflective thinking);

- contexts within which the curriculum is found (for example a curriculum is to develop the individual learner in all aspects of growth); or
- strategies used throughout the curriculum (for example a curriculum is to develop problem-solving processes).

Portelli (1987), drawing on a metaphor developed by Soltis (1978), notes: 'Those who look for the definition of curriculum are like a sincere but misguided centaur hunter, who even with a fully provisioned safari and a gun kept always at the ready, nonetheless will never require the services of a taxidermist' (p. 364).

The incompleteness of any definition notwithstanding, certain definitions of the term can provide insights about common emphases and characteristics within the general idea of curriculum. Consider, for example, the following definitions of curriculum:

- Curriculum is the 'permanent' subjects that embody essential knowledge.
- Curriculum is those subjects that are most useful for contemporary living.
- Curriculum is all planned learnings for which the school is responsible.
- Curriculum is the totality of learning experiences so that students can attain general skills and knowledge at a variety of learning sites.
- Curriculum is what the students construct from working with the computer and its various networks, such as the Internet.
- Curriculum is the questioning of authority and the searching for complex views of human situations.

Definition I

Curriculum is such 'permanent' subjects as grammar, reading, logic, rhetoric, mathematics, and the greatest books of the Western world that best embody essential knowledge.

An example is the National Curriculum enacted in the United Kingdom in 1988, which prescribed the curriculum in terms of three core and seven foundational subjects, including specific content and specific goals for student achievement in each subject.

The No Child Left Behind (NCLB) legislation introduced into the US in 2001 requires tests in reading and maths annually for students in grades 3–8 and once in high school. This is an unprecedented focus on two traditional subjects, reading and maths. What is not tested are subjects such as history, art, civics, music and physical education and these are deemed by many students as not worth knowing (Guilfoyle, 2006).

Problems posed by the definition   This definition suggests that the curriculum is limited to only a few academic subjects. It assumes that what is studied is what is learned. It does not address questions such as: does the state of knowledge change? If so, shouldn't the subjects making up the curriculum also change? What makes learning such subjects essential? Goodson and Marsh (1996) point out that the National Curriculum in the United Kingdom is simply a reconstitution of the subjects included in the Secondary Regulations of 1904, suggesting that 'historical amnesia allows curriculum reconstruction to be presented as curriculum revolution' (p. 157). Griffith (2000) contends that a knowledge-based curriculum such as the National Curriculum does not exist independently of space and time. It should not be considered ahistorically, for it is neither neutral, factual nor value free.

Definition 2

Curriculum is those subjects that are most useful for living in contemporary society.

The subjects that make up this curriculum are usually chosen in terms of major present-day issues and problems within society, but the definition itself does not preclude individual students from making their own choices about which subjects are most useful.

According to Rothstein, Wilder and Jacobsen (2007) a balanced curriculum should be concerned about contemporary living skills such as critical thinking, project-based learning and social skills.

Wilson (2002) argues that curriculum must include higher-order skills such as teaching students to think critically and to communicate complex ideas clearly.

Problems posed by the definition   This definition seems to imply that what is contemporary has more value than what is long-lasting. It encourages schools and students to accommodate themselves to society as it exists instead of attempting to improve it. It leaves open questions such as: what accounts for stability in the curriculum? What is useful knowledge? If useful practical skills are increasingly emphasized, what becomes of intellectual development?

Definition 3

Curriculum is all planned learnings for which the school is responsible.

'Planned learnings' can be long written documents specifying content, shorter lists of intended learning outcomes, or simply the general ideas of teachers about what students should know. Exponents of curriculum as a plan include Saylor, Alexander, and Lewis (1981), Beauchamp (1981) and Posner (1998).

Problems posed by the definition   This definition seems to assume that what is studied is learned. It may limit 'planned learnings' to those that are easiest to achieve, not those that are most desirable. It does not address questions such as: on what basis does the school select and take responsibility for certain learnings while excluding others? Is it possible for teachers to separate the ends of instruction from the means? Are unplanned, but actual, learnings excluded from the curriculum?

The NCLB Act in the USA is forcing schools to plan very carefully for the teaching of reading and maths (and science since 2007). By implication there is less pressure to plan for other subjects. There are penalties for schools if their students do not reach specified levels of proficiency. The National Literacy Strategy and the National Numeracy Strategy in the UK are also forcing schools to concentrate their planning and their respective school timetables on maths and literacy.

Armstrong (2007) suggests that education policy-makers are building a superhighway across today's education landscape: 'All byways in the journey from early childhood to early adulthood are now being aligned – test scores and benchmarks and accountability are the bulldozers, cement mixers and asphalt pavers that are constructing this curriculum superhighway' (p.16).

Definition 4

Curriculum is the totality of learning experiences provided to students so that they can attain general skills and knowledge at a variety of learning sites.

Emphasis is on learning rather than teaching, especially learning skills and knowledge at sites other than schools. The assumption is that all sites – including workplace sites – can be conducive to learning general knowledge. This approach to curriculum has been heavily publicized in a number of countries and is usually supported for economic reasons by business organizations, other vocationally oriented groups and advocates of explicit competency standards.

Problems posed by the definition   This definition usually leads to a narrow technical-functionalist approach to curriculum, requiring that unduly large numbers of outcomes and high levels of specificity be identified. Walker (1994) and Cairns (1992) are critical of the uniformity and the focus on minimum standards the definition encourages. Moore (2006) points out that the economic well-being of a nation depends on much besides vocational training.

Kennedy (2005) concludes that a curriculum which only focuses on key competencies for the world of paid employment is deficient. The curriculum should 'include a full range of skills and competencies relevant throughout the life span' (p. 56). Reid (2007) also takes a wider view of competencies, which he terms 'capacities', such as communication, civic participation, health and well-being.

Definition 5

Curriculum is what the student constructs from working with the computer and its various networks, such as the Internet.

Obviously, this is a modern definition. It assumes that computers are every-where – in the home, school and office – and students, perceiving them as part of the natural landscape, are thriving. Advocates argue that the new comput-ing technologies have created a culture for increasingly active learning; stu-dents can construct their own meanings as they locate sources on the Internet, explore issues and communicate with others. Social skills are also developed through chat groups, conferences and e-mail communications.

Problems posed by the definition   Although some writers such as Vine *et al.* (2000) contend that schools in the near future will change drastically as students access more electronic resources from the home, others such as Reid (2000) and Westbury (2000) believe that schools will remain long-enduring institutions.

Pinar (2004) suggests that administrators are wrongly fantasizing the future as technological and information-based. He concludes that 'information is not knowledge, of course, and without ethical and intellectual judgment – which cannot be programmed into a machine – the Age of Information is an Age of Ignorance' (p. xii).

Budin (1999) reminds us that technology is not a neutral tool. What is now available on the Internet, for example, is not necessarily what should be on it or what will be on it tomorrow. Furthermore, not all students have the same level of access to the Internet, and the learning it promotes may prove to be far more passive than is now commonly believed. We should, therefore, be wary of exces-sive claims about active or constructivist learning made possible by computers.

Definition 6

Curriculum is the questioning of authority and the searching for complex views of human situations.

This definition is consistent with the ancient Socratic maxim 'the unexamined life is not worth living'. However, it may also overly encourage rejection of what is, making it a postmodernist definition. The term postmodernist implies opposition to widely used ('modern') values and practices. Hence, postmodernists are disparate in their own views, usually sharing only a desire to challenge what is modern, a readiness to accept the unaccepted and a willingness to conceptualize new ways of thinking (see also Chapter 21).

Reynolds and Webber (2004) use such terms as 'advocating multiplicity' (p. 3); 'the struggle is to keep finding lines that disrupt and overturn and tactically weave through the globalised corporate order' (p. 4).

Problems posed by the definition Postmodernism reduced simply to the process of questioning may not be helpful in identifying in practice how students should spend their time and energy. Although many authors are enthusiastic about the general potential of postmodernist thinking (Atkinson, 2000; Pinar, 2004), others (Barrow, 1999) contend that it is overly general, vague and confused. It is subject to the charge of relativism. Moore (2006) contends there is a fatal, internal contradiction among those postmodernists who state that all truth is relative, when this statement itself would have to be nonrelative in order to be true.

Characteristics of curriculum

Some curriculum experts, such as Goodlad (1979), contend that an analysis of definitions is a useful starting point for examining the field of curriculum. Other writers argue that there are important concepts or characteristics that need to be considered and which give some insights into how particular value orientations have evolved and why (Westbury, 2007).

Walker (2003) argues that the fundamental concepts of curriculum include:

- content: which may be depicted in terms of concept maps, topics and themes, all of which are abstractions which people have invested and named;
- purpose: usually categorized as intellectual, social and personal; often divided into superordinate purposes; stated purposes are not always reliable indicators of actions;
- organization: planning is based upon scope and sequence (order of presence over time); and can be tightly organized or relatively open-ended.

Other writers such as Beane (2001) produce principles of curriculum but they are more value-oriented and less generic. For example, he lists five major principles about curriculum:

- concern with the experiences of learners;
- making decisions about both content and process;
- making decisions about a variety of issues and topics;
- involving many groups;
- decision-making at many levels.

It is evident that these authors have a particular conception of curriculum; perhaps a combination of student- and society-centred. Inevitably, if specific principles are given a high priority, then a particular conception of curriculum emerges. Longstreet and Shane (1993) refer to four major conceptions of curriculum:

- society-oriented curriculum: the purpose of schooling is to serve society;
- student-centred curriculum: the student is the crucial source of all curriculum;

- knowledge-centred curriculum: knowledge is the heart of curriculum;
- eclectic curriculum: various compromises are possible, including mindless eclecticism!

The conceptions or orientations of curriculum produced by Eisner and Vallance (1974) are often cited in literature, namely:

- a cognitive process orientation: cognitive skills applicable to a wide range of intellectual problems;
- technological orientation: to develop means to achieve pre-specified ends;
- self-actualization orientation: individual students discover and develop their unique identities;
- social reconstructionist orientation: schools must be an agency of social change;
- academic rationalist orientation: to use and appreciate the ideas and works of the various disciplines.

It is interesting to note that Vallance (1986) modified these orientations twelve years later by deleting 'self-actualization' and adding 'personal success' (pursuing a specific, practical end) and a 'curriculum for personal commitment' (pursuing learning for its inherent rewards).

These conceptions of curriculum are useful to the extent that they remind educators of some value orientations that they may be following, whether directly or indirectly. Yet others, such as Pinar *et al.* (1995), argue that these conceptions are stereotypes and are of little value.

Who is involved in curriculum?

Curriculum workers are many and include school-based personnel such as teachers, principals and parents and university-based specialists, industry and community groups, and government agencies and politicians.

A large number of those working in the curriculum field are involved in serving the daily and technical needs of those who work in schools. This has been the traditional role over the decades where the focus has been upon curriculum development for school contexts.

Pinar *et al.* (1995) refer to the 'shifting domain of curriculum development as politicians, textbook companies, and subject-matter specialists in the university, rather than school practitioners and university professors of curriculum, exercise leadership and control over curriculum development' (p. 41). In a later publication, Pinar (2004) argues that 'public-school teachers have been reduced to domestic workers instructed by politicians' (p. xi) and that '[e]ducation professors are losing – have lost? – control of the curriculum we teach' (p. xi).

It is certainly the case in most OECD (developed) countries that a wider range of interest groups are now involved in curriculum development (Ross,

2000). Curriculum in the twenty-first century is indeed moving in many directions and some would assert that this reflects a conceptual advance (Jackson, 1992) and a more sophisticated view of the curriculum. Others would argue that curriculum as a field of study is still conceptually underdeveloped (Goodlad and Su, 1992) and rather like 'trying to nail Jell-O to the wall'! (Wright, 2000).

Reflections and issues

1 There are very divergent views about the nature of curriculum. What definition of curriculum do you support? Justify your choice.
2 Trying to clarify central concepts by proposing definitions for them has been popular in many fields (Portelli, 1987). Have these concepts and definitions proven useful in the field of curriculum?
3 'The struggle over the definition of curriculum is a matter of social and political priorities as well as intellectual discourse' (Goodson, 1988, p. 23). Reflect upon a particular period of time and analyse the initiatives, successes and failures which occurred in terms of curriculum development or policy development.
4 'If the curriculum is to be the instrument of change in education, its meanings and operational terms must be clearer than they are currently' (Toombs and Tierney, 1993, p. 175). Discuss.
5 'The term "social subjects" rarely occurs in the current formulations of the National Curriculum or the whole curriculum in the United Kingdom; indeed the very word "society" is notable by its infrequency' (Campbell, 1993, p. 137). This indicate deficiencies in the conceptions of curriculum incorporated into the National Curriculum. Discuss.

Web sources

Web Definitions for Curriculum, wordnet.princeton.edu/perl/webwn – extracted 20 February 2008.
What is Curriculum?, www.uwsp.edu/education/wilson/curric/definigcurriculum.htm – extracted 20 February 2008.
Issues of Teaching and Learning, www.csd.uwa.edu.au/newsleter/issue0795.html – extracted 20 February 2008.
What Is Curriculum – Based Measurement?, www.studentprogress.org/families.asp – extracted 20 February 2008.

Chapter 2

Introducing key concepts

Introduction

We make sense of our world and go about our daily lives by engaging in concept building. We acquire and develop concepts so that we can gain meaning about persons and events and in turn communicate these meaning to others.

Some concepts are clearly of more importance than others. The key concepts provide us with the power to explore a variety of situations and events and to make significant connections. Other concepts may be meaningful in more limited situations but play a part in connecting unrelated facts.

Every field of study contains a number of key concepts and lesser concepts which relate to substantive and methodological issues unique to that discipline/field of study. Not unexpectedly, scholars differ over their respective lists of key concepts, but there is, nevertheless, considerable agreement (see, for example, Hayes, 2006). With regard to the curriculum field there is a moderate degree of agreement over key concepts.

Searching for key concepts

To be able to provide any commentary on key concepts in curriculum assumes of course that we have access to sources of information that enable us to make definitive statements.

A wide range of personnel are involved in making curriculum, including school personnel, researchers, academics, administrators, politicians and various interest groups. They go about their tasks in various ways such as via planning meetings, informal discussions, writing reports, papers, handbooks, textbooks, giving talks, lectures, workshops, etc.

To ensure that a list of key concepts is comprehensive and representative of all these sources would be an extremely daunting task. A proxy often used by researchers is to examine textbooks, especially synoptic textbooks (those books which provide comprehensive accounts and summaries of a wide range of concepts, topics and issues in curriculum).

Schubert *et al.* (2002) undertook a detailed analysis of textbooks over the period 1861–2000 and this volume provides a valuable overview of curriculum thought over major historical periods. Marsh and Stafford (1988) provided a similar historical analysis of major curriculum books written by Australian authors over the period 1910–88. Green (2003) undertook a comprehensive review of Australian authors writing in the curriculum field.

Major synoptic texts published in the USA include Doll (1996), Oliva (2004) and Marsh and Willis (2007). All of these are longstanding texts in the USA and have undergone subsequent editions.

Pinar *et al.*'s (1995) *Understanding Curriculum: An Introduction to the Study of Historical and Contemporary Curriculum Discourses*, an encyclopaedic volume of diverse discourses, represents a very important but different form of synoptic text.

In subsequent volumes, Pinar (2004) and Reynolds and Webber (2004) continue with presentations of diverse discourses – a complex, cacophonous chorus from competing theoretical points of view.

These texts tend to be very comprehensive and cover a number of key concepts within the broad categories of:

- conceptions of curriculum/models/approaches;
- curriculum history;
- curriculum policy and policy-makers, politics of curriculum;
- curriculum development procedures/change/improvement/planning steps;
- issues and trends/problems/future directions;
- discourses of gender, race – postmodern, political, historical, phenomenological (especially Pinar *et al.*, 1995).

A text published in the United Kingdom (Ross, 2000), has a major focus upon historical developments in curriculum in that country, but also includes sections on curriculum and reproduction, hidden curriculum, content-driven, objectives-driven and process-driven curricula.

In Australia, three major texts focus directly upon curriculum concepts. Brady and Kennedy (2007) examine social contexts, curriculum planning models, assessment and evaluation, and curriculum change. Marsh (2008) examines student learning, curriculum planning models, providing for individual differences, assessment and reporting, school culture, standards, innovation, and change. Smith and Lovat (2003) examine the origins and nature of curriculum, curriculum and ideology, curriculum and the foundational disciplines, critical theory, assessment and evaluation, curriculum change, and curriculum futures.

Taken overall, it is very evident that there are a number of common key concepts that are included in these synoptic texts.

Categories of concepts included in this volume

After examining a wide range of synoptic curriculum texts, including those described above, a decision was made to include material relating to two sets of categories:

1 generic issues in curriculum; and
2 alternative perspectives.

By concentrating upon a single concept in each chapter, it is possible, of course, to have many different groupings, and readers are encouraged to explore their own interests and swap around their order of reading chapters. Each chapter focuses upon a key concept in terms of its major characteristics, strengths and weaknesses. Follow-up questions and references are also included in each chapter.

Generic categories

The generic categories include the following:

- curriculum planning and development;
- curriculum management;
- teaching perspectives;
- collaborative involvement in curriculum;
- curriculum ideology.

Curriculum planning and development

This is Part II of the book (after the introductory section) and, together with the opening chapter, includes six chapters dealing with the following topics:

- using curriculum models as a planning tool (Chapter 3);
- curriculum frameworks (Chapter 4);
- objectives, learning outcomes and standards (Chapter 5);
- selecting and organizing teaching and learning modes (Chapter 6);
- assessment, grading and reporting (Chapter 7);
- curriculum implementation (Chapter 8).

These chapters represent the standard planning processes in developing curriculum.

Curriculum orientations have moved over the decades and previous inviolable principles have been overtaken by postmodern uncertainties (Chapter 1). Teachers are turning more to curriculum models to assist them with planning their units of work. A range of different models are analysed in Chapter 3.

In many countries curriculum frameworks have been established to guide (some would argue, enforce) curriculum planning and development (Chapter 4).

'Objectives', 'Outcomes' and 'Standards' continue to stir educationalists. Arguments for outcomes approaches were very dominant in the 1990s but subsequently standards, especially subject standards, are being given a higher priority (Chapter 5).

Teaching and learning modes are widening as teachers attempt to match teacher and student priorities. There is considerable research support for specific learning modes, such as cooperative learning (Chapter 6).

Assessment and grading methods are also diversifying due to pressures from educators proposing 'authentic' and 'performance-based' assessment (Chapter 7).

Curriculum implementation is a critical phase in curriculum development because this is where a plan becomes a reality with real students in a real classroom (Chapter 8).

Curriculum management

This is Part III of the book and includes five chapters dealing with the following topics:

- innovation and planned change (Chapter 9);
- leadership and the school principal (Chapter 10);
- school-based curriculum development (SBCD) (Chapter 11);
- school evaluations/reviews (Chapter 12);
- curriculum reform (Chapter 13).

These span recurring and ongoing issues in curriculum, largely viewed from a management perspective. Curriculum reform (Chapter 13) can also, of course, be a grassroots/teacher-driven initiative, but over recent times curriculum reform has been decidedly top-down by political/executive directives.

Teaching perspectives

This is Part IV of the book and includes two chapters dealing with the following topics:

- learning environments (Chapter 14);
- teacher appraisal (Chapter 15).

Learning environments both within and outside the school are an integral part of the learning process and are of major concern to teachers and students (Chapter 14). Teacher appraisals have loomed large in recent years as accountability pressures continue to increase. However, there are some positive elements which can lead to improved teacher performances and skills (Chapter 15).

Collaborative involvement in curriculum

This is Part V of the book and includes three chapters dealing with the following topics:

- decision-makers, stakeholders and influences (Chapter 16);
- teachers as researchers: action research and lesson study (Chapter 17);
- parent–teacher participation (Chapter 18).

There are a myriad of stakeholders in curriculum and the list continues to grow (see Chapter 16)!

Action research and lesson study are powerful tools for individual teachers and groups of teachers to enquire about and improve their practices (Chapter 17).

Parents' work with schools can vary enormously but there is a powerful pedagogical reason for their close involvement (Chapter 18).

Curriculum ideology

This is Part VI of the book and includes three chapters dealing with the following topics:

- curriculum theorizing (Chapter 19);
- gender, sexuality and the curriculum (Chapter 20);
- postmodernism and the curriculum (Chapter 21).

Curriculum theorizing is a general process whereby individuals discern emerging patterns in curriculum, identify common patterns and issues and relate these patterns to their own teaching context. There are many diverse approaches to curriculum theorizing ranging from prescriptive to critical-exploratory theorizers (Chapter 19).

Theorizing about the unequal ways in which people are treated because of their gender and sexuality is the focus of gender studies. This includes an analysis of feminist pedagogy and theorizing about male identity, especially challenges to heteronormativity (Chapter 20).

Postmodernism refers to both social conditions and practices. Postmodernists challenge the standardized and traditional, positivist approaches to curriculum development.

Alternative perspectives

As indicated above, every reader of curriculum will have his or her unique experiences and priorities and may want to read the book in different ways. A small number of possible alternative perspectives are listed below.

Student-centred perspective

The concepts included in the chapters which follow emphasize student interests and problems of unequal power relationships between students and teachers. Questions are raised about functions of schools, about schools as a

source of conflict for students and about the legal and moral rights of students
as clients and consumers.

The following chapters have relevant sections.

- student outcomes (Chapter 5);
- student-oriented modes of learning (Chapter 6);
- authentic assessment (Chapter 7);
- classroom and out-of-school learning environments (Chapter 14);
- students as stakeholders (Chapter 16);
- gender inequalities (Chapter 20).

Politics of curriculum perspective

A perspective which is very evident in the curriculum literature relates to
'politics of curriculum'. According to Longstreet and Shane,

> Politics of every sort and at every level of society affect the processes of
> curriculum, complicating many times over what appears at first glance to
> be no more than a simple process of translating the overall curriculum
> design in to a practical plan for students learning.
>
> (Longstreet and Shane, 1993, p. 93)

The following chapters have relevant sections:

- curriculum models (Chapter 3);
- restriction of curriculum frameworks (Chapter 4);
- standards and political mandates (Chapter 5);
- assessment uses and accountability (Chapter 7);
- measuring curriculum implementation (Chapter 8);
- change leaders (Chapter 9);
- curriculum development (Chapter 11);
- reform reports (Chapter 13);
- why do teacher appraisals (Chapter 15)?;
- decision-makers and influences (Chapter 16);
- critical exploratory theorizers (Chapter 19);
- poststructuralism and postcolonialism (Chapter 21).

Future studies and the curriculum perspective

Another theme which is also frequently cited in the literature is 'future studies
and the curriculum'. As we come to the close of the first decade of a new
millennium there are new emerging pressures and priorities. Various predictions
have been made about likely issues for teachers and students in the twenty-first
century. Yet the most daunting aspect of all is the profound uncertainty of the
future and the need to make decisions despite the uncertainty.

Chapters which allude to future orientations include the following.

- making use of technology (Chapter 6);
- change strategies and tactics (Chapter 9);
- categories of reform (Chapter 13);
- learning settings outside school (Chapter 14);
- decision-makers (Chapter 16);
- critical exploratory theorizers (Chapter 19);
- gender analysis and feminist pedagogy (Chapter 20);
- gender analysis and male identity (Chapter 20);
- postmodernism and schooling (Chapter 21).

Many other themes might be also described but these examples are sufficient to illustrate the combination that can be formed. There are benefits for the reader in reflecting upon each concept and considering examples from their teaching experiences which tend either to support or not to support the statements included in a chapter. The questions at the end of each chapter and the web sources should also stimulate the reader to ask probing questions and to explore matters further, perhaps by making use of the references at the end of the book.

There are no simple answers or recipes for major issues in curriculum. However, the time spent in reflecting extensively on curriculum matters can be most rewarding. It is to be hoped that the key concepts presented in this volume provide an accessible entry-point for readers embarking upon this journey.

Concluding comments

It is important to read this book in terms of your major interest in curriculum. The illustrated perspectives included here give an idea of how the chapters can be grouped in various ways. However, the final task of reflection comes back to the reader, who must decide his or her personal priorities.

Reflections and issues

1 From references you have read to date what do you consider are major curriculum concepts? Make a list of these and provide a brief reason for each selection.
2 To what extent do you consider that curriculum philosophies (for example constructivism, humanism, critical social theory) influence which key concepts are selected? Give examples.
3 Is it possible to give priority to several emphases such as student-centred and teacher management or are they diametrically opposed? Give examples.

Web sources

Key Concepts in Maths and Language Arts, http://www.bced.gov.bc.ca/irp/irp.htm – extracted 20 February 2008.

Curriculum Concepts, Theoretical Perspectives and Themes, www.uwd.ca/nursing/ CurriculumConcepts – extracted 20 February 2008.

What Is Concept-Based Curriculum?, www.d18.s-cook.k12.il.us/central/curriculum/ what.html – extracted 20 February 2008.

Curriculum Terms and Concepts, webinstituteforteachers.org/2001/modules/termsconcepts/index.htm – extracted 20 February 2008.

Key Concepts Manual, www.bced.gov.bc.ca/irp/key_concepts.pdf – extracted 20 February 2008.

Part II

Curriculum planning and development

Chapter 3

Using curriculum models as a planning tool

Introduction

When we choose to teach in a certain way in a classroom we are really following some kind of personal theory or model. It may be implicit rather than explicit but it is still evident.

The value of curriculum models

There are a number of fundamental questions that always need to be asked in curriculum. Kliebard (1977) suggests that the fundamental question for any curriculum theory is: what should we teach? This question then leads us to consider other questions, such as:

- Why should we teach this rather than that?
- Who should have access to what knowledge?
- What rules should govern the teaching of what has been selected?
- How should various parts of the curriculum be interrelated in order to create a coherent whole?

Beyer and Apple (1998), Posner (1998) and Ross (2000) extend this list to include broader, more politically sensitive questions:

- What should count as knowledge? As knowing? What does not count as legitimate knowledge?
- Who defines what counts as legitimate knowledge?
- Who shall control the selection and distribution of knowledge?
- Who has the greatest access to high-status and high-prestige knowledge?
- How shall curricular knowledge be made accessible to students?
- How do we link the curriculum knowledge to the biographies and personal meanings of students?

If there was only *one* simple answer to these questions then the process of curriculum planning would indeed be very simple. Alas, this is not the case. It seems that the diverse classroom settings and circumstances that curriculum decisions need to take into account defy any attempt to provide straightforward answers to these questions. Even the most fundamental question about curriculum seems, therefore, to lead to an infinite regress of sub-questions.

As a consequence we have to turn to curriculum models which can identify basic considerations that must be accounted for in curriculum decisions and can show their interrelationships. Curriculum models can provide useful, detailed perspectives on some particulars of the curriculum in action, but not the total picture. Some curriculum writers distinguish between 'curriculum models' and 'curriculum algorithms'. 'Models' refers mainly to conceptualizations, while 'algorithms' refers mainly to procedures (Rapaport and Kibby, 2003).

The line dividing algorithms from models is not always clear. Deschamp (1983) suggests that many of the so-called 'models' in curriculum planning are really algorithms because they establish certain step-by-step procedures. On the other hand, in Orpwood's (1985) view the author of one of the best-known models (Tyler, 1949) never intended his model to be used as a prescribed series of planning steps, but some of his followers have given it a specific, means–end, algorithmic thrust.

There has been a proliferation of curriculum models developed over the years, varying from simple to complex. Some models might merely contain base descriptions of preferred modes of action. Others can be a sophisticated set of principles of order and structure.

In the UK, Ross (2000) refers to content-driven models (especially objectives-driven approaches) and process-driven curriculum models. Kelly (2004) takes a similar stance when he advances the dichotomy of 'curriculum as content and education as transmission' and 'curriculum as process and development'.

On the other side of the Atlantic, American scholars such as Posner (1998) propose a wider set of groupings, characterized by different questions. They consider that curriculum models can be divided into four groups:

- the procedural approach: what steps should one follow?;
- the descriptive approach: what do curriculum planners actually do?;
- the conceptual approach; what are the elements of curriculum planning and how do they relate to one another?;
- the critical approach: whose interests are being served?

Not surprisingly, there have been critics of individual models or groups of models. For example, there have been numerous critics of procedural approaches such as Tyler's (1949) model (Lawn and Barton, 1981; Kliebard, 1970; Walker and Soltis, 2004; Kelly, 2004). Criticisms have also been levelled at descriptive models, such as Walker's (1971) naturalistic model (Glatthorn and Jailall, 2000). Conceptual models have not received the same attention, but a recent example, Wiggins and McTighe's (1998) Understanding by Design, is now being widely used, especially in the USA. Critics of this model contend that it is too prescriptive and linear (Marsh, 2006).

Commentaries on curriculum models

Critical approaches are very diverse and can examine various aspects of social structures and mainstream curriculum practices. Some take a postmodern stance while others focus on fundamental issues such as gender and race. Some writers focus on a specific context and make little attempt to develop models for use by groups of teachers or schools. For example, Pinar (1980) does not believe that curricula should have predetermined goals toward which all decisions are directed. Planning should remain as personal, individual and informal as possible. Because Pinar (1980) does not believe it is possible to design a curriculum for others, he does not advocate that curriculum planning proceed through specific steps or phases.

The listing of curriculum models used in this chapter is similar to Posner (1998) but the examples included in each category do vary. Of course, interpretations of how specific models should be categorized can also vary widely. Some educators might argue that some models straddle several of the groupings.

Procedural models

A large number of models are included under this category (see Table 3.1). By far the most influential, and the earliest one, was Tyler's (1949) model. This model was a classic example of how to simplify complex teaching situations sufficiently so that plans and procedures can be carried out rationally.

Taba's (1962) model is based on the four steps of the Tyler rationale but adds a preliminary step 'diagnosis of needs'. Taba emphasized an inductive reasoning approach in her planning model.

Goodlad and Richter's (1966) model follows the Tyler rationale but adds in three levels of planning, the instructional level; the institutional level; and the societal level.

Table 3.1 A classification of curriculum models

Procedural models	
Tyler (1949)	Rational Planning Model
Taba (1962)	Induction Model
Goodlad and Richter (1966)	Planning Levels Model
Posner (1974)	Intended Learning Outcomes Model
Cohen (1974)	Interaction Model
Skilbeck (1976)	Situational Analysis Model
Johnson (1967)	P-I-E Model
Wiggins and McTighe (1998)	Understanding by Design Model

Posner's (1982) model is another rational approach to planning based upon intended learning outcomes (ILOs), an instructional plan and an evaluation plan.

Cohen (1974) produced a highly simplified planning model entitled the 'Interaction Model'. This approach emphasizes a non-linear approach to selecting objectives, selecting learning experiences, organizing learning experiences and evaluation. Cohen argued that the four elements could be selected, and revisited in any order.

Skilbeck's (1976) model highlights the culture of the school and so the first planning step focuses on situational analysis. The following steps include goal formulation, programme building, implementation and monitoring.

Johnson's (1967) rational planning model revolves around planning elements, implementation elements and evaluation elements (P-I-E).

It is interesting to note that in the 1960s and 1970s there was intense interest in developing curriculum models (see Table 3.1). To a large extent, all of these models were trying to improve school systems. They grew out of experiences that the authors had at specific schools. They were largely described by various authors as rational/managerial (Reid, 1993), traditionalist (Pinar, 1978) and quasi-scientific (Apple, 1979).

Of the curriculum models described above only Tyler's model is still widely used in a number of countries. The others are largely of historical interest (see Table 3.2). The Tyler model is described in more detail on pp. 29–31.

It is fascinating to note that, after a lack of interest for nearly twenty years, a new curriculum model has emerged which is now being widely used in a number of countries. Wiggins and McTighe published their model, 'Understanding by Design' (UBD), in 1998. They contend that design must be done backwards in a series of three steps, namely identify desired results, consider evidence of understanding needed, plan learning experiences. Whether the wide interest in this new model is due to the appropriateness of the three linear components, or due to the massive advertising and professional development programmes sponsored by an American professional association, is difficult to ascertain. The UBD model is also described in more detail on pp. 32–34.

Table 3.2 Date of publication of selected curriculum models

Tyler's Objectives Model	Tyler (1949)
Taba's Inductive Model	Taba (1962)
Schwab's Deliberation Model	Schwab (1970)
Walker's Naturalistic Model	Walker (1971)
Stenhouse's Process Model	Stenhouse (1975)
Posner's Intended Learning Outcomes Model	Posner (1974)
Resnick's Constructivist Model	Resnick and Klopfer (1989)
Wiggins and McTighe's Understanding by Design Model	Wiggins and McTighe (1998)

Descriptive models

Proponents of descriptive curriculum models contend that better curricula will result when those engaged in it understand the complexity of the process. Objectives are relegated to a less central position. Two examples of descriptive models are included below (see Table 3.3).

Walker (1971) was especially interested in how curriculum planners 'actually' went about their task, rather than following Tyler's advice about how they 'should' go about the task. He had an excellent opportunity to find out when he was appointed as participant observer and evaluator for the Kettering Art Project during the late 1960s in California. For a period of three years he meticulously recorded the actions, arguments and decisions of the project team. By analysing transcripts of their meetings and other data, Walker was able to isolate important components in the curriculum development process. During the 1960s and 1970s a number of major, national curriculum projects were in operation and so he was able to compare his findings from the Kettering Art Project with several other projects. He developed his concepts into a process framework which he termed 'naturalistic'.

Stenhouse (1975) argues that a process planning model can be developed which is not means–ends. There can be intrinsic justification of knowledge in itself: 'A form of knowledge has structure, and it involves procedures, concepts and criteria. Content can be selected to exemplify the most important situations in which the criteria hold' (Stenhouse, 1975, p. 85). Stenhouse developed a discussion-based form of teaching in the Humanities Project, using procedures emanating from his process model.

Conceptual models

Proponents of conceptual models typically focus upon 'deep' issues and are less concerned about planning procedures (see Table 3.4). Schwab (1970) published a series of papers about developing a 'practical language' for developing curricula. A major concept is 'deliberation', where curriculum planners take the necessary time to sort out relevant facts, to consider alternative solutions and to weigh alternatives and their costs and consequences. Schwab also used the term 'commonplaces' to identify four considerations that must be included in any practical curriculum decision – 'subject matter', 'learner', 'teacher', 'milieu'. Curriculum deliberation is always directed toward all four of these commonplaces simultaneously.

Table 3.3 Descriptive models

Walker (1971)	Naturalistic Model
Stenhouse (1975)	Process Model

Gardner (1983) conceptualized a set of intelligences based on studies he undertook in child development and cognitive science. The eight intelligences highlighted the importance of intelligences other than the traditional ones, linguistic and logical-mathematical. For example, he highlighted spatial, bodily kinaesthetic, musical, interpersonal, naturalist and intrapersonal. Gardner left it to others such as Armstrong (1994) and Campbell (1997) to provide practical ways to demonstrate how multiple intelligences could be incorporated into classroom activities.

Resnick and Klopfer (1989), along with a number of cognitive psychologists, have focused upon constructivism – the stance that views knowledge as something constructed by individual human beings and not merely discovered. Resnick and Klopfer (1989) argue that teachers and students go through inner cognitive conflicts and, in the process, explore ideas and concepts to create knowledge.

Critical-exploratory theorizers

In the late 1970s a change of focus became evident when curriculum scholars abandoned these traditional approaches and favoured instead a 'reconceptualist' approach – a new form of theorizing – they criticized existing conceptual schema and political structures. These critical approaches are described in detail in Chapter 19. See also Table 3.5.

Some writers, for example Jackson (1992), describe Tyler's book as the 'Bible of Curriculum Making'. Hlebowitsh (1992) lauds Tyler for providing a practical theory that informs and guides the conduct of schooling. Yet, there

Table 3.4 Conceptual models

Schwab (1970)	Deliberation Model
Gardner (1983)	Multiple Intelligences Model
Resnick and Klopfer (1989)	Constructivist Model

Table 3.5 Examples of critical theorizers

Social & Cultural Control	Bernstein (1973)
Social Reproduction	Bowles and Gintis (1976)
Cultural Reproduction	Giroux (1982)
Literacy Artist	Eisner (1974)
Existential/Psychoanalytic	Pinar (1980)
Phenomenological	Van Manen (1980)
Autobiographical/Biographical	Miller (1992)
Gender Analysis & Feminist Pedagogy	Lather (1991)
Gender Analysis & Male Identity	Sears (1992)
Race	McCarthy (1988)
Postmodern/Poststructural	Slattery (1995)

are many others who criticize Tyler's model for being behaviouristic, theoretical, managerial, means–end, objective and rational (see Grundy, 1987; Eisner, 1979). Rogan and Luckowski (1990) see the Tyler model as representing a pre-paradigmatic stage because it does not seek to develop a theoretical explanation of curriculum.

A critical analysis of two models

Tyler's (1949) planning model

Major principles

Tyler's model states *how* to build a curriculum. He argues that there are really four principles or 'big questions' that curriculum makers have to ask (see Figure 3.1). These questions are concerned with selecting objectives, selecting learning experiences, organizing learning experiences, and evaluating. For Tyler, these questions can be answered systematically, but only if they are posed in this order, for answers to all later questions logically presuppose answers to all prior questions. There is therefore some basis for critics labelling Tyler's approach 'rational-linear'.

Educational purposes

The first question to ask is: what educational purposes do you seek to attain? Many would argue that this is a logical first step to take. Only when you have decided what you want to teach can you select and organize your content and teaching activities. However, do you select as your criteria what 'students' need to know, or what 'society' thinks should be taught, or what 'subject specialists' consider is important to their academic discipline?

Tyler maintains that all three sources are important and appears to be quite eclectic in his stance.

According to Tyler, the dilemma can be resolved by identifying a number of potentially useable objectives derived from these three sources and then using 'educational philosophy' and 'psychological principles' as screens to sieve off the important objectives (see Figure 3.1).

Tyler's book provides no way of deciding which educational philosophy should be used. In one sense this explains the popularity of Tyler's approach because *it* caters for a diversity of value stances. On the other hand, it might be argued that Tyler's response to this dilemma is to state that each school has its own values, stated or implied, about the nature of a good life and a good society, and in principle it can discover and use these in planning its curriculum. How this task can best be accomplished Tyler leaves vague.

He is more specific about how psychology might be used as a screen when he discusses certain principles in the psychology of learning, such as how

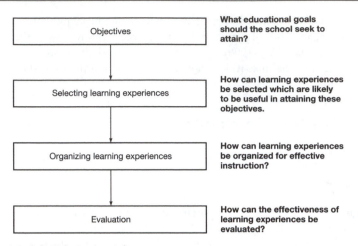

Figure 3.1 Ralph Tyler's principles.

maturation levels and environmental conditions affect learning. But here, too, he still throws the onus back upon the curriculum planner to make choices of objectives with very little guidance about how to undertake the task:

Selecting learning experiences

The second question is: how can learning experiences be selected which are likely to be useful in attaining these objectives? It is important to note that Tyler was referring to more than just 'content', although subsequent writers have simplified it to just that term. Tyler was concerned about students getting the learning experiences they needed to satisfy the intentions (objectives) of the curriculum. Further, he felt that students should be aware of the behaviours expected of them from undertaking these learning experiences. They should have the opportunity to practise the desired behaviours.

Tyler does assert that learning experiences must be selected so that students have sufficient opportunity to experience and successfully complete the tasks required of them. He also asserts that learning experiences must enable students to gain satisfaction from carrying on particular kinds of behaviour. Both assertions about designing learning experiences were quite advanced for the late 1940s, when *Basic Principles of Curriculum and Instruction* (Tyler, 1949) was published.

Organizing learning experiences

The third question is: how can learning experiences be organized for effective instruction? Tyler introduces a range of helpful suggestions. Still, the ends–means character of his thinking is apparent here, for his use of the phrase 'effective instruction' clearly carries within it the idea of efficiency. In other words he suggests that a learning experience should be organized for precisely the same general reason that it was selected in the first place: as a means of helping students reach certain ends (the previously specified objectives).

Evaluation

The fourth question is: how can the effectiveness of learning experiences be evaluated? Tyler emphasizes the need for curriculum planners to see how far the learning experiences that they have developed and organized actually produce the desired results. His notion of evaluation is determining the degree of fit between the results specified in the objectives and the results actually achieved.

Ends–means notions of evaluation have, of course, been widely accepted and used in education, yet some ideas that Tyler described in 1949, over a half-century ago, can still seem innovative, including the need to evaluate students throughout a unit and not just at the end. Indeed, Cronbach (1986) claims that Tyler invented formative evaluation by teachers. Tyler emphasizes that evaluation involves getting evidence about changes in the behaviour of students and that doing so is not confined merely to giving paper-and-pencil tests.

Advantages of the Tyler model

1   It can be applied to any subject and to any level of teaching (Hlebowitsh, 1992).
2   It provides a set of procedures which are very easy to follow and which appear to be most logical and rational.
3   At the time the model was first published (1940s) it broke new ground by emphasizing 'student behaviours' and 'learning experiences' (Helsby and Saunders, 1993). The guidelines for evaluation were also far more comprehensive than others available in the 1940s.

Disadvantages of the Tyler model

1   No explicit guidelines are given about why certain objectives should be chosen over others.
2   Research evidence on teacher thinking and teacher planning indicates that few teachers use objectives as their initial planning point (Bolin and McConnel Falk, 1987; Connelly and Clandinin, 1988). Nor do they use a set series of steps.
3   Tyler is only concerned about evaluating intended instructional objectives. He ignores the unintended learnings which invariably occur.
4   The separation of the four steps tends to underestimate the interrelationships which occur in any curriculum planning activity (Reid, 1993).

Wiggins and McTighe's (1998) Understanding by Design model

The volume *Understanding by Design* (UBD), authored by Grant Wiggins and Jay McTighe, was first published in 1998. The two authors have had extensive experience in lecturing about designing curriculum and have published widely on aspects dealing with performance assessment and standards-based education. In the preparation of this volume it is evident that they consulted widely with experts from various sources, including Howard Gardner, Arthur Costa and William Spady. The publication was produced by the Association for Supervision and Curriculum Development (ASCD) and they have been largely responsible for a very comprehensive and successful marketing activity for UBD.

Understanding by Design (1998) is a very readable book. The authors argue that it is not a prescriptive programme; rather it is a conceptual framework and provides a set of design processes and design standards.

Wiggins and McTighe argue that teachers are designers and that one of their major tasks is to design curriculum and learning experiences to meet specified purposes. They contend that if design is done backwards it is more purposeful. It is like task analysis. You settle on the task to be accomplished and then you work out how to get there. Another difference with this volume is that assessment has been thought about at the beginning of the design and not at the end. The authors argue that it is most important to work out what will be accepted as evidence that students have obtained the desired understandings and proficiencies before proceeding to plan these experiences.

Stage 1: identify desired results

In this first stage goals and established content standards are analysed. The authors suggest that four filters or criteria should be used in helping decide what ideas and processes should be included. The filters include:

- Filter 1: to what extent does the idea, topic or process represent a 'big idea' having enduring value beyond the classroom?
- Filter 2: to what extent does the idea, topic or process reside inside the heart of the discipline?
- Filter 3: to what extent does the idea, topic or process require uncoverage?
- Filter 4: to what extent does the idea, topic or process offer potential for engaging students?

These are certainly very useful criteria. The emphasis upon the ideas of enduring value is important to select out concepts of major significance. The authors are also mindful that the disciplines have a major role to play as it is important to select insights from these sources. The authors also talk about misconceptions or uncoverage and this is a useful concept to remind teachers about the values they might bring to planning without necessarily being aware of them. The need for ideas to engage students is a major element and one that is very significant for all teachers.

Stage 2: determine acceptable evidence

This stage is all about planning what kinds of evidence will be needed to indicate that students have reached a particular proficiency in understanding. The authors are mindful of using a range of assessment methods and they consider that a variety should be used. The authors consider both formal and informal assessments. They are certainly not concentrating on end of term teaching tests. They are also concerned about the need to use performance tasks to enable students to demonstrate their levels of understanding.

Stage 3: plan learning experiences and instruction

The authors argue that teachers, having experienced the first two stages, would then be in a good position to make decisions about what will be included in their curriculum design.

They contend that there are several key questions that must be considered at this stage, namely:

- What enabling knowledge (facts, concepts and principles) and skills (procedures) will students need to perform effectively and achieve desired results?
- What activities will equip students with the needed knowledge and skills?
- What will need to be taught and coached and how should it best be taught, in light of performance goals?
- What materials and sources are best suited to accomplish these goals?
- Is the overall design coherent and effective?

Since the first edition of *Understanding by Design* (UBD) was published in 1998, ASCD has been very active in promoting the UBD approach by a range of marketing developments. These include:

- the development of a companion book entitled *Understanding by Design: Professional Development Workbook* (McTighe and Wiggins, 2004);
- the development of audios and videotapes on UBD;
- online professional development courses;
- Understanding by Design exchange on-site training;
- conferences and workshops;
- Understanding by Design: The Backward Design Process – this six-lesson course is the third in a series designed to help practitioners describe, explain and design principles and strategies with the UBD framework;
- on-site training by UBD experts is available and arrangements can be made for these experts to visit – the ASCD has a range of experienced consultants

available to travel to various locations around the world, where they design workshops, provide keynote speeches and help plan conferences;
• conferences and workshops – the ASCD provides a number of summer conferences and professional development workshops on UBD.

It is interesting to note that the UBD approach is the first detailed curriculum model to be published since the 1970s. It does appear to be well received by teachers in a number of countries.

Advantages of the UBD model

1 It provides a sense of ownership for teacher-planners.
2 There is a strong alignment between the use of outcomes and objectives.
3 It is a systematic, outcomes-based approach to planning.
4 It encourages teachers to check prior misunderstandings before commencing the planning process.

Disadvantages of the UBD model

1 The design-backwards approach is very prescriptive and linear.
2 It has too much emphasis on outcomes and insufficient detail on selecting learning experiences or how to use them.
3 Many of the concepts included are not new – they are new titles for concepts developed much earlier by Tyler (1949) and Bloom (1956).

Concluding comments

The recent upsurge in the use of curriculum models, as typified by the use of the UBD model, indicates that teachers and planners see some value in their use. Teachers are being encouraged to do school-based planning of topics and themes and so curriculum models may be used more frequently in the future.

Reflections and issues

1 What are the characteristics of good curriculum planning? What priorities would you give to such matters as:

• sequenced learning experiences;
• comprehensive goals and objectives;
• group deliberation?

2 If teaching is so unpredictable is it folly to attempt to produce a model at all? Are there common aspects of teaching situations which can be included in a model? Give details.

3   'Schools persist in using curriculum models grounded in technical ration-
    ality (for example, Tyler's model) because it fits well with the bureaucratic
    organization of schools' (Olson, 1989, p. 25). Is this the major reason?
    Consider other reasons why schools might support or reject the Tyler
    approach.
4   The use of technical/rational administrative solutions to complex social
    issues of equity and access in schools is wrong-headed, superficial and fun-
    damentally flawed, according to Smyth (1989). Discussion.
5   Critically analyse this statement: the Tyler model and the UBD model use
    'metaphors of "construction" and "building"'. These are indicators of a
    technical, product-centred approach to curriculum. Do you agree? Develop
    an argument for or against this stance.

Web sources

Curriculum models – objectives based model, www.ssdd.uce.ac.uk/crupton/curriculum-
    design/key-concept-map/obj-based-proc-model.htm – accessed December 2007.
Tyler model of curriculum design, coe.sdsu.edu/people/mora/Mora/Modules/TylerCurr
    Model.pps – accessed December 2007.
Understanding by Design, www.ascd.org/portal/site/ascd/ – accessed December 2007.
Lesson planning, lesson plan formats, www.adprima.com/lesson.htm – accessed December
    2007.
Lesson plans: teaching strategies, www.adprima.com/lesson.htm – accessed December 2007.
Preschool curriculum models, www.adprima.com/lesson.htm – accessed December 2007.
Arkansas curriculum models, www.adprima.com/lesson.htm – accessed December 2007.
Econ Ed Link, www.adprima.com/lesson.htm – accessed December 2007.
Examples of classroom-based assessments, www.eed.state.ak.us/tis/frameworks/sstudeis/
    part4a3.htm – accessed December 2007.

Chapter 4

Curriculum frameworks

Introduction

Curriculum frameworks have been adopted in many countries under various names such as 'core subjects', 'foundation subjects', 'key learning areas'. Supposedly they facilitate curriculum planning and provide greater flexibility for teachers. Yet, they can also be a tool of control and direction.

It is important to consider the claims and counter-claims about curriculum frameworks. Harris' (2005) question is an important one: 'are they a force for pedagogical change or a façade for continued conservation?' (p. 53).

What is a curriculum framework?

A 'curriculum framework' can be defined as a group of related subjects or themes which fit together according to a predetermined set of criteria to appropriately cover an area of study. Each curriculum framework has the potential to provide a structure for designing subjects and a rationale and policy context for subsequent curriculum development of these subjects. Examples of school-oriented curriculum frameworks include 'science' (including, for example, biology, chemistry, physics, geology) and 'commerce' (including, for example, accounting, office studies, economics, computing). In the USA the term 'social studies' was first used by the National Education Association in 1894 to describe predominantly history, but also geography, economics, government and civics. However, there have been many other frameworks which have been proposed by educators over the decades, and these are examined next.

Frameworks produced by theorists and educators

Educational theorists over the years have produced their ideal framework groupings. For example, Hirst (1974) has argued convincingly that knowledge can be classified into eight forms, which he labels as follows:

- mathematics;
- physical sciences;

- human sciences;
- history;
- religion;
- literature and the fine arts;
- philosophy;
- moral knowledge.

As noted by Ribbins (1992), Hirst distinguishes between 'forms' and 'fields' of knowledge, and in some cases there is considerable overlap with school subjects and university disciplines but in other cases very little. Hirst states:

> I have argued elsewhere that although the domain of human knowledge can be regarded as composed of a number of logically distinct forms of knowledge, we do in fact for many purposes, deliberately and self-consciously organize knowledge into a large variety of fields which often form the units employed in teaching. The problems that arise in teaching such complex fields as ... geography ... are much more difficult to analyse than those arising in such forms as, say, mathematics, physics and history.
>
> (Hirst, 1967, p. 44)

Phenix, in his work *Realms of Meaning* (1964), maintains that there are six fundamental patterns of meaning that determine the quality of every humanly significant experience (see Table 4.1).

Young (1971) argues that society selects, classifies, distributes, transmits and evaluates educational knowledge. He maintains that academic curricula assume that some kinds and areas of knowledge are much more worthwhile than others. Young argues that frameworks based upon subject-based academic curricula are rarely examined and that they should be seen for what they are – 'no more than historic constructs of a particular time'.

In a similar vein, Stengel (1997) contends that there are no stable meanings for either 'academic subject' or 'school subject' – they are not sacrosanct bodies of knowledge.

Table 4.1 A framework based on 'Realms of Meaning'

Realm of Meaning	Disciplines
Symbolics	Ordinary language, mathematics, non-discursive symbolic forms
Empirics	Physical sciences, life sciences, psychology, social sciences
Aesthetics	Music, visual arts, arts of movement, literature
Synnoetics	Philosophy, psychology, literature, religion; in their existential aspects
Ethics	The varied special areas of moral and ethical concern
Synoptics	History, religion, philosophy

Goodson (1983) has examined the evolution of a number of school subjects in the UK and noted their paths towards acceptability and status. He argues that the differential states of school subjects derives from their origins in the academic disciplines and in different educational sectors.

Goodson (1981) is not entirely convinced about the historical basis for the control by dominant groups. Based upon a number of studies, he argues that sociologists such as Young have 'raided' history to support their theory:

> Studies develop, so to speak, horizontally working out from theories to social structure and social order. When historical evidence is presented it is provided as a snapshot from the past to prove a contemporary point.
>
> (Goodson, 1985, p. 358)

Lawton (1993) notes that in the United Kingdom conventional subjects that any Member of Parliament could immediately recognize were supported strongly in developing the National Curriculum – any other versions, such as areas of experience (the HMI Entitlement Curriculum Model), were ignored and derided as educational theory, 'an increasingly taboo concept in right-wing circles' (p. 6).

Recent approaches

Curriculum frameworks that were developed in the 1990s and the twenty-first century are predominantly guides that have been explicitly designed and written to assist school communities of teachers, students and parents in their curriculum 'decision-making' about K-10 programmes (infants to junior secondary, Australia) (Kerr, 1989). This statement sounds very positive but in practice the impacts on teachers, students and parents may be far less. There is also the more sinister element of frameworks being used by system-level personnel to review teacher and school performance.

Features of curriculum frameworks

Ideally, curriculum framework features are comprehensive and detailed. Most important is a rationale or platform – a statement of the values, principles and assumptions which have guided those who produced the framework.

In addition, a framework should include content examples, teaching and learning principles and guidelines for evaluation of subjects included in the framework.

When curriculum frameworks are published there are often optimistic claims about their quality and coverage. For example, when the Australian collaborative national curriculum was published, the following claims were made:

- strong links between theory and practice;
- up-to-date and relevant information about pedagogy, learning and resources;

- evocative and inspiring to teachers – they become impressed by its potential as a curriculum area.

(Marsh, 1994)

Impact upon teachers

Again, developers often make overly optimistic claims about the impact upon teachers. Consider the following:

- frameworks provide greater coherence across subjects and across the grade levels K-12 (infants to senior secondary, Australia) – they demonstrate the commonalities between subjects within a framework and enable content and skills to be sequenced across grade levels;
- frameworks encourage teachers to evaluate the total learning environment – teachers need to consider the effectiveness of the taught curriculum, and their teaching effectiveness as well as student performances;
- frameworks enable curriculum boundaries to be reconsidered and sometimes redefined – they highlight the changing emphases and the evolving boundaries of subjects;
- frameworks encourage teachers to reconsider their packaging and delivery of subjects – it enables them to develop new emphases (for example vocational, recreational) and career pathways;
- frameworks enable relatively low-status subjects to be given a more prominent place in the school programme because equal status is given to all frameworks.

It might be argued that the creative teacher would always do many of the above activities.

A curriculum framework might encourage more traditional teachers to experiment with their lesson planning but this would depend upon many contextual factors. The claim that frameworks give more prominence to the low-status subjects is often not realized in practice as priority for more time given to literacy and numeracy on the school timetable precludes this from happening.

In summary, the claimed advantages of using curriculum frameworks should be treated with caution. A framework may give the appearance of coherence and order but this may not be how classroom teachers perceive it. However, it is likely that the inclusion of generic skills (for example problem-solving or critical thinking) can be accommodated more effectively and widely in a curriculum framework:

- the curriculum will be more coherent and orderly because the framework for each curriculum area is arranged, usually from kindergarten to secondary levels, and priorities are established for each level;
- high-quality curriculum development is likely to occur because planning criteria and standards apply consistently across all curriculum frameworks;

- there are opportunities for curriculum frameworks to include subjects which are highly prescriptive and those that allow considerable flexibility and variation at the school level;
- new content areas and skills can be easily accommodated in curriculum frameworks, including various multidisciplinary and interdisciplinary variations;
- curriculum frameworks developed at a state or regional level have the potential to become accepted as national frameworks;
- there are opportunities to incorporate desirable skills into each framework, such as communication and language skills, numeracy skills, problem-solving skills.

In practice, teachers have found a number of difficulties in using a curriculum framework. In many cases the complex educational terms used by the framework writers are not easily comprehended by classroom teachers. They now have too many options and it is difficult for teachers to choose which content or teaching strategies to use. There is also the accountability requirement lurking close at hand, which can become very stressful for teachers:

- classroom teachers have insufficient time to understand the new approaches;
- there is insufficient professional training available on the framework;
- the technical terms used by developers may be difficult for teachers to comprehend;
- the accountability requirements of the framework can be daunting for teachers.

Examples

United Kingdom

In the United Kingdom, a national curriculum framework was established under the Education Reform Act of 1988. It was considered by the government that

> it is vital to ensure that all pupils between the ages of 5 to 16 study a basic range of subjects – including maths, English and science. In each of these basic subjects syllabuses will be published and attainment targets set so the progress of pupils can be assessed at around ages 7, 11 and 14, and in preparation for the GCSE at 16. Parents, teachers and pupils will then know how well each child is doing.
>
> (Conservative Party, 1987)

The National Curriculum consists of three 'core' subjects (mathematics, English and science) and 'foundation' subjects (history, geography, technology, music, art, physical education, modern foreign languages). Subsequently the number of foundation subjects has been increased to include citizenship and personal, social, health and economic education (Qualifications & Curriculum Authority, 2007).

For each subject, programmes of study have been developed that cover a range of knowledge, skills and understandings. Some of the subjects reflect the traditional academic subject boundaries (for example mathematics), whereas others are used as a broad area or framework (for example design and technology). These subjects are intended to comprise 70 per cent of the total school time and students are expected to study all core and foundation subjects.

A tightly prescribed structure has been organized whereby 'attainment targets' (specifying up to ten levels of attainment, covering the ages 5–16) have been established for each subject; assessment activities are for four 'key stages' at ages 5–7, 7–11, 11–14 and 14–16; and 'standard assessment tasks' (SATs) have been designed for each key stage.

There have been major criticisms of the national framework. Goodson (1994) contends that the National Curriculum is a retrogression to the subject-based framework developed in 1904. McCulloch (1998) claims that the implementation of the National Curriculum has proved to be highly bureaucratic and intrusive in its effects.

Ball (1994, p. 46) describes the National Curriculum as 'one which eschews relevance and the present … Made up of echoes of past voices, the voices of a cultural and political elite; a curriculum which ignores the past of women and the working class and the colonized – a curriculum of the dead'. Ross (2000) contends that the ten-subject curriculum has an unworkable overload of content and assessment. It produces antagonism from teachers and alienation of the profession. Elliott (2002) considers that the National Curriculum in England and Wales is inexorably 'audit-driven', values have been systematically disconnected from the target specifications, and the division between core curriculum subjects and foundation subjects creates a lack of balance and a narrowing of the range and variety of learning opportunities for students.

However, there have been some revisions to the National Curriculum since 2000, including reductions in the level of detailed prescription for many subjects and more opportunities for school initiatives at Key Stages 3 and 4 in the areas of Personal, Social and Health Education (PSHE) and Citizenship Education.

Being a subject-centred framework there are clearly difficulties in including integrated or cross-curricular approaches. The Qualifications & Curriculum Authority (QCA) recommends that schools include 'cross-curriculum dimensions' (for example identity and cultural diversity; creativity and critical thinking) but it is unclear whether schools become heavily involved in these.

The new secondary curriculum for Key Stages 3 and 4 launched in 2007 is an attempt to 'modernize' the traditional subject-based framework. New programmes of study are included involving in-class and beyond-the-school activities. Also included are new approaches to assessment (Qualifications & Curriculum Authority, 2007) and teaching and learning (Teaching and Learning Research Programme, 2007). Personalized learning activities, developed by the Department for Children, Schools and Families (2007), are also given prominence in the new Key Stage 3 and 4 subjects.

Australia

The creation of eight learning areas in Australia in April 1991 was billed at the time as an innovatory consultative approach to national curriculum development. Although some exploratory mapping of mathematics/numeracy content occurred across all states and territories in 1988, followed by mapping of some other areas in 1989 (for example science, technology), a total design was not introduced until several years later by the Australian Education Council (AEC); a new but powerful curriculum player (Grundy, 1994).

At the AEC meeting in April 1991, eight areas of learning were confirmed, namely:

- English;
- science;
- mathematics;
- Languages Other Than English (LOTE);
- technology;
- studies of society and environment;
- the arts;
- health and physical education.

No amplification of these eight areas was produced at this AEC meeting apart from a recognition that a small working group should focus on structures and processes for national collaboration.

Hannan (1992), the then Director of Curriculum in Victoria, notes that the creation of the eight learning areas was both pragmatic and conservative – 'this is the break-up nearest to that already in use around the country' (p. 29).

Of the eight learning areas, four were established subjects, namely English, LOTE, mathematics and science. The remaining four represented collections of subjects or even new studies. The latter four areas were a curious combination, perhaps reflecting pragmatic decisions and not a little idiosyncratic preference. For example, the inclusion of business studies mainly in studies of society and environment reflected the strongly established grouping of the social sciences and commerce in Victoria. As another example, media studies was included in the arts learning area even though in some states, such as Western Australia, it was incorporated with English at the secondary school level.

For each of the eight learning areas in the framework, national statements and profiles were produced, all within an outcomes-based system. Although Directors-General from each state education system had confirmed in 1992 their strong commitment to implementing national statements and profiles, the political climate had changed a year later (Marsh, 1994). At the AEC meeting in July 1993, state ministers were divided about intentions to implement national statements and profiles, which led to a motion of deferment and subsequent 'posturing' and/or 'killing' of the national curriculum initiative by individual state education systems (Marsh, 1994, p. 164).

In the subsequent decade, individual state education systems supported to varying degrees the implementation of the national curriculum statements and profiles (Watt, 1998). Although the framework remained intact in most states, there were extensive revisions to the structure of each of the eight learning areas, especially the inclusion of more standards-based outcomes (Watt, 2000). In the state of Victoria, the grouping of the eight learning areas was reviewed, leading to individual subjects being reinstated at secondary school levels. The decision to use syllabuses in the state of New South Wales also led to major variations in that state. Other states, such as South Australia, introduced major variations to the original framework (Blyth, 2002).

As happened in the United Kingdom, there have been criticisms of the national framework in Australia. Willmott (1994) argued that the eight learning areas of the framework lacked a rigorously developed theoretical base – that the division into eight learning areas was a confusing amalgam of traditional subjects and pragmatic expediency.

Reid (1992) argues that there was no research evidence for the profiles approach. He contends that the National Collaborative Curriculum Project 'has been shaped by progressive bureaucrats who are seeking to ward off the worst excesses of the market-driven educational philosophy of the New Right' (p. 15).

Hughes (1990) noted that the professional development implications for teachers were enormous and should not be underrated. Collins (1994b) criticized the eight areas of knowledge as being 'largely artificial creations with varying degrees of coherence' (p. 45).

It is evident that the four learning areas which were a conglomeration of previously distinct subjects (for example Studies of Society and Environment (SOSE)) have not been very successful. They had the potential to offer students valuable interdisciplinary learning experiences 'but territorial and sometimes divisive subject sub-cultures and the challenge of preserving depth of student understanding in the face of enormous curriculum breadth' undermined these opportunities (Harris, 2005, p. 53).

Criticism of SOSE in particular has been wide ranging, including by the then prime minister and by many government ministers:

> There is something both deadening and saccharine in curriculum where history has been replaced by the broader 'time, continuity and change' and geography by 'place, space and environment'. Both should be stand-alone subjects.
>
> (John Howard, as reported by Rhianna King, *West Australian*, 9 February 2007, p. 6)

A recent paper by the Adelaide Declaration Review Steering Committee (2007) recommends the re-establishment of the traditional disciplines of History, Geography and Economics.

Concluding comments

Curriculum frameworks appear to offer coherence and streamlined planning for teachers, yet they inevitably include specific values, choices and priorities which may or may not be acceptable to teachers and the wider community. Attempts at including integrated subjects/cross-curricular programmes may have had considerable merit but have not been able to secure a lasting foothold. As noted by Harris and Marsh (2007), 'the long-term impact of various integrated, interdisciplinary, multi-disciplinary and trans-disciplinary approaches does not look all that promising' (p. 12). Frameworks in the future in many countries may return to single subjects/disciplines.

Reflections and issues

1   'Curriculum frameworks provide opportunities for an education system to include new subjects to suit a country's present and future social and economic needs.' To what extent can this occur? Give examples of where such initiatives have been successful.

2   'There has been an almost total lack of argument for the National Curriculum (UK), both in general terms and in detail' (Wiegand and Rayner, 1989, p. 12). Why do you think the foundation subjects were selected for special attention in the framework? What might have been some alternative ways of organizing the curriculum? What opportunities are there for themes and for interdisciplinary work?

3   'We are left with a curriculum (UK) founded upon a myth about the educational excellence of the old grammar school curriculum. Central to this myth is the idea that the traditional disciplines or subjects encapsulate standards of educational excellence' (Elliott and Chan, 2002, p. 20). Discuss.

4   The national statements (Australia) represent a summation of the best available knowledge about the content in the eight learning areas. 'It builds upon some of the best of current practice and provides moral support for the continuance of a range of good practices' (Willis, 1991, p. 4). Discuss.

5   'The enthusiasm Australian educational agencies have shown for diverting resources into centrally-driven curriculum development has not translated well into useful products' (Blyth, 2002, p. 21). Discuss.

6   'Frameworks improve the quality of curriculum by assisting in the evaluation of existing curriculum and helping to revise and develop curriculum' (Hardy, 1990, p. 5). In what ways is this likely to occur?

7 'Schools should operate within the general guidelines of central office personnel – curriculum frameworks enable this to occur.' Discuss.

Web sources

Curriculum frameworks, www.cde.ca.gov/be/st/fr/ – extracted 4 October 2007.

Curriculum frameworks, www.curriculum.wa.edu.au/pages/framework/framework00. htm – extracted 4 October 2007.

Qualifications & Curriculum Authority, www.qca.org.uk/14–19/ – extracted 4 October 2007.

National Curriculum Homepage, curriculum.qca.org.uk – extracted 4 October 2007.

Personal Learning, www.standards.dfes.gov.uk/personalisedlearning/ – extracted 4 October 2007.

Victorian Essential Learning Standards, vels.vcaa.vic.edu.au/ – extracted 4 October 2007.

Chapter 5

Objectives, learning outcomes and standards

Introduction

Learning within a school environment is typically goal directed. Students are at school because they want to learn certain things, attain specific standards and perhaps satisfy the requirements for a particular diploma or award. The majority of students are not there, as described mischievously by Postman and Weingartner (1987), to serve out a sentence! Teachers, too, are not serving 'time' in schools but are wanting their students to achieve particular goals or ends.

Objectives provide an answer to what it is that students want to learn and what it is that teachers are trying to teach them. There are many other terms that are used as synonyms, such as 'outcomes', 'goals', 'aims', 'purpose', 'intentions'. Some authors, such as Moore (2001) and Glatthorn and Jailall (2000), make distinctions between some of these terms, but, based upon widespread use and application, the major terms are undoubtedly 'objectives', 'outcomes' and 'standards'.

Objectives

Objectives greatly assist the planning process for teachers. The foundation for well-planned teaching is, unquestionably, clearly stated objectives. Some teachers resist using objectives because they consider they are too limiting or are inappropriate for certain content that cannot be specifically defined or evaluated. Yet measurement experts such as Mager (1984) point out that 'if you are teaching things that cannot be evaluated, you are in the awkward position of being unable to demonstrate that you are teaching anything at all. Intangibles are often intangible because we have been too lazy to think about what it is we want students to be able to do' (p. 5).

In terms of the teaching role, objectives provide the opportunity for teachers to formulate, and, it is hoped, act upon, clear statements about what students are intended to learn through instruction. We are probably all aware of anecdotes which refer to the guessing games which can occur between a teacher and students. For example: what does our teacher want us to learn? I don't know what he/she wants. Is it to memorize/regurgitate certain content or is it to apply and explain certain content? Objectives, if conveyed to students, can eradicate a lot of these misunderstandings and can lead to a higher level of communication between the teacher and students.

Objectives are also likely to lead to higher levels of achievement by students, but only under certain conditions. For example, objectives can lead to better learning in lessons which are loosely structured, such as research projects or a film. However, for lessons which involve very structured materials, such as a tightly sequenced laboratory experiment or a computer program, objectives seem to be less important (Tobias and Duchastel, 1974). Objectives assist teachers and students to focus upon what will be evaluated. There should be a close relationship between the assignments, tests and checklists used by the teacher and the objectives for the particular teaching unit or lessons. The feedback received by students from particular assessments lets them know whether they are achieving the standards required.

Outcomes

Willis and Kissane (1997) define outcome statements as 'broad descriptions of student competencies which reflect long term learning of significance beyond school, and which are superordinate to the details of any particular curriculum content, sequence or pedagogy' (p. 21). Outcome statements concentrate upon the outputs rather than the inputs of teaching. Exponents of this approach argue that objectives only concentrate upon the inputs of teaching.

To a certain extent, the approach represents a recycling of earlier movements, especially in the USA, such as mastery learning and competency-based education. Yet it does not incorporate specific behavioural statements. Rather, the emphasis is upon broad outcome statements to be achieved, eight to twelve statements per learning area (which typically comprises several teaching subjects).

A very successful and leading exponent of outcome-based education in the USA has been William Spady. According to Spady (1993), 'outcome-based education' means focusing and organizing a school's entire programme and instructional efforts around the clearly defined outcomes we want all students to demonstrate when they leave school (p. ii).

That is, the intended learning results are the start-up points in defining the system (Hansen, 1989). A set of conditions are described that characterize real life and these are used to derive a set of culminatory role performances. Students are required to provide a culminating demonstration – the focus is upon competence as well as content but not on the time needed to reach this standard (students can cover a common set of requirements in varying periods of time (Killen, 2007)). Specifically, an outcome is an actual demonstration in an authentic context.

Moore (2001) notes that in the USA there have been many versions of out-come-based education (OBE) but all of them promote system-level change – 'observable, measurable outcomes; and the belief that all students can learn' (p. 98). This may have been their major attraction and the cause for their demise; they promised far-reaching reform but could not deliver.

Some states within the USA were enthusiastic about OBE at first, such as the Pennsylvania Department of Education, which recommended it be used throughout the state (Glatthorn and Jailall, 2000). However, by the mid-1990s OBE was being widely criticized in terms of:

- its overemphasis on outcomes rather than processes;
- schools inflicting values that conflicted with parental values;
- lack of hard evidence that OBE worked;
- fears that OBE would 'dumb down' the curriculum and lead to lower standards;
- concerns that content becomes subservient under an OBE approach;
- student outcome statements being difficult and expensive to assess.

As a result, OBE in the USA rapidly declined in the 1990s, to be overtaken by standards-based (content standards) and constructivist approaches (Glatthorn and Jailall, 2000).

Standards

The raising of educational standards is a constant cry in educational reform. In the USA there was a major impetus in the 1990s to create 'unified national standards that would ensure consistent delivery and outcomes across diverse state systems and districts via the Educate America Act, 1994' (Blyth, 2002, p. 7).

Knowledge experts in the various subject fields have produced standards for their respective subjects (see Table 5.1). These standards have been taken up by individual states in the USA and incorporated into state curriculum frameworks and mastery tests. According to Arends (2006), 'state frameworks have an important influence on what is taught in schools because mastery tests are usually built around the performance standards identified in the frameworks' (p. 52).

Table 5.1 Examples of subject-matter Curriculum Standards (USA)

English	Standards for the Assessment of Reading and Writing
Foreign languages	Standards for Foreign Language Learning
History	US History Standards
Mathematics	Curriculum and Evaluation Standards for Social Mathematics
Science	National Science Education Standards

Note: see also http://project2061.aaas.org/; http://putwest.boces.org/standards.html.

Since 2002 there has been an additional standards requirement, in the form of No Child Left Behind (NCLB) legislation. All states have had to develop achievement standards in mathematics, language and science for students in grades 3 to 8. Standardized tests are used by the states to measure students' adequate yearly progress. Schools that do not make adequate yearly progress can, after three years, be closed down. NCLB has placed enormous pressure on teachers to raise standards in these three subjects, often by reducing instruction in other subjects. This squeeze provides teachers with little incentive to 'engage students in relevant, authentic and challenging learning experiences' (Plitt, 2004; Guilfoyle, 2006).

In the UK, literacy and numeracy standards have become a requirement through the National Literacy Strategy and the National Numeracy Strategy (Webb and Vulliamy, 2006). Standards have been established via attainment targets for the three core subjects and foundation subjects.

A distinction needs to be made between content and performance standards. Content standards declare knowledge to be acquired, whether it is processes or content. Performance standards are tasks to be completed by a student where the knowledge is embedded in the task and where a student has to use the knowledge and skills in a certain way.

Marzano and Kendall (1996) contend that both content and performance standards need to be used. Further, they suggest that content standards are articulated at a general level but with specific sub-components at developmental levels, or 'benchmarks'. As noted by Blyth (2002), 'benchmarks are essential in describing the developmental components of the general domain identified by a standard' (p. 14).

Standards seem to be welcomed by many teachers and citizens (see Table 5.1). Various writers extol the virtues of the new standards – they are a better way to develop conceptual understanding and reasoning (Goldsmith and Mark, 1999). Rosenholtz (1991) and Swanson and Stevenson (2002) assert that standards provide a common focus, clarify understanding, accelerate communication and promote persistence and collective purpose.

Yet other educators are more cautious. Schmoker and Marzano (1999) raise the question: will the standards movement endure? They contend that educators have to be very disciplined about writing clear standards and that the standards must be limited in number. Moore (2001) notes that the standards must be carefully linked to assessment. Glatthorn and Jailall (2000) assert that many of the standards are too vague about content.

The relative merits of objectives, outcomes and standards

In the 1970s, various educators criticized what they perceived to be undue attention being devoted to objectives in teaching, and especially behavioural objectives. For example, Eisner (1979, p. 103) developed the terms 'expressive objective' and later 'expressive outcome' to demonstrate that not all teaching requires the same degree of certainty.

It is evident that outcome statements together with pointers and work samples do provide considerable guidance for teachers about the standard required in a specific subject or learning area. Whether they are a better planning mechanism than objectives is problematic – there is insufficient empirical evidence available to be categoric about this matter (Ellis and Fouts, 1993). All that we can list at this time are the possible advantages:

- they are more explicit statements about what students should be able to do;
- they allow teachers more flexibility in planning their teaching;
- there is less emphasis upon content to be covered and more emphasis upon skills/competencies to be achieved;
- they provide more concrete details about student performance for parents;
- they will enable teachers and school principals to be more accountable for student standards;
- they can address higher-order thinking skills;
- they acknowledge differing learning styles and forms of intelligence.

It should be emphasized that none of these purported advantages has been substantiated in the research literature. Further, educators are still searching for solutions to some major problems, such as the following:

- enormous workloads for teachers (especially primary school teachers) to assess students on outcome statements even when using special computer software such as KIDMAP;
- providing sufficient professional development training for teachers on the outcomes-based approach – teachers need substantial training to arrive at a shared commitment to the achievement of a common set of outcome statements (Griffin, 1998);
- developing outcome statements (and pointers) which are meaningful and assessable – it cannot be assumed that all teachers will interpret them in the same way (Willis and Kissane, 1997);
- developing an economical system to monitor whether the outcomes have been achieved or not (Brady, 1996);
- obtaining evidence that an outcomes approach will lead to improved learning (Darling-Hammond, 1994).

Educators reacting to the national profiles in Australia have also been critical of attempts to specify in advance the outcome levels for students. Collins concludes that

> [the] profiles are just, quite literally, cultural artefacts ... the levels do not mark a necessary ordering of any developmental sequence (more accurately, we have no evidence that they do), but are simply a setting out of particular, and likely to change, majority cultural patterns.
>
> (Collins, 1994a, p. 14)

It can also be argued that objectives share many of the advantages listed for outcomes without incurring the disadvantages. For example, objectives enable teachers and students to focus upon major concepts, they can be communicated easily to parents and students and they enable assessment procedures to be directly related to the objectives. Furthermore, objectives do not have some of the inherent weaknesses of outcome statements in that there are no assumptions about developmental/growth levels or necessity for semi-arbitrary areas of knowledge to be divided into strands.

Types of objectives

Objectives can range from the general to the highly specific. It can be argued that the two extremes have relatively little impact upon teachers. General abstract statements about such affairs as intellectual development or citizenship provide little insight for the teacher. On the other hand, objectives that are so tightly focused that they concentrate upon low-level, insignificant facts or processes are also of very limited use to teachers.

Behavioural objectives

Behavioural objectives are perceived by some educators to be at a middle position between these two extremes. These objectives focus upon observable and measurable changes in students. Typically, adherents of behavioural objectives require three criteria to be met, namely: evidence of achievement, conditions of performance and acceptable levels of performance.

Evidence of achievement

The performance by learners must be stated as an observable student behaviour. Hence it is suggested that teachers should use terms which are observable, such as:

* list;
* define;
* add;
* calculate;
* demonstrate.

Example: Students will list the states and territories of Australia.

Conditions of performance

This criterion requires that the important conditions under which the behaviour is expected to occur must also be specified.

Example: Using a compass and a ruler, construct two tangents to a circle of 6cm diameter from an external point 12cm from the circle centre.

Acceptable levels of performance

It is also necessary to state the minimum acceptable levels of performance, or, in other words, the criterion for success. This defines the desired performance and may be expressed in terms of speed (amount of time taken), accuracy or quality.

Example: Students must spell accurately 90 per cent of the fifteen words presented.

By combining these three criteria, we get detailed behavioural objectives which can be readily observed and measured.

Example: Students will match up accurately 90 per cent of the rivers listed with their location in states of Australia without using their workbooks.

Instructional objectives

A case can be made for instructional objectives (behavioural or non-behavioural) to be used by teachers to assist with the instructional process. They provide a clearer direction and overcome vague ideas that might not have been fully developed. Further, they assist the teacher in selecting appropriate content, teaching strategies, resources and assessment. Having instructional objectives can also assist the teacher in demonstrating accountability to the principal, to parents and to the head office education system personnel (Cohen *et al.*, 1998).

For each major unit of instruction it is reasonable and useful for a teacher to develop a number of instructional objectives – for example between two and six. Of course, the teacher will have help in formulating objectives – help from national and state, governmental and professional, local district and school resources. And these objectives should be statements of the major purposes to guide the teacher and the student through the curriculum. As noted earlier, objectives can act like a roadmap. A roadmap need not specify every town and creek to be useful. Likewise objectives for a unit of instruction need not specify every change in student behaviour.

Without following the strict criteria described above for behavioural objectives, there are some criteria which enable teachers and curriculum developers to produce effective instructional objectives. These include:

- scope: the objectives must be sufficiently broad to include all desirable outcomes, presumably relating to knowledge, skills and values;
- consistency: the objectives should be consistent with each other and reflect a similar value orientation;

- suitability: the objectives should be relevant and suitable for students at particular grade levels;
- validity: the objectives should reflect and state what we want them to mean;
- feasibility: the objectives should be attainable by all students;
- specificity: the objectives should avoid ambiguity and be phrased precisely.

To follow each of these criteria closely would be an exacting task. Nevertheless, it is important to keep them in mind when devising appropriate instructional objectives.

Classifying objectives

During the 1970s experts in educational evaluation, led in particular by Benjamin Bloom, began exploring the possibility of classifying objectives in terms of cognitive, affective and psychomotor behaviours. Cognitive objectives deal with intellectual processes such as knowing, perceiving, recognizing and reasoning. Affective objectives deal with feeling, emotion, appreciation and valuing. Psychomotor objectives deal with skilled ways of moving such as throwing a ball, dancing and handwriting. Of course, it is important to remember that in real life behaviours from these three domains occur simultaneously. Notwithstanding, by focusing upon one domain at a time we can gain important insights about planning lessons.

To celebrate the fortieth anniversary of the publication of *Taxonomy of Educational Objectives, Handbook 1: Cognitive Domain* (Bloom *et al.*, 1956) notable educators in the United States produced critiques which were included in the volume edited by Anderson and Sosniak (1994). Some of the conclusions made by these authors are worth noting:

- Teacher educators at universities have used the *Taxonomy* to help teachers plan their lessons, prepare their tests and ask questions.
- Teachers have made little use of the *Taxonomy* because it is too time-consuming, it is not practical to spend time on the higher-order objectives (which takes away time from content), and it is too rational and complex.
- The *Taxonomy* concentrates upon categorizing and does not provide any guidance about how to translate these objectives into teaching programmes – as a result it has had limited impact.
- The major enduring influence of the *Taxonomy* has been to convey the notion of higher- and lower-level cognitive behaviours.
- The *Taxonomy* has been used extensively by experts preparing tests.
- Although the *Taxonomy* purports to be descriptive and neutral, it concentrates upon overt student behaviours only.
- The *Taxonomy* has been a major focus for discussion in most countries of the world; it has forced educators to raise questions as to whether they have varied the cognitive level of tasks, exercises and examinations they propose, and whether they sufficiently stimulate their students to think.

Concluding comments

Teachers undertake purposeful activities in schools. To give direction to what the teacher and students are doing involves the communication to all parties of particular intentions. Over the decades, 'objectives' in their various forms have been used to communicate intent. 'Outcomes' and 'standards' are currently being highlighted as more user-friendly approaches to communicate intent. It is problematic whether their popularity will continue into the next decade (Glatthorn and Fontana, 2002).

Reflections and issues

1 Instructional objectives can be powerful directives in the teaching process. Discuss.
2 Objectives appear to stand for an excessive interest in efficiency, an undue and misplaced zeal for things rather than process or experience. They seem to portray little heaps of knowledge, rather than an integrating structure or matrix. Critically analyse this statement.
3 To what extent is it possible in practice to devise outcomes for which all students can achieve satisfactory standards? Outline some of the possibilities and problems in achieving this end.
4 Compare and contrast the benefits of 'behavioural' objectives and 'instructional' objectives.
5 Compare the advantages and disadvantages of using an outcome-based and a standards-based approach to curriculum planning.
6 How are the standards established by central policy-makers more desirable than the standards currently set by texts and high-status tests?
7 In outcomes-based education you start your planning by examining the output intended. How difficult is this to do? Take an outcome statement and explain how you would plan learning activities to achieve it.
8 'The hardest part of introducing essential learning outcomes is to work out how to assess them'. Discuss.
9 By international standards, countries that perform highly on TIMSS (Trends in International Mathematics and Science Study) typically use syllabuses and not outcomes. Is there a stronger relationship between the use of syllabuses and student achievement?

Web sources

National Assessment Agency 14–19 reforms, http:/www.naa.org.uk – extracted December 2007.
Qualifications & Curriculum Authority, http://www.qca.org.uk – extracted December 2007.

Victorian Essential Learning Standards, http://vels.vcaa.vic.edu.au/ – extracted December 2007.

Outcomes Based Education, http://comnet.org/cpsr/essays/obe.htm – extracted December 2007.

What's Wrong with Outcome-Based Education?, http://www.faithchristianmin.org/articles/wwobe.htm – extracted December 2007.

Outcomes and Standards Framework, http://www.det.wa.edu.au/education/curriculum/cip2/ondex.asp – extracted December 2007.

Board of Studies NSW, http://www.boardofstudies.nsw.edu.au – extracted December 2007.

Chapter 6

Selecting and organizing teaching and learning modes

Introduction

There are an increasing number of learning modes available for teachers to use, ranging from computer-based simulations and on-line learning, through problem-based learning and inquiry to cooperative learning (see Box 6.1). Yet the emphasis on standards and accountability, especially No Child Left Behind (2001) legislation in the USA and the National Literacy Strategy and the National Numeracy Strategy in the UK, is having a restrictive emphasis on the modes of instruction that teachers use. Teachers are now required to be more directive and to provide activities that directly engage students. According to Webb and Vulliamy (2006) this has led to a narrowing of the curriculum in the UK and a further de-professionalization and deskilling of teachers.

Matching teacher and student priorities

It might appear to be merely commonsense that teaching styles need to be matched with students' learning styles. We have all experienced at first hand teaching situations where the teacher's style and students' learning styles have been very different, to the extent in some 'war' stories of being diametrically opposed!

Various authors such as Dunn *et al.* (1989), Hendry *et al.* (2005) contend that it is crucial for teachers to match their styles with students' learning styles. Every person has a learning style – it's as individual as a signature. Knowing students' learning styles, we can organize classrooms to respond to their individual needs. There is significant research evidence to support this stance (Liu and Read, 1994; Witkin *et al.*, 1977). A study by Ford and Chen (2001) concluded that students who learned in matched conditions scored significantly higher in conceptual knowledge. However, in their study the males outperformed females in matched conditions, so there are other complications to consider such as the role of gender in the interactions between matching/mismatching.

Box 6.1   Overview of eighteen alternative teaching and learning modes

- cooperative learning
- constructivist learning
- debates
- demonstrations
- direct instruction
- discussion
- field work
- independent study
- inquiry
- learning centres

- lectures and presentations
- mastery learning
- on-line learning
- oral reports
- practice drills
- project learning
- problem-based learning
- small group brainstorming
- questioning
- simulations and role plays

McIntyre, Pedder and Rudduck's (2005) study of pupil voice concluded that pupils who offered ideas, and where teachers responded to these ideas, were able to develop highly consensual views about learning – that is, by a process of interaction they developed a closer matching. Zembylas (2007) takes a similar stance with his emphasis on teachers and students developing emotional understanding of each other or of the subject matter they explore.

However, it can be very difficult to diagnose learning styles of students. What criteria do you use? For example, is performance in certain subjects more important than potential? How do you take account of students' needs and interests (Paris and Ayres, 1994) Although it might be laudable to argue that you match learning tasks to the needs, interests, abilities and previous experiences of students, how do you do this in practice?

Slack and Norwich (2007) refer to the reliability and validity of Smith's (2001) student self-report inventory, which focuses on visual, auditory and kinaesthetic styles. Their study of 160 students in south-west England in Key Stage 2 mixed-age classes found that the visual and auditory scales were directly related to learning mode preferences. They concluded that the use of this inventory to match students' learning styles was a promising way of bringing about government policy on inclusive, differentiated and personalized learning.

Another element to consider is whether students care about learning. Who or what invites students to learn? Tomlinson (2002) and McIntyre, Pedder and Rudduck (2005) contend that students seek an affirmation that they are significant in the classroom. As a consequence, matching factors should be couched in terms of:

- their acceptance in the classroom;
- making them feel safe – physically, emotionally and intellectually;
- making them consider that people care about them and listen to them.

Morrison and Ridley (1988) use a similar argument when they suggest that teachers need to consider the following questions when matching their students:

- How is each student's self-concept being developed?
- How is each student's motivation being developed?
- How does a teaching style(s) meet students' individual differences in need, interest, ability and skill?
- How does a teaching style(s) develop individual learning styles and rates of learning?
- How is autonomy being developed in each student?
- How does the organization of the class and school facilities foster security in each student?

The other side of the equation is to consider the teaching styles of teachers, which are often the result of personal attitudes and values, personality, previous experience and availability of resources (Howes *et al.*, 2005). Hargreaves (1995) distinguishes between three major teaching styles, which he labels 'lion tamers' (i.e., firm discipline, teacher as expert); 'entertainers' (i.e. multiple resources, active group work); and 'new normalities' (i.e. negotiated, individualized teaching).

Ryan and Cooper (2006) use the terms 'concrete sequential', 'abstract sequential', 'abstract random' and 'concrete random' to categorize four dominant teaching styles. A 'concrete sequential' teacher relies on hands-on materials, working models and displays to help students learn and tends to use task-oriented lessons. 'Abstract sequential' teachers value depth of knowledge and assist students to think about topics and to generate ideas. 'Abstract random' teachers capitalize on student interest and enthusiasm rather than adhering strictly to a lesson plan. 'Concrete random' teachers rely upon a variety of resources and organize their classes so that students operate independently or cooperatively.

These are just a few of the many groupings and stereotypes which have been produced about teaching styles. The major point to stress is that there are many differences and that we need to be aware that teaching styles will be dependent upon such factors as:

- type of activity in the classroom;
- type of organization of the classroom;
- use of resources;
- grouping and organization of students;
- students' roles in the classroom;
- criteria used for assessing students;
- nature and amount of student and teacher talk.

Yet it is also important to heed Joyce and Weil's (1986, pp. 433–34) caveats about learning styles, namely:

- it is not possible for teachers to assess the developmental levels of all their students and then create totally personalized curricula exactly matching their levels;
- students can and will adapt to different teaching styles if we give them the chance;
- the simplest way to discover the environments students progress best in is to provide them with a variety and observe their behaviour.

These authors are emphasizing the adaptability of teachers and of students. No teacher has a fixed style of teaching and no student has a fixed style of learning. In teaching–learning situations it is crucial that participants are flexible and adaptable.

Joyce and Weil (1986) provide additional insights into learning and teaching styles by their use of the term discomfort. They argue that a discomfort factor is necessary for teachers and students. If an environment is perfectly matched to the developmental levels of learners, it can be too comfortable and there will be little advance beyond that level. That is, discomfort is a precursor to growth. Teachers need to be constantly trying out new teaching styles even if they are unfamiliar and cause discomfort. For their part, teachers must assist students to acquire the necessary skills to adapt to new, unfamiliar learning styles.

Making use of technology

All modes of instruction make use of some form of technology, ranging from chalk to elaborate computer packages. Some forms of technology we take for granted, such as chalk, marker pens and whiteboards, especially if they do not interfere with a well-proven, traditional mode of instruction. Even the use of overhead projectors and powerpoint projectors causes minimal interference in teacher-directed forms of delivery.

It is when major behavioural changes are called for that teachers espouse concerns about using technology. There may be good reason for this techno-phobia if it involves different grouping patterns of students, if the authority of the teacher role is reduced or if the teacher has to learn new skills. Fear of using computers in schools, 'cyberphobia' (Russell and Bradley, 1996), may be quite deep seated and may occur in young teachers as well as older, highly experienced teachers.

There are currently many proponents who extol the virtues of incorporating computers into classroom activities – that is, technology-infused instruction. 'Multimedia (computers) create rich learning environments where kids really thrive' (Betts, 1997, p. 20). Within a few short years computer technology for educational use has expanded rapidly. There is now a range of software programs available, which can provide highly sophisticated functions relating to computer-managed instruction (CMI) and computer-assisted instruction (CAI).

CMI assists teachers with various organizational tasks, including recording student activities, resource investigations and presentation, and recording of students assessments. Instructional opportunities for students (CAI) are forever increasing (Williams, 2000). Norton and Wiburg (2003) include the following examples:

- skills software for drilling and practising: skills software programs offer interactive experiences, generally with immediate feedback about performance;
- computer graphics programs: these enable students to experience the world other than through verbal and print language – according to Norton and Wiburg (2003), 'shape, size, proportion, relationship, scale, surface, texture and rhythm are all expressed more rapidly through image making than through using words' (p. 53); as an example Franklin (2004) uses the floating staircase out of Harry Potter movies as a video clip to demonstrate how figures can be drawn in art classes ascending and descending stairs;
- data bases: text-based data bases include only text information; hypermedia data bases provide information with access through links; multimedia data bases include a variety of media forms including pictures, video clips, text and sound;
- telecommunication opportunities: these include e-mail messages; listservs distribute a single message to multiple receivers; bulletin boards post a public message to multiple receivers; chatrooms allow on-line conversations with multiple participants; synchronous communication allows two or more persons to interact at the exact same time;
- Internet-access to teaching/learning programs: this is readily available and they are fun to use – for example, Jones (2002) refers to 'The Human Race', an interactive Internet site that enables students to enjoy regular physical activity away from their computers;
- simulations: many educational software publishers produce simulations – '[s]tudents are given the power to "play" with a model of the subject being studied and to experience the effects of changing different variables in the model' (Norton and Wiburg, 2003, p. 57).
- mathematical devices: these provide students with the opportunity to explore real-time data – for example, probeware allows students to measure temperature, humidity, distance and many related variables; large amounts of data can be collected in a class period.
- assessment of student performance software: the number of such programs is increasing rapidly – there are now programs available which create a variety of rubrics (criteria for judging performance); electronic portfolios of work can be created; students' problem-solving processes can be observed and recorded; and a new set of interpretive tools is being created to monitor higher-level thinking and group collaboration;
- on-line courses: these are being developed at all levels of schooling – Lifter and Adams (1997) describe a Virtual Enrichment Program for primary students living in outback areas of New South Wales, Australia; secondary students living in small towns and outback areas of Queensland, Australia,

are being offered on-line (asynchronous) and real-time (synchronous) forms of instruction (Gibbs and Krause, 2000).

In summary, computer technology enables classroom instruction to be greatly benefited because it:

- provides the flexibility to meet the individual needs and abilities of each student (Norton and Wiburg, 2003);
- provides students with immediate access to rich source materials beyond the school and beyond the nation – that is, it fosters cross-cultural perspectives (Norton and Wiburg, 2003);
- presents information in new, relevant ways;
- encourages students to try out new ideas and to problem-solve (Means, 2000);
- encourages students to design, plan and undertake project-based multimedia learning (Simkins *et al.*, 2002);
- motivates and stimulates learning (Norton and Wiburg, 2003);
- enables students to feel comfortable with the tools of the Information Age.

Yet, it is evident in many schools that modes of instruction have been little affected by computer technology – 'with all of the investment of time and money that has gone into putting the hardware and software in place in schools, students will spend most of their school days as if these tools and information resources had never been invented' (Becker, 1998, p. 24). Various reasons have been given for the limited amount of take-up in schools, including the following:

- teachers are unfamiliar with the equipment, and the time and resources are not available for comprehensive, ongoing training (Frid, 2001);
- there is insufficient school budget for adequate numbers of personal computers, software, network wiring or support technicians to be available (Cradler and Bridgforth, 2004);
- there is limited pre-service preparation of teachers in the use of computer technology (Norton and Wiburg, 2003) and resultant student teachers show anxiety about using computers (Orlich *et al.*, 1998).●
  there is no overwhelming research evidence that teachers can be more effective using computer-based lessons rather than non-computer-based lessons (Russell and Bradley, 1996);
- the problems of equity for poorly funded schools could be heightened;
- computer-based technology threatens teachers – they are likely increasingly to lose control over the work they do (Bigum, 1997);
- computer technology is not a neutral force in the classroom – it concentrates upon speed and power and downplays student reflection and ethics (Schwartz, 1996);
- there is increasing evidence that it may discourage social interaction and lead to isolate behaviours;

- there are reports of considerable health risks for teachers (eye strain, wrist and shoulder pain) and students (the effects of carrying heavy laptops to and from school) (Norton and Wiburg, 2003);
- there are a growing number of cases of students cheating (cybercheating) at all levels of teaching (Varnham, 2001; Franek, 2006; Poole, 2004);
- substantial daily use of computers by young children may deprive them of important social and physical experiences (Monke, 2006).

Perhaps Means' (2001) warning is timely: 'We should reflect on "Online and offline: Getting the mixture right", or expressed another way "E-world and R-world: Getting the mixture right"' (p. 13).

Impact of standards on teaching and learning modes

The impact of standards and standards testing has been most notable in the USA and the UK. In the USA the No Child Left Behind Act (NCLB, 2001) aims to improve the standards of accountability by the use of standardized assessments (Fuhrman and Elmore, 2004). If a school does not meet the proficiency standards for all sub-groups of the student population (including African Americans, Latinos, low-income students, special education students) corrective action is taken, such as requiring additional tutoring of students, or poorly performing staff are transferred.

As might be anticipated, NCLB has put teachers under considerable pressure to 'teach to the test' and to use instructional modes involving direct instruction and practice drills (Marsh and Willis, 2007; Guilfoyle, 2006).

In the UK, national initiatives such as the National Literacy and Numeracy Strategies have been implemented to improve learning and to raise standards. Teachers are encouraged to use up to fifteen minutes of whole-class teaching in literacy and numeracy each day for primary school students. Myhill's (2006) study concludes that the whole-class discourses are typically teacher directed, to lead students to a predetermined destination. Burns and Myhill (2004) conclude that teaching in the UK is now 'a heavily accountable teaching culture, highly instructional, objectives-based pedagogy' (p. 47).

There are indications that the national testing of literacy and numeracy in Australia may also be leading to restrictive modes of teaching (Woods, 2007). Woods suggests that a reliance on high-stakes testing and 'scientific' evidence to justify the mandatory and some teaching methods is indeed destructive.

Teaching and learning modes

Teachers are often urged to use a variety of modes to ensure that diverse student interests and abilities can be accommodated (Greatorex and Malacova, 2006). Yet, teachers are limited in the modes they can use because of:

- restricted student abilities and interests;
- the high number of students in a class;
- the limitations of the teaching room;
- insufficient background or knowledge about a specific instructional mode;
- the type of technology available.

It is evident from Table 6.1 that a wide variety of modes is available and most teachers have the opportunity to expand their repertoire. There is only space here to describe three instructional modes.

Examples of modes

Directed questioning

The use of questions directed at students, both oral and written, is a very common mode of instruction. There are various reasons why teachers use questions and not all are related to student learning! Questions are used to:

- get immediate feedback during a demonstration;
- focus a discussion;
- pose a problem for solution;
- help students sharpen their perceptions;
- attract a student's attention;
- get a particular student to participate;
- diagnose a student's weaknesses;
- allow a student to shine before his or her peers;
- build up a student's security to an extent where the teacher is quite sure the student will respond correctly.

Questions can be used in rapid-fire succession or they can proceed more slowly with time for thoughtful responses. The types of questions a teacher asks will determine the kind of thinking they want their students to do. Various writers have provided different classifications of questions. Some of these include:

- high- and low-order questions
  - low-order – mainly recall of facts and specifics
  - high-order –mainly application analysis

- convergent and divergent or closed and open questions
  - convergent/closed – lead to expected answers
  - divergent/open – allow new directions in answers

- what, when, how, who and why?
  - a useful range to use which proceeds in sequence from low-order to high-order.

Table 6.1 Teacher-directed (T) and student-centred (S) emphases in lessons

Models of instruction	Introduction	Major activity	Conclusion	Teacher's role	Students' role	Organization mode
Lecturing/teacher talks	T	T	T	Presents information	Listen and respond	Total class
Practise drills	T	T/S	T	Repeats examples until skill mastered	Respond and practise	Total class/small groups
Directed questioning	T	T/S	T	Presents questions	Respond with answer, occasional answers	Total class/small groups/individual
Direct instruction	T	T/S	T/S	Presents task	Master task	Total class
Demonstration	T	S	T/S	Presents information materials	Observe, listen, practise	Total class/small groups
Constructivism	T/S	T/S	T/S	Raises issues	Active learning	Total class/small groups
Discussion	T	T/S	T/S	Questions, listens, responds	Listen, respond, question	Total class/small groups/individual
Cooperative learning	T/S	T/S	T/S	Presents goals	Work in groups	Small groups
Problem-solving/enquiry	T	S	T/S	Directs activities	Engage in activities	Small groups/individual
Role playing, simulation games	T	S	T/S	Introduces, monitors	Participate/act out	Small groups
Project-based learning/problem-based learning	T	S	T/S	Introduces, monitors	Active learning	Individual or small groups
Independent study	S	S	S	Facilitates, monitors	Initiate, engage in activities	Individual
On-line learning	T	S	S	Introduces, monitors	Initiate, engage, self-assess	Individual or group

Asking appropriate questions is a difficult task and requires considerable practice. A useful starting point is to choose an appropriate topic and then write down a range of questions which cover the sequences listed above. Ensure that the questions are concise and at an appropriate level of difficulty for students. Eliminate questions that appear to be ambiguous or vague.

Often students are very anxious about teacher questions and, in particular, their answers, because they realize that they will be judged by their peers as well as the teacher. They may be cautious in answering because of a lack of self-confidence. If the climate of the classroom is positive and supportive, students may be more prepared to take personal risks. It is up to the teacher to support students who are not confident about answering questions by rephrasing questions, asking supplementary questions or providing additional information.

Cooperative learning

Cooperative learning is a form of small-group instruction that has become especially popular with teachers and students. It is advocated as a complement to direct instruction and to teaching which is often highly competitive. Research evidence indicates that students gain considerably from cooperative learning across all grade levels of schooling (Ellis and Fouts, 1997; Gillies and Ashman, 2003).

A number of different approaches to cooperative learning have been developed but most share the characteristics listed in Box 6.2. Cooperative learning is a technique where a group is given a task to do that includes efforts from all students.

According to Cruickshank *et al.* (2005) cooperative learning occurs when learners work together in small groups and are rewarded for their collective accomplishments (see Box 6.3). Groups or teams of four to six work on particular tasks. The members of the group are selected so that they are heterogeneous in terms of gender, academic ability, race and other traits. The rules of behaviour for participants involve responsibility and accountability to one's self and the team, and a willingness to encourage peer help and cooperate with other team members. The rewards or marks are based on the team's achievement.

A number of different cooperative learning models have been developed and used in school settings. The Jigsaw method involves the following:

1 The teacher divides the class into teams of five or six students, ensuring that there is a mix of abilities in each team.
2 The assigned team activity has subtasks so that there is one task for each team member, which is variously labelled as A, B, etc.
3 The persons assigned to do task A in each team come together and form a new team. New teams are also formed for B, etc.
4 The newly formed teams (A team, B team, etc.) work on completing their task by discussing issues and then working individually or collectively.

Box 6.2   Characteristics of cooperative learning classrooms

- Most classroom activities involve using small groups of three to five students.
- Each group is as heterogeneous as possible in terms of gender, ethnicity, and knowledge and ability.
- The teacher and students set clear, specific, individual and group goals.
- Each student has to achieve certain individual goals as well as being accountable for group success.
- The teacher provides worthwhile group rewards on the basis of group members' individual achievements.
- Each group divides up group work into individual tasks.
- Each group member soon learns that interdependence is needed for the group to function effectively. This involves a considerable amount of face-to-face interaction.
- Each group member learns effective listening and communicating skills as well as group processing skills.
- Each group evaluates how successfully each student has contributed to the group. Students need to interact with and support each other in completing the overall task and the sub-tasks.

5 When the tasks have been completed, the students reassemble in their original teams. Each team member (A, B, etc.) shares his or her information and this is compiled into the overall assignment, which is then submitted to the teacher.

Once a teacher has selected a particular approach it is then necessary to undertake the following planning steps:

1 Develop materials – this may involve a mini-lecture to be given by the teacher for the preparation of text, worksheets and study guides for each group to use directly.
2 Plan the tasks and roles for students in each group – students need to have a clear understanding of their roles. It may take several sessions before students are familiar with what to do.
3 Plan for the use of time and space – don't underestimate the time needed for cooperative learning lessons.

Once the planning sequence has been completed the steps involved in the actual lessons include:

1 Teacher goes over goals for the lesson.
2 Teacher presents information to students either verbally or with text.

Box 6.3   Benefits of cooperative learning

- improves learning of academic content
- improves student strategies for acquiring information
- develops social skills
- boosts students' self-esteem
- allows student decision-making.

3 Teacher explains to students how to form their learning teams.
4 Teacher assists learning teams as they do their work.
5 Teacher tests knowledge of learning materials or groups present the results of their work.
6 Teacher finds ways to recognize both individual and group effort and achievement.

(Arends, 2006, p. 332)

Not all lessons are conducive to cooperative learning. Ideally, topics are used which require the searching out of answers and the exploration of alternative solutions. The teacher also has to make organizational decisions which may only be possible in certain circumstances – for example rearranging the room furniture and organizing materials. There can also be difficulties in groups and personality conflicts still occur. Students may need considerable help in developing problem-solving skills (Barry et al., 1998).

To overcome some of these difficulties, especially with lower grades, it may be necessary for the teacher to assign roles. Chapin and Messick (1999) suggest the following:

- one student as chairperson to organize the group's work;
- one student as recorder or secretary to write down the group's answers;
- one student as check person to check that everyone can explain and agree with completed answers;
- one student as encourager to keep participants interested and excited.

The research evidence on cooperative learning is extremely positive and includes literally hundreds of published studies (see, for example, Ellis and Fouts, 1993; Orlich et al., 1998; Emmer and Gerwell, 1998). Some of the major findings include:

- achievement effects of cooperation learning are consistently positive – that is, experimental groups have significant positive effects over control groups;
- positive achievement effects occur across all grade levels from 2 to 12 (infants to senior secondary, Australia), in all major subjects, and the effects are equally positive for high, average and low achievers.

On-line teaching

On-line teaching can range from the use of multimedia resources accessible from digital repositories to complete instructional courses (Freebody and Muspratt, 2007). The on-line environment is quite unique because of the capacity to shift the time of delivery and the place of delivery compared with traditional teaching (Jury, 2004).

Developing on-line teaching courses is expensive and there are a number of issues to consider:

- Does the need exist?
- The design of the course must consider the existing technology available; how to maintain interactivity between instructors and students (Melton, 2004).

Yet it is evident that electronic on-line learning communities are developing rapidly.

Synchronous tools (such as chatrooms, instant messaging) and asynchronous communication tools (such as e-mail, discussion boards and blogs) are now available to facilitate the implementation of on-line courses.

Concluding comments

Teachers and students both benefit from initiating/experiencing a range of modes of instruction. How a particular mode of instruction is used in a classroom is dependent upon a number of factors and there will be many variations and hybrids from an idealized mode. Further, it is a learning process for all participants and early experimentations with different instructional modes are likely to cause discomfort – for both the teacher and the students. Yet it is essential that a varied combination of modes are used to ensure that all students are exposed to at least some approaches which are closely amenable to their interests and preferred ways of learning.

Reflections and issues

1 Reflect upon the modes of instruction you have used/typically use in the classroom. Why do you prefer these approaches? List some possible advantages and disadvantages of each.
2 'Students are not failing because of the curriculum. Students can learn almost any subject matter when they are taught with methods and approaches responsive to their learning style strengths' (Dunn *et al.*, 1989, p. 15). Do you support the view that students have dominant learning styles? Should students be 'matched' with modes of instructions that suit their learning styles? Give details of how this might be achieved.

3 'Teaching cannot simply consist of telling. It must enlist the pupils' own active participation since what gets processed gets learned' (Tomlinson and Kalbfleisch, 1998). What modes of instruction can a teacher use to encourage more active pupil participation?

4 Plan a unit that could be taught using cooperative learning. How would the plan differ from other approaches? What might be some possible advantages and disadvantages?

5 Discuss how modern technology can enrich modes of instruction. What are some of the problems for teachers and students in using computers in classrooms? What personal goals do you have for using computers in your various modes of instruction?

6 How do you react to the following statements? 'When I think of using computers in the classroom, I feel anxious'; 'I am unable to evaluate educational software' (Russell and Bradley, 1996, p. 237). Describe your level of competence and confidence in using computer-based instruction. Are you actively trying to upgrade it? Give details.

7 To what extent is the selection of appropriate study materials crucial to the success of cooperative learning lessons?

8 Teachers should not assume that all their students possess the social skills needed to work effectively in small groups. What can the teacher do to assist students with limited social skills?

9 Middle schooling programmes rely heavily upon cooperative learning strategies. What are the strengths and weaknesses of using this approach with students (Years 5 to 9)?

Web sources

Technology in schools, http://www.nea.org/technoogy/ – extracted December 2007.

Constructivism, http://www.funderstanding.com/constructivism.cfm – extracted December 2007.

Competition and student learning, http://www.ascd.org/portal/site/ascd/template. MAXIMIZE/menuitem.1eb2de4 … – extracted December 2007.

Teaching strategies – early childhood education, http://www.teachingstrategies.com/index.cfm – extracted December 2007.

No Child Left Behind Act, http://en.widipedia.org/wiki/No_Child_Left_Behind – extracted December 2007.

Chapter 7

Assessment, grading and reporting

Introduction

As noted by Black (2001), 'reformers dreaming about changing the education system for the better almost always see a need to include assessment and testing in their plans and frequently see them as the main instruments of their reforms' (p. 80). However, one of the main problems is that assessment is about several things at once. It is about grading and about learning (Carless, 2007). This causes major problems for teachers whereby they might value innovative assessment ideas but in practice what they do is far more limited (James and Pedder, 2006).

Assessment can take many forms and is certainly much wider than traditional forms of objective tests and essay tests. We should never forget that assessment can have a dramatic effect on the lives of students (Cunningham 1998). Wherever possible, forms of assessment should be used that raise student's self-esteem – learning experiences are needed which enable students to create success criteria and to organize their individual targets (Clarke, 2001).

There are significant and deep-rooted differences in the assessment systems of different countries. Black and Wiliam's (2005) survey of England, France, Germany and the USA provides some fascinating differences:

- England: there has been a deep distrust of teachers; many new formal tests have been initiated; there is some school-based assessment.
- France: they use a range of different assessment systems; teachers concentrate on formative assessment and pedagogy; all summative assessment is handled externally;
- Germany: they rely on national tests; teachers are trusted to make summative judgments;
- USA: there has been an increase in testing for accountability purposes; there is rigid pacing of teaching to ensure that adequate progress is made to the standards in the No Child Left Behind Act (2001) (US Department of Education, 2002);
- Australia: Cumming and Maxwell (2004) consider that assessment practices across Australian states and territories are very uneven; the new frameworks

are now specifying student outcomes; there are some opportunities for teachers to collaborate on formative assessment.

It is evident, as noted by Black and Wiliam (2005) that 'assessment practices and initiatives are determined at least as much by culture and politics as it [*sic*] is by educational evidence and values' (p. 260).

Some of the newer approaches to assessment, such as 'authentic' and 'assessment for learning', examined in this chapter may be more inclusive and user-friendly for students than traditional approaches.

Assessment

Assessment is the term typically used to describe the activities undertaken by a teacher to obtain information about the knowledge, skills and attitudes of students. Activities can involve the collection of formal assessment data (e.g. by the use of objective tests) or the use of informal data (e.g. by the use of observation checklists). Teachers typically assign a grade or mark (numerical score, letter, grade, descriptive ranking) for work undertaken by students such as a project or a written test. Some of the basic principles of assessment are listed in Box 7.1.

Reasons for assessment

Assessment is usually undertaken for the following reasons:

- diagnosis of learning and monitoring progress;
- grading students;
- predicting future achievements;
- motivating students;
- diagnosis of teaching.

Diagnosis of learning that has occurred and monitoring progress are major reasons for assessment (Chase, 1999). This information may be gleaned by a teacher asking questions of individual students or by student comments. The diagnosis should help each student understand his or her weaknesses and it also guides the teacher about where to direct his or her instructional energies.

In most cases, student grades are assigned to indicate achievement at the end of a unit or term, semester or year. Sufficient evidence needs to be collected by a teacher to enable the person to assign accurate grades. Generally, the more frequent and varied the assessments used, the more informed the teacher will be about the grades to assign to students.

Assessment can also be used to predict students' eligibility for selection in future courses. This is usually of importance at upper secondary school levels.

Box 7.1   Some basic principles of assessment

1   Assessment can only be based on samples of behaviour and therefore inaccuracies will always occur (Salvia and Ysseldyke, 1998).
2   Assessment must communicate to teachers how to make instruction more effective. Assessment is an integral and prominent component of the entire teaching and learning process (McInnis and Devlin, 2002).
3   Assessment of knowledge and skills must be clearly aligned with expected learning outcomes.
4   Assessment is not done mainly to grade students but to promote instruction.
5   Assessment must be fair to all individuals and groups (Willingham and Cole, 1997).
6   Assessment must measure a broad range of abilities (Darling-Hammond and Falk, 1997).
7   Assessment results should be meaningful to all participants, students, teachers and parents (Wiggins, 1998).

Assessment can often increase the motivation of students even though the teacher may not consciously highlight it as an incentive to work hard! It depends on the individual learner, as some students will be highly motivated by an impending test whereas others might suffer excessive stress and/or be demotivated.

Assessment data can provide valuable diagnostic information for the teacher – some reasons why lessons fly or flop (Eisner, 1993). They may indicate, for example, that aspects of content or processes were not understood fully by students, or that the material presented was too difficult or too easy for a particular class.

Of course, it is also important to be mindful of the distorting effects of assessment (Gipps and Murphy, 1994). Different forms of assessment will promote particular kinds of learning (e.g. rote learning) and downgrade other kinds, especially if these are difficult to measure (e.g. higher-order thinking).

Assessing for whom?

There are close links between reasons for assessment and their intended audiences. Possible audiences include the following:

- learners: they should be the main audience but typically they are not given a high priority – they are rarely involved in planning the assessment activities;
- teachers: need feedback about the effectiveness of their teaching – student assessment data are being used increasingly as a data source for appraising teachers;

- parents: want regular feedback – media efforts to publicize school results and 'league tables' of schools have led to increased clamouring for assessment information;
- tertiary institutions: universities and technical and further education (TAFE) colleges require specific assessment information from applicants intending to enrol;
- employers: are demanding more specific information, especially in terms of literacy and numeracy and key competencies.

Important emphases in assessment

ICT developments in assessment

The widespread use of computers in schools is now well established. There has been a significant investment in educational information and communication technologies (ICT) around the world (Quellmalz and Kozma, 2003). According to Ridgway and McCusker (2003), ICT 'is at the centre of a cultural vortex which is bringing about radical social change. ... It has had a profound effect on the cultural practices associated with every academic discipline over the last 20 years' (p. 310).

ICT enables assessment of real-world problems and gives students and teachers more opportunities for feedback and reflection. Yet, according to Baker (2003), technology-enhanced assessment is still emerging even though development is rapid. Raikes and Harding (2003), with reference to our current 'horseless carriage stage' (p. 268), argue that there are still many barriers to overcome, namely:

- cost and expected return on investment;
- establishing the equivalence of pencil and paper and computer test forms;
- security;
- coping with the diversity of ICT environments and cultures in schools and colleges;
- software and hardware reliability, and resilience of the system in the face of breakdown (Raikes and Harding, 2003, p. 270).

But the opportunities using ICT do look promising. Consider, for example, the coordinated ICT Assessment Framework, funded by the US National Science Foundation and using a working group of international experts in ICT from Chile, Finland, Norway, Singapore and the USA (Quellmalz and Kozma, 2003). As illustrated in Figure 7.1, the ICT strategies and tools that are currently being used by many teachers are quite impressive.

ICT tools are many, including the Internet, word-processors and data bases. These can be used to accomplish multiple ICT strategies, such as 'communicate' and 'critically evaluate': the knowledge being assessed can include content

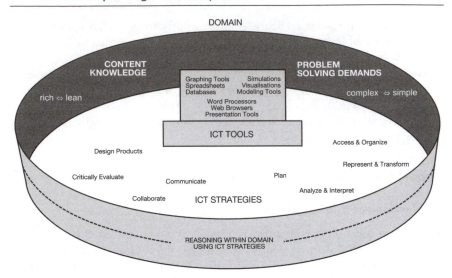

Figure 7.1 Coordinated ICT assessment framework.
Source: Quellmalz and Kosma (2003).

knowledge ('lean' factual knowledge to 'rich' schematic knowledge); and a process knowledge dimension (which can range from simple, procedural knowledge to complex, strategic knowledge).

It is also interesting to note from this study of 174 classrooms that 78 per cent of teachers and students used the ICT tools listed in Figure 7.1, 71 per cent used web resources, 68 per cent used e-mail and 52 per cent used multimedia software.

Geh (2006) refers to curriculum-embedded assessment programs developed by the Rapid Assessment Corporation. For example, he argues that the Reading Assessment is highly successful – it alerts teachers to learning difficulties and encourage teachers to provide highly targeted individual tutoring or small-group instruction. Books in the school's existing library are labelled according to reading level; students select books to read based on their interests and reading level according to a STAR reading test. After finishing a book students take a computer-based quiz unique to each book. All the information on the computer is instantly updated. Reports can be organized by building, classroom, teacher or student.

Landauer, Laham and Foltz (2003) refer to recent successful efforts to develop automatic essay assessment. The Latent Semantic Analysis (LSA) Scheme uses a combination of content, style and mechanics to assess essays. Various empirical trials have revealed that LSA produced reliabilities equivalent to that of humans.

Although the many examples of ICT for assessment are encouraging, other writers issue various caveats. For example, McFarlane (2003) suggests that the safest route to progress is to computerize conventional tests. There are issues still to be resolved over the equivalence of paper and computer-based tests, such as the fact that the lack of scratch workspace on mathematics tests can cause underachievement on some computer-based tests (Russell *et al.*, 2003).

Baker (2003) and Raikes and Harding (2003) note that an ongoing problem with ICT for assessment is the competitive branding and positioning of rival groups developing very expensive assessment initiatives. Baker (2003), for example, suggests that approaches are needed to 'appropriately and rigorously test and publicly report findings of competing strategies' (p. 422).

Assessment for learning

Over the last decade there has been major interest in a number of countries, but especially Scotland and England, the USA, Australia and Canada, in 'assessment for learning' or 'formative assessment'. One of the driving forces for this has been the seminal work of Black and Wiliam (1998) from the Assessment Reform Group in London. Subsequently, major projects have been directed by Mary James and David Pedder (2006) (Learning How to Learn Project) and Priestley (2005) in England, and Assessment is for Learning (AifL) in Scotland.

In Canada, Earl's (2005) work has been very influential. In California, the Classroom Assessment Project to Improve Teaching and Learning (CAPITAL), as outlined by Coffey, Sato and Thiebault (2005), attempts to analyse teachers' assessment practices, how they are shaped and how they are able to improve their day-to-day assessment efforts.

Baker (2007) describes another major project, CRESST POWERSOURCE, an international collaborative project which examines the use of multiple interim assessments of problem-solving and explanation (formative assessment) in the teaching of middle school algebra.

It has been very evident to researchers that to encourage classroom teachers to use assessment for learning effectively is indeed very complex. Mary James, as reported in Marshall and Drummond (2006), notes the tension between the 'letter' and the 'spirit' of formative assessment. That is, many teachers use formative assessment practices superficially but do not integrate practices into their curriculum planning.

Hargreaves (2005) argues that there are various conceptions of assessment for learning, which he groups into six categories:

- it means monitoring students' performance against targets or objectives;
- it means using assessment to inform next steps in teaching and learning;
- it means teachers giving feedback for improvement;
- it means learning about children's learning;
- it means children taking some control of their own learning and assessment;
- it means turning assessment into a learning event.

She concludes that these various definitions can be interpreted as two major categories for conceptions of learning: learning as attaining objectives; and learning as constructing knowledge. She notes that the majority of teachers still hold the measurement/objective conception, which is understandable in the light of a National Curriculum which has been operating in the UK since 1988.

Conceptually there are problems in treating formative assessment and summative assessment as separate entities. For example, Taras (2005) contends, after Scriven (1967), that 'all assessment begins with summative assessment (which is a judgment) and that formative assessment is in fact summative assessment plus feedback which is used by the learner' (p. 466).

Kennedy (2007) argues that modifications are needed to forms of summative assessment so that the two can co-exist more successfully. Negative wash-back effects of high-stakes summative assessment can greatly limit opportunities for formative assessment.

In terms of practising assessment for learning, numerous researchers point to practical issues for teachers, such as Lee and Wiliam (2005); Coffey, Sato and Thiebault (2005); Brandom, Carmichael and Marshall (2005); Guskey (2002); Fisher and Frey (2007); and Priestley and Sime (2005). For example, Priestley and Sime (2005) concluded from their AifL study in Scotland that four factors for successfully engaging staff members included the following:

- proactive leadership;
- professional trust in the capacity of teachers to drive change and adapt teaching;
- the creation of space for collaboration between teachers;
- the use of 'start-small' strategies.

Priestley and Sime (2005) argue that these four factors combine to 'stimulate high levels of socio-cultural interaction within a school' (p. 482)

Assessment: value continua

System-level values and classroom teaching preferences can have a major influence on the types of assessment which can actually occur (see Table 7.1). In many cases the preferences can be depicted on continuums which illustrate opposing points and many points in between.

Diagnostic–formative–summative

Let us look first at diagnostic assessment. Obviously students come into classrooms with varying backgrounds and interests so it is inefficient to start a new teaching unit without checking their knowledge and understandings. Some may lack the prerequisite skills to undertake the lessons required of them and, worse still, others may have certain negative attitudes to the topic, which will provide a major difficulty unless the teacher is aware in advance of these

Table 7.1 Value continua in assessment

Diagnostic	Formative	Summative
Informal	Formal	
Norm-referenced	Criterion-referenced	
Process	Product	
Learner judged	Teacher judged	
Internal	External	
Technicist	Liberal	Postmodernist

emotional attitudes. On the other hand, if the students already have a number of skills or understandings that the teacher intended to teach them, their interest and enthusiasm would be reduced if the same activities were repeated. Diagnostic evaluation simply reminds teachers that they must start their instruction at the level the students have reached. What is more, the teacher needs to be continually aware of students' levels in their progress through the curriculum unit. In this sense, the teacher is undertaking diagnostic evaluation through all the stages of instruction.

Formative assessment provides data about instructional units in progress and students in action. The data help to develop or form the final curriculum product and help students adjust to their learning tasks through the feedback they receive. Formative evaluation is important, therefore, because it provides data to enable 'on-the-spot' changes to be made where necessary. Students' learning activities can be refocused and redirected and the range and depth of the instructional activities of a curriculum can be revised in 'mid-stream' (Tunstall and Gipps, 1996). It applies, therefore, to both course improvement and student growth, although some writers tend to concentrate only upon the former (Pryor and Torrance, 1996).

By contrast, Clarke (2001) concentrates very much on the importance of formative assessment to bring about student growth. She cites Black and Wiliam's (1998) research findings that formative assessment strategies do raise standards of student achievement, especially for children of lower ability (see the section on 'Assessment for learning' on pp. 75–76).

Summative assessment is the final goal of an educational activity. Eventually, teachers need to know the relative merits and demerits of a curriculum package. Also, they need to have collected appropriate information about the levels of achievement reached by students. Of course, this information may be used in a diagnostic way as a preliminary to further activities, but it must be emphasized that summative evaluation provides the data from which decisions can be made.

Over recent years, related summative assessment terms have become widely used, such as benchmarking (the process of measuring standards of actual performance against those achieved by others with broadly similar characteristics) and value-added assessment (where raw scores from test results are adjusted to allow for the characteristics of the intake of the school; Clarke, 1998). These forms of summative assessment usually involve 'high-stakes' standards and the publication of results for parents and community to make comparisons (Hess, 2003) (see Table 7.2).

Informal–formal

Informal assessment is inevitable, ongoing and very useful. Informal observations of natural situations are especially valuable for gaining information about student

Table 7.2 Commonly used assessment techniques

Techniques	Diagnostic	Formative	Summative
Informal observing and recording of student behaviour	Anecdotal records	Anecdotal records	Anecdotal records
	Case histories	Case histories	Case histories
	Checklists	Checklists	Checklists
	Rating scales by teacher	Rating scales by teacher	Rating scales by teacher
	Unobtrusive techniques	Unobtrusive techniques	Unobtrusive techniques
Informal collecting of information from students	Interest inventories	Interest inventories	Interest inventories
	Rating scales by students	Rating scales by students	Rating scales by students
	Questionnaires	Questionnaires	Questionnaires
	Interviews	Interviews	Interviews
	Sociograms	Sociograms	Sociograms
	Self-reports	Self-reports	Self-reports
Analysis of student work examples	Individual and group projects	Individual and group projects	Individual and group projects
	Content analysis of work book	Content analysis of work book	Content analysis of work book
	Logbooks and journals	Logbooks and journals	Logbooks and journals
	Portfolios	Portfolios	Portfolios
Testing of students	Objective test	Objective test	Objective test
	Standardized tests	Standardized tests	Standardized tests
	Essay tests	Essay tests	Essay tests
	Semantic differentials	Semantic differentials	Semantic differentials
	Attitude scales	Attitude scales	Attitude scales
	Simulation and role plays	Simulation and role plays	Simulation and role plays
	Projective techniques	Projective techniques	Projective techniques

Note: Italics refer to the optimal time to use each of the listed techniques; that is, they could be used at diagnostic (early) or formative (middle) or summative (end) levels but some periods are better than others.

interactions. The less obvious it is to students that they are being assessed, the more natural will be their behaviour. Informal assessment is especially important in early childhood and lower primary classes. Teachers use various techniques such as observations, running records, anecdotal records and written notes to assess the development of the whole child (Carr, 2001).

Formal assessment is planned and often is an obtrusive activity. Thus any weekly tests and planned assignments could be categorized as formal assessments. There are a number of forms of informal and formal assessments that can be used.

Norm-referenced–criterion-referenced

Norm-referenced measures are used to compare students' performance in specific tests. These measures simply provide comparative aged-based data on how well certain students perform in a test (e.g. maths or reading). Of course, they are open to misinterpretation. Students who receive special coaching or good teaching are likely to outperform those who do not have these opportunities. Norm-referenced measures provide valuable evaluative data about the performance of students on specific tasks but do not tell us anything about an individual's potential or his or her attitude toward certain subjects.

Criterion-referenced measures avoid the competitive elements of norm-referenced measures because information is obtained about students' performance in terms of their previous performances rather than in relation to the performance of others. Once the skill level for a particular task has been defined (the criterion) it is presumed that a student will persevere until it is attained. The difficulty lies in defining learning activities in terms of tasks to be mastered. Certain subjects such as mathematics and topics such as motor skills and mapping are particularly amenable to this approach, but it is more difficult to establish criterion-referenced tasks for 'creative writing' or 'art'.

Performance-based assessments have gained considerable support over recent years. They can be criterion- or standards-referenced but typically the former. In the USA thirty-four states are now using tests that include performance tasks (Heck and Crislip, 2001). These performance tests require students to demonstrate their acquisition of problem-solving and critical thinking (Yeh, 2001) or writing skills (Heck and Crislip, 2001). Some writers link these kinds of performance tests with constructivism – the theory that knowledge is constructed by individual human beings and not merely discovered (see, for example, von Glaserfield, 1995; Phillips, 1995).

The intention may be to develop criterion-referenced measures but in many cases they finish up as norm-referenced measures. For example, Elliott and Chan contend that

> in theory the assessment [for the National Curriculum in England and Wales] was supposed to be criterion-referenced and therefore linked to

task specific standards of achievement. However, the standardized tests developed for each key stage have not been able to avoid a considerable element of norm-referencing and are too crude to inform teaching and learning.

(Elliott and Chan 2002, p. 8)

Process–product

Most assessment involves making judgements about products such as an assignment, project or object. Products are often perceived to be the major priority of the course. Yet, processes such as thinking skills, working cooperatively in groups and problem-solving are very important (Withers and McCurry, 1990).

Payne (2003) contends that assessing processes such as interpersonal relationships and performance is important and that process and product are intimately related. He suggests that if the steps involved in arriving at the product are indeterminate and measuring the processes leading to the product is impractical, then the emphasis has to be on the product. Wiggins (1998) considers that although a number of practical techniques are available for assessing processes, this still requires the teacher to make judgements: is the process observed/rated 'exemplary' or 'on course' or 'grounds for concern'? Notwithstanding, various computer programs are now available whereby multiple process measures can be taken (Asp, 2000).

Learner-judged–teacher-judged

At most levels of schooling the teacher does the judging about standards. Typically, individual teachers set and mark their tests and other forms of assessment. Rarely are students consulted or given responsibility for self-assessment. Yet there are very promising developments if students are involved (Francis, 2001). Clarke (2001) contends that learners must ultimately be responsible for their learning. She states that the greatest impact on students is an overall rise in their self-esteem, as revealed by such student behaviours as the following:

- being able to say where they need help without any sense of failure;
- beginning to set their own targets and goals;
- now being able to speak about their learning when they would not have done so before. (Clarke, 2001, p. 44)

Munns and Woodward (2006) contend that there are strong theoretical and practical connections between student engagement and student self-assessment. Their study of primary school students in the Fair Go Project (action research into student engagement among low social-economic status students in Sydney's south-west) noted that students' reflections about their learning and the use of higher levels of thinking greatly improved their engagement.

McDonald and Boud (2003) undertook a study of ten high schools in Sydney where senior school students and their teachers were trained in the use of self-assessment. The experimental group achieved higher examination results than the control group. McDonald and Boud (2003) concluded that the 'use of self-assessment training as part of the curriculum provides a way of laying the foundation for the kinds of skills students will need as lifelong support after school' (p. 219).

Internal–external

Internal assessment involves those directly participating in the teaching–learning process, usually classroom teachers. External assessors become involved when 'high-status/high-stakes' assessments are to occur state-wide or nationally, typically at the completion of senior secondary schooling.

In the USA high-stakes, standardized assessments are widely used and have been very popular over recent years in many states because it is argued that they raise the academic performance of students and contribute to them earning at least basic educational credentials (Schiller and Muller, 2000). Yet there are many critics of high-stakes testing. Some of the major concerns include:

- test scores are mainly used for sorting and ranking students – there are serious adverse effects on low-income and minority students (Casas and Meaghan, 2001; Brennan et al., 2001);
- tests divert valuable instructional time to prepare for testing (Froese-Germain, 2001; Pedulla, 2003; Egan, 2003);
- the impact of high-stakes summative assessment can have negative effects on student motivation (Harlen and Crick, 2003).

Guskey (2002) contends that in the USA the large-scale assessments are successful in rank-ordering schools and students. However, he argues that the assessments best suited to guide improvements in learning are teacher administered quizzes, tests and assignments.

In the UK large-scale summative assessment tests for the National Curriculum in English, maths and science have been in use since the late 1980s (Newton, 2003). Leading experts such as Wiliam (2003) and James and Pedder (2006), are extremely critical of these summative tests and assert that an alternative model is needed which uses teacher assessment for formative, diagnostic and summative purposes.

In Australia, with the exception of Queensland and the Australian Capital Territory, all other states and territories use external assessments at Year 12.

These are quite evidently high-stakes tests – they enjoy considerable public confidence and credibility, despite their limitations. More recently, tests have been introduced in all states in Australia: literacy and numeracy tests for all students in Years 5 and 7. The federal government is attempting to develop nationally agreed minimum acceptable standards for literacy and numeracy at a particular year level (Meadmore, 2001). Although it is problematic whether these tests fairly and justly represent the diversity of Australian students, they are likely to be retained as a major, highly visible platform of centralized testing.

Inclusive–exclusive

The production of forms of assessment should, ideally, provide access to all learners and be inclusive, regardless of gender, ethnicity or disadvantage. Studies have indicated that in many cases assessment is far from inclusive and that it is exclusive. Salvia and Ysseldyke (1998) cite examples where minority ethnic groups and females are not given equal opportunities. It is evident that a number of multiple-choice tests tend to be biased against females (Gipps and Murphy, 1994; Willingham and Cole, 1997). Teachers' assessment of ethnic minority students can often be biased, as reported by Cunningham (1998).

Gipps raises three fundamental questions about inclusivity:

1 Whose knowledge is taught?
2 Why is it taught in a particular way to this particular group?
3 How do we enable the histories and cultures of people of colour, and of women, to be taught in responsible and responsive ways?

(Gipps, 1994, p. 151)

Inclusivity also applies to students with special needs. There is a need for all students to have access to appropriate forms of assessment. Kopriva (1999) notes that there has been considerable interest in developing alternative assessments and alternative testing formats for students with special needs.

Technicist–liberal/postmodernist

A number of writers argue that traditional forms of assessment are technicist and are used to identify and perpetuate the social hierarchy (Blackmore, 1988; Broadfoot, 1979). Many forms of assessment, especially traditional written examinations, concentrate upon a narrow view of student achievement which emphasizes the outcomes of the academic curriculum. Hargreaves *et al.* (2002) contend that technological advances in assessment also have this narrow focus – using advanced computer skills to devise and refine valid forms of assessment.

The other option, according to Hargreaves *et al.* (2002) is to consider the postmodern perspective and to highlight uncertainties and diversities. After all, 'human beings are not completely knowable and so no assessment process or system can therefore be fully comprehensive' (Hargreaves *et al.*, 2002, p. 83).

Authentic assessment

Authentic assessment and, sometimes, the assessment of authentic learning are two names that were popularized in the 1990s and continue to be widely used in the assessment literature in the twenty-first century. Authentic assessment encompasses far more than what students learn as measured by standardized tests or even by ordinary teacher-made tests. Authenticity arises from assessing what is most important, not from assessing what is most convenient. Fundamentally, then, there is nothing new about authentic assessment as a reaction against narrowness in education and a return toward the kind of education that connects feeling, thinking and doing, as advocated by John Dewey and other progressives early in the twentieth century. Applied to the curriculum, authentic assessment suggests that the curriculum must be directed at learning in the broadest possible sense; hence the curriculum itself should be evaluated in terms of how well it contributes to students' deep understandings not only of subject matter but also of their own lives. In this sense, the popularization of authentic assessment represents another manifestation of grassroots, bottom-up approaches to curriculum planning.

Fundamentally, authentic assessment is a way of capturing and somewhat formalizing the myriad things that perceptive teachers have always considered – although often intuitively – about what is happening to their students (Gipps *et al.*, 2000). The advantages of formalizing the process are in making it increasingly accessible to more and more teachers and in keeping it viable as an integral part of flexible curriculum planning and development against the inroads of centralized curriculum control. The basic danger in formalizing the process is that the more widely it is used, the more likely it is to be reduced to a formula coopted by centralizing influences and thus to lose much of its flexibility and value.

In authentic assessment, therefore, the tasks students undertake are more practical, realistic and challenging than traditional paper-and-pencil tests (Pryor and Torrance, 1996). Students are engaged in more meaningful, context-bound activities, focusing their energies on 'challenging, performance-oriented tasks that require analysis, integration of knowledge, and invention' (Darling-Hammond *et al.*, 1995, p. 2). Eisner (1993) states that the tasks of authentic assessment are 'more complex, more closely aligned with life than with individual performance measured in an antiseptic context using sanitized instruments that were untouched by human hands' (p. 224). Some general characteristics of authentic assessment are listed in Box 7.2.

Although there are many enthusiastic supporters of authentic assessment (for example Wiggins and McTighe, 1998; McTighe and Wiggins, 2004; Tomlinson, 2005) there are many accounts of problems in implementing it.

Box 7.2   Some characteristics of authentic assessment

- Teachers collect evidence from multiple activities.
- Assessments reflect the tasks that students will encounter in the world outside schools.
- Assessments reveal how students go about solving problems as well as the solutions they formulate.
- Procedures for assessments and the contents of assessments are derived from students' everyday learning in schools.
- Assessments reflect local values, standards and control; they are not imposed externally.
- The tasks students are assessed upon include more than one acceptable solution to each problem and more than one acceptable answer to each question.

Franklin (2002) notes three major difficulties: parental unfamiliarity with the goals of authentic assessment; teacher preferences for traditional methods; and the greater amounts of time required to undertake authentic assessment. Hargreaves *et al.* (2002) note that teachers have great difficulty in knowing how to measure outcomes, with the need to harmonize assessment expectations between home and school and with the issue of time and resources.

Hargreaves *et al.* (2002) are also critical on the grounds that from a post-modern perspective, authentic assessment is not knowable; it is contrived – schools are highly artificial places. Meir (1998) considers that 'much of what passes for authentic curriculum and authentic assessment is the jargon of contemporary pedagogy' (p. 598).

Commonly used assessment techniques

A number of assessment techniques are available to teachers and they can be used at various diagnostic, formative and summative stages. On the one hand, it is very desirable for teachers to use a variety of techniques to ensure that the multi-dimensionality of student performance is adequately explored (Haney and Madaus, 1989). But there is also the danger of over-assessing and collecting vast arrays of data that have limited use.

McMillan *et al.*'s (2002) research study of the assessment practices of over 900 primary school teachers concluded that they use direct observation as a major technique; they only tap students' higher-level thinking skills to a limited extent; and they place greater importance on social behaviour than academic achievement.

Trepanier-Street *et al.* (2001), in their study of 300 lower primary and upper primary teachers, discovered that lower primary grade teachers mainly used one-on-one assessment of specific skills, written observational notes, checklists, rating scales and portfolio information. Upper primary grade teachers used more teacher-made tests and published tests from textbooks and reading series.

The examples listed in Table 7.2 are wide ranging and are repeated in all columns, depending on their applicability at diagnostic, formative and summative stages. They are presented in italics at the perceived ultimate stage of use. Despite the range of informal techniques included in Table 7.2, it is likely that teachers still tend to use a number of the written tests, such as objective tests and essay tests.

Space precludes a detailed discussion of each of these techniques but the one example given below includes a brief description and a reminder of respective merits and demerits. Every teacher has to make judgements about which techniques to use from a wide selection.

Portfolios

In the USA, student portfolios developed as a major form of assessment in the mid-1990s largely due to the writings and acceptance of cognitive psychologists – for example Resnick and Klopfer (1989) and the New Standards Project by Simmons and Resnick (1993).

The use of portfolios of student work has been central to the movement for authentic assessment. Their use has been based on the belief that what is most significant in any educational situation arises from the student's perception of that situation. Thus authentic assessment emphasizes individual-centred curricula, in which the teacher helps the student identify his or her interests and makes suggestions about how the student can deepen and broaden those interests in ways that lead to a wide variety of worthwhile and concomitant learnings.

Despite the teacher's help, however, authenticity requires the student to take responsibility for what is learned. Only in this way does learning become integrated with the rest of the student's life rather than remaining something apart, as an isolated lesson selected by someone else. Given the responsibility that students must take for their own learnings, it becomes incumbent upon them to demonstrate what they have learned and not simply to wait for their teachers to make these discoveries. Therefore such use of student-initiated projects is an integral part of authentic assessment, and portfolios of student work are perhaps the most telling form of demonstration.

Portfolios can include any number of things – not only finished work but also notes, drafts, preliminary models and plans, logs and other records; not only written work but also audiotapes, videotapes, photographs, three-dimensional creations and other artefacts. Students decide what to create and what to include in their portfolios; hence the portfolios reveal not only what individual students have done but also the strategies they have used in making their decisions.

Teachers, therefore, can assess not only the finished products portfolios contain but also the processes students have followed in carrying out their projects. What kind of decisions have been made? How wise have they been? Where have they led? What are the alternatives? There may be numerous opportunities as projects unfold for teachers to discuss these questions with students and thus to offer advice and constructive criticism. Much of the authenticity of assessing portfolios is in the opportunities they provide to both teachers and students for considering the development of interests, attitudes and values as well as skills and conventional academic learnings (Lyons, 1999; Orland-Barak, 2005).

Computer-assisted instruction enables students to do a variety of projects (individually or in groups) and these are useful inclusions in portfolios because they provide tangible evidence of a range of problem-solving skills. For example, Lifter and Adams (1997) claim that many of the eight levels of multiple intelligence are incorporated into computer software CD-ROMs. Eisner (1997) argues that computers can now create multimedia displays which capture meanings from alternative forms of data.

Box 7.3 lists some examples of what can be included in a portfolio, although in practice there is virtually no limit to what a portfolio might contain.

An increasing number of teachers are exploring the use of portfolios as an important 'authentic' assessment tool because:

- students can reflect on what they have learned (Calfee and Perfumo, 1996; Orland-Barak, 2005);

Box 7.3   Examples of what a student portfolio might contain

- essays
- journals
- summaries
- records, such as daily logs
- self-assessments, such as collect-checklists and rating forms
- experiments
- demonstration of skills
- rough drafts and finished products
- research notes
- team or group activities
- creative works
- major projects or products, such as dioramas, oral history collections, audio- and videotapes, photographs, charts, cards and timelines
- tests
- teacher comments.

- students do the selecting of what to include and have to justify their choices (Klenowski, 2002);
- students value the opportunity to assemble their materials;
- students can demonstrate what they have done and, by inference, what they are capable of doing (Salvia and Ysseldyke, 1998);
- students have to demonstrate thinking and expressive skills;
- portfolios provide an equitable and sensitive portrait of what students know and are able to do (Mansvelder-Longayroux *et al.*, 2007);
- portfolios enable teachers to focus on important student outcomes;
- portfolios are a tangible way to display and celebrate students' achievements (McTighe, 1997);
- portfolios provide credible evidence of student achievement to parents and the community (Hebert, 1998).

Many states in the USA have moved toward mandating school systems to use portfolios as a required form of assessment. This involves some topics being chosen by the district or state, and other quality controls over the criteria to be used for grading the portfolios. These external controls may be necessary to demonstrate the credibility of portfolios to the general public, but some educators have questioned whether moving to state-level acceptance so quickly can be justified. For example, Herman and Winters (1994) note that:

- inter-rater agreement on portfolio assessments from state reports is very low;
- portfolio grades have only moderate correlations with other forms of assessment (e.g. a moderate correlation of 0.47 between writing portfolio scores and direct writing assessments);
- portfolios may not represent an individual student's work but the efforts of several supporting peers, teachers or parents;
- teachers' time taken for choosing portfolio tasks, preparing portfolio lessons and assessing portfolios is burdensome;
- there are major costs involved in staff training, development of portfolio specifications, administration of portfolio records and their storage.

Torrance and Pryor (1995), referring to 'authentic' assessment trials in the United Kingdom, also voice caveats about being too ambitious and over-enthusiastic about these approaches because the additional responsibilities for teachers in busy classrooms will be enormous.

Merits of portfolios

- Students find it meaningful and good for their self-esteem.
- Students have to justify their choices.

Demerits of portfolios

- It is very time-consuming to assess portfolios.
- It is difficult to establish appropriate rubrics.

Record-keeping and reporting

Record-keeping for many teachers might be perceived as a chore but it is impossible to rely on one's memory for details about students' learning and achievements. Record-keeping is typically undertaken because:

- it helps teachers monitor the progress of individual students and to use this as a basis for planning future learning experiences – it serves a formative function;
- parents require detailed reporting of their child's achievements at regular intervals;
- the information can be used for placement of students in subsequent years;
- the information is required by the school or state system or nationally, as an accountability measure (Sutton, 1992).

Record-keeping can be very time-consuming and it is often quite instructive to reflect upon the range and type of record-keeping that is currently used. Some pertinent questions to ask about each item include:

- Why do this?
- Who is it for?
- Does it really match up with the original purpose?
- What happens to the data collected and recorded?
- Who actually uses it and for what purpose?
- Could it be organized more rationally to save time and effort?
- Would computerized records assist?

Many innovatory computer-based packages are already available to assist teachers with the task of assessing and recording students' achievements. Schools have to balance up the cost of these programs versus teachers devoting much of their daily time to assessing, recording and reporting so that their time for teaching is greatly reduced.

Trends in reporting

Parents have a major role in schools and they have a right to receive regular school reports about the achievements of their children. However, because all parents have experienced schooling in the past, they have expectations about the format of reports and what they consider to be the highest priorities in reporting. There can also be a considerable generation gap between parents' experiences at school and current education provisions.

The new and more complex forms of assessment clearly demand new forms of reporting (Wiggins, 1998; McTighe and Wiggins, 2004). Yet changes to reporting are not welcomed by parents if they create, in turn, further anxieties for them. Most educators agree about basic principles of reporting, namely:

- the process of communication must be fair, timely, confidential and clear (Loyd and Loyd, 1997);
- the basis for comparing students' performance must be made known and be credible;
- the relative weight attached to categories that make up the final grade must be made explicit and kept uniform across students and teachers;
- any summary judgements made in the report must be supported by data (Wiggins, 1998).

A number of schools are now changing the type of communication they send to parents. The mailing to the parents of a single-sheet report form once a term or once a semester as the only form of communication has changed dramatically. Schools now use the following:

- a variety of written reports;
- parent–teacher meetings/interviews;
- parents' information evenings;
- leaflets to explain new curriculum or assessment procedures;
- newsletters.

New developments in assessment and reporting

Two major factors are currently driving assessment developments: the emphasis upon performance assessment and the priority given to standards and accountability. Recent efforts to develop a comprehensive picture of student learning have involved systematically combining multiple-choice formats and performance formats.

There are many other developments which are likely to make assessment more flexible and tailored to the needs of students and teachers in the future. Consider the following.

- Computer adaptive testing (CAT) customizes the assessment process so that the computer determines which level of questions to pose to the student. If a student answers a question correctly then he or she receives a more difficult item. Although expensive to develop at present, more customized versions are likely to be developed.

- Large-scale testing can now be done at computerized testing centres – students take their test on-line and receive their score instantaneously.
- In the classroom (or at home) students can download specific assessment programs and then transmit them to the teacher or computer for scoring.
- Technology allows a variety of test-and-response formats using the computer's video and audio capabilities. Students can answer orally or by constructing answers on the screen. Computer software can translate items into many languages.
- Automated essay grading has made major advances and prototypes are now available for use on a standard Windows PC (Williams, 2001).
- Much of the paper testing done today will become an anachronism. As students come to do the majority of their learning with technology, they will want the medium of assessment also to be technology (Bennett, 2002).

Concluding comments

Assessment of students is a constant part of life in schools and a very important element. Although some forms of assessment have stood the test of time and are still used widely (e.g. external examinations), there have been enormous pressures over recent decades to widen the range of assessments and procedures.

It is likely that norm-referenced assessment will decrease as accountability focuses more on what students actually know and can do. Performance assessment is likely to become far more prominent in both classrooms and for high-stakes testing. Electronic assessment will be integrated into the educational process along with on-line delivery of instruction.

Reflections and issues

1 With reference to a specific group of students, reflect upon the assessment techniques you would use. Why do you use these? Which others might you use in the future? Which ones would you not use? Give reasons.
2 'Assessments should reflect on tasks students will encounter in the world outside schools and not merely those limited to the schools themselves' (Eisner, 1993, p. 226). How might this be done? Give details of techniques you would use to achieve this end.
3 What does it mean to be more focused on student performance? Why is this necessary? What assessment techniques would facilitate this emphasis?
4 How can assessment help a student to learn? What information/feedback do they need to have, when and how? Describe an assessment technique that illustrates how assessment can help a student.
5 'Technology opens up new design choices for assessment so there is great importance on making these wisely. When attention is focused on

technology at the expense of thinking through the assessment argument, worse assessment can actually result' (Mislevy, 2002, p. 27). Discuss.

6 'Technology is becoming a medium for learning and work ... as schools integrate technology into the curriculum, the method of assessment should reflect the tools employed in thinking and learning' (Bennett, 2002, p. 8). Discuss.

Web sources

Formative v. Summative Evaluation, http://jan.ucc.nau.edu/edtech/etc667/proposal/evaluation/summative_vs._formative.htm – accessed December 2007.

Authentic Assessment, http://www.funderstanding.com/authentiqjissessment.cfm – accessed December 2007.

Ideas for Assessment Tasks, http://intranet.cps.k 12.il.us/Assessments/Ideas and Rubrics/Assessment_Tasks/Ideas Ta ... – accessed December 2007.

Performance Tasks, http://www.aea267.k12.ia.us/cialframework/tasks/ – accessed December 2007.

Automating Authentic Assessment with Rubrics, http://stone.web.brevard.k12.fl.us/htrnl/comprubric.html – accessed December 2007.

Online Portfolios, http://www.electricteacher.com/onlineportfoliol – accessed December 2007.

Digital Portfolios, www.richerpicture.com – accessed December 2007.

Chapter 8

Curriculum implementation

Introduction

Curriculum starts as a plan. It only becomes a reality when teachers implement it with real students in a real classrooms (Ornstein and Hunkins, 2004). Careful planning and development are obviously important, but they count for nothing unless teachers are aware of the product and have the skills to implement the curriculum in their classrooms.

Definitions and terms

As noted by Fullan (1999) and Scott (1999), a curriculum, however well designed, must be implemented if it is to have any impact on students. Although this is obvious, there are thousands of curriculum documents now gathering dust on storeroom shelves because they were never implemented or because they were implemented unintelligently. The obvious importance of curriculum implementation has not necessarily led to widespread understanding of what it entails or of what is problematic about it.

The term 'implementation' refers to the 'actual use' of a curriculum/syllabus, or what it 'consists of in practice' (Fullan and Pomfret, 1977). It is a critical phase in the cycle of planning and teaching a curriculum. Adoption of a curriculum refers to somebody's intentions to use it, be it a teacher or a head office official, but it does not indicate whether the curriculum is implemented or not.

Implementation refers to actual use, as outlined above, but there is also an important 'attitudinal' element. In education systems where teachers and principals have the opportunity to choose among competing curriculum packages (i.e. acting as 'selectors') attitudinal dispositions are clearly important. For example, if a teacher perceives that the current curriculum he or she is using is deficient in certain areas, then an alternative will be sought which overcomes these problems. Leithwood (1981) maintains that teachers will only become involved in implementing new curricula if they perceive a dysfunction – they have a desire to reduce the gap between current and preferred practices – with reference to their teaching in a particular subject.

But for many subjects a revised or new curriculum is produced to be used by teachers in all schools in a school district and no choice is available. There is no opportunity for teachers to consider alternatives. Their task is to find out how to use the new curriculum as effectively as possible. In these circumstances, the dominant implementation questions for the teacher might be:

- How do I do it?
- Will I ever get it to work smoothly?
- To whom can I turn to get assistance?
- Am I doing what the practice requires?
- What is the effect on the learner?

This emphasis on how to use a new curriculum is a major concern for teachers because as 'craft specialists' they gain most of their intrinsic satisfaction from being successful in using a particular approach and materials with their students. However, the implementation of any new curriculum will take a teacher a considerable period of time as he or she needs to become competent and confident in its use. It is only when a new curriculum is completely accepted by teachers in a school and the activities associated with it are a matter of routine that the phase 'institutionalization' is said to have been reached.

Nonetheless, some writers (for example Snyder et al., 1992) argue that the idea of institutionalization unduly implies that the curriculum is something concrete and static. These writers suggest that 'curriculum enactment' is a more useful way of describing the ongoing process of implementation because it emphasizes the educational experiences that students and teachers jointly undergo as they determine what the curriculum will be like in each classroom.

There is also the matter of commitment to change (Cuban, 1992). Spillane (1999) argues that commitment depends in great part on the capacity and will of teachers. Not all teachers will automatically accept the notion that a newly proposed curriculum is what they should use, nor will all want to use it with their students (Fullan and Hargreaves, 1991). Most would no doubt welcome the opportunity to choose among several alternatives. In fact, some teachers might be perfectly satisfied with their existing curriculum. In situations where teachers have no choice about whether or not to use a new curriculum, they may embrace the new curriculum with enthusiasm, becoming what is known as 'consonant' users (willing to conform to the new curriculum), or they may be reluctant, making considerable alterations in the curriculum, thus becoming what is known as 'dissonant' users (unwilling to conform). In extreme cases, a dissonant user may erect a façade of compliance while adopting Machiavellian tactics to resist or even to undermine the new curriculum. Again, the attitudes of individual teachers are extremely important in implementation.

Some subjects in schools are considered to be important core areas and are given detailed treatment in syllabus documents. For these subjects, teachers may be expected to cover particular content and to follow a certain instructional sequence. The term used for this adherence to prescribed details is 'fidelity of use'. Alternatively, there may be other subjects where teachers can exercise their creative flair and implement very special, individual versions of a curriculum. This is then termed 'adaptation' or 'process orientation'.

It is doubtful that complete prescription of, and control over, everything teachers do has ever occurred. Although guidelines about curriculum and teaching may be prescribed in detail, there are countless ways in which teachers can responsibly and professionally get around both the spirit and the substance of such prescriptions (Fullan, 1991). For example, teachers can easily vary the content of a course or the sequence in which it is taught. They can emphasize particular values or issues or dismiss them entirely. Unless a superior is observing a teacher constantly, little can be known about what really goes on behind the classroom door (Goodlad and Klein, 1970).

A realistic view of curriculum implementation lies, therefore, between these two extremes. Some subjects in a school may be considered the essential core of the curriculum and be spelled out in detail in a curriculum guide. Especially for such subjects, teachers usually are expected to cover certain topics in a certain sequence. The most commonly used term in the professional literature for adherence to prescribed details in implementing a curriculum is 'fidelity of use'. Alternatively, for some subjects, teachers are expected to exercise their creative flair and implement their own individual versions of the curriculum. Doing so is commonly referred to as adaptation.

Influences on implementation

Researchers have investigated the process of curriculum implementation and what makes it successful. In the early 1980s, Fullan (1982) produced a list of what he called 'factors affecting implementation', and this list has been widely cited in the professional literature ever since. He suggested that the process could be analysed in terms of characteristics of the curriculum innovation or change, characteristics of the school, characteristics of the school district and characteristics external to the school system. Table 8.1 is a listing of the specific characteristics Fullan identified.

Later, Fullan and some colleagues (Fullan et al., 1989) reviewed the professional literature on curriculum implementation since the 1950s and suggested that it emphasized four themes, which they labelled (1) adoption, (2) implementation, (3) standardization and (4) restructuring.

In the 1960s, the first theme – adoption – was prominent. A common but naïve assumption of the time was that a formal decision by a district or a school to adopt a curricular innovation was sufficient to ensure its use in all classrooms. A vast number of failed innovations were recorded during this decade.

Table 8.1 Factors affecting implementation

A *Characteristics of the change*
  1. Need for and relevance of the change
  2. Clarity
  3. Complexity
  4. Quality and practicality of programme (materials, etc.)

B *Characteristics at the school district level*
  5. The history of innovative attempts
  6. The adoption process
  7. Central administrative support and involvement
  8. Staff development (in-service) and participation
  9. Time-line and information system (evaluation)
  10. Board and community characteristics

C *Characteristics at the school level*
  11. The principal
  12. Teacher–teacher relations
  13. Teacher characteristics and orientations

D *Characteristics external to the local system*
  14. Role of government
  15. External assistance

Source: Fullan (1982, p. 56).

During the 1970s, the attention of researchers shifted toward the second theme – implementation – and numerous studies of the implementation of individual innovations were undertaken. Some of these were large scale, such as the Rand Study (Berman and McLaughlin, 1975) and the Study of Dissemination Efforts Supporting School Improvement (DESSI) (Crandall and associates, 1983). Fullan *et al.* (1989) argued that these studies were of little value in understanding implementation because they focused on single innovations: 'Schools are not in the business of implementing innovations one at a time, they are in the business of managing multiple innovations simultaneously' (p. 3).

Fullan *et al.* (1989) found the third theme – standardization and testing of students and teachers – to be ongoing during the four decades they considered. However, they concluded that despite enormous investments of resources, energies and expectations, this approach to curriculum implementation is doomed to failure because it trivializes the teaching profession.

Their fourth theme – restructuring – was considered by Fullan *et al.* in 1989 to be typical of contemporary approaches to implementation. Fullan and his colleagues found that such approaches focus on changing the characteristics of schools to include practices such as partnerships, career ladders, coaching and mentoring. However, events of the 1990s and 2000s may have altered what is typical. Now standards-based reform linked to high-stakes testing (as in theme three) has become the driving force in curriculum implementation (Hargreaves *et al.*, 2001).

Glatthorn and Jailall (2000) note that standards-based approaches have increased in appeal for state governments as more people have come to believe that the quality of American education has been in decline. Furthermore, the passage of the No Child Left Behind Act (NCLB) in 2001 and its renewal in 2004 have required states to develop standards for English-language arts, mathematics and science at every grade level and to test student progress in grades 3 to 10. Additionally, NCLB threatens federal sanctions against states that do not comply or that do not by 2014 reach the NCLB goal of raising all students to proficiency as measured by state tests (Nelson *et al.*, 2004).

Standards-based education appears to be taking a toll on teachers, particularly in forcing them to adopt a technological rationality for their practice, one that threatens to de-skill and de-professionalize them: 'Outsiders are increasingly controlling the teacher's competence and performance in ever-increasing detail' (Hargreaves *et al.*, 2001, p. 23). Fullan (2003) asserts that, exacerbating this trend, curriculum implementation is increasingly being done in large-scale, developmental, multi-year partnerships involving many states and even entire countries, thus removing teachers from their traditional roles as decision-makers. Fullan (2000) describes a large-scale reform project that had begun in the United Kingdom in 1997, identifying some areas of attention that seemed to make it successful. These include the following:

- the need to upgrade the school system's context: this involves revamping policies, incentives and standards for the teaching profession;
- the need for coherence: it is often necessary to eliminate ad hoc, uncoordinated innovations and policies so that schools and school systems can be selective, integrative and focused;
- the need for cross-over structures: national and regional agencies must be coordinated in a critical mass required for long-term success;
- the need for investment in quality materials: high-quality materials are essential for success;
- the need for integrated pressure and support: a balance between pressure and support keeps the project moving in appropriate directions;
- the need for developing strategies for involving whole-school systems: large-scale reform is not likely to be successful if targeted at individual schools.

House (1979), a prominent researcher on curriculum implementation in the 1970s and 1980s, provides another way of looking at curriculum implementation. He identified three perspectives (the technical, the political and the cultural) as useful in explaining how and why certain approaches to implementation have persisted over the decades. Many other researchers, such as Hargreaves *et al.* (2001), have built on and extended these three perspectives.

The technical perspective assumes that systematic planning and a rational approach to implementation can overcome the typical problems teachers face, such as lack of time and expertise. In a later paper, House (1996) suggests that the political perspective recognizes that, in practice, people do not behave entirely rationally. This perspective emphasizes the balance of power among stakeholders as what determines the success or failure of an innovation. The cultural perspective suggests that the deeply ingrained beliefs and values of stakeholders, which are socially shared and shaped, are what ultimately affect what happens in classrooms. This perspective suggests that successful implementation usually depends on transforming the culture that stakeholders share. In practice, it is likely that all three perspectives can be used to explain what happens in any school. Indeed, Corbett and Rossman (1989) and Hargreaves *et al.* (2001) argue that the three perspectives depict processes that actually operate in schools, that they are closely intertwined and that they often occur simultaneously.

Lusi (1997) contends that state officials face extremely difficult tasks in curriculum implementation; they are required to improve the academic achievement of all students in all schools: 'This requires changing the core processes of teaching and learning which in turn requires changing the behaviours of teachers' (Lusi, 1997, p. 10).

Cohen and Hill's (2001) study of a major project to improve mathematics teaching and learning in California came up with similar conclusions. They noted that when teachers had opportunities to learn about student materials or assessments, students achieved higher scores: 'When Californian teachers had significant opportunities to learn how to improve students' learning their practices changed appreciably' (Cohen and Hill, 2001, p. 6).

Despite the alternative views debated in the professional literature, movement since the 1990s has been decidedly toward an increasingly rigid approach to curriculum implementation. Examples are Porter (1993), who argues for strict standards for the delivery of the enacted curriculum and cites the professional standards for teaching mathematics developed by the National Council of Teachers of Mathematics, and Schmidt *et al.* (1996), who urge the adoption of a multi-category curriculum framework for measuring the alignment of various phases of implementation. Reactions to the No Child Left Behind Act (NCLB) itself have ranged from exhortations about its potentially positive impact on how teachers implement curricula (Christie, 2004; Hirsch, 2004) to trenchant criticisms of its negative impact on teachers themselves (Abedi and Dietel, 2004; Jones, 2004; Plitt, 2004).

Problems of describing/measuring implementation

Attempts to describe the implementation of new curricula are fraught with all kinds of difficulties. For example, do you focus upon the curriculum materials, or what the teacher is doing, or what the students are doing? If the intention is to try to do all three things, what criteria do you use to select instances of each, since they are all occurring simultaneously in the classroom? Are there optimal times to examine how a curriculum is being implemented, such as after six months of operation, or a year, or even longer?

Trying to measure degrees of implementation is even more difficult than trying to describe them (Desimone, 2002). Decisions have to be made about what kinds of data should be collected, such as observational data, document analysis or self-report data. Measurement data also tend to have a punitive air about them and so this can lead to concerns about who is doing the measuring and who is to receive the results.

Measuring student activities and achievements

A major reason for producing a new curriculum is to provide better learning opportunities for students, such as higher achievement levels in terms of particular understandings, skills and values. Rarely is it possible, however, for measurements to be obtained on student achievements so that it can be stated unequivocally that a new curriculum is superior to the previous one, in terms of particular dimensions. There are so many confounding variables which affect student scores. A single test is unlikely to be suitable for use and to be able to provide valid and reliable comparable data between a new curriculum and the previous one.

Despite the lack of empirical evidence linking testing with student achievement, high-stakes testing of students became a political priority in the USA during the 1990s (Nave et al., 2000), and there is pressure from some quarters for a single national test for all students (Porter, 1993). A differing point of view holds that a more promising development is authentic assessment of student learning, such as through the use of portfolios of student work or through increasingly sophisticated ways of measuring problem-solving, reasoning and critical thinking (Resnick and Tucker, 1992).

Measuring use of curriculum materials

In most teaching programmes, curriculum materials figure prominently in the day-to-day activities undertaken by the teacher and students (Allwright, 1990). In fact, surveys have revealed that school students can spend up to 80 per cent of their time engaged with particular curriculum materials (Cornbleth, 1990).

It is clearly important in any study of implementation to gather information about how curriculum materials are used. Some of the curriculum materials analysis schemes developed in the 1970s provide convenient criteria for evaluating curriculum materials (for example Piper, 1976; Eraut et al., 1975). However, these schemes are often very time-consuming to complete and tend to emphasize the characteristics of the curriculum materials in isolation.

During the 1980s more attention was paid to developing checklists which provide ratings of curriculum materials 'in use' (for example the Innovations Configuration developed by Hall and Loucks, 1978; and the Practice Profile developed by Loucks and Crandall, 1982).

The Innovations Configuration (IC) describes the different operational forms of an innovation that result as teachers implement it in their classrooms. The checklist can be structured to indicate the variations that are considered to be ideal, acceptable and unacceptable uses of an innovation (Hord and Huling-Austin, 1987).

Harlen (1994) argues that it is very important that teachers use curriculum materials as intended. She urges groups of teachers (for example in professional subject associations) to undertake a comprehensive series of steps in evaluating K-12 (infants to senior secondary, Australia) curriculum materials. The steps she considers essential include:

- deciding on the criteria to be used;
- gathering information by studying how the curriculum material is used in classrooms – for example making notes during lessons; discussing the work with students; sound and video recording;
- analysing the information – using a grading scheme for each of the criteria;
- reporting the judgements – profiles of the curriculum materials can be produced and/or full reports written.

Clearly, this would be a major undertaking. Analysis schemes devised in the USA for mathematics (Kulm and Grier, 1998) and science (National Science Resources Centre, 1999) are also extremely comprehensive, time-consuming and expensive.

The rapid growth in the use of the Internet by teachers and students has also spread numerous new ideas about what can be included in checklists of curriculum materials and how they can be used (Means, 2001). In particular, the Internet has become a huge new resource for teachers and students (Molnar, 2000; Schofield and Davidson, 2000).

Measuring teacher activities

Various methods have been used over the decades to measure teachers' implementation activities, ranging from formal visits to observation checklists, questionnaires, interviews and self-report techniques. In the USA, where implementation studies have been very extensively undertaken since the 1970s, observation checklists and rating scales are commonly used. In these studies, particular categories of behaviour are determined in advance and used as the basis for the checklist items and rating scales.

For example, self-report techniques are incorporated into the Stages of Concern (SoC), an instrument developed by Hall et al. (1977) and subsequently used widely in many countries. The SoC focuses upon teachers' feelings as they become involved in implementing an innovation. These will vary in both type and intensity. Hall et al. argue that there is a definable set of major stages of concern and that as teachers become involved in implementing an innovation they will move developmentally through these stages (see Table 8.2).

The SoC has been widely used in a number of countries, as noted in studies by Wells and Anderson (1997), Bailey and Palsha (1992), Guan (2000), Vaughan (2002) and Ingvarson (2004). Of special interest is a confirmatory study by Marsh and Penn (1988), who found that the concerns of students engaged in a remedial reading programme progressed in a sequence similar to the SoC.

Second-generation research in Belgium and the Netherlands (Vandenberghe, 1983; Van den Berg, 1993; Van der Vegt and Vandenberghe, 1992) has produced an alternative version of the SoC that includes an increased number of self-oriented concerns.

Van den Berg (2002) highlights the major impact of concerns theory on the professional development of teachers and the extent to which concerns-based

Table 8.2 Stages of Concern (SoC)

	Stages of Concern	Definitions
Impact	6 Refocusing	The focus is on exploration of more universal benefits from the innovation, including the possibility of major changes or replacement with a more powerful alternative. Individual has definite ideas about alternatives to the proposed or existing form of the innovation.
	5 Collaboration	The focus is on coordination and cooperation with others regarding use of the innovation.
	4 Consequence	Attention focuses on impact of the innovation on student in his/her immediate sphere of influence. The focus is on relevance of the innovation for students, evaluation of student outcomes, including performance and competencies, and changes needed to increase student outcomes.
Task	3 Management	Attention is focused on the processes and tasks of using the innovation and the best use of information and resources. Issues related to efficiency, organizing, managing, scheduling and time demands are utmost.
Self	2 Personal	Individual is uncertain about the demands of the innovation, his/her inadequacy to meet those demands, and his/her role with the innovation. This includes analysis of his/her role in relation to the reward structure of the organization, decision making, and consideration of potential conflicts with existing structures or personal commitment. Financial or status implications of the programme for self and colleagues may also be reflected.
	1 Informational	A general awareness of the innovation and interest in learning more detail about it is indicated. The person seems to be unworried about himself/herself in relation to the innovation. He/she is interested in substantive aspects of the innovation in a selfless manner such as general characteristics, effects and requirements for use.
	0 Awareness	Little concern about or involvement with the innovation is indicated.

Source: Hall *et al.* (1979); Hall and Hord (1987).

instruments, such as the SoC, have been used to examine levels of curriculum implementation in a variety of subjects, including new innovations such as School Net technology.

Nonetheless, weaknesses in the SoC have also been uncovered. One major weakness is that the fixed stages do not discriminate completely between how different teachers in different schools might implement a new curriculum.

Research on implementation

Fullan and Pomfret's (1977) review of research on implementation has been widely cited in the professional literature on curriculum. Not only did the authors bring into prominence implementation as a distinct step in curriculum planning and development, they also helped define and shape much subsequent research on implementation. Among their greatest influences on researchers was their use of the terms 'fidelity perspective' and 'process perspective', as introduced on pp. 93–94.

Fidelity of implementation

The fidelity perspective on implementation is now well established in the literature. Proponents emphasize the importance of the planned curriculum and assume that when the planned curriculum is exemplary and demonstrably effective it will be readily and completely accepted by teachers. House (1979) referred to the 'firm faith in the technological process' (p. 10) held by proponents of fidelity in curriculum implementation. Roitman and Mayer (1982) noted that hard-line proponents insist that curriculum innovations enacted in the classroom should closely – if not completely – correspond to what is planned. Why else devote considerable resources, time and energy to planning the best possible curriculum for use in schools if teachers do not actually use it? And if teachers use it in only partial or modified form, won't its effectiveness be likely to suffer from dilution?

Ariav (1988) used the phrase 'curriculum literacy' to suggest that many teachers lack understanding of what the curriculum should be and lack skill in how best to teach it. The fidelity perspective assumes that because teachers have a low level of curriculum literacy, the planned curriculum must be highly structured and teachers must be given explicit instructions about how to teach it. Because both the curriculum and instructions to teachers are specified, the fidelity perspective leaves little room for a curriculum to be tailored to any particular or changing circumstances of the specific schools or classrooms in which it is intended to be taught. Current writings tend to discredit this hardline approach to fidelity of use. Tyack and Cuban (1995) and Carless (2004) contend that curriculum developers who take a fidelity of use approach ignore teachers' prior experiences, almost as if it were a virtue to have amnesia about teachers' backgrounds.

A fidelity of use approach treats teachers as passive recipients of the wisdom of the curriculum developers; teachers must be thoroughly trained to use the new curriculum, but, once trained (it is argued), they will be able to teach it at a high level of technical proficiency. This is a dubious assumption. For example, Datnow and Castellano (2000) found that after teachers had special training in the Success for All program, not all followed the developers' demand to implement the curriculum with fidelity. Some did because they thought doing so would be beneficial; others did not because they thought doing so constrained their autonomy. Drake, Spillane and Hufferd-Acles (2001) noted that teachers implemented National Council of Teachers of Mathematics (NCTM) standards only if they had previously had positive experiences that shaped their identities as teachers and helped them interpret how the curriculum could be implemented.

Fidelity of curriculum implementation seems to lend itself more readily to some situations than to others, particularly those where the content of the curriculum is unusually complex and difficult to master, where it requires definite sequencing or where students' understanding of it depends on their being appropriately matched with specific curricular strands. Many of the national curriculum projects undertaken in the United States in the 1960s and 1970s (some federally sponsored, some privately sponsored) were developed from the fidelity perspective on implementation. For example, in the Biological Sciences Curriculum Study Project (BSCS) the teacher's role was tightly prescribed:

> A programmed discussion is provided via a series of single topic films. At certain points in the presentation, there is teacher intervention with specified questions, which are provided for his/her use. The teacher is also provided with prototypes of the kinds of answers he/she may receive, and with suggested ways of handling these answers so that he/she does not cut off discussion or discourage inquiry.
>
> (Grobman, 1970, p. 117)

Many of these national projects undermined whatever chance they had of success by taking the idea of fidelity of implementation to the extreme of attempting to design teacher-proof curriculum packages. In such packages, not only were both the curriculum and the directions to teachers spelled out in extreme detail, but the teacher's role as mediator between the curriculum and the student was reduced to the barest possible minimum in order not to dilute the work of the developers of the curriculum. Naturally, for both good reasons and bad, such packages were viewed extremely negatively by many teachers. In districts and schools where teacher-proof curricula were adopted, often they were never implemented or implementation was quickly abandoned; and in the relatively few schools where they were implanted, teachers almost always found ways to modify them in practice to fit specific classroom realities that developers had been unable to foresee.

Fidelity of use in curriculum implementation never completely disappears. The New Standards developed by Tucker and Godding (1998) demand strict adherence (fidelity) by teachers, and many comprehensive reform models developed in the late 1990s also are highly prescriptive. For example, Fullan (2000) asserts that Slavin's Success for All Model (1999) has been successful because it has five mandatory pre-implementation requirements and the implementation of the reading curriculum requires one-to-one reading tutors, continual assessment of student progress and the use of local facilitators. Fullan (2000) concludes that Success for All is a predefined program that is carefully developed, implemented and monitored.

The current emphasis on national standards means that in many schools 'testing is now used to control curriculum and teaching' (McNeil, 2003, p. 26). A number of states have prescribed standardized testing and standardized procedures for teaching a subject or for using a particular curriculum package (Segall, 2003). This emphasis has led to an alignment of goals, objectives, instructional materials, teacher education and other standardized measures (McNeil, 2003), a powerful combination supporting fidelity of use.

Adaptation in implementation

The alternative approach to curriculum implementation was termed the 'process perspective' by Fullan and Pomfret (1977), but it has also became known as 'adaptation' or 'mutual adaptation'. Proponents of this approach maintain that the differing circumstances facing schools and teachers require on-site modifications to the curriculum (Berman and McLaughlin, 1975). They suggest that in reality all planned curricula become modified during the process of implementation and that such modification to suit the specific and changing situations faced by the teachers who enact them is essential if the curricula are to have the greatest possible benefits for students. In their own work, Fullan and Pomfret seemed to favour this approach, particularly in their analysis of the Rand Study, which, at the time, was possibly the most comprehensive research study on implementation ever undertaken, encompassing 293 projects in school districts in different regions of the United States. The researchers in the Rand Study concluded that successful innovations occurred when planned curricula were not highly specified or packaged in advance but were mutually adapted by users within specific institutional settings (Berman and McLaughlin, 1975).

Mutual adaptation

The term mutual adaptation was first used by Dalin and McLaughlin (1975) to describe implementation in which adjustments are made to both the innovative curriculum and to the institutional setting. In mutual adaptation, the process is a two-way street between developers and users. Since the 1970s, many researchers have argued that mutual adaptation consists of agreed-on modifications arranged between developers and users and, as such, represents the most effective way of ensuring successful implementation of a new curriculum. House (1979) maintained that implementation is really a political decision and emphasized personal, face-to-face interaction as a key part of it. MacDonald and Walker (1976) maintained that implementation really involves negotiation and that there are trade-offs to be made between curriculum developers and teachers. Farrar, Desanctis and Cohen (1979) and Rudduck and Kelly (1976) interpreted curriculum implementation in terms of the culture of the school. For example, mutual adaptation can be characterized as evolution, in which what at first appears to be a precise blueprint is increasingly perceived by teachers as something malleable: 'The needs and values of those within the organization add, subtract, modify and invent. ... Some variations are less discordant than others, but virtually none is a single composition with everyone playing from the same score' (Farrar et al., 1979, p. 96). Spillane (1999) concludes that it is the social dimension that underscores how teachers implement a curriculum. Teachers' sense-making can vary widely. They operate in enactment zones. As Spillane explains, 'the more teachers' enactment zones extend beyond their individual classrooms to include rich deliberations about the reforms and practicing the reform ideas with fellow teachers and other experts, the more likely teachers are to change the core of their practice' (p. 170).

The continuing debate: fidelity of use versus mutual adaptation in the 1990s and beyond

In the 1990s both fidelity of use and mutual adaptation continued as influences on curriculum implementation, especially as a follow-up to some of the major curriculum trends of the 1980s. For example, in the United States, the George H. W. Bush administration sponsored a well-publicized national conference in 1989 that recommended seven national goals for schools, ranging from improving literacy to decreasing dropout rates. Though such general goals are not a curriculum (and the federal government lacks the constitutional authority to enforce a national curriculum on the states and local school districts), the goals themselves were clearly promoted in order to create uniformity, thus also promoting the idea of fidelity of use among both citizens and educators alike. In contrast, although in the 1990s the Clinton administration supported the setting of national performance standards for schools to meet, it suggested that schools could meet them in a variety of ways, thus promoting the idea of mutual adaptation.

The numerous reports by national commissions in the 1980s (Boyer, 1982; National Commission on Excellence in Education, 1983) have also been interpreted in a variety of ways. Ginsberg and Wimpelberg (1987) suggested that these reports created a lot of dialogue and publicity but had very limited actual impact on schools, perhaps just enough to be characterized as trickle-down reform. Yet when foundations, state governors and state legislatures have taken recommendations of these reports seriously, the result has been changes for schools, such as longer school days, more time devoted to certain subjects and more formal graduation requirements. Desimone (2002) terms these 'first wave changes'. Although most state mandates may not affect day-to-day teaching very much, the overall emphasis on efficiency and setting standards of minimal achievement – all within an ethos of a technical-rational outlook – has had an impact on many schools (Ornstein and Hunkins, 2004; Walker, 2003).

In the 1990s, policies promoted by the federal government as well as by state mandates influenced curriculum development and in general pushed in the direction of fidelity of use. In contrast, increased professionalization among teachers and grassroots demands for local curriculum development pushed in the direction of mutual adaptation (Fullan, 2000), In the 2000s, the No Child Left Behind Act (NCLB) (2001) has created far greater pressures for fidelity of use. In placing responsibility on states to produce and use their own standards and tests or face the loss of federal funding, NCLB has changed the lives of teachers, forcing them to narrow their range of teaching techniques in order to attempt to optimize students' test scores. This squeeze provides teachers with little incentive to 'engage students in relevant, authentic, and challenging learning experiences' (Plitt, 2004, p. 745).

In the United Kingdom, pressures for fidelity of use have markedly increased over recent years. Elkins and Elliott (2004) point to actions by the central Department of Education and Employment to hold schools and teachers accountable for the outcomes of teaching. Teachers' professional careers are now heavily influenced by their students' test scores. Kelly (2004) refers to excessive political interference in the school curriculum in the United Kingdom through which politicians and administrators have forced teachers to become merely operators and technicians, noting that 'even their responsibility for teaching methods has been continuously eroded in key areas such as the teaching of reading and of numbers' (Kelly, 2004, p. 190).

In Australia, similar developments are occurring. The federal government, which constitutionally does not have the right to determine curriculum, is in fact narrowing the curriculum and how it is implemented by teachers by emphasizing national literacy surveys and by requiring states (through funding incentives) to implement various standardized tests and benchmarks (Reid, 1999a). Vidovich (2004) notes that teachers' implementation of curricula in language arts and mathematics is strongly influenced by the reporting of results of national literacy and numeracy tests.

Researchers have also drawn attention to how the professional careers and personal lives of teachers influence how they participate in curriculum implementation (Hargreaves and Fink, 2000; Wise, 2000). Curriculum projects that require protracted periods of time for the completion of implementation can provide many new professional opportunities for teachers. Some teachers seek out these opportunities, while others – especially those in different phases of their careers – find these opportunities threatening (Huberman, 1993). Goodson (1992) has emphasized the importance of teachers' life histories and has been highly critical of curriculum implementation that depersonalizes teachers. Noddings (1986, 2000) holds a similar view, arguing for an ethic of caring and suggesting that such an ethic is what fidelity is really about.

In the USA, many states increased their requirements for high school graduation and even in times of financial austerity devoted more funds to improving curricula at both the secondary and elementary levels (Kirst, 1993). Throughout this period, however, the general trends in the United States were mixed and the underlying tensions between fidelity of use and mutual adaptation remain unresolved (O'Neil, 2000).

Funding opportunities and incentives from the federal government in the USA improved in the late 1990s. The Comprehensive School Reform Programs (CSRP) were created by the US Congress in 1998. Thousands of schools across the nation each received awards of at least $50,000 to implement whole-school models. In many cases the models are quite prescriptive, indicating that fidelity of use is a priority.

The NCLB of 2001, supported by large majorities of both Democrats and Republicans in both houses of Congress, is the major federal initiative of the 2000s. Whether NCLB will or will not lead in the long run to a stronger and more humane American educational system is extremely problematic (Nelson *et al.*, 2004). Some states and school districts are embarking enthusiastically on the path NCLB sets forth; others are balking. Will a single national curriculum eventually be implemented, or will time-honoured curricular differences among states (Swan, 1998) and local districts (Sandholtz *et al.*, 2002) remain indefinitely?

Specific examples of curriculum implementation

Hong Kong

The coordinated and concerted effort to reform the education system in the Hong Kong Special Administration Region is an interesting example. In 2000, the Curriculum Development Council produced a major reform document *Learning to Learn*. The components of *Learning to Learn* were not dissimilar to many others introduced in industrialized countries. They included the following:

- eight key learning areas within a curriculum framework;
- a number of generic skills (for example communication skills);
- changes in assessment, with a greater emphasis upon formative assessment;
- diversified learning and teaching materials;
- life-long learning;
- whole-person development.

What is very different is the commitment of the education department to ensure that the new curriculum is implemented effectively. Some of the implementation strategies include:

- a major emphasis on teacher development – each year approximately 100 teachers are selected to become 'seed teachers' who work full time developing materials, giving workshops to teachers in schools and generally acting as change agents;
- creation of a new promotional position in all primary schools, 'curriculum development' leader, who acts as a catalyst and curriculum leader in each primary school;
- provision of research projects and lighthouse schools, which experiment with new student-centred approaches to individual differences;
- provision of a range of workshops and courses for school principals and vice-principals;
- creation of web pages providing teachers with a wealth of practical examples;
- hiring of a large number of overseas experts to give presentations and workshops to teachers and principals;
- provision of information sessions and materials for parents.

Above all, the education department wisely decided upon a long lead time for implementing the new curriculum, and targets for different elements of curriculum reform are moderate and achievable.

The progress to date is most impressive. There is evidence that a number of schools are developing very well towards their implementation targets (Marsh, 2007).

United Kingdom

The Blair government's education reforms after taking office in 1997 focused especially on higher standards for all students. The White Paper *Excellence in Schools* set out specific details, especially with regard to literacy and numeracy, namely:

- the introduction of a National Literacy Strategy into every primary school from September 1998;
- the introduction of a National Numeracy Strategy into every primary school from September 1999;
- the setting of numerical targets for pupils' attainments in every school, linked to the government's pledge to increase pupils' scores in national assessment tests by the year 2002 (Southworth, 2000).

Again, what is especially interesting is the implementation strategies used to bring about these reforms. Fullan and Earl (2002) describe the strategies as an effective combination of accountability mechanisms and capacity-building strategies. They include:

- ambitious standards (high standards and tests);
- devolved responsibility (the school and especially the school head as the unit of accountability);
- good data/clear targets (benchmark data for every school, results shared annually);
- access to Best Practice and Quality Professional Development (professional development for all, leadership development through the National College for School Leadership; Mackay, 2002);
- accountability (through national inspections by the Office for Standards in Education (OFSTED) and publication of results in the media);
- intervention in inverse proportion to success (rewards are given to success-ful schools, schools with poor results are supported in the first instance, or closed; Fullan and Earl, 2002).

Fullan and Earl (2002) contend that in terms of literacy and numeracy gains from the base years, the implementation strategies have been very successful (18 per cent increase in achievement levels in literacy, 17 per cent increase in achieve-ment levels in numeracy). However, Fullan and Earl caution the government about the continuance of such a strong centre-directed approach. Although this top-down initiative may have been required at the beginning, there now needs to be a greater 'investment in local capacity-building, followed in turn by greater attention to local creativity, reflection and networking' (Fullan and Earl, 2002, p. 4).

Concluding comments

How a planned curriculum is implemented as the enacted curriculum in any school is a complex process that can vary enormously from school to school. The only certainty about curriculum implementation is that there is no one right way of going about it for all teachers in all schools. The ongoing issues concerning curriculum implementation are not likely to be resolved, but in recent years there has been growing awareness of the complexity of the pro-cess, and hence more reason for both caution and guarded optimism.

Reflections and issues

1   Some common implementation problems, according to Clough et al. (1989), include the following: too little time for teachers to plan and learn new skills and practices; too many competing demands, making successful

implementation impossible; failure to understand and take into account site-specific differences among schools. Explain why these could be major problems. What solutions would you offer?

2 'For a new curriculum project to be fully implemented there are four core changes required of a teacher – changes in class groupings and organization, materials, practices and behaviours, and in beliefs and understandings' (Fullan, 1989, p. 8). Do you agree with these four core changes? Give examples to illustrate their importance. Alternatively, put forward other more important factors.

3 'Because implementation takes place in a fluid setting, implementation problems are never "solved". Rather they evolve ... new issues, new requirements, new considerations emerge as the process unfolds' (McLaughlin, 1987, p. 174). What are the implications of this statement for implementing new curricula in schools? What implementation elements can or cannot be planned in advance? What contingency plans should be developed?

4 'Successful implementation is an individual development process within certain organizational conditions and strategies' (Fullan, 1989, p. 24). To what extent are individual development factors (for example commitment, skills, willingness to experiment) important? What are some important organizational conditions?

5 'Testing certain content in certain ways will result in an alignment of classroom practices with the official view of what and how subjects should be taught' (Matheison, 1991, p. 201). Does testing ensure that fidelity of use implementation occurs? What are some problems associated with curriculum controlled by testing?

6 Pressure and support are both needed to ensure that implementation occurs. Do you agree? How might pressure and support occur simultaneously within your school or school district?

Web sources

Teachers' experiences in curriculum implementation, www.minedu.govt.nz/index.cfm?id = 8226 – extracted 15 November 2007.

Curriculum Implementation – Issues and Challenges, www.wested.org/tal/five_film_categories/CURRICULUM/curriculum-implementation.html – extracted 15 November 2007.

Curriculum Implementation Plan – Strategic Overview, members.iinet.net.au/~westps/eight/ciplan.html – extracted 15 November 2007.

Teachers as Learners: Curriculum Implementation: Issues and Challenges, http://www.wested.org/tal/five_film_categories?CURRICULUM/curriculum-implemene – extracted 15 November 2007.

Part III

Curriculum management

Chapter 9

Innovation and planned change

Introduction

We live in an era in which change has become a familiar term. In fact, one frequently used phrase implies that the only permanent feature of our time is change. There is hardly any social institution which escapes the process of change, and education is no exception (Stoll and Fink, 1996). Formal education in schools in the last five decades has been marked by significant and frequent changes in its aims and objectives, its content, teaching strategies, methods of student assessment, provisions and the levels of funding. Yet it might also be argued that education is the social anchor, a stabilizing force 'in the midst of an ever changing society and economy buffeted by globalised market forces' (Kennedy, 2005, p. 33).

Glatthorn and Jailall (2000) use a 'streams' metaphor to explain all the changes which are ongoing in educational systems – some streams ebb, some gather strength, sometimes the streams are widely separated, at other times they flow together. Not always have the changes led to something better – some innovations have been disappointing and brought about yet another turn in the search for the 'best' education (Seashore Louis, 2007). Fullan (2004) contends that the major problem in education is that educational systems are fundamentally conservative – they want to retain the status quo – and when change is attempted 'it results in defensiveness, superficiality or at best short-lived pockets of success' (p. 3). Yet there is a moral purpose for education (Fullan, 2001). Teachers and schools should be making a difference to the lives of students – 'they are in the business of making improvements, and to make improvements in an ever changing world is to contend with and manage the forces on an ongoing basis' (Fullan, 1993, p. 4).

Developing a new mindset for teachers is indeed a major challenge (Spillane *et al.*, 2002; Kridel and Bullough, 2007). Some educators contend that 'teachers have the reputation of being inherently and universally stubborn when facing change' (Corbett and Rossman, 1989, p. 36). Much of this purported stubbornness could be attributed to the selection process in recruiting teachers and the socialization process experienced by teachers.

On the other hand, it might be argued that the problem lies with the naïveté of educational leaders and their inept ways of bringing about change. Some leaders simply assume teachers will carry out their proposals; others use regulations and mandates to enforce change. Too many leaders focus upon change as a product and overlook the processes – the human face of change (House, 1996).

Then again, perhaps educators underestimate what it takes to make fundamental changes in an organization. Hatch (2000) contends that the private sector will use up to 20 per cent of their resources to make substantive changes to their organization, whereas in education we rarely spend more than 1 per cent on change efforts. Staff members are often expected to donate their time. Expecting change at bargain basement rates is unlikely to be successful.

Yet there have been some massive financial outlays by certain countries recently. They include the United Kingdom's capacity building (Barber, 2006); the building of a knowledge-based globalized economy in Hong Kong (Law, 2002); and the PETALS framework for excellence and engagement in learning in Singapore (Shanmugaratnam, 2006).

Some basic terms

'Change' is a generic term which subsumes a whole family of concepts such as 'innovation', 'development' and 'adoption'. It can be either planned or unplanned (unintentional, spontaneous, accidental movements or shifts). The literature tends to focus upon 'planned change', which for Fullan (1991) is multidimensional, involving possible changes in goals, skills, philosophy or beliefs, and behaviour, but above all is change in practice. Poppleton (2000) notes that planned change can refer to innovations at classroom or school level as well as to reforms and reconstructions of the whole or parts of the educational system of a country.

The term 'innovation' may mean either a new object, idea or practice, or the process by which a new object, idea or project comes to be adopted by an individual group or organization. Early studies in the curriculum literature tended to view innovations as objects or events, similar to a new item of machinery for farmers or a new apothecary line. Much more emphasis is now placed upon innovation as a process. A working definition of innovation is the planned application of ends or means, new or different from those which exist currently in the classroom, school or system, and intended to improve effectiveness for the stakeholders.

This definition, with its emphasis upon 'intention' and 'application', is indicating that the innovation process is not only an awareness but a definite intention to implement one or more of the alternatives. Many early studies of innovations tended to focus upon knowledge, awareness and adoption decisions, but few penetrated the crucial area of implementation, to find out how teachers were actually using an innovation.

The definition also directs attention to 'improving' effectiveness for the stakeholders. Educators do not always agree with the contention that a change has to be an improvement to quality to be classed as an 'innovation'. Whether an innovation is regarded as an improvement or not depends of course upon the judgement of the adopting agency or individual, as they will perceive an innovation in terms of their past experiences and aspirations. If it is 'new' to them, and different to what they have done before, then they will probably choose it because it is considered likely to bring about an improvement. Innovations are not objective and unchanging, but are constantly being changed and redefined as a result of experience. In other words, the initial perception of an innovation by teachers and other individuals or agencies may be that it is 'new' and an 'improvement' to what they were doing, but the final judgement of worth cannot really be known until some time later when they have become fully conversant with the innovation and how it might be applied to their situation (Poppleton, 2000).

The inclusion of the attribute 'improvement' in the concept of an innovative process emphasizes the political nature of curriculum innovations. Whilst other educational terms such as 'child development' or 'age grading' tend to be analysed and discussed by educationalists as important concepts and ends in themselves, 'innovations' are initiated in school situations because certain authorities are not satisfied with particular directions or levels of learning and want to do something different (Soder, 1999).

There is no doubt that politicians are taking a leading role in determining directions for innovations (Angus, 1995; Peddie, 1995; Sarason, 1990; Reid, 2005). Caldwell (1993) suggests that governments are adopting a more powerful and focused role in terms of setting goals, establishing priorities and building frameworks for accountability. Yet the literature is also replete with examples to demonstrate that many current reforms and innovations are contradictory and illogical. Postmodernists contend that many of the assumptions about Western society need to be dismantled and exposed. Many of the policies of politicians and bureaucrats need to be challenged (Giroux, 1992; Glatthorn and Jailall, 2000; Cook-Sather, 2002).

Teachers need to enter into dialogue about the uncertainties, the concerns, doubts and questions about teaching and so-called improvement projects. It is a challenge for teachers to transcend traditional, positivist approaches – it can indeed be emancipatory for them even if the context of schooling appears to be constraining and antagonistic (Ball, 1994; Day and Roberts-Holmes, 1998).

The process of educational change

A number of writers have coined phrases to describe the process of educational change. Fullan (2001) on many occasions in his writings has produced interesting phrases to 'capture' the spirit of the change process. He lists the six components thus:

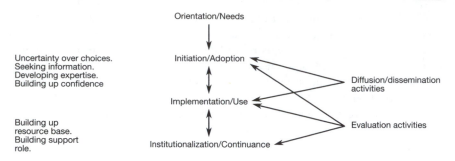

Figure 9.1 Educational change process.

1 The goal is not to innovate the most.
2 It is not enough to have the best idea.
3 Appreciate the implementation dip.
4 Redefine resistance.
5 Reculturing is the name of the game.
6 Never a checklist, always complexity (Fullan, 2001, p. 34).

A more traditional approach to educational change processes is to separate out the phases involved:

1 Orientation/needs phase: dissatisfaction, concern or need is felt and expressed by one or more individuals who seek answers to such dominant questions as:
    – What is the problem that is concerning me (us)?
    – How and why has it arisen?
    – Is it important enough to rectify?
    – Do I (we) want to take the necessary steps to overcome the problem?

2 Initiation/adoption phase: a person (or a group of persons) initiates and promotes a certain programme or activity – dominant questions of this phase are:
    – What should I (we) do?
    – What will it look like?
    – What will it mean for me (us)?

3 Implementation/initial use phase: attempts are made by teachers to use the programme or activity and this can have varied results, from success to disastrous failure – dominant questions for the teacher at this phase include:
    – How do I do it?
    – Will I ever get it to work smoothly?
    – To whom can I turn to get assistance?

- Am I doing what the practice requires?
- What is the effect on the learner?

4 Institutionalization/continuation phase: the emphasis here is to ensure that structures and patterns of behaviour are established so that the use of the innovation will be maintained over time – the dominant questions for the school are:
   - How do I (we) make sure that the innovation will continue?
   - Who will take responsibilities to ensure the adequate operation of it?

Although these four phases can be separated for purposes of analysis, in practice they will merge imperceptibly into each other. There can be forward and backward modifications between the phases (as indicated by the two-way arrows in Figure 9.1), and the time periods for each phase can vary tremendously.

The 'initiation/adoption' phase is often termed 'the front end' of an innovation. This is the period when basic decisions are made by external agencies and publishers, for whom numbers of adopters (and therefore sales) are of crucial importance. They can expect that schools and teachers will adopt a curriculum package only if it fulfils a special need for them, although there are other factors which can influence their decision. Fullan (1991) listed a number of factors which co-determine adoption rates, including existence and quality of related innovations, access to information, advocacy from central administrators, change agents, availability of federal or state funds, community pressures, and decrees by state governments.

The 'implementation phase' has been defined as 'what an innovation consists of in practice' (Fullan and Pomfret, 1977). But this simple statement does not reveal the complex realities and problems associated with the phase. Leithwood's (1981) definition raises some of the complexities: 'Implementation is a reduction in the gap between current and preferred status.'

Whilst the answer to the question of whether an innovation has been adopted can be simply 'yes' or 'no', the same cannot apply to implementation. There is a continuum of degrees of implementation ranging from major to minor adaptations through to high fidelity of use level. The only definite point on the continuum is for non-implementation.

'Institutionalization' occurs when an innovation is supported in schools after an initial period of use (usually two to five years). The real test for continuance or disappearance of an innovation comes after external funds have been terminated or after consultant assistance has stopped. It can be argued that institutionalization has to be reached before it is possible to judge the outcomes or effects of an innovation since otherwise an adverse evaluation would lead to the removal of the innovation. Institutionalization is facilitated by such factors as administrative commitment, pressures and support (Scott, 1999). It is weakened by staff mobility and changing student populations.

The above phases are useful in establishing likely stages in the change process but they ignore the 'emotional' work of change (Hargreaves *et al.*, 2001) or the 'personality of change' (Goodson, 2001). Goodson maintains that a teacher's personal beliefs and missions are a crucial building block in the change process.

Carless (2004) reminds us that frontline teachers are faced with multiple innovations and they have to juggle a variety of commitments. Hargreaves (1997) suggests that 'the chaos of multiple innovations and intensified reform efforts is often a sign of governments in panic' (p. 62).

Churchill and Williamson (1999) conclude from their study that teachers' experiences with previous educational changes affect their receptivity to future changes. Those teachers who had a high level of commitment to a recent change are more likely to adopt a positive approach to future innovations. Those who played resistant roles previously are likely to respond negatively in the future.

Change leaders

There can be a number of change leaders within a school or agency. According to Binney and Williams (1995), 'they are clear about what they want to change and they are responsive to others' views and concerns' (p. 52). They need not be senior-level teachers or administrators. Any person who helps other teachers with the curriculum (both content and processes of teaching) or who helps teachers identify problems and search out resources and linkage groups is a change leader.

Southworth and Doughty (2006) suggest that leadership must extend beyond the principalship and consider other leaders in a school and the community – the need for distributed leadership. According to Scott, an effective change leader:

- gives positive support and doesn't put people down;
- is enthusiastic and cares about education;
- is committed to doing things well;
- can tolerate ambiguity;
- accepts change as inevitable;
- is action-oriented;
- possesses a wide repertoire of communication skills;
- understands and can work with the dynamics of change (Scott, 1999).

Fullan (2002) focuses especially upon school principals – 'only principals who are equipped to handle a complex, rapidly changing environment can implement the reforms that lead to sustained improvement in student achievement' (p. 16). He suggests that 'the principal of the future – the Cultural Change Principal – must be attuned to the big picture ... Cultural Change Principals display palpable energy, enthusiasm and hope' (p. 17).

Fullan and Earl (2002) extend the concept further by asserting that school leaders need to be able to use the extensive ongoing data that is now available about students and teachers as they go about their decision-making. This may cause tensions for many principals who are unaccustomed to interpreting data which has been collected centrally, but it is now a reality in a data-rich world. Principals need to use this data, not as a surveillance activity but in the service of improvement.

Fullan, Hill and Crevola (2006) take a similar stance when they provide a model for teachers so that they can target precise instructional strategies for specific students. They encourage teachers to analyse performance data to be able to carry out precision teaching.

Sulla (1998) notes that change leaders external to the school are often a crucial element in ensuring that an educational change is implemented successfully. She maintains that external change leaders are better placed to take into account the local context and to help teachers engage in reflective inquiry.

Diffusion and dissemination

'Diffusion and dissemination' activities are crucial for an understanding of how innovations are communicated. Rogers (1983) defines 'diffusion' as 'the spontaneous, unplanned spread of new ideas'. It involves a special type of communication between individuals and groups because the messages are concerned with 'new' ideas. Groups and individuals will often seek out further information about an innovation before they make a decision to adopt it or not. If they are unable to decide between several alternatives, the diffusion of information enables them to make an informed choice.

Information transfer is rarely a one-way process: most frequently it is effected by an exchange of ideas and information between individuals. Diffusion activities typically involve a two-way communication of information. Information about an innovation can of course be diffused by different communication channels, from mass media to face-to-face exchange.

The term 'dissemination' is often used synonymously with diffusion but it really has a narrower focus and applies to the specific procedures used to inform individuals or groups about an innovation and to interest them in it (Coulby, 2000). The emphasis is upon goal-directed activities and upon the arousing of interest in the innovation among potential clients. Some writers (for example Zaltman et al., 1977; Rosenau, 1973) see dissemination very much like marketing activities and provide detailed guidelines about how a range of tactics such as direct mail, workshops, visits or telephone calls can be used in certain educational situations. They analyse each of these tactics according to various criteria such as relative cost, coverage, impact and user convenience.

For other writers (Simpson, 1990; Sarason, 1990), curriculum dissemination occurs within a cultural framework. They maintain that change agents need to be aware of a school system's attitudes and administrative structure and to use only those dissemination activities which are suited to these prevailing norms. Craig (2006) takes a similar stance when she states that dissemination is about meaningfully portraying ideas or practices to others so that they might be inspired but they have to decide within their own unique circumstances.

Change strategies and tactics

'Strategy' in the area of educational change means, reduced to its simplest form, a plan for replacing an existing programme with an innovation. Several such strategies have been proposed by education writers. The difficulty with some of them is that they have been devised for curriculum change in quite specific educational settings at a particular point in time. The temporal factor is understandable as strategies suggested for the 1960s would necessarily differ from those for the 2000s, with their different sets of relationships. Nevertheless they are helpful for the purposes of analysis.

Major strategies have been classified in the typology by Bennis *et al.* (1976), who allocated each of them to one of three groups which they labelled as 'power-coercive', 'normative/re-educative' and 'empirical-rational'.

'Power-coercive' strategies are based on the control of rewards and punishments and are relatively easy to apply. The recipients simply have to comply if they want to obtain the rewards offered. The motivation for complying is of course not meaningfully related to the innovation. That is, it is extrinsic in nature, and teachers on the receiving side will have no inner self-generated need for accepting and implementing an innovation (intrinsic motivation).

'Normative/re-educative' strategies refer to actions intended to manipulate recipients so that they see the situation differently. This can be achieved by biased messages, persuasive communication and training workshops. The recipients are trained or re-educated to appreciate the beneficial aspects of a particular innovation.

'Empirical-rational' strategies rely upon the recipients realizing that they should change to the new innovation in their best interests. The strategies rely upon providing detailed knowledge about the innovation by holding workshops, seminars and demonstrations.

It is not difficult to identify any of these strategies included in educational changes which have occurred in the past. All education systems will on occasions use a 'power-coercive' strategy if a major change is envisaged and it is seen to be necessary for all students (for example a new core area in computing). But there will also be occasions when the authorities will be less coercive and they will appeal to teachers' rational judgements or, if this fails, they may try to re-educate teachers to their point of view. All three strategies may be used concurrently and at different levels with different groups of teachers and administrators (Hess, 2003).

Table 9.1 Dissemination tactics and their effects

	Rel. Cost of Imp.	Rel. Coverage	Relative Impact	User Convenience	Feedback	Ideal for	Unsuited to	Incentives required
IMPERSONAL *Information*								
Direct Mail	L	H	L	H	H	Installing or replacing visible, low-risk, familiar innovations	Complex innovations	Low price, ease of ordering, guarantee, bonus, etc.
Mass Media	L	H	L	M	L	Awareness, arousal	Complex, high-cost innovations	Stimulus to act on information (limited time, special introductory offer, etc.)
Printed Matter	L	M	L	H	L	Awareness, interest	Complex innovations requiring hands-on trial	Stimulus to act on information
Professional Association	L	M	M	M	M	Awareness of innovations, data on trials	Mass-market adoptions	Professional membership status, interaction with peers, prepaid travel to meetings
PERSONAL *Demonstration*								
On-Site	M	L	M	H	H	Trial of high-risk innovations in large LEAs	Low-risk, routine adoptions	Released time for observation testimonials
Visitation	H	M	M	L	M	Demonstration of complex, high-risk innovations	Low cost, routine adoptions	Released time, prepaid travel, materials to take home, testimonials
Workshop	M	L	L	M	M	Hands-on trial	Persuasion of university personnel	Free registration, credit, materials to take home, snacks
INTERPERSONAL *Field Agents*								
Non-commercial	H	M	M	H	H	Implementing high-risk, unfamiliar, complex training or organizational innovations	Mass-market adoptions	Free consultation, technical assistance, targeted information retrieval system, etc.
Commercial	H	H	H	H	H	Installing high mark-up, low-risk, consumable innovations	Low mark-up, complex innovations	Free samples, entertainment, volume discounts, special deals, etc.

L=low M=medium H=high

The particular strategies used will vary from situation to situation, but to maximize their effect certain 'tactics' will tend to be associated with them. A change agent may not systematically plan to use particular tactics but some tactics can clearly reinforce or reduce the potential impact of specific strategies. Examples of the wide range of tactics available, including personal contact, user involvement, information distribution and training/installation tactics, are shown in Table 9.1.

At different times particular tactics might appear to be the most appropriate. For example, a busy school principal might prefer to send a general e-mail/memo (impersonal information) to all staff because of the time saved (relative cost). However, the impact on the teachers is likely to be far less than if the principal had called a meeting or met up with key teachers (personal) (see Table 9.1).

The categories included in Table 9.1 have a distinct marketing orientation. This is deliberate because it is argued that educators can gain important insights from how commercial businesses embark upon change.

The strategies and tactics used will depend on the scale of the change. Fullan and Earl (2002) describe a 'large-scale and sustainable reform' for the United Kingdom in terms of the English National Literacy and Numeracy Strategy (NLNS). The strategies were largely power-coercive (prescribed targets, scripted lessons, monitored progress). Although the results in the first year were very impressive (achievement levels rose from 54 per cent to 71 per cent for mathematics), Fullan and Earl (2002) contend that strategies for subsequent years for UK schools must involve 'local capacity-building, followed in turn by greater attention to local creativity, reflection and networking' (p. 4). Gordon and Whitty (2000) note the influence of the Office for Standards in Education (OFSTED) in gaining these higher standards – their monitoring of the literacy hour in schools with stopwatches (Hewitt, 2001) would have to be construed as being a power-coercive strategy! By contrast, Hannay et al. (1997) describe the strategies and tactics used with eight secondary schools in a school district in Ontario, Canada. These schools embarked upon a restructuring/recapturing process. School-based restructuring committees were set up in each school to design new positions of responsibility (POR) models for their individual schools. In each school new cross-departmental collaborative groupings of teachers emerged. There was increased attention to curriculum integration and more active learning strategies. The strategies used with these eight schools were largely 'normative-re-educative' and to a lesser extent 'empirical-rational'.

In Australia, it is interesting to note the strategies used by the Commonwealth Government to bring about 'innovatory' practices to the states. Power-coercive and normative-re-educative strategies are very evident in the linking of funding grants to specific requirements such as in literacy and numeracy. A recent requirement is that national testing will replace state-based tests in literacy and numeracy and that student reports should include an A–E component (Wilson, 2006; Moss and Godinho, 2007).

Another example of a power-coercive strategy is the requirement by the Australian Schools Assistance Act (2004) that all states and territories will implement Statements of Learning (English, mathematics, civics and citizenship, science, ICT) by 2008 and will use common national tests in these five domains by 2008 (Kerr, 2006).

At the state and territory levels various strategies, including power-coercive ones, are used. Gardner and Williamson (2005) refer to the power-coercive strategies used by the Minister of Education in Tasmania to force through a new Key Teacher (Behaviour Management) program. Harris and Marsh (2005) use the term 'disjunction' to explain the differences between stakeholders involved in educational change. They contend that the minister and government school systems have the resources to highlight their policy options whereas other stakeholders such as independent schools and unions have to look to other political tactics to contest these policies.

Table 9.2 Categories of models of change

External to school	*Internal to school*	*External/ internal/ personal*	*External*
High control Example: Research, Development and Diffusion (Clark and Guba, 1965) Authority Model	Interactive Example: Concerns Based Adoption Model (Hall *et al.*, 1979)	Interactive Example: Goodson's Model (2000)	Research-based Example: Comprehensive school reform programmes (Education Commission of the States, 1998)

Table 9.3 Eight basic lessons of the new paradigm of change

Lesson 1	You can't mandate what matters (the more complex the change the less you can force it)
Lesson 2	Change is a journey not a blueprint (change is non-linear, loaded with uncertainty and excitement and sometimes perverse)
Lesson 3	Problems are our friends (problems are inevitable and you can't learn without them)
Lesson 4	Vision and strategic planning come later (premature visions and planning blind)
Lesson 5	Individualism and collectivism must have equal power (there are no one-sided solutions to isolation and group think)
Lesson 6	Neither centralization nor decentralization works (note top-down and bottom-up strategies are necessary)
Lesson 7	Connection with the wider environment is critical for success (the best organizations learn externally as well as internally)
Lesson 8	Every person is a change agent (change is too important to leave to the experts; personal mindset and mastery are the ultimate protection)

Source: Fullan (1993, pp. 21–2).

Contexts of innovations

Schools in which innovations are implemented can vary enormously in terms of staff interest and expertise, organizational structures and resources. The staff will have their own special identity based upon their attributes, informal and formal values and norms, leadership traits and organizational climate. Students at a particular school will have certain characteristics in terms of socio-economic status, social orientation, norms, values and skills (Wideen, 1994).

Persons in the local community may have interests that can affect, or be affected by, their school (Prawat, 2000). Parents and community groups may develop a number of initiatives about the type of curriculum they wish to have taught at their school, but the teachers may then respond differently and try to influence their students and, indirectly, the parents. Differing points of view represented by the numerous 'cultures' of a school (parents, teachers, head office bureaucracy) may then create tensions on particular curriculum issues (Grundy, 2005).

Because of these differences it is not possible to predict in advance how participants at a specific school will react to a proposal to implement an innovation (Scott, 1999). Readiness for change is clearly a major factor, but this will depend in turn on such aspects as advocacy from central administrators; access to information; teacher pressure and support; community pressure, support, opposition or apathy; availability of external funds; and new legislation or policy. In many cases, innovative successful schools lose their creativity and atrophy as a result of loss of leadership, and internal divisions and conflicts (Azzara, 2000).

Models of change

Various education writers have outlined models of change that they contend have been successful in particular contexts. In general terms we can classify them as being either 'external' to the school or 'internal' to a school (see Table 9.2). The external model typically relies upon authority to exercise influence over people, processes and the use of resources (Desimone, 2002). The internal model relies upon interaction, group processes and consensus.

There are, of course, many other variations that might be located at different points on the continuum depicted in Table 9.2. Sometimes top-down, external models are effective but on many occasions they are not. Furthermore, not all internal, school-focused models are successful.

Some writings on educational change tend to differ from model-building assertions but the principles they espouse have a particular value orientation. Take, for example, Fullan's (1993) 'eight basic lessons about change', as depicted in Table 9.3. It is evident from these lessons or principles that Fullan is espousing a process-oriented model with an emphasis upon individual and organization variables.

Box 9.1   The longevity of innovations

Innovations that have lasted

- teacher aides
- cooperative learning
- whole language learning
- site-based management

Innovations that have not lasted

- homogeneous grouping
- merit pay
- 8mm projectors.

Principals also have to make some difficult decisions relating to a proposed innovation too (Southworth, 2000). They may not have any choice if the change is a system-wide one (Male, 1998). The proposed innovation may be at a considerable personal cost to them if they have to find the time to lead it, along with other responsibilities such as managing the academic performance of students, curriculum and instruction, professional performance of staff, administrative organization, school facilities and external relations.

As noted by Murphy and Rodi (2000), principals develop different coping strategies and some might have a well-developed resistance to any changes which threaten to undermine the present organizational pattern and behaviours at their school. Other principals may not be confident with initiating change, preferring to have an orderly well-organized approach and established procedures for all routine tasks.

Which innovations last?

A simple answer to the above question is 'not many'! Many traditional school practices continue to endure, despite attempts over the decades to bring about change.

Tyack and Cuban (1995) suggest that there is a kind of 'grammar of schooling'. Farrell (2001) suggest that there is a 'set of expected patterns we have historically constructed regarding what a "real" school is – anything which deviates substantially from that "real school" image will, by their analysis, be resisted by teachers, parents, students and public policy-makers' (p. 268).

Critical theorists such as Giroux (1997) contend that the enduring forms are maintained by those with most economic and political power in society. There will not be fundamental change until there are border crossings of these structures.

At different periods particular innovations appear to be the catchcry for all stakeholders, only to fall into oblivion a few years later (Ferrero, 2006).

Cuban (1988) reminds us that innovations keep on appearing. There may be all sorts of reasons for this, such as previous practices failing to remove the problems they were intended to solve; or because the politics of the problem were emphasized rather than the problem itself. He suggests that few educational innovations make it past the schoolroom door permanently.

The two lists included in Box 9.1 reveal that there are a number of innovations which were widely used in earlier decades that are no longer in use today. Some are products, while others are processes. Those that have survived appear to have done so because they have had a relative advantage, were easily managed and stimulated active involvement by teachers (Vanterpool, 1990).

Teachers have a number of responsibilities including providing a stable, supportive learning environment for their students. Some innovations and changes have the potential to bring about valued school improvement but no educational change is simple or without cost. Stakeholders have to make informed choices about whether to become involved in an innovation or not. As concluded by Ellis and Fouts (1993), some of the innovations that sweep through the school scene are nothing more than fads, while some have greater staying power. We have a responsibility to take change seriously, to be aware of the motivations and pressures for change and the implications and demands on all stakeholders (Chatterji, 2002).

Reflections and issues

1 Examine an innovation in education that occurred recently and with which you are quite familiar. Who initiated it? What steps were taken to implement it? How were impediments overcome? Is it still being used in schools? If not, when did it cease and why?

2 Compare and contrast the following statements using examples from schools with which you are familiar:
   • 'Most innovations that have lasted began with teachers involved in the planning' (Vanterpool, 1990, p. 39).
   • 'Teachers are not willing to explore innovations because they guard jealously the privacy of their own classroom and their established procedures' (Marsh, 1997, p. 24).

3 'Real change is always personal, organizational change is always painstaking. Success will require both high strivings and realistic acceptance – and authentic leaders who keep a steady focus on the human face of reform' (Ross, 2000). Discuss.

4 School reform has failed because we have focused too narrowly on academic achievement. Give some examples to support or refute this statement.

5 'Sustaining school-wide reform programs past the initial stage of enthusiasm is one of the biggest problems that schools face' (McChesney and Hertling, 2000, p. 14). How might a principal sustain a high level of enthusiasm? What would be the incentives for teachers?

6 'The essential nature of an innovation can be eroded with small, almost imperceptible alterations so that the school 'tames' it' (Jansen and Van der Vegt, 1991, p. 33). To what extent should adaptation be permitted in school settings? Is it necessary for all of a planned innovation to be maintained? Can strict fidelity of use be maintained without violating the autonomy of teachers and students?

Web sources

Reed, J. (2005) 'Sense and Singularity', *Times Educational Supplement*, 8 April 2005, www.tes.co.uk/search/story/?storey_id = 2088555 – extracted December 2008.

Whittaker, M. 2004) 'Take a Risk and Talk to Heads', *Times Educational Supplement*, 15 October 2004, www.tes.co.uk/search/story/?storey_id = 2042414 – extracted December 2008.

Credaro, A., 'Innovation and change in Education', http://www.geocities.com/koalakid_1999/UNIVERSITY/change.htm – extracted December 2008.

Principles of Innovation and Change, http://www.uwm.edu.Dept/CUTS/bench/princp.htm – extracted December 2008.

Planned Change and Innovation, http://web.syr.edu/~cspuches/change.htm – extracted December 2008.

Chapter 10

Leadership and the school principal

Introduction

In many countries over the last decade, the emphasis upon standards has dominated the educational agenda. According to Joseph, Mikel and Windschiti (2002) the work of teachers has become increasingly routinized by the use of standardized curricula and standardized achievement tests to assess the performance of students, teachers and schools. School principals have to operate in this very exacting environment and performativity has been a major focus (Woods, 2000). Although the term 'leadership' is being highlighted for school principals, especially in the UK, structural conditions are ensuring that tight accountability regimes and curriculum specifications are in place (Glatter, 2006).

There is a major tension still to be resolved between 'leadership' and 'management' for school heads. On the one hand the expectation for principals is to be proactive and transformational leaders but in reality the management requirements are closely linked to a narrow technicist orientation, hierarchical approaches and a market ideology (Grace 1995):

- Governments have national agendas and want 'compliant' principals who will accept national values which are imposed upon them (Glatter, 2006). Brundrett (2006) describes the standards-based national intervention in leadership development in England under the National College for School Leadership (NCSL).
- The wider community wants school principals to have purpose, commitment and creativity and have a broad understanding of the environmental contexts in which their schools are located (Lucas and Valentine, 2002).
- Teachers are interested in distributed leadership and to explore how all members of a school can play complementary roles (Firestone and Martinez, 2007).
- Students want principals who are caring and who can listen (Noddings, 2006). They want school principals to be the final arbiter on matters of justice, discipline and penalties, but above all to be an inspirational, charismatic figurehead.

The expectations in total are overwhelming and, in most cases, quite unrealistic (Grace, 1995). Copland (2001) contends that expectations for the principalship in the USA have steadily expanded, always adding to and never subtracting from the job description. Because of these additional expectations, the principal's role has come under ever closer scrutiny – it is increasingly difficult to recruit 'quality' principals. Shortages of school principals have been reported in many countries, including Canada, Australia, New Zealand, UK and the USA (Rhodes and Brundrett, 2006).

According to Copland (2001), 'we have reached the point where aggregate expectations for the principalship are so exorbitant that they exceed the limits of what might reasonably be expected from one person' (p. 529).

Woods (2000), in describing the scene in the United Kingdom, argues that it is not only the additional expectations but the enhanced emphasis upon market and public regulatory mechanisms that are the problem. School principals have to demonstrate performativity – 'to amend their identity nearer to innovative, enterprising, competitive entrepreneurs modelled on the private sector' (Woods, 2000, p. 15)'. Male (1998) refers also to the marketplace environment and a move to individuality and isolation for head teachers.

There is a further complication in that many of the expectations described above are based on 'dated' stereotypes. For example, there is the expectation that effective school principals are males, and as a result females are in the minority in positions of authority even though women are in the majority in the teaching service (Porter, 1994). Lee et al. (1993) refer to a recent empirical study which revealed that male teachers assess the leadership of female principals they work for as relatively ineffective even though measures of self-efficacy and staff influence demonstrate higher results for both male and female teachers working for female rather than male principals!

Solutions to the leadership shortages are elusive. Rhodes and Brundrett (2006) argue that schools should focus on growing their own leaders – there need to be specific approaches to leadership talent identification and leadership succession planning. Eckman (2006) suggests a co-principal leadership model as a way of addressing the shortage of qualified educational leaders in the USA. Respondents in co-principal positions reported high levels of job satisfaction and more opportunities for leadership experience – particularly for females. In her study of fifty schools having co-principals, Eckman (2006) noted that females were represented on 83 per cent of the co-principal leadership teams.

Another major problem apart from shortages of school principals is the special difficulties of leadership in low-achieving schools. Clearly these problems are related. In the US, the No Child Left Behind legislation (2001) focuses especially on students in high-poverty, low-performing schools (Duke et al., 2006). Principals in low-performing schools have especially difficult personnel problems and often a dysfunctional school culture.

Hopkins and Higham (2007) contend that school principals must help develop other leaders – they must connect with the bigger picture and link up

Box 10.1   Domains in which the principal is expected to demonstrate leadership

Curriculum and instruction

- reviewing or revising an existing subject
- influencing specific teaching methods
- introducing new subjects/units

Academic performance of students

- influencing achievement standards in all subjects
- encouraging high attainments by students in accordance with their abilities
- monitoring tests and examinations in specific subjects

Non-academic development of students

- managing or controlling student behaviour
- influencing student welfare/attitudes
- influencing students' extracurricular activities

Professional/personal performance of staff

- influencing the performance of teachers
- influencing the performance of administrators
- influencing induction of newly graduated teachers
- influencing the performance of student teachers
- supporting teacher welfare and their personal development

Administration/organization

- influencing schedule of teaching
- influencing student enrolment priorities
- influencing student decisions
- influencing operational efficiency

School facilities

- managing use of buildings, grounds and furnishings
- initiating changes to improve instruction
- initiating changes to improve aesthetics

External relations

- maintaining regular communication with school board members
- maintaining regular communication with regional and state education department officials
- providing positive public relations with the local community.

with other principals. 'System leadership', according to Hopkins and Higham (2007), 'can contribute decisively to a full range of government and local agenda by sharing of expertise, facilities and resources' (p. 163).

Earley and Weindling (2006) take a similar stance when they argue that head teachers should be involved as 'consultant leaders'. In the UK consultant leaders are now playing a major role in educational developments such as the New Relationship with Schools and the Primary Leadership Strategy (Earley and Weindling, 2006).

Functions and standards

Priorities for leadership and management, from one perspective are relatively similar in many countries. Webb *et al.* (2006) contend that as a result of globalization there is growing uniformity, particularly as a result of marketization and managerialism. Thus a typical listing of functions such as those shown in Box 10.1 is applicable in many countries.

Yet there are also differences between countries due to different cultural influences and local school factors. Webb *et al.* (2006) contrast the narrow educational outcomes to be achieved through curriculum and pedagogical prescription allied to national testing and school inspections in England with the strong tradition of trust in teacher professionalism in Finland. Goddard (2007) highlights differences between countries especially in terms of how principals facilitate or deny access to schools for children from minority and marginalized cultural groups.

It is certainly the case that in England over the last decade there has been massive commitment by the government to improving school leadership. The NCSL was established in 2000 and there is now a Centre for Excellence in Leadership. Six key areas of leadership are included in the National Standards for Head Teachers (DFES, 2004), namely:

- shaping the future;
- leading learning and teaching;
- developing self and working with others;
- managing the organization;
- securing accountability;
- strengthening the community.

There is now some research evidence emerging which indicates that these national leadership programmes are impacting positively on leadership in schools, although the level of impact varies with different programmes (Brundrett, 2006). Yet other authors, such as Wallace and Hoyle (2005) and Bottery (2004), are more sceptical.

In the USA a number of frameworks are available, such as the standards framework produced by the Interstate School Leaders Licensure Consortium

(Council of Chief State School Officers, 2007). The standards are based on five career stages, including identifying qualified aspirants, entry-level leaders, early career leaders and advanced career leaders.

In Australia, the Australian Institute for Teaching and School Leadership was established in 2005. Now renamed Teaching Australia, its officers are undertaking exploratory steps in developing professional standards for school leaders. A National Standards Drafting Group of volunteer principals is currently drafting principal standards (Teaching Australia, 2007). As noted by Ingvarson *et al.* (2006), there are problems when government agencies are responsible for assessing and recognizing attainment of standards in school leadership, but on the other hand it is difficult to have school leaders devise their own system.

An alternative to standards frameworks is proposed by Louden and Wildy (1997) based upon a probabilistic framework, utilizing written case studies and Rasch modelling. Performance of principals is located on a set of continua, offers only an estimate of performance and describes what normally can be expected rather than judging mastery of a skill.

Leadership qualities and styles

The reality of the school day, with its constant interruptions, can put a principal under considerable stress. Typically, a principal will adopt a particular 'leadership style' which emphasizes certain priorities and limits others. This is his or her coping mechanism and it is quite understandable.

A leadership style commonly listed is instructional leadership (Lezotte, 1997). This emphasis was a development of the effective schools movement and it involved principals actively participating in the instructional process – collecting weekly lesson plans from teachers, reading about different instructional strategies, undertaking the clinical supervision process (pre-observation conferences, classroom observations, post-observation conferences) (Du Four, 2002).

Transformational leadership

A leadership style which has been championed in the 1990s and the 2000s is transformational school leadership. Bass and Avolio (1994) developed a model of transformational leadership which they considered was exemplified by the four 'I's:

- idealized influence – being a role model for their followers;
- inspirational motivation – motivating and inspiring followers;
- intellectual stimulation – stimulating followers to be innovative and creative;
- individualized consideration – paying special attention to each individual's needs.

Leithwood *et al.* (1996) and Yu *et al.* (2002) have identified specific dimensions of transformational school leadership as well as behaviours associated with each of the dimensions. Their dimensions include:

- charisma/inspiration/vision;
- individual consideration;
- intellectual stimulation;
- structuring;
- culture building;
- high performance expectations;
- modelling.

This leadership style focuses especially on visionary concerns while largely ignoring routine managerial concerns. It emphasizes the significance of the person and personal traits in bringing about social and cultural change (Crowther *et al.*, 2000).

Although transformational leadership has had a major influence some educators argue that it overstates the importance of individuals. For example, Gronn (2000) criticizes transformational leadership because it exaggerates the sense of agency attributed to leaders – naïve realism, the belief in the power of one.

Glanz (2007) argues that strategically minded leaders want to transform their work in schools deeply, not artificially and superficially. Fullan (2003) concurs that change without addressing a change in core beliefs is doomed to remain temporary and superficial.

Distributive leadership

This perspective is very different to an individual-centred, transformative approach. According to Spillane *et al.* (2004), a distributive leadership perspective is complex, fluid and emergent, involving tasks and practices stretched over personnel and other resources within a field or organization. It involves interactions and dynamics between persons because leadership is not embodied in a designated leader. Individuals take on organizational leadership roles such as public relations spokesperson in the community or IT expert (Daresh, 2006).

Ritchie *et al.* (2007) contend that it is the 'collective' element in distributive leadership which is so important. It will not happen in a hierarchically structured organization – successful interaction chains need to be established.

Entrepreneurial leadership

Both in the UK and USA, initiatives have been taken to introduce private participation and entrepreneurialism into schooling. In the UK 'academies' were established in 2002 – the sponsors can be from business, faith or voluntary groups. These private sponsors contribute up to £2 million of the capital for a new academy in return for a formal role in its governance (Woods *et al.*, 2007). The number of academies is now over fifty and is likely to grow considerably. Yet the results to date are mixed. Woods *et al.* (2007) contend that academics are creating new relationships but it is a very contested area – 'the boundaries and extent of public control and of enhanced private influence are likely to be tested over time' (p. 254). Davies and Hentschke (2006) are equally cautious when they conclude that only under certain circumstances will public–private partnerships yield a number of potential benefits.

In the USA charter schools were developed to fulfil a similar function. Essentially, charter schools are public schools specifically designated by a state as exempt from some state regulations that apply to ordinary public schools. The idea is to provide considerable latitude to a charter school and the people within it to pursue their own views about what education should be (Hess, 2004). Thus charter schools are schools of choice for the parents, students and teachers involved in them and are conducive to on-site curriculum decision making. Although laws differ from state to state, in general charters for such schools may be granted to local school districts, to groups of parents or teachers, even to business organizations. Recently Arizona has had the highest number of charter schools (464), followed by California (537), Florida (227), Texas (221) and Michigan (196). The total number of charter schools is more than 3,000, the total number of students enrolled is more than 685,000, and these numbers are almost certain to grow. Charter laws are now in place in more than forty states.

Charter schools have emerged with strong bipartisan support at the federal level as well as at state level. Since 1994, the United States Department of Education has provided a competitive grant programme (the Charter Schools Program) to assist with start-up costs, and there is now an additional aid programme (the Credit Enhancement for Charter School Facilities Program). Total funding available each year for charter schools is now over $225 million. Also, significant links have been established with NCLB; one of the options for non-performing schools is for them to opt for charter school status. Good and Braden (2000) contend that charter schools embody a widespread belief that market-driven organizations will outperform traditional bureaucratic ones.

According to Gresham, Hess, Maranto and Milliman (2000), teachers in Arizona's charter elementary schools experienced a sense of empowerment. Good and Braden (2000) describe charter schools as 'the liveliest reform in American education'.

Yet, in practice charter schools have not lived up to all the glowing rhetoric. Wells (1999) considers that there is little evidence to indicate that students actually learn more in charter schools than in ordinary public schools. The studies available to date provide modest results in favour of charter schools. Hoxby's (2004) comparison of charter schools and regular public schools demonstrated a slight advantage for charter schools in state examinations in reading (4 per cent) and mathematics (2 per cent).

Inclusive leadership

Tillman et al. (2006) contend that 'school leadership must place social justice front and centre to all actions within the school' (p. 208). School leaderships

must be informed by social justice lenses of race, gender, sexual orientation, social class and language. Ryan (2006) argues for a model of inclusive
leadership which should include:

- advocating for inclusion;
- educating participants;
- developing critical consciousness;
- adopting inclusive decision- and policy-making strategies.

These authors contend that schools are about deeper moral purposes like
social justice.

Cultural change leadership

Fullan (2002) refers to essential qualities that he considers are needed for the
principal of the future – the Cultural Change Principal – namely:

- moral purpose: the school principal treats students, teachers and parents
  well – the principal seeks to make a difference in the lives of students;
- understanding change: the school principal helps others find collective
  meaning – he or she works on transforming the culture;
- improving relationships: the school principal builds relationships with
  diverse people and groups – the principal tries to motivate and energize
  disaffected teachers;
- knowledge creation and sharing: the principal is the lead learner and shares
  with others;
- coherence making: the principal concentrates on student learning as the
  central focus and then brings together other elements to facilitate this – the
  principal does not take on too many projects for the sake of it.

Lucas and Valentine (2002) argue that creating a school culture that accepts
and encourages experimentation, risk-taking and open dialogue is likely to be
successful.

Concluding comments

Governments and organizations in a number of countries are funding major
initiatives related to school leadership and management. As might be anticipated, various diverse approaches are being developed.

Yet there is the danger of overload for school leaders. As noted by Copland
(2001), if these different leadership styles are considered en masse rather than
separately, it may be the case that additional understandings are grafted onto a
comprehensive definition of the principal's role and in turn lead to even further
overwhelming expectations for principals.

Reflections and issues

1 'We need to move away from the notion of how the principal can become master implementer of multiple policies and programmes. What is needed is to reframe the question: What does a reasonable leader do, faced with impossible tasks?' (Fullan, 1988, p. 12). Is it more productive to consider schools as operating in a non-rational world – with complex, contradictory happenings occurring daily? What realistic priorities should a 'reasonable' leader select?

2 'Women principals are found to act in a more democratic and participative style, whereas male principals are more directive and autocratic' (Lee *et al.*, 1993, p. 156). Discuss.

3 'Leadership is and must be oriented toward social change, change which is transformative in degree' (Foster, 1989, p. 52). To what extent is this a major concern for school principals? What impediments may limit this as an option?

4 'Principals, as middle managers, must simultaneously manage at least four sets of relationships: upward with their superiors; downward with subordinates; laterally with other principals; and externally with parents and other community and business groups. Managing one set of relationships successfully may interfere with or hinder another set of relationships' (Goldring, 1993, p. 95). Explain this management problem, giving examples.

5 'A leader in the postmodern world needs a clear sense that nothing is guaranteed; that nothing, certainly, will be easy' (Starratt, 1993, p. 157). Discuss with reference to the school principal as leader.

6 To what extent does a distributive leadership perspective give insights about how to improve school leadership?

7 How can we contribute to the raising of standards, not only in our own school but in others too? To what extent can system leaders bring about a 'sea change'?

8 What kinds of leadership tasks can teachers share in a distributed leadership environment? What are some limiting factors on teachers' capacity to play this complimentary role?

Web sources

Transformative leadership, literacy.kent.edu/oasis/leadership/over2.htm – extracted 2 October 2007.

Distributed Leadership, www.ncsl.org.uk/mediastore/image2/bennett – extracted 2 October 2007.

Transformative Leadership for Social-Emotional Learning, www.lions-quest.org/documents/TransformativeLeadershipfor SEL2006.pdf – extracted 2 October 2007.

Social Equity Leadership, www.has.vcu.edu/gov/selc/ – extracted 2 October 2007.

Headmaster, www.hdmaster.com/ – extracted 2 October 2007.

Chapter 11

School-based curriculum development
Idealized or actual?

Introduction

Schooling is often characterized by turbulence and change. Organizational structures, leadership and financial underpinnings are constantly in a state of flux and ferment. To a large extent the turbulence is due to politicians, who in their zeal to appeal to voters constantly invent (and reinvent) reforms to perceived educational problems.

School-based curriculum development (SBCD) in its various guises of 'decentralization' and 'school-focused' is exhorted by politicians in many countries. Currently SBCD is a vogue priority in a number of Asian countries such as Singapore, China, Hong Kong and Taiwan (Juang *et al.*, 2005). It is not a new approach. It has been widely practised in Israel for over thirty years (Ben-Peretz and Dor, 1986).

In the UK, politicians are advocating personalized learning, which encourages teachers to seek out and promote individualized learning in local school settings (Miliband, 2004), but also high on their agenda are standards and accountability priorities across the system.

Similarly, it might be argued that at the school district level in the USA school-managed activities are practised, yet with the advent of the No Child Left Behind (NCLB) legislation, centrally planned and controlled standards are now firmly in place, especially for core subjects.

This chapter examines some of the key factors for promoting SBCD and what is possible in current educational climates of accountability.

Some basic terms and issues

School-based management (SBM)

Although it is difficult to define precisely what is meant by 'self-managing schools' or 'site-based management' it is important to exclude what is not. As noted by Caldwell and Spinks (1998), 'a self-managing school is not an autonomous school nor is it a self-governing school, for each of these kinds of schools involve a degree of independence that is not provided in a centrally determined framework' (p. 15).

Caldwell links the emergence and popularity of SBM with decentralized tendencies in business. In terms of business and industry, 'responsibility, authority and accountability are being shifted to the level of the operational unit' (Caldwell, 2002a, p. 1).

Within the education sector, a similar major push toward management at the school level has been occurring and continues to gain momentum. Regardless of the philosophies of different governments, the trend seems to be irreversible and is characterized by the following:

- centrally determined frameworks;
- a leaner bureaucracy;
- the shift of responsibility, authority and accountability to schools;
- a better-informed community exercising more choice in schooling;
- empowered leadership, especially for school principals/heads (Gamage, 2005).

However, these changes to the management of schools do not necessarily generate better-quality curricula, teaching and learning (Dimmock, 1993). As noted by Burrow (1994), the shifting of responsibility to the local level has occurred for other than pedagogical reasons. Smyth (1994, p. 2) argues that the concept of the self-managing school is deceptive in that:

- the rhetoric of devolution is really about recentralization of education;
- it is closely linked to structural changes in the economy;
- the trends are not emancipatory or liberating for teachers.

Research on SBM

Studies undertaken in the USA and Canada in the 1990s have not shown positive impacts of SBM.

Rossi and Freeman's (1993) study of SBM in twelve high schools in eleven states in the USA (half selected because they had implemented SBM, the other half because they had tradition-led school principals) found that schools implementing SBM did not pay any more attention to issues of curriculum, pedagogical issues and student concerns than the traditionally managed schools.

Leithwood and Menzies' (1999) review of eighty-three empirical studies of SBM found little evidence for or against. Their overall conclusion was that 'there is virtually no firm, research-based knowledge about the direct or indirect effects of SBM on students ... There is an awesome gap between the rhetoric and the reality of SBM's contribution to student growth' (p. 34).

By contrast, Caldwell (2002a) contends that the connection between SBM and improved student learning is now becoming clear. Caldwell (2002a) cites a

UNESCO forum held in February 2001 at which participants 'shared international experience of success with strategies that linked SBM, enhanced professional development for teachers, community support for schools and making learning for students more active and joyful' (p. 9).

Many education systems operating in the twenty-first century are maintaining some centralized control mechanisms such as by the use of centrally determined frameworks and centrally determined funding mechanisms.

A number of descriptive accounts have been published about the benefits of self-managing schools or SBM. Yet despite the positive rhetoric it is difficult to find any research-based evidence on the direct or indirect benefits of SBM.

School-based curriculum development

The term school-based curriculum development (SBCD) has been used as a rallying cry for various innovatory educational practices. There have been variations in terms, such as 'school-focused' rather than 'school-based' and 'curriculum decision-making' rather than 'curriculum development'. Further, some would argue that SBCD is a slogan, while others prefer to conceptualize it as a method or technique. These variations need to be considered before proceeding any further with an analysis of SBCD.

A literal definition of 'school-based' might imply that all educational decisions are made at the school level. Apart from independent and 'alternative' schools operating as separate entities, it is highly unlikely that this situation pertains in systemic schools (for example government schools, schools in a school district). The term 'school-focused' is a weaker interpretation in that it suggests that decision-making, at whatever level it occurs and by whomever, is undertaken in terms of the interests and needs of school communities. This latter term could apply to a whole range of highly centralized decision-making activities. Expressed along a continuum, 'school-based' is closer to the extreme of individual schools being responsible for all curriculum decisions, whereas 'school-focused' could be represented as a middle position between the centralized and decentralized extremes.

The term 'curriculum development' has wide connotations and is used to describe the various curriculum processes of planning, designing and producing associated with the completion of a particular set of materials. It can also include teaching activities associated with the implementation and evaluation of a set of materials. One might ascribe such elaborate activities to a well-funded curriculum project team, but the scale and range of these activities could well be beyond the scope of individual school communities. As a result, the term 'curriculum-making' is preferred because it signifies a less grandiose range of activities for school personnel. SBCD can involve *creating* new products or processes but that can also involve *selecting* from available commercial materials and making various *adaptions*. The latter two processes, of course, require less time, fewer funds and a lower level of commitment from

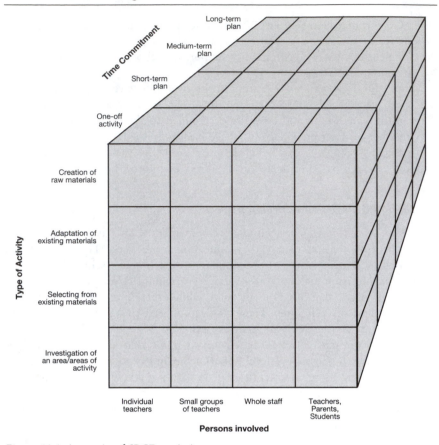

Figure 11.1 A matrix of SBCD variations.

participants. Yet it can be argued that SBCD tasks should be embarked upon only if they are manageable and can be achieved within a reasonable timeframe.

There is yet another interpretation of curriculum development which is far less materials oriented than those mentioned above. It can be argued that teachers should not merely be involved in activities which enable them to implement curriculum materials more effectively, but that they should engage in wide-ranging inquiries of concern to them. Connelly and Ben-Peretz (1980) argue that teachers engaging in educational enquiry will grow professionally from these activities even though, as a result of these experiences, they may be less inclined to implement curricula designed by others.

Without doubt, education systems and agencies have used the term SBCD as a *slogan*. It conjures up action at the local level, it connotes participation, grassroots control and many other attributes which are held to be near and dear to the general public. In a more cynical vein, it could also be stated that

Table 11.1 A conceptual map: facilitating school-based curriculum development (SBCD)

Major factors	Processes in a school to support SBCD	Innovative outcomes and practices of SBCD in a school
Levels of dissatisfaction with central controls	Exploring alternatives, distributed leadership, personalized learning, action research, collecting data	• Celebration of small- and large-scale successes • Plans for continuity and linkage at three levels (school, region, system, data valuing) • Collaboration by most teachers, parents, students –positive school atmosphere • Improved student results • Improved levels of camaraderie among staff • Attracting more resources to the school
Empowerment	• Team projects • Developing individual strengths • Providing extra time for discussions and planning • Sharing beliefs and skills • Professional development	• Rewards (financial, emotional) for individual teachers and the school as a whole • Ongoing comprehensive evaluations
Knowledge and skills of curriculum planning	• Teachers communicate and share skills • External experts used • Group planning and action research • Study visits and sharing	
Resources	• Expanding human resources, especially teacher leadership • Using resources to free up time for teachers • Obtaining additional external resources	

SBCD has been used by senior officers in some educational systems to deflect the blame for educational crises or is used as a means of cost-cutting in head-office budgets (Dimmock, 1993).

Other writers argue that SBCD is an amalgam of ideas which can be construed as an *educational philosophy*. Skilbeck (1990) puts together such terms as 'teacher and learner working together to produce the curriculum', 'freedom for both teacher and pupil' and the 'school's responsiveness to its environment' to produce a theoretical position about SBCD. He argues at length for structures and policies to be developed at the school level and for there to be shared decision-making by all participants, especially teachers and students. Fullan (2002) supports teacher involvement in change at the school level and he has produced various factors and strategies which could be viewed as a model for SBCD.

The literature is also replete with various accounts of SBCD as a *technique*. Case study accounts in particular have focused upon particular techniques which seem to work. Some writers have produced particular procedures such as person-centred approaches (Department of Education, 2002) or management-centred approaches (Joyner *et al.*, 2004). Others have concentrated upon ways of making SBCD work more effectively by the training of special in-house consultants (Sabar, 1983) and leadership skills and qualities for school principals (Leithwood and Menzies, 1999).

Conceptual analysis of SBCD

In an earlier volume on SBCD the authors provided a simplified analysis based upon a three-dimensional model (Figure 11.1) (Marsh *et al.*, 1990). Three variables are considered, namely *type of activity* (creation, adaptation, selection of curriculum materials) on one axis; *people involved* (individual teachers, pairs of teachers, groups, whole staff) on another axis; and *time commitment* (one-off activity, short term, medium term, long term).

Taking an example from the matrix in Figure 11.1, a typical SBCD activity might be the *adoption* of a primary science workbook by a *small group of teachers* as part of a *short-term plan* to upgrade their teaching of science in the upper primary grades. A more ambitious undertaking based upon the matrix cells in Figure 11.1 could be the creation of new *materials* for a local community unit by a *team of teacher, parents and students* as a *long-term plan* to be completed over a period of one calendar year.

A more detailed conceptual model is provided in Table 11.1 based upon four major factors which are progressively linked across processes in a school to support SBCD; and innovative outcomes and practices of SBCD in a school.

Factor One: levels of satisfaction/dissatisfaction with central controls

Teachers have a major interest in their craft. Maximum satisfactions are achieved if they are able to teach in ways which suit the majority of their students. The occasional successes they have with extremely difficult students make their endeavours well worth the effort. They guard very jealously those particular strategies or 'recipes' which seem to work (Lortie, 1975; Huberman, 1980).

Sometimes the problems are beyond the resources of an individual teacher and he or she needs to exchange ideas with others and perhaps even work collaboratively with a colleague on a particular problem. These experiments in cooperative ventures will only occur if the conditions are amenable and psychologically safe for the individual teachers.

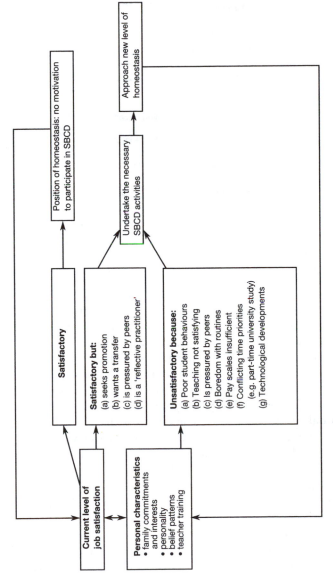

Figure 11.2 Levels of dissatisfaction/satisfaction.

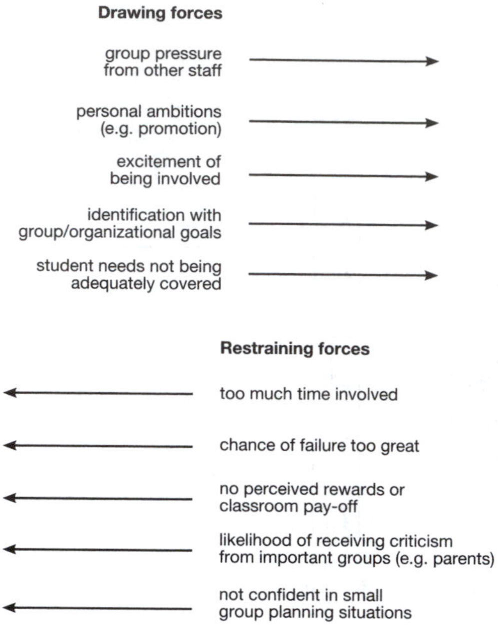

Drawing forces

group pressure
from other staff

personal ambitions
(e.g. promotion)

excitement of
being involved

identification with
group/organizational goals

student needs not being
adequately covered

Restraining forces

too much time involved

chance of failure too great

no perceived rewards or
classroom pay-off

likelihood of receiving criticism
from important groups (e.g. parents)

not confident in small
group planning situations

Figure 11.3 Force field for using an educational innovation.

Teachers may be deeply dissatisfied with how the curriculum is controlled centrally or they might cherish a desire to experiment with others in designing a curriculum more suitable for their respective schools.

Stated another way, teachers may embark upon SBCD activities if they have particular *needs* but these will be tempered by the *limits* of their particular teaching environment. There has to be a balancing of these two factors. Teachers will be highly motivated to participate if there are important needs to be satisfied, but only if these can be accommodated within the value system of the school community. Day *et al.* (1985) point to four factors which can affect the directions that teachers might take and that some compromise between them is always needed. These four factors include *predilections* of what teachers would like to do, *situations* that have to be taken into account and wider external factors of *expectations* and *prescriptions* (such as by legislation).

It is argued that job satisfaction is a key variable. If teachers are satisfied with what their students are achieving, especially as this often requires some very careful attention to the use of particular resources and methods, then they will be reticent about changing this state of affairs. The frenetic activities which can typically occur in a day's teaching make many teachers long for periods of stability and even homeostasis. Teachers, as a result of their socialization into the profession, do not tend to opt for avant-garde initiatives. Few want to be labelled as radicals or mavericks. The majority want the security of regular and predictable patterns of classroom activity.

However, as indicated in Figure 11.2, there will be some teachers who want to participate in SBCD activities even though they are relatively satisfied with their current teaching position. For example, those teachers seeking promotion realize that they need to do something extra to give themselves a chance of earning promotion. They might consider that their active participation in an SBCD activity could be a useful way of highlighting their particular strengths and details of this activity could be included in their curriculum vitae. Then again, there might be teachers who are prepared to reflect upon their current practices – they have the ability and the desire to problem-solve about their teaching (Schon, 1983) even though they are relatively satisfied with their current position.

In addition to those teachers who might be in the category of being satisfied but mobile, there is the much bigger group of teachers who would be dissatisfied with their present teaching position. A major reason for their dissatisfaction might be poor student attainment in their particular subjects or individual students performing poorly across a range of subjects. Another reason could be their dissatisfaction with inadequate resources, timetabling constraints or insufficient preparation time. A related reason might be sheer boredom with the system of rules and regulations and teaching practices.

Teachers have to balance out competing forces when making decisions about whether to become involved in SBCD or not. As indicated in Figure 11.3, as a result of considering needs and constraints teachers may decide to try out some innovations and not others. The process they undertake may be akin to the force field of 'driving' and 'restraining' forces noted by Lewin (1948) many decades ago. As indicated in Figure 11.3 some of the driving forces can be very influential but so too are the restraining forces. Clearly, only those innovations which are perceived to have a majority of dominant driving forces will in fact be adopted. The majority, in all likelihood, will be rejected. Fullan makes this point succinctly when he states that:

> It should be clearly understood that I am not saying that teachers are 'intrinsically' uninterested in serious education change. The truth of the matter is that the culture of the school, the demands of the classroom, and the usual way in which change is introduced do not permit, point to, or facilitate teacher involvement in exploring or developing more significant changes in educational practice.
>
> (Fullan, 1982, p. 120)

Every teacher develops his or her own unique configuration of driving and restraining forces, as outlined in Figure 11.2. Two or more teachers will only be willing to interact on SBCD activities if they perceive mutually supportive results from sharing their ideas and preferences (a mutual linking of configurations).

The final phase of the model, as indicated in Figure 11.2, is for pairs or groups of teachers to undertake their chosen innovatory SBCD activities on the assumption that improved teaching and learning situations for themselves and their students will be the result. They are likely to be seeking a new position of stability, a different set of relationships and procedures which will provide them in turn with a reasonable degree of homeostasis.

As indicated on pp. 212, 243–44, SBCD can involve parents and students as well as teachers. It is argued that the conceptual model (Table 11.1 and Figure 11.2) applies also to parents and students. For example, parents, through their formal contacts (for example school councils) and informal meetings, can lobby for changes and the adoption of certain innovations if they perceive that there are problem areas and issues to be resolved. On the other hand, they may be the restraining forces who feel strongly that certain innovations proposed by the teaching staff should not be adopted.

Students, especially through their student councils, can also provide opinions and advice which can be influential in determining final decisions about certain innovatory programmes. However, it has to be conceded that students' level of influence is likely to be minimal in many school communities.

Factor Two: empowerment

Empowerment assumes that persons holding power (for example state or local managers or school principals) give the power to someone else (for example teachers or students) in the interests of improving schools (Elmore, 1988). However, it is not always clear who has the power and how it might be transferred. Then there is the matter of responsibility. If persons are empowered, to whom are they responsible: to parents and students? To the community? To the teaching profession?

'Power' can be defined as control, but in terms of educational settings it is more useful to consider power as 'doing or acting'. Opportunities for teachers to try out new approaches, to problem-solve and to enquire, can assist them in becoming 'empowered'. Empowerment of teachers (and students) occurs when they have opportunities to create meaning in their respective schools. By contrast, 'disempowered' teachers are those who teach defensively and control knowledge in order to control students (McNeil, 1988). In these situations schooling becomes an empty ritual, unrelated to personal or cultural knowledge.

Teacher empowerment is seen by writers such as Giroux (1992) as a significant concept in understanding the complex relations between schools and the dominant society. He argues that teachers and students need empowerment to resist and to struggle against the domination in society produced by capitalism.

Some writers argue that teachers are becoming steadily disempowered (Apple, 2000; Whitty, 1994). For example, Apple (2000) argues that teachers face the prospect of being deskilled because of the encroachment of technical control procedures into the curriculum in schools. He cites as examples behaviourally based curricula, pre-specified competencies for teachers and students, and testing activities.

Southworth (2000) and Poppleton (2000) have reviewed the major reforms that were introduced by the Thatcher and Major governments and the Blair government in the United Kingdom. They have cited the following:

- the construction and implementation of a National Curriculum;
- introduction of a national system of testing pupils at the age of 7, 11, 14 and 16 years;
- the publication of schools' test results and the use of league tables to rate schools' apparent success;
- the creation of the Office for Standards in Education (OFSTED), which sets in place week-long inspections of all schools;
- the setting of numerical targets for pupils' attainments in every school;
- the intention to link teacher performance to rewards and pay.

It is evident that both political parties have severely curtailed opportunities for teacher empowerment, brought about a resultant loss of autonomy and increased teachers' resistance to change.

Yet in SBCD activities it is very evident that teacher empowerment must be encouraged. Devolution of significant authority to teachers over matters of budget and curriculum decisions is important. This requires actively restructuring schools to involve a variety of stakeholders. Practical ideas for bringing about distributed leadership have been advanced by the National College for School Leadership (2005) in the UK. (See also Marzano *et al.*, 2005.)

Factor Three: knowledge and skills of curriculum planning

Participants in SBCD need to have knowledge and skills of curriculum planning if they are to be effective. All teachers have particular values and beliefs about teaching. Within a school staff there are likely to be different beliefs about the following:

- what content should be taught;
- how students learn;
- how students interact with others;
- how learning should be monitored and assessed.

As a consequence, open dialogue is necessary to ascertain as a school staff what will be the consensual directions. Walker's (1972) Naturalistic Model (see Chapter 3) is a useful planning vehicle where staff openly discuss various opinions/beliefs and gradually move from establishing a platform to a deliberation about agreed options and then to a design. Other curriculum planning approaches, such as Tyler's (1949), Taba's (1962) and more recently Wiggins and McTighe's (1998) models, all provide useful background knowledge about how to develop a curriculum within an SBCD framework.

Factor Four: resources

SBCD, like other school-related activities, relies heavily upon human and non-human resources. Self-nurturing SBCD within a school is extremely difficult. External funding from education authorities or by direct grants is usually essential for schools to reorganize staff to bring about SBCD. As an example, a common essential to undertake SBCD is to have extra staff allocations made to allow free time for staff to have planning and feedback sessions.

Of course the major resource of all is the human resource. A strong core of teachers within a school is needed to successfully bring about SBCD. Some of their tasks include:

- developing a clear vision for their school;
- a willingness to share their beliefs and to be involved in working parties;
- a willingness to take on specific leadership roles.

Another important human resource is outside experts, especially change agents who can assist staff with their problem-solving, developing collegial group processes, and providing support in resolving particular curriculum problems.

Processes in a school to support SBCD

As depicted in Table 11.1, there are numerous processes that can be initiated by the principal and by school leaders. Some pertain specifically to one of the four factors described above but most are wide-ranging and apply to all factors.

Innovative outcomes and practices of SBCD in a school

It is critical that all efforts at SBCD, whether they be small-scale or large-scale are recognized and celebrated by school staff (see Table 11.1). It is essential that efforts be made to evaluate the various successful and unsuccessful elements of each SBCD endeavour. The following apply especially to the four factors depicted in Table 11.1.

This conceptual model is intended to demonstrate key factors and stages in doing SBCD but also there is built-in flexibility between the stages. On occasions there might be considerable merging between processes and outcomes.

SBCD research

Undertaking SBCD can be both fulfilling and draining. For teachers there are the attractions of involvement in an SBCD project, with all the bonhomie, excitement and camaraderie that can develop, and a welcome relief from isolation, but this is only the positive side. On the negative side there is the very real danger that a person will overextend himself or herself and become fatigued. It is also possible that earlier convivial meetings can be transformed into sessions of friction and conflict.

Consequently, it is difficult for teachers to find the time to carry out research on their SBCD. Usually it is external facilitators who produce case study reports. Not unexpectedly, many of these case studies are superficial and non-probing, but largely positive in their descriptions. Examples include Cocklin, Simpson and Stacey's (1995) analysis of a secondary school in New South Wales, Australia; Day's (1990) analysis of a primary school in the UK; Hannay's (1990) study of a high school in Canada; Ramsay et al.'s (1995) study of eighteen secondary schools in New Zealand.

There is a paucity of recent research studies on SBCD. Cousins, Goh and Clark (2006) studied four secondary schools in Canada. They concluded that the role of the principal was crucial.

Macklin's (2004) case studies of a primary school in Queensland and a Prep–Year 9 school in Queensland demonstrated the value of teachers in a school experimenting with innovative pedagogies within an action research framework. Chen and Chung (2000) studied twelve primary schools doing SBCD in Taiwan. They concluded that the most significant factor was to have a standing committee for curriculum development and this was crucial to bring about successful SBCD.

Ben-Peretz and Dor's (1996) fascinating thirty-year longitudinal study of twenty-eight schools doing SBCD in Israel concluded that 'for SBCD to be a viable process, the school must have a unique ethos and a distinct philosophy and must also have the power to maintain pedagogic and economic autonomy' (p. 25).

In keeping with the use of technology, Juang, Liu and Chan (2005) developed a web-based performance support system using three critical factors of continuity, sequence and adaptability. This was implemented in a primary school in Taiwan over a two-year period, with successful results. The authors acknowledged that SBCD is a complex and highly knowledge-intensive task but that the four web-based modules did assist teachers with the main SBCD processes of analysis, design implementation and evaluation.

Concluding comments

Undertaking successful SBCD is a long-term process involving a redesign of the whole school organization (Wohlstetter et al., 1997). Unless teachers have access to additional intellectual and financial resources, the SBCD produced may be quite limited (Rudduck and Hopkins, 1985).

Yet there are promising examples emerging in many countries, despite the tightening central controls exerted by central authorities.

Reflections and issues

1   What has been the main driver of school-based curriculum development? Is it simply the result of decentralization or is it a deeper desire for student-focused learning?

2   'To develop a sound SBCD you must have experienced, skilled staff along with specialized curriculum support staff. High quality classroom resources are not as important as key staff' (Macklin, 2004, p. 6). Discuss.

3   'Taking small steps, while easier to take in the beginning, are in the long run riskier than bold steps; incremental changes that do not address the fundamental problems, get in the way of powerful student learning and simply put off the day of reckoning' (Sizer, 1989). Do you agree? Select some examples to illustrate your stance on the use of small steps versus bold steps.

4   The three major factors that facilitate empowerment include acquisition of support (for example endorsement by the principal), information (for example technical data) and resources (for example human services). Do you agree that these are important factors? Give examples to support your answer.

5   'Teachers seeking empowerment have to resolve the common tensions between management and curriculum. Decisions are often made in favour of management which emphasizes the need to survive above the urge to learn and to develop' (Walker and Kushner, 1991). Is this the typical pattern in your experience? How can both groups' ends be served more appropriately?

6   'We are certain of one thing. We will never move within the bureaucratic structure to new schools, to free schools. That structure was invented to assure domination and control. It will never produce freedom and self-actualization. The bureaucratic structure is failing in a manner so critical that adaptations will not forestall its collapse. It is impractical. It does not fit the psychological and personal needs of the workforce' (Clark and Meloy, 1990, p. 21). Discuss this statement and, in particular, point to what some alternatives might be.

Web sources

School-based curriculum development, www.nzcer.org.nz/pdfs/1314bib.pdf – extracted 15 November 2007.

A study of the problems and coping strategies for SBCD, www.ntnu.edu.tw/acad/epub/j47/ed471–1.htm – extracted 15 November 2007.

Curriculum as conversation: the teachers' voices, dlibrary.acu.edu.au/Faculties/tres-cowthick/conferences/papers/Nuttall.htm – extracted 15 November 2007.

Chapter 12

School evaluations/reviews

Introduction

Accountability and school improvement continue to be major driving forces as we near the end of the first decade in the twenty-first century. Evidence-based organizational change is now a major focus. Schools and systems are now producing objective and reliable evidence of school performance. Increasingly, school self-evaluation is being encouraged or a combination of internal/external modes of evaluation. There are changing roles as the inspectorate is now being given a new role as a 'critical friend'.

In principle, these are interesting developments but there are complexities still to be resolved relating to levels of mandated changes, time availability and stages of development of schools in their self-evaluation journey (Swaffield and MacBeath, 2005).

Some basic terms

'Evaluation' is a process of collecting and communicating information and evidence for the purpose of informing judgement and ascribing value to a particular programme (Worthen and Sanders, 2003). It can refer to small-scale activities involving a very limited number of clients (such as a teacher and his or her class) or to massive large-scale studies involving many schools and teachers (and other interested parties such as parents and community members).

Nevo (2001) examines the relative advantages of external school evaluation (for example by OFSTED inspectors in the United Kingdom), where the emphasis is upon accountability, setting standards and benchmarks, and internal school evaluations, where the emphasis is upon self-evaluation, empowerment evaluation, reflection and the professionalization of teachers. He argues the case for a combination of external and internal evaluation. Specifically, external evaluation can:

- stimulate internal evaluation – to motivate persons and organizations to do internal evaluation;

- expand the scope of internal evaluation – by providing benchmarks and comparative data;
- legitimize the validity of internal evaluations.

Further, internal evaluations can benefit external evaluations by:

- expanding the scope and examining unique elements;
- improving the interpretation of findings;
- increasing the utilization of the evaluation results.

However, we must delve further because this dichotomy of evaluations does not indicate some of the complexities (Vanhoof and Van Petegem, 2007). For example, Wroe and Halsall (2001) and Lachat, Williams and Smith (2006) argue that the enormous amount of performance data now collected in the UK by OFSTED and by schools themselves will only act as a spur to improve performance if teachers are willing and able to scrutinize the data, make sense of them and decide what action to take.

Swaffield and MacBeath (2005) contend that the combinations of external and internal evaluations take various forms, but especially the following:

- parallel – the two systems run side by side, each with their own criteria and protocols;
- sequential – external bodies follow on from a school's self-evaluation;
- cooperative – external agencies cooperate with schools to develop a common approach.

Swaffield and MacBeath (2005) favour the cooperative model by the use of critical friends, but they are very mindful of the complexities involved.

McGehee and Griffith (2001), Visscher (2001) and Ainscow, Booth and Dyson (2006) acknowledge that large-scale evaluations have become an important part of the education culture. Fullan and Earl (2002) undertook a large-scale evaluation of the National Literacy and Numeracy Strategy in the United Kingdom and noted that it is a prime example of the intricacies of national

---

Box 12.1   Elements of school-level evaluation

- collecting and presenting information from teachers and administrators, students and parents
- analysis of information collected and making judgements
- strategic planning
- development – improving quality
- accountability – proving quality.

reform (see also Fullan, 2000). Ainley *et al*. (2002) noted the renewed interest in large-scale evaluation in Australia with regard to literacy and numeracy.

School self-evaluation is now the focus in many countries, accompanied usually by large-scale evauations (Wroe and Halsall, 2001; Swaffield and MacBeath, 2005; Department of Education and Training, Victoria, 2005). Various on-line supports are now available to assist schools undertake self-evaluations (School Poll, OFSTED, 2007; AdvancEd, 2007).

School self-evaluation can be undertaken as a small-scale or large-scale activity. Skilbeck (1990) supports the use of small-scale activities rather than elaborate, comprehensive, managerial evaluations, and suggests that they should be at the level of 'intelligent forms of reflection on experience, self-appraisal and forward thinking'. In his opinion, educators often amass vast quantities of unmanageable data, and this should be avoided by being quite clear about such questions as the following:

- What do I need to know about this activity?
- How can I most economically find out?
- How can I use what I know?
- What do I need to make known to others?

School self-evaluation differs from other kinds of educational evaluation in that it focuses upon how teachers and students interact over a particular curriculum or syllabus at one school site. It is not just an analysis of how students perform in a teaching/learning unit, nor is it just an analysis of the lesson plans which teachers use in instruction. Rather, school self-evaluation involves an examination of the goals, rationale and structure of teachers' curricula, a study of the context in which the interaction with students occurs (including parent and community inputs) and an analysis of the interests, motivations and achievements of the students' experiences.

School self-evaluations also focus on the needs and interests of the constituent groups involved in the school community (Department of Education and Early Childhood Development, Victoria, 2005). Particular interest groups operating at the school level, mainly teachers, administrators, students and parents, may have very different views about the purposes of schooling. Consequently, evaluation studies have to reflect different orientations and not give undue emphasis to single dimensions such as the behaviour of individuals (students), an analysis of materials, or the behaviours of a school as a social institution.

Riley and Macbeath (2000) suggest that school evaluation is about accountability and development. Accountability is crucial to prove quality – to ensure that standards in a school are rising. Development is also most important because it establishes a positive staff climate – staff are more aware of the data that need to be collected as an aid to certain developmental goals.

Wilcox (1992) emphasizes the developmental aspect also (see Box 12.1), along with four other important aspects of curriculum evaluation:

1   It is based on evidence which is systematically collected.
2   The evidence is seldom unambiguous and therefore needs to be interpreted.
3   Judgements of value are made about the entity being evaluated and its effects.
4   It is action oriented, intended to lead to better practices and policies.

Purposes

The two fundamental questions to be answered before considering any evaluation are:

1   Why do you want to evaluate?
2   What do you want to evaluate?

Why do you want to evaluate?

In large-scale studies, the purposes of evaluation are usually related to policy concerns at the head offices about the widespread implementation of programmes in an entire school system. At the local school level, evaluation activities may be undertaken for a multitude of highly personal reasons. These could include:

- concerns about providing better teaching and learning for students within a particular school community;
- the need to examine the impact of a new programme or organizational processes;
- the need to ascertain school strengths in relation to system priorities and goals;
- collecting and presenting information from teachers and administrators, students and parents;
- analysis of information collected and making judgements;
- strategic planning;
- development – improving quality;
- accountability – proving quality;
- the need to substantiate the value of a particular programme or organizational structure to parents and/or to local business;
- a response to dissatisfaction expressed by individual teachers or a group/association.

When establishing purposes of evaluation at the school level it must be realized that any teaching situation brings about some unintended outcomes (Morell, 2005). Any comprehensive evaluation study must therefore provide for the collection of data on side-effects and unintended learnings (Elliott and Kushner, 2007).

Because evaluations at the school level rely upon conviviality and cooperation, it is essential that disparate motivations such as those listed above are discussed by staff, who, in a series of informal and formal meetings, may come to a consensus about what are the most important purposes for them in doing the evaluation (Flinders and Thornton, 2004). Nevo (2001) argues that one of the best ways to develop effective curriculum practices is to grant schools the authority to formally evaluate in addition to external agencies. However, in many cases individual schools cannot avoid external accountability forces – they are the driving force above and beyond the personal needs of a school community.

As an example, all government primary schools operating in Western Australia are required, under the School Accountability Framework:

- to produce, in partnership with their school community, a school plan setting out their objectives, priorities, major initiatives and evaluation measures;
- to assess their performance in terms of standards of student achievement and the effectiveness of the school;
- to make available to the public and to the District Director a School Report that describes the school's performance;
- to be accountable for the performance of the school – school staff to the principal and school principals to the District Director (Department of Education, Western Australia, 2002a, p. 5).

	Early planning discussions	Working party meetings	Documents produced	Materials provided	Implementation phases
Colleague evaluation checklists					
Rating scales					
Anecdotal reports					
Observation category systems					
Interviews					
Questionnaires					
Self-evaluation checklists					
Diary entries					
Questionnaires					
Student evaluation checklists					
Rating scales					
Interest inventories					
Attitude scales					
Questionnaires					
Objective tests					
Essay tests					
Standardized tests					
Interviews					
Photographs					

Figure 12.1 Techniques for collecting data at different phases of implementing new programmes.

Table 12.1 Techniques used to obtain evaluative data about teacher–student interactions (processes)

Informal observing and recording	Audiotaping and videotaping Observation Category systems Unobtrusive techniques Colleague observation
Informal collection of information from students	Interviews Questionnaires Rating scales Group discussions
Formal visits by senior supervisors (superintendents, inspectors, principal education officers)	Combination of observations and check lists

Yet the accompanying documents for schools are couched in the language of 'self-assessment' and schools are encouraged 'to see this document as a resource to augment their existing self-assessment practice' (Department of Education, Western Australia, 2002b, p. 8).

What do you want to evaluate?

In the terms of Schwab (1969) these factors are 'commonplaces' of curriculum and consist of 'learner', 'teacher', 'subject matter' (curriculum) and 'milieu'. Any evaluation activity must necessarily examine the impact and interaction of these elements.

The sources of information about these four commonplaces can vary considerably. For example, information about the school milieu might be obtained from parents, community members and employers; information about the subjects taught at school might come from school administrators, external subject specialists, publishers, superintendents and parents. The range and choice of sources of data relates back to the purposes of the evaluation, the scale of the activity, the time and funds available (Matthews *et al.*, 2007).

Once the focus of an evaluation has been determined, it is then possible to plan the kinds of information needed. For example, the evaluators may decide that information about students should include data about their previous academic levels, ongoing information about their class performance and interactions with the teacher, and information about their achievements. This type of information is obviously collected at different time periods and the examples listed above refer to all three types of data: that is, diagnostic data collected prior to the beginning of a curriculum unit to find out interests and achievement levels of students; formative data collected during the teaching of a unit to pinpoint aspects of the teaching that are mismatched and not being successfully implemented; and summative data, which are collected on completion of a unit and focus upon specific student outcomes and achievement levels.

Techniques that can be used to collect diagnostic, formative and summative data about students are included in Figure 12.1. Similar techniques can be used for collecting information about teachers and teacher–student interactions, as depicted in Table 12.1.

Collecting evaluative data about teachers requires considerable support and goodwill. George *et al.* (1998) highlight some of the problems and issues. They suggest that the ideal situation is for teachers to work in peer panels comprising three to five teachers. The important considerations are as follows:

- that they choose each other and there are no superordinate–subordinate relationships;
- that matters that are discussed are private to them but generally focus upon skill development;
- that they agree to meet regularly, ideally once a week;
- that they give low-inference feedback to each other (observe/record/report).

They do not make high-inference judgements as this would interfere with their peer relationships.

As depicted in Table 12.2 teaching-partner observer or peer panels can use a variety of techniques to collect useful data over the various phases, ranging from informal observations, through rating systems to the use of interviews and questionnaires.

Self-reflection and analysis are extremely valuable activities for all teachers and especially important for school-level evaluation (Wroe and Halsall, 2001). Schon (1987) refers to the need for teachers to be reflective practitioners. He focuses specifically upon how and why teachers should reflect upon their experiences.

The evaluative techniques listed in Figure 12.1 can be used in terms of both self-evaluation and using a teaching-partner or peer panel. However, the most common techniques include some form of written recording sheet (e.g. keeping a diary) and a variety of observational techniques. Diaries represent a 'shorthand' method of recording the significant happenings of a teacher's day. It is recommended that diaries should concentrate on one or two aspects that are considered most important. Points that may be useful as foci for diary entries include such questions as:

- Is my teaching behaviour having the desired effect in classroom management?
- Has a particular seating arrangement encouraged the desired behaviour from the students concerned?
- Has a particular teaching strategy improved the performance of a specific group of students?
- Is a special project being positively accepted by the class or is there a lack of interest?

Table 12.2 School objectives and performance indicators

School objectives	Performance indicators
1. The school provides students with suitable opportunities to learn domains of knowledge and skills	• Student attendance rates • Destinations of students after leaving school • Survey of students
2. The school encourages hard work and achievement from its students	• Attitude survey of students • Parent questionnaire
3. The teachers at the school create and implement effective programmes of learning	• Teacher time for planning per week • Administrative and clerical support time per week

Observation is a direct, systematic way of determining what is happening in the classroom. Observations of classrooms can often be very revealing! For example, the literature contains examples of teachers who have complained that certain students in their class do not contribute to their lessons. However, observations by colleagues revealed that these same teachers did not encourage the students in question to participate and in some instances prevented their interaction with other students. There are often massive discrepancies between what teachers state they are teaching compared with what actually occurs in classrooms.

Several alternatives are available for the classroom teacher who wishes to collect his or her own observational data. These include using audiotaping or, if resources are available, videotaping. Student observations can also be sought via informal discussions and interviews or by the use of checklists and questionnaires.

It should be clear that self-evaluation techniques for the teacher are fairly limited, and that far more data, including important additional perspectives, are available if colleagues on a school staff assist each other cooperatively with their evaluation activities. However, this requires colleagues to collect data about each other and to submit themselves to self-reflective activities, as listed in Figure 12.1. The challenge may be troublesome for some teachers unless peer panels (as described above) or similar pairings are organized. It is suggested that if teachers are willing from the outset to collect evaluative data about their own activities and those of their colleagues, then the feedback they obtain will enable them to be more successful and presumably more fulfilled.

There are, of course, many hidden assumptions involved in all this. Not all colleagues will want to submit themselves to all of the types of data collection listed in Figure 12.1 and to peer and panel procedures. Teachers in a planning group have to be sufficiently empathic toward each other to accept feedback even if it is low-inference feedback. The kinds of evaluative activities, therefore, have to be carefully negotiated with the individuals concerned. Some readers might consider that the types of self-evaluation listed in Figure 12.1 are too superficial and are likely to lead to over-concentration upon the frequency of occurrence of activities rather than the quality of the actions. Also, time constraints are often so pressing that it is not always feasible to undertake many, if any, of these evaluative activities.

A combined qualitative/quantitative technique, which is widely used in the USA, in the United Kingdom and in other European countries (Visscher, 2001), is the performance indicator (see Table 12.3). These can be directed specifically at teacher performance (especially teacher competence tests in the USA), at student performance (e.g. the General Achievement Test in Victoria, Australia) or at school-wide issues.

Performance indicators are linked directly to specific objectives or goals for a school programme and are intended to indicate the extent of progress made towards a specific objective. Rogers and Badham (1992) suggest that performance indicators should be capable of being collected on several occasions over a period of time.

As examples, three objectives for a school are listed in Table 12.3 along with possible performance indicators. It is evident that performance indicators should not be used in isolation but they can add an important perspective to an evaluation.

Persons involved

Depending upon the size and scope of school-level evaluation, those involved may be a team of one or two external experts, the entire school staff (together with selected school council members) or just one classroom teacher taking up the role of an evaluator. The US evaluation scene is normally dominated by the experts who are hired as consultants to evaluate school district programmes and similar large-scale activities. The literature on evaluation contains numerous references to the characteristics of 'good' evaluators (Simons, 1987; Popham, 1995; Wood, 1991), which include such attributes as technical competence, personal integrity and objectivity.

External, full-time professional evaluators are not very evident on the Australian scene. External evaluators, as members of a team to undertake school evaluations, are found in all states but they are mostly experienced teachers and school principals who serve on evaluation panels for short periods of time, including site visits of one or two days.

In the United Kingdom, the Office for Standards in Education (OFSTED) has recruited a wide range of registered inspectors and inspection contractors, who are in turn subject to inspection quality audits (OFSTED, 1997).

More recently, OFSTED has been emphasizing the need for more school self-evaluation and the use of critical friends to work with schools as school improvement partners. As noted by Swaffield and MacBeath (2005), head teachers are 'being trained as consultant leaders to form a cadre of people who may be appointed as critical friends' (p. 251).

Internal evaluators, by contrast, are persons who are involved in, and responsible for, duties in a specific school. A pair of teachers in a primary school or a small team of teachers from within a subject department at the secondary school level might undertake small-scale evaluation activities. These individuals may turn to external experts for particular forms of assistance – for instance in designing the appropriate data-gathering instruments or in developing appropriate criteria for validating the evidence. On occasions, school staff may be able to obtain small grants to employ external consultants for particular tasks, such as initiating the evaluation exercise, coordinating the diverse activities or collecting some of the data (e.g. observing teachers in the classrooms). Checklists of specific questions are a very useful way of providing evaluators (individual evaluator or a team) with the necessary guidelines.

Concluding comments

The management of schools, system wide or individually, brings attention to bear on performance issues and matters of evaluation. Various stakeholders want information about achievements (especially in terms of the students, teachers, subject matter and milieu) to justify the substantial financial expenses. In addition to accountability reasons, participants in a school community need to 'sample the temperature' of what is going on so that development plans can be targeted to areas of need.

A range of techniques are available for obtaining evaluative data about teachers, students and the milieu. However, if participants at a school are not committed to regular evaluation activities and are not willing to produce developmental, strategic plans based upon evidence obtained from these evaluations, little can be achieved.

Reflections and issues

1 'Evaluations are designed increasingly to be used, to accompany or initiate changes in schools and central offices' (Rogers and Badham, 1992). Do you agree? If this is the case what are the implications for the time taken and who initiates the evaluation?
2 'Value-added' measures indicate the educational value that a school adds over and above that which could be predicted given the backgrounds and prior attainments of the students within the school' (Department of Education and Early Childhood Development, Victoria, 2007, p. 6). What are some examples of value-added measures? Comment on their potential successes and problems.
3 'In the last ten years we have witnessed a rapid growth in school self-evaluation models and practices ... What is least clear and most controversial in this range of activity is who has control of the process, who has access to any product that emerges and whose interests are served' (Simons, 1987, pp. 319–20). What groups do you consider are controlling school evaluation processes? Are you aware of successful evaluation efforts? What do you consider are some of the major inhibiting factors?

4 'Evaluation can be a constructive process leading to stronger professionalism, but only if teachers grasp the opportunity for reflection and growth that it presents' (Granheim, 1990, p. 1). Do the evaluation approaches with which you are familiar allow teachers to 'reflect and grow'? What are some important safeguards you would propose to allow this to happen?

5 'In the final analysis the evaluator's role is to assess the educational quality of the curriculum policy or program. But (s)he can still do this democratically through dialogue and discussion with a variety of interest groups, including practitioners. Through such dialogue an evaluator can deepen and extend his or her own understanding of the nature of educational values and how they can be best realized in particular contests' (Elliott, 1991, p. 231). How important is the dialogue and discussion between interest groups in a school evaluation? What techniques can be used to achieve it? Elaborate upon some of the restrictions.

6 'Evaluation is a form of inquiry whose end product is information. Information is power, and evaluation is powerful' (Guba and Lincoln, 1989, p. 56). Can school evaluations be powerful? Which stakeholders are most affected by school evaluations? How can their needs be communicated and respected? Use examples to illustrate your point of view.

7 The UK Education Acts legislate for the local management of schools. 'Any school which seeks to use management information effectively for planning purposes will need to devise systems for integrating a review of:
   • Curriculum delivery and pupil outcomes;
   • Staff appraisal and development;
   • Use of finance and other material resources' (Rogers and Badham, 1992, p. 85).

Describe how you would plan an integrated evaluation of these elements. What might be some potential constraints?

Web sources

Five Generations of Evaluation, http://web.syr.edu/~bvmarten/evalact.html – extracted 19 November 2007.

School Poll Helping UK Schools with Self-Evaluation Form, http://www.schoolpoll.com/sef – extracted 19 November 2007.

Evaluation and Assessment, www.cmu.edu/teaching/assessment/index.html – extracted 19 November 2007.

School Self-Evaluation, http://www.sofweb.vic.edu.au/stndards/account/eval.htm – extracted 19 November 2007.

School Improvement Resources, http://www.advanced.org/products_and_services/school_improvement_resources/ – extracted 19 November 2007.

Whole School Evaluation, http://www.into.ie/ROI/WorkingConditions/InspectionProbation/WholeScoolEvalua ... – extracted 19 November 2007.

National Study of School Evaluation, http://www.nsse.org/ – extracted 19 November 2007.

Chapter 13

Curriculum reform

Introduction

As noted by Reville (2006), 'in our zeal for solutions, we are quick to condemn the strategies of reformers who preceded us because they have obviously not achieved the desired results' (p. 1). The frequency of reforms is wide ranging, so apparently there must be many curriculum problems to solve.

Although there appear to be some promising and worthwhile directions for exploration and experimentation we need to be wary of panaceas and exaggerated claims. In particular, we need to be aware of claims that large-scale testing will result in quality education for all students – in fact this might run the risk of narrowing the scope of curriculum (Medina and Riconscente, 2006).

As noted by McCaslin (2006), successful reform should start with a clearer understanding of how to learn from previous reform efforts. 'Reforms should build on each other, not serve as sequential correctives' (p. 489).

What is curriculum reform?

Bourke (1994) notes that the term 'reform' is typically used to refer to changes instituted from above – 'the implication in much of the rhetoric is that only government decision-making can reform education' (p. 1). He questions whether governments are always able to reform (to make better) – on many occasions the changes implemented by a government are worse for at least some groups. Kennedy (1995) asserts that curriculum reform is really about changes to the content and organization of what is taught, within the constraints of social, economic and political contexts. Curriculum content and organization are of central importance but unless a reform effort is consistent with the values of the wider society it is unlikely to be successful. Glatthorn and Jailall (2000) consider that curriculum reform not only involves content and organization but that it is mainly directed at students and teachers. Clearly, curriculum reform is multifaceted and can include an analysis of teaching staff, students, content and school structures.

School principals are often targeted as the key player to bring about reform. Fullan (2004) contends that the challenge for the principal is to share and sustain ideas about change so as to transform what is essentially a conservative system. Teachers are also a critical link in any curriculum reform – educational change depends on what teachers do and think – it is as simple and complex as that (Fullan, 2004). Boyle and Bragg's (2006) longitudinal study of over 2,000 primary schools in the UK concluded that teacher's professional identities were characterized by fragmentation and discontinuities within an increasingly intensive external audit policy culture.

Student voice is becoming increasingly noticed as administrators and researchers try to tap young people's unique perspectives on learning, teaching and schooling (Thiessen, 2006; Thomson and Gunter, 2006). As noted by Thiessen (2006), it is important to understand the 'experiences of students in and out of school in their own terms and to find ways to engage students in their own development' (p. 346).

Curriculum content is being increasingly targeted in terms of specific subject-matter standards; this is especially the case for literacy and numeracy and science (Galton, 2002; Marx and Harris, 2006).

Reformers have also focused upon differing structures of schools and the linkages between individual schools, districts and regions. Seller (2005) contends that individual schools may become innovative but they cannot stay innovative without district action.

Hargreaves (1995) notes the interconnectedness of curriculum reform in terms of societal change. For example, he argues that secondary schools are the prime symbols and symptoms of 'modernity' (for example bureaucratic complexity, inflexibility) and that 'postmodern' conditions of the 1990s (and beyond into the twenty-first century) require very different principles.

Ideology and reform

Kennedy (1995) refers to the similarities in reform efforts occurring in the United Kingdom, the USA and Australia. He concurs with Coombs (1985) that in all these countries there has been 'a crisis of confidence in education itself' (p. 9). No longer is curriculum decision-making the preserve of professional educators – governments are now playing a central role in terms of broad social, political and economic agendas.

In the United Kingdom, the National Curriculum introduced in 1988 was based on the Right ideology of a market economy and a consumer-oriented emphasis. A number of schools have opted out of local education authority control, supposedly to allow parents more choice. A policy of open enrolment and local management of schools is now in place (Bennett and Anderson, 2005). The Left ideology since 1997 (New Labour government) has been conservative and pragmatic and focused squarely on literacy and numeracy standards for students (Crump, 1998).

Barber's (2006) personal commentary reflects the Right ideology: school systems do need sustained investment if high standards are to be achieved; accountability for results is critical because parents have a right to know how schools are doing; market disciplines are important so that poor schools can be promptly turned around.

Galton (2002) argues from a researcher perspective that the National Curriculum in the UK has not improved the quality of teaching and learning in the primary school. The 'high-stakes' national tests have reduced the time available for non-core subjects and so the purported 'balanced curriculum has become an increasingly impoverished one' (p. 18).

Osborn and McNess (2002) are critical of the increasingly prescriptive National Curriculum, driven by external targets. This has led to teachers having reduced time for affective and pastoral aspects of education.

Other writers such as Smyth (2006), writing about Australian education, argue that decisions in the UK and in Australia are 'blatant neo-liberal ideology dressed up as rational analysis' (p. 301).

Reform reports

Reform reports are often a popular means of bringing a purported problem to the consciousness of the public. The reports tend to focus on one or two key elements, often dramatizing the problems so as to elicit the solutions. Examples include:

USA
- National Council of Teachers of Mathematics (1991) *Professional Standards for Teaching Mathematics*. Virginia: NCTM;
- National Center on Education and the Economy (1997) *New Standards: Performance Standards: English Language Arts, Mathematics, Science, and Applied Learning. Vol. 1: Elementary School; Vol. 2: Middle School; Vol. 3: High School*. Washington, DC: NCEE;
- Charles Schools Program (1994);
- Comprehensive School Reform Program (CSRD) (1998);
- No Child Left Behind Act (NCLB) (2001);
- No Child Left Behind Reauthorization Act (NCLB) (2007).

United Kingdom
- Department for Education and Skills (1997) *White Paper, 'Excellence in Schools'*. London: HMSO;
- Department for Education and Skills (2001) *Education and Skills: Investment for Reform*. London: HMSO;
- Department for Education and Skills (1998) *Framework for Teaching* (National Literacy Strategy);
- Department for Education and Skills (2003) *A New Specialist System: Transforming Secondary Education*;
- Department for Education and Skills (2005) *Education Improvement Partnerships – Local Collaboration for School Improvement and Better Service Delivery (Academics)*.

Examples

United Kingdom

Fullan and Earl (2002) refer to the National Literacy and Numeracy Strategies in the United Kingdom as 'large-scale reform'. Commencing in 1997, when it came to power, the Labour government established literacy and numeracy as its first-order priorities. The government used 1996 as the baseline to check on the targets achieved by 11-year-olds in literacy and numeracy. The results in 2001 were impressive: 75 per cent of children achieved the desired target for literacy (compared with 57 per cent in 1996) and 71 per cent of children achieved the desired target for numeracy (compared with 54 per cent in 1996).

It has been a heavily directed top-down approach to reform (Fullan and Earl, 2002). Some critics consider that the costs to teachers have been very high. For example, Furlong (2002) criticizes the rigorous forms of quality control and inspection carried out by the Office for Standards in Education (OFSTED) inspectors. Brown *et al.* (2002) note the amount of teacher stress and teacher burnout for primary school teachers. Southworth (2000) contends that recent central initiatives by the government have added to the power of primary school heads and that the emphasis upon the head as chief executive has increased heads' authoritarian power and limited any democratic sharing by teachers. Jolliffe (2006) concludes that although some of the practical ideas of the National Literacy Strategy were innovative (for example, all teachers have a daily literacy hour), interactive teaching has rarely occurred and teachers receive insufficient training in the underlying pedagogy.

The central government's *Education and Skills: Investment for Reform*, published in 2001, is an attempt to reform and transform secondary education by driving school leadership, school structures, teaching and learning, and partnerships beyond the classroom. The emphasis is upon recognizing and rewarding advanced schools (high-performing schools with particular expertise) and using them to drive reforms in secondary education.

It is evident that many of the teachers working in these specialist schools 'can and do benefit from the opportunities that specialism and the specialist system can provide' (Jupe and Milne, 2005, p. 52). They note that more than two-thirds of England's secondary schools are already specialist and by 2008 there will be a fully specialist system, with each school having developed at least one specialism.

Academies have been set up to try to provide 'federations' or groups of schools working in close collaboration. Rutherford and Jackson (2006) describe the Collegiate Academies established within the Birmingham local education authority. For example, the Birmingham Catholic Partnership provides a sustainable network of nine secondary schools in Birmingham. Each school contributes 0.5 per cent of its base budget to employ a full-time coordinator and administrative officer. They develop and lead programmes to support professional development of staff. Rutherford and Jackson (2006) and Ingall (2005) conclude that Collegiate Academies are providing a dynamic for school improvement.

USA

Standards-based approaches are currently strongly supported in the USA. The majority of the standards are subject based and have been developed by the major professional subject associations, such as the National Council of Teachers of Mathematics. Standards-based approaches call for high standards for all students oriented around challenging subject matter, acquisition of higher-order thinking skills and the application of abstract knowledge to solve real-world problems (McLaughlin and Shepard, 1995).

More importantly there are various reinforcing processes (or drivers) to ensure that standards are introduced, namely:

- curriculum frameworks that state the academic content to be covered;
- provision of curriculum materials to support teachers;
- professional development to ensure that teachers have the requisite content knowledge and instructional abilities;
- assessment and accountability systems to monitor student progress;
- leadership and support by discipline-based professional organizations;
- state requirements for all schools, including:
  - content standards that all students should learn,
  - performance standards – levels of mastery required,
  - aligned assessments – state-wide testing of students,
  - training and certification requirements for all teachers (Swanson and Stevenson 2002).

However, there are critics of standards-based reform in the USA. Donmoyer (1998) argues that standards-based reform is largely rhetoric and myths about what politicians and educators 'believe' will happen.

In a similar vein, Chatterji (2002) concludes that there has been little coherence in the way in which reforms have filtered down to districts, schools and classrooms. Levin (1998) contends that standards-based reform has been formulated to create economic benefits, yet there is little evidence to demonstrate any marked improvements in worker productivity. Lea and Fradd (1998) argue that the idea of high standards for all is creating problems for students from non-English-language backgrounds because the new academic curriculum does not have the flexibility to accommodate students' different cultural experiences.

It is evident that there are a number of issues still to be resolved with standards-based reform. To a certain extent, the reform uses a 'big stick' approach to wake up and challenge unmotivated students and unmotivated teachers (Nave *et al.*, 2000). Yet it is more than this. It does provide detailed curriculum support for teachers so that they can inspire their students to achieve at higher levels. Professional associations are providing strong collaborative support to schools. Despite the fiery opposition to this powerful, nation-wide movement (Thompson, 2001) it is proving to be a very durable reform (Sirotnik and Kimball, 1999).

Charter Schools was a United States Department of Education programme established in 1994. Charter schools are schools of choice for parents, students and teachers involved in them. Each charter school has a board that governs it. Usually charter schools are small, with 150–250 students, and they establish their own unique educational programmes. The number of charter schools has grown rapidly. Charter laws are now in place in forty states and the total number is now over 3,000 schools.

Wells, Lopez, Scott and Holme (1999) enthuse that in a postmodern manner charter schools provide liberation from the constraints of the bureaucratic and modern public education system. Yet other studies provide only modest results in favour of charter schools. Hoxby's (2004) comparison of charter schools and regular public schools demonstrated a slight advantage for charter schools in state examinations in reading (4 per cent) and mathematics (2 per cent). To the extent that charter schools do offer liberation and autonomy for parents, students and teachers, they are places that run against the national current toward top-down curriculum decision making (Buckley and Schneider, 2006; Huerta et al., 2006).

Comprehensive school reform programmes

The Comprehensive School Reform Program (CSRP) was passed by the US Congress in 1988. The idea behind CSRP is that previous efforts to reform or even to improve schools have been unsuccessful because they were piecemeal, failing to focus comprehensively on the 'whole school' and to design fully what were to be the new innovations.

Thousands of schools across the United States have received awards of at least $50,000 to implement CSRP (McChesney and Hertling, 2000); however, a participating school must select the particular reform programme it will use from a catalogue of thirty-three approved research-based models. Some of the models available focus on school processes, such as Sizer's (1992) Coalition of Essential Schools; others focus on the curriculum itself, such as Slavin and Madden's (2001) Success for All.

Although principals are seen as playing a critical role in providing the leadership for successfully implementing a reform model, the majority of programmes have external design teams to assist schools in the process of implementation. According to McChesney and Hertling (2000), the tasks of the design teams are as follows:

- to integrate all aspects of reform;
- to provide a strong vision that sustains schools;

- to maintain a strong focus on results;
- to use research and development skills.

Some external design teams have proved to be highly prescriptive (thus supporting fidelity of curriculum implementation), whereas others have been more flexible (thus permitting considerable adaptation).

Many thousands of schools are now involved in trying out CSRP. Proponents such as Slavin (2001) contend that the approach has enormous potential for creating programmes and models that are strongly research based and that will lead to great improvement in student achievement in a variety of schools. Other educators are more cautious. Hatch (2000) reports that even schools receiving large amounts of CSRP funding have great difficulty in 'breaking the mould' and finding 'the right balance between exploiting current practices and exploring new ideas that may lead to success in the future' (p. 565).

Using case study data from twenty-two schools, Datnow (2000) studied how and why schools adopt reforms and the consequences of their decisions for implementation and sustainability. She concluded that 'power relations often thwarted genuine initial buying and interest in change among local educators' (p. 357).

Similarly, Borman, Hewes, Overman and Brown (2003) undertook a meta-analysis of the implementation of twenty-nine widely used CSRP models, concluding that CSRP models that were most clearly defined and implemented with fidelity tended to have the strongest effects, that strong effects start to occur only after the fifth year of implementation and that effects seem to vary with local circumstances.

The No Child Left Behind Act (NCLB) was passed by the US Congress in 2001. According to Marsh and Willis (2007), it is based on the same assumptions as *A Nation at Risk* – an educational crisis that can be cured by emphasizing a few basic academic subjects, spending more time on task, testing students more and measuring the results more often. Yet it must also be acknowledged that 'NCLB represents the most substantial involvement of the federal government in public schools in the history of the US education' (Good, 2006, p. 453). In summary, the requirements are as follows:

- all states develop achievement standards in mathematics and language arts (and science in 2007);
- all students are tested in grades 3–8 to measure students adequate yearly progress;
- states which fail to comply lose federal financial aid;
- schools that don't make adequate yearly progress are eligible for federal aid for two years but after three years will be taken over or closed down;
- students from such schools are eligible to transfer.

Proponents of NCLB argue that 'school systems must be held accountable for equipping all students with the academic skills on which America's future depends (Paige, 2006, p. 461). NCLB will close the achievement gap between students of different races. It forces school officials to address the disparity among different students' academic performance.

Reauthorization of the NCLB is currently being considered. There is a diversity of views on the benefits or problems with the current NCLB. Some of the perceived problems are as follows:

- the goal of 100 per cent student proficiency is impossible to meet;
- the focus on reading and mathematics testing takes time away from the rest of the curriculum (Au, 2007);
- it judges school performance on mathematics and reading scores only;
- it is drastic with respect to how it measures 'failure' in certain sub-groups;
- early achievement gains in mathematics have not continued.

(Fuller *et al.*, 2007)

Certainly, teacher articles in many teacher journals are very negative. For example:

> NCLB is the main reason that I left the classroom (I taught science and math) because I was unable to be the kind of teacher that I wanted to be. Instead of teaching my students to think, I was required to drill them endlessly, filling their heads with information that has little meaning in order to perform well on tests that they did not respect.
>
> (Elisheva H. Levin, New Mexico)

> Get rid of NCLB. Perhaps we should have a No Person on Federal Government Left Behind act and test our legislators according to standards. If they don't pass, they should be replaced immediately.
>
> (Mary L, former teacher, Pennington, Ill.; Neill, 2007)

Miner (2007) notes that the NCLB law is due for reauthorization and 'if pro-NCLB forces get their way, teachers, students and schools will have many more years of ever-increasing tests and sanctions' (p. 28).

Concluding comments

As we near the end of the first decade of the twenty-first century it is revealing that some perennial challenges in terms of curriculum reform have continued but there have also been some promising developments. A number of reforms are cyclical – at certain periods they have strong support while at other times they can be quite minimal.

The strength and influence of standards-based reforms in several countries is impressive. It is interesting to ponder on which are the main factors driving it. Is it a general world-view and the economic status of the society? Is it due to the recommendations of prestigious committees? Or is it due to the emergence of new technology (Glatthorn and Jailall, 2000)?

Despite the enthusiasm that can be generated by new reforms it is important to remember that making reform proposals is only part of the process and that there are many problems in getting reforms implemented. The factors affecting innovation and change, and implementation, as noted in Chapters 8 and 9, respectively, are most pertinent.

Reflections and issues

1   'Educational reform cannot progress without financial resources. People, time and materials are necessary costs that are not considered to any great degree in most reform reports' (Presseisen, 1989, p. 135). Why is it that reform reports rarely include detailed budgets? Who should determine priorities for finance for reform proposals?

2   Some of the most difficult dilemmas we face currently have been around for a long time. Give examples of reforms that have been proposed over the decades to solve a particular curriculum problem. Have any proposals been more successful than others? Give reasons.

3   'Do schools exist to increase the nation's productivity or for other equally important personal and social goals?' (Passow, 1988, p. 254). What is your stance on this matter?

4   The reform proposals in the USA reflect and help perpetuate practices that are at odds with equity goals. Why do you consider that equity goals which were being advanced in the 1960s and 1970s are not being given a high priority in the twenty-first century? Are equity and excellence diametrically opposed goals?

5   'Schools and especially classrooms, are remarkably resistant to change, much to the consternation of politicians, policy-makers and innovators ... Professional and institutional structures are resilient. They withstand many an assault and have powerful capacities to maintain and reproduce themselves despite surface changes' (Hargreaves, 1994). Can this claim be substantiated? Give examples to support your response.

6   'English education has a history of power domination rather than power sharing. The recent and current reforms in English education ensure that schools endure as organised hierarchies' (Southworth, 2000, p. 14). What are the implications for the success of transformational reform if such hierarchies exist?

Web sources

Curriculum Reform Movement, http://www.ncrel.org/sdrs/areas/issues/methods/assmen t/as5curri.htm – extracted 3 January 2008.

Teacher Roles in Curriculum Reform, www.cels.bham.ac.uk/ELTED/Vol2Issue1/ kennedyc.pdf – extracted 3 January 2008.

Education Policy: Curriculum Reform and Implementation in the 21st Century, www. soros.org/initiatives/esp/articles_publications/publications/epcnljune_2005713/ – extracted 3 January 2008.

Outcomes Driven Curriculum Reform, www.leeds.ac.uk/ducol/documents/000000860.htm – extracted 3 January 2008.

Curriculum Reform Project University of Aberdeen, www.abdn.ac.uk/cref/ – extracted 3 January 2008.

Part IV

Teaching perspectives

Chapter 14

Learning environments

Introduction

The classroom environment is an integral part of the learning process and no teacher or student can be unaffected by it. For students, classroom environments represent sources of security and identity for individuals (Judson, 2006). Teachers need to be able to adapt classroom environments for creative and innovative initiatives (Loi and Dillon, 2006). Yet many classroom buildings are 'old and in poor condition, and may contain environmental conditions that inhibit learning and pose increased risks to the health of students and staff' (US Environmental Protection Agency, 2006, p. 3).

In any school, the class teachers and students have to adjust to the building architecture – the overall space, the position and number of doors and windows, the height of the ceiling and the insulation qualities of the walls. Yet, as Bennett (1981) reminds us, '[t]his does not indicate architectural determination. Architecture can certainly modify the teaching environment, but teachers determine the curriculum and organization' (p. 24).

Teachers and students have the opportunity to 'express their "personalities" through the arrangement and décor of the environment and the arrangement of space' (Ross, 1982, pp. 1–2). However, creative arrangements need to be undertaken in the knowledge that specific physical conditions and space allocations can have important consequences for the attitudes, behaviours and even the achievements of students.

There is growing interest in very different classroom environments. Fully electronic learning environments are being planned and prototypes already exist, 'The Classroom of the Future', located at the National Institute of Education, Singapore, showcases how technology will influence pedagogical methods and improve the learning environment (Back Pack Net Centre, 2005). Educators such as Edwards (2006) argue for 'green schools' which use passive solar heating and natural cross-ventilation.

Classroom settings

How an area of space is used in a teaching/learning situation is clearly important, but it is often taken for granted. The particular pattern of juxtaposing furniture and spaces within the confines of a classroom (or open teaching area) has a variety of purposes. In some instances, the teacher arranges a particular pattern because he or she is convinced that this configuration aids learning. As examples, single rows of desks might be considered to be most useful for students listening to an expository, teacher-directed science lesson; a grouping of desks in clusters of four might be far better for sharing materials in an art lesson; and a circle of chairs with the desks pushed to the sides might be the most appropriate for a literature lesson.

However, the teacher may have other reasons in mind that explain a particular pattern. Perhaps the teacher is concerned about a general atmosphere of restlessness in the class and wants convenient aisles and spaces so that 'seat work' can be continuously surveyed. In this case, the classroom spaces take on a greater significance than the furniture, because the opportunities for supervising are uppermost in the teacher's mind. It is impossible to separate these 'emotional climate' needs from the physical setting (Konza *et al.*, 2001).

Schools are contradictory places. As noted by Cullingford (2006) 'the emphasis of school, the organisation of classes, the physical conditions and the ambience of schooling are based on an industrial model of inputs and outcomes' (p. 211). Students, in the main, are very critical of this system even though they give the impression of politeness and submission.

Room arrangement principles

The following guidelines may be helpful in making decisions about the classroom – the teacher's special learning environment along with thirty or more students!

First, use a room arrangement that facilitates a teaching and learning style and does not impede it. The classroom teacher needs to be aware of whether the physical environment he or she has provided facilitates the student behaviours desired. That is, unless the two are interrelated or congruent (the technical term is synomorphic) undesirable effects are likely to occur.

In broad terms, a teacher may desire to organize the class on the basis of territory or by function; the former focuses on a teacher-dominated purpose, while the latter emphasizes a resource specialization, student-initiated focus. In classrooms organized by territory, the major decision is how to allocate and arrange student desks and chairs. It is assumed that each student has his or her own domain or work space and that this is the basis for considering how certain learning activities will occur. Classrooms organized on the basis of function enable students to engage in generative learning (Harris and Bell,

1990). They are commonly found in junior grades in primary schools in specialist subject areas (e.g. media or science) and subjects using computer-based projects (Anderson-Inman and Horney, 1993) in many secondary schools. In this case, the allocation of space is based upon what specialist material/activities can be accommodated in a given area, and the matter of the location of desks is only of minor consideration.

Second, ensure that high-traffic areas are open and not congested. There are always high-traffic areas such as around doorways, the pencil sharpener, computers, certain bookshelves and the teacher's desk. According to Emmer *et al.* (2000), high-traffic areas should be kept away from each other, have plenty of space and be easily accessible.

Floor space

There are numerous classroom shapes and sizes but it is possible to highlight the common elements of classrooms. The typical classroom is 12 metres long and 8 metres wide and is designed to accommodate approximately thirty students. One wall is typically taken up with blackboards or whiteboards and another wall often contains several pin-up boards. The teacher's table is usually at the front of the room and students' desks are arranged in four rows of seven or eight.

In this relatively formal classroom situation it is likely that the 'action zone' (Brophy, 1981) for interaction between the teacher and students will be found in the front and centre. That is, students seated near the front and centre desks facing the teacher are more likely to be the focus of the teacher's attention, rather than the students seated on the margins or at the rear of the room.

Many teachers are able to devise very different, creative patterns of use within the confines of the standard classroom (Cohen *et al.*, 2002; Loi and Dillon, 2006). Small-group activities are facilitated by clusters of desks. A common area formed by the combination of five or six desks may be ideal for spreading out documents and charts as well as providing close physical contact between a small group of students. The desks can still be oriented towards the blackboard and the teacher or they can be located at points in the room which maximize space between groups.

Arrangement of student desks

Depending on space available, many different arrangements are possible. In devising the location of students' desks it is important to remember their needs, including:

- a need to be seated at points in the classroom where they can comfortably undertake the learning activities;

- a need for them to be located at desks or tables adjacent to peers with whom they have a close and mutually positive relationship;
- a need for them to have access to the teacher and to resources in the room.

Arrangement of furniture and equipment

Large items of furniture such as cupboards can be used as dividers within a room. Pieces of pegboard can be used to cover the sides of a cupboard and thereby provide additional display space. It is also helpful to have one or two large tables in a classroom even though they take up a lot of space. These tables can be used for a multitude of purposes including storing audiovisual materials, storing unfinished work or for displays of completed projects/units.

The placement of computers in the room is an additional complication. A single computer might be located in any convenient corner but a pod of five or more computers can cause difficulties in an already crowded room. Some primary schools have all their computers located in a separate computer laboratory.

Learning stations and work centres

Learning stations and work centres are areas where a small number of students come to work on a special activity. These areas need to be located so that they do not distract from major learning activities.

Box 14.1   Checklist to evaluate the use of classroom space

1 Is there too much furniture?
2 Is the best use made of the whole space of the school?
3 How does the use of space reflect the range and nature of different activities?
4 How effectively is shared space used?
5 How attractive and stimulating is the space?
6 How does the grouping of tables and work areas reflect the needs of the students and the tasks, especially computer-based tasks?
7 How well do students understand the classroom organization?
8 How appropriately and effectively are the resources deployed?
9 How accessible are resources and spaces?
10 How easy is pupil and teacher movement?
11 How effectively does the organization of space promote pupil interaction?

Learning stations are examples of functional areas which are often established in primary schools. A learning station is simply an area in a room where a group of students can work together at well-defined tasks. Usually, all resource materials are provided at the one location and tasks are included on colour-coded cards so that individuals or groups can involve themselves with minimal supervision by the teacher.

Materials can be at different difficulty levels to provide for differentiated instruction (Tomlinson, 1999). Many educators applaud the use of learning centres – 'they provide children with opportunities for making choices, working with others, being involved in hands-on activities and becoming fully engaged in learning' (Bottini and Grossman, 2005, p. 274).

Tablet PCs and laptops and other recently developed computer products are ideal for using at learning stations. Students can work individually, in pairs or in small groups on projects (Bitter and Peirson, 2005).

A classroom might contain three or four learning stations, located so that there is sufficient space between each to minimize noise interruptions and provide convenient access to other support areas, such as a 'conference' section where the teacher can discuss completed work units with students.

In addition to the traditional specialist rooms in secondary schools, such as design and technology centres, home economics rooms and science laboratories, it is interesting to note how these have been extended to include sophisticated language laboratories, media centres and micro-computer laboratories (Cohen et al., 2002; de Castell, 2000).

Pin-up boards and bulletin boards

Pin-up boards are a major element in any classroom because they can be used to display various items of interest such as student work, charts, posters, class rules and routines. Primary school students might have class banners, class photographs, birthday charts and monitor charts (Konza et al., 2001). Secondary school students might prefer posters on media topics, environment and sporting figures (Glickman, 2003).

Interactive whiteboards

Interactive whiteboards are clearly a resource for the future. They are essentially a large computer screen which is sensitive to touch. The content of the computer screen is displayed on the board using a data projector. Interactive whiteboards can be used to replace whiteboards and overhead projectors. Students can display their work, add notes, and even include video, music and picture files. They will be a boon to student-initiated activities and small-group work.

Special items

Plants can add a very positive effect to a classroom and of course students learn to be responsible for their watering. At primary school level, various animals may be kept such as fish, birds, tadpoles and mice. They add novelty and colour and are further opportunities for students to develop responsibilities for the animals' safety and welfare. The task for each teacher is to work out how to make the best use of available furniture and facilities. It is often amazing how the rearrangement of particular desks or cupboards leads to unforeseen increases in space/access. Mezzanine floors suspended above the tables and chairs, withdrawal areas complete with lounge chairs and occasional tables, are just some of the more adventurous schemes which have been implemented by some teachers. The checklist included in Box 14.1 provides useful reminders about space utilization.

Other physical and psychological factors in the classroom

Winston Churchill once remarked: 'We shape our buildings, and afterwards our buildings shape us.' This statement underlines the importance of the physical buildings in which we work and play, and especially the environments in the checklist in Box 14.1 to evaluate the use of classroom space in which schoolchildren spend at least twelve years of their lives. However, Churchill also appears to be attributing a considerable degree of determinism to the physical buildings, and it is far from clear whether this stance can be supported.

Research evidence indicates that relationships between the physical environment and students are far from clear. There are some patterns emerging related to crowding, privacy and territoriality, but few conclusive studies relating to specific physical environment factors. In fact, it is very difficult to disentangle the physical from the psychological factors. The research studies that have provided conclusive results are those that have demonstrated particular interrelationships between the two, such as the density of students in a classroom and student attitudes of dissatisfaction. The examples which follow indicate the interrelationships between physical environment factors and the affective states of students rather than direct influences on achievement measures.

Colour

The communications media are very aware of the use of colour and it is little wonder that colour television, colour inserts in daily newspapers, glossy colour magazines and full-colour computer games and graphics are so popular (Cohen *et al.*, 1998). So it is in classrooms. The list of items that can add colour to a classroom are endless and not limited to those listed above. Newspaper clippings, pamphlets and photographs are an integral part of many classrooms and they can add to the visual impact. So, too, can three-dimensional models (e.g. of landscapes, buildings and animals) and dioramas. Personal computer nooks and cubicles found in many classrooms add to the diversity of colours. However, a variegated assortment of colours, vying for students' attention in a classroom, needs to be considered in terms of educational purposes (Emmer *et al.*, 2000). Colours may be used by the teacher to gain students' attention and motivation, but they are also included to provide satisfaction and 'belonging-ness' to the student members of each classroom (Konza *et al.*, 2001). As Field (1980) notes, 'classrooms belong to the children, and teachers need to help them identify with them more readily' (p. 197). If students are involved in the planning of materials to be displayed and in the regular changing of them, then it is likely that they will identify far more readily with their teacher and the classroom endeavours he or she is trying to pursue.

Despite the many assertions from education writers about the value of colour in classroom environments, there is little research evidence to support or refute its use. At the primary school level, Santrock (1976) studied first- and second-grade children in a specially designed room, which was decorated alternately with happy, sad and neutral coloured pictures. The results indicated that the type of pictures in the room had a strong influence on the children and that they worked longer at a task when they were in the setting with the happy pictures.

Related to colour is the amount of natural light available to students in a classroom. Rosenfeld's (1999) research demonstrated that primary school students in Seattle, Washington, who studied in light-filled schools scored higher in maths and reading tests than those students working in classrooms with the least light.

Noise

Sounds are all around us but when certain sounds are unwanted they are generally termed 'noise'. Bell *et al.* (1976) make this point when emphasizing that noise involves a physical component (by the ear and higher brain structures) but also a psychological component when it is evaluated as unwanted.

As far as the classroom is concerned, it is important that the physical environment provides acoustics which enable participants to hold discussions in a normal conversational voice. The level of desirable noise will vary in different settings, from a manual arts workshop with noisy lathes and electric drills to an extremely quiet library. Each instructional setting has its own noise-level requirements to the extent that each person can hear clearly what is needed to be heard and is not distracted by other noises (Eriksen and Wintermute, 1983).

Research studies on the effects of noise in classrooms have been considerable over the last six decades, but the results are inconclusive and often contradictory. Some of these studies have examined short-term exposure of students to noise within the school, while others have monitored long-term exposure to severe noise from external sources. As an example of the former, Slater (1968) examined seventh-grade primary school children's performance on a standardized reading test under three conditions. The first classroom of students was isolated from surrounding background noise, the second had normal background neighbouring noise of 55–79 decibels (dB) and in the third room additional noise sources were used (lawnmower tape recordings) to maintain a background noise level of 75–90 dB. The results indicated that the students' performance on the reading test was not affected either positively or negatively by the different levels of noise. In another study of primary school students, Weinstein and Weinstein (1979) compared the reading performance of fourth-grade students under quiet (47 dB) and normal background noise (60 dB) and also found that there were no significant differences in performance.

Noise affects all teachers and students but the problem is compounded for students with hearing problems (Anderson, 2001). Ray (1992) noted in his study that 20–43 per cent of primary school students had minimal degrees of permanent or fluctuating hearing impairment that could adversely affect listening and learning. The problem is especially acute with special education students, many of whom have significant histories of hearing loss (Reichman and Healey, 1993). Dockrell and Shield (2006) note that poor classroom acoustics can create a negative learning environment for many students, especially those with learning impairments.

Temperature

Common sense would indicate that there is a fairly limited temperature range in which school students might be expected to work at their best. High temperatures will tend to make some students irritable and uncomfortable. In extreme cases students can become lethargic and even nauseous. Then again,

Table 14.1 Important psychosocial and physical factors in computer-networked classrooms

Psychosocial factors	• student cohesiveness
	• autonomy/independence
	• involvement
	• task orientation
	• cooperation
Physical factors	• spatial environment
	• visual environment
	• computer environment
	• workplace environment
	• air quality

cold temperatures seem to bring out aggression and negative behaviour in some students.

Judgements about temperature control in schools are typically made at head office, in that decisions about the architectural design of schools and the use of specific building materials are made at this level. The use of particular designs, the siting of buildings and the use of insulating material will clearly affect maximum and minimum temperatures.

Seating comfort

Having comfortable seating in classrooms is of major importance. If students are confined to uncomfortable seats for extended periods of time they become distracted from the learning task (Gay, 1986). Uncomfortable seating may also lead to negative attitudes about the teacher (Tessmer and Richey, 1997). Mann (1997) reports on a study where students were given modular, modern furniture and noted major changes in attitude. Lieble (1980) states the problem succinctly: 'the mind can only absorb what the seat can endure' (p. 22).

Class size

Of course, interactions between the teacher and students can be increased when class numbers are small. Small classes result in less desk space being necessary and therefore more free space is available for informal activities or for specialist equipment.

However, research evidence is contradictory on whether class size affects student achievement. For example, Murphy and Rosenberg (1998) and Finn *et al.* (2001) contend that there is compelling evidence that reducing class size, especially for younger children, will have a positive effect on student achievement. By contrast, Rees and Johnson (2000) and Galton *et al.* (2003) conclude that there is no evidence that smaller class sizes alone lead to higher student achievement. O'Donnell (2000), commenting on the funding resources in the Australian education systems, notes the reluctance of governments to make significant reductions in class size. By contrast, Scotland's Education Minister announced in May 2007 that infant classes will be reduced to eighteen children per class (Paton, 2007, p. 2). Biddle and Berliner (2002, p. 20), in a major synthesis of research studies, on class size, form several conclusions:

- small classes in the early grades generate substantial gains for the students and those extra gains are greater the longer the students are exposed to those classes;
- extra gains from small classes in the early grades are larger when the class has fewer than twenty students;

- students who have traditionally been disadvantaged in education carry gains forward into the upper grades;
- the extra gains appear to apply equally to boys and girls;
- evidence for the possible advantages of small classes in the upper grades and high school is inconclusive.

Psychosocial environment

A number of studies have been carried out on students' perceptions to obtain information on a better person–environment fit in classrooms (Fraser and Walberg, 1991). At the primary and secondary school levels, students can be surveyed to obtain data on their present levels of personal satisfaction and adjustment, and their respective teachers can then use this information to make changes where appropriate (Griffith, 1997).

A number of student inventories have been developed which provide this information. The Classroom Environment Scale (Moos and Trickett, 1974) has been widely used in the USA. This instrument measures nine different dimensions of the classroom environment, including students' interpersonal relationships, personal growth and teacher control. My Class Inventory is an instrument developed by the Australian researchers Fisher and Fraser (1981) and is used to gain information about primary school students' perceptions of classroom goals and value orientation. The items require students to make ratings on actual classroom environments as well as preferred environments. This information can be of great interest to class teachers who are concerned about providing instructional environments which are more in accord with those preferred by students. A questionnaire instrument developed by Fraser *et al.* (1996), What Is Happening in this Class?, measures students' perceptions of their classroom environment. Items are included which provide data on seven dimensions: student cohesiveness, extent of teacher support, extent of student involvement, investigative activities, task orientation, cooperation and equity.

Zandvliet and Frazer (2005) studied the learning environments in computer-networked classrooms (see Table 14.1). They isolated important psychosocial and physical factors, namely, that there were statistically significant associations with satisfaction for psychosocial environment variables but not for physical environment variables.

Ability groupings

Ability groupings and cross-setting arrangements have been the subject of considerable controversy over the years. Although some educators argue that homogenous ability groups have many benefits for teachers and students, others argue that it leads to unfair stigmatism of some students and inappropriate allocations to groups, with little hope for these students to be moved to higher-ability groups.

Davies, Hallam and Ireson (2003) note that there has been an increase in the use of ability grouping in primary schools in the UK because of increased pressure on schools to raise the performance of their students. They conclude that many factors need to be considered when embarking upon the setting up of ability groups, such as the physical layout of the school, staff levels and the availability of resources.

Single-sex schools and single-sex classes in co-educational schools

In many Western countries over the last decade there have been growing concerns about boys' apparent underachievement relative to that of girls. Within the UK, governments have highlighted the underachievement of boys in national assessments at 7, 11, 14 and 16 years of age (Younger and Warrington, 2006). In Australia the boys' lobbies have been very successful in demonstrating that boys are the new disadvantaged group (Ailwood, 2003).

Independent single-sex schools have been popular in many countries and achievements of boys and girls in their respective schools have been noteworthy. The emergence of single-sex classes within co-educational schools in the UK and Australia has been marked. The arguments in favour of single-sex classes for boys assert that these classes enable boys to share their feelings and emotions without embarrassment; they are less distracted by girls (Sukhnandan *et al.*, 2000; Swan 1998).

There is evidence also that single-sex classes can benefit girls as much as or more than boys (Herr and Arms, 2004). According to Younger and Warrington (2006), such an approach enables teachers to challenge some girls' stereotypical responses to subjects such as mathematics and science and enables girls to develop confidence in their own abilities. Yet there are concerns that many of the initiatives for single-sex classes for boys are 'rooted in the agenda of male disadvantage and repair and situated strongly within recuperative masculinity politics' (Younger and Warrington, 2006; Karlsson, 2007).

It is evident that the use of single-sex classes in co-educational schools is a complex matter and for it to be successful there must be wide-ranging staff development programmes and appropriate teaching and learning strategies that engage and motivate students (Martino and Pallotta-Chierolli, 2005). In the short term, recuperative masculinity agendas are unhelpful and do not address the real needs of girls currently being failed by the school system (Younger and Warrington, 2006).

Private and public schools

Debates continue to rage over whether private schools provide a better education compared with government schools (Loader 1999; Townsend, 1999: Blackmore, 1998; Hiatt, 2007). A study by Beavis (2005) noted that the learning environment was a major factor in parents opting for private schools. Parents cited such reasons as the following:

- better discipline in private schools;
- smaller classes;
- more individual attention given to students.

Home schooling

An option that is becoming increasingly popular for parents is to opt for home schooling (Hiatt, 2006). All state and territory education systems in Australia make provision for this. Parents are required to develop their curriculum based upon the relevant syllabus documents. Typically, education officers will inspect the parents to check the progress of children. There can be a number of reasons why parents might take this option, including moral and religious grounds and/or a strong motivation to develop the perceived (or actual) special talents of a child.

Various organizations are available to provide resources for home schooling. With current major developments in computers it is now possible for home schoolers to undertake electronic learning.

Tutoring services provided by commercial interests

Although tutoring of primary and secondary school students is not a major industry in Australia, it is expanding rapidly. In Asian countries it is widely practised and in the US it has increased dramatically as a result of the No Child Left Behind Act (NCLB). For example, schools in the US that miss the NCLB goals are provided with free tutoring by the state. Such is the pressure on states to meet the NCLB targets (ASCD, 2006a, 2006b).

Other learning settings

The school is not the only learning environment for young and older children. There are other non-formal agencies such as church and other groups which provide organized, systematic and educational activities.

Community schools

Dryfoos (2004) has evaluated a number of community schools in the US. These are schools which are jointly operated through a partnership between the school system and community agencies. These schools typically emphasize community service and service learning. He concludes that community schools are having a positive impact and reducing social barriers to learning.

Participation in these community activities enables students to realize the value of life skills – they develop self-confidence and understand more about personal dependability (McLaughlin, 2001). Full service youth and community centres provide additional learning environments apart from classrooms. They have family resource centres, healthcare facilities, pre-school, before and after school childcare, auditoriums and other facilities. These sites are open day and night and do capture the spirit of a community school (Dryfoos, 2000).

Service learning

Service learning has become an important priority in recent years whereby students visit other environments (e.g. senior citizen homes, disabled hostels) and provide caring services to others in need. Doing these community services gives students an opportunity to reflect on their own development (Dinkelman 2001). Seitsinger (2005) researched the use of service learning in middle schools in the US and concluded that these experiences enabled students to develop their higher-order thinking skills.

In Canada, Ellis (2003) reports how a storefront school has been working out of a shopping centre in Ottawa. It is a creative partnership between the school board and the shopping mall owners. It provides a valuable opportunity for 19–21-year-old students with disabilities to take part in a work experience/ life skills programme.

Yet there are issues with service learning. Butin (2003) argues that there are at least three major problems:

- there is limited research evidence on community impact resulting from service learning even though it might provide knowledge and insight to some students and teachers;
- research on students involved in service learning shows only small increases in academic, social and personal outcomes;
- it is difficult to undertake rigorous and authentic assessment of service learning.

Butin (2003) contends that service learning must be 'understood through multiple conceptual frames – technical, cultural, political and post-structural' (p. 1690).

Concluding comments

Descriptions of classroom environments run the full gamut from invective criticism:

> Judging from what is said and from what is available as a measuring stick, schools are architecturally and environmentally sterile ... Their structure is insipid, cavernous and regimented. They are only now and then really creature-comfortable. Their designs maximize economy, surveillance, safety and 'maybe' efficiency.
>
> (George and McKinley, 1974, p. 141)

to unbridled praise: 'Open planned classroom environments are a liberatory measure capable of emancipating children from the authority of teachers' (Cooper, 1982, p. 168).

In this chapter an attempt was made to place judgements about classroom environments on a more substantial footing and not to subscribe to either extreme view. Classroom instruction is affected by different uses of space and physical conditions. It is not possible to have knowledge of all the inter-relationships but it would be less than professional to ignore the evidence that is available. Creative arranging of the classroom is one thing, but it must be tempered by careful consideration of the effects of the classroom environment in all its complexities.

Reflections and issues

1   'In my space there must be a wide range of ways to succeed, multiple interests to pursue, a variety of possible contributions to make. This means the room is decentralised and characterised by lively work stations or interest areas, rather than by straight rows' (Ayers, 1993, p. 60). How achievable is this? Describe how you have developed classrooms in terms of multiple interests.

2   To what extent is it possible to cater for students' individual learning styles in terms of environmental elements such as noise, temperature and colour? Give examples from your classroom experiences or from classes you have visited.

3   'A certain level of adequacy must be attained in seating, acoustics, temperature and lighting for high level learning to occur' (Tessmer and Richey, 1997, p. 85). Explain, giving examples from your classroom experiences.

4   'Machines change relations within the traditional classroom. Film, video, computer software and web sites act as teachers and partially displace the human teacher' (De Vaney, 1998, p. 3). Discuss.

5   'School is diffusing spatially, merging into the physical backdrop of society. Schools are losing their architectural individuality, becoming increasingly difficult to recognize as places of learning' (Hopmann and Kunzli, 1997, p. 262). What are other places of learning? Are schools losing their individuality? If so, what will the impact be in the short and medium term?

6   'Children's attitude and behaviour [are] determined, to a considerable extent, by the design of school grounds' (Titman, 1997, p. 2). What messages do school grounds convey to schoolchildren? What are positive and negative elements of school grounds for children? How might this affect their behaviour in and out of the classroom?

7   'Teachers have little training in how to arrange a room. Perhaps every new teacher should receive an empty classroom and then plan what they want to do in it and how they want to operate' (Cohen et al., 2002, p. 31). If you were given an empty room how you would arrange it?

8   'The classroom environment is such a potent determinant of student out-
    comes that it should not be ignored by those wishing to improve the effec-
    tiveness of schools' (Fraser, 1986, p. 1). In what ways does the classroom
    environment determine student outcomes? What can a class teacher do to
    maximize the positive elements of a classroom environment?

9   According to Evans (1990), a school is both the temple and the exhibition
    hall of the modern world. Brightly coloured curtains and carpets are part of
    the intentions to display desired features to the public. But important
    aspects of teaching and administration remain hidden. In fact, care is often
    taken to indicate the 'official' way into the school. Do you agree with this
    statement? To what extent do the physical forms of schools give out mes-
    sages to the public?

Web sources

Changing the Environment, D. Fisher, http://www.scre.ac.uk/spotlight/spotlight2.html –
    extracted November 2007.
Individualized Classroom Environment Questionnaire, http://www.buros.un1.edu.
    buros/jsp/reviews.jsp?item = 06001207 – extracted November 2007.
Classroom Environment Questionnaire, http://www.jalt.org/pansig/PGL1/HTML/
    FinchD.htm – extracted November 2007.
Classroom Environment, http://www.det.wa.edu.au/education/Abled/BestPrac/classen.
    htm – extracted November 2007.
Classroom Environment: The Basics, http://www.learnnc.org/articles/BasicEnv1 –
    extracted November 2007.
Creating an Effective Physical Classroom Environment, http://www.teachervision.fen.
    com/classroom-management/decorative-arts/6506.html/ – extracted November 2007.
Elementary Approach: Classroom Environment, http://www.highscope.org/Educational
    Program/Elementary/environment.htm – extracted November 2007.
Redesigning the Classroom Environment, http://www.schoolzone.co.uk/resources/arti-
    cles/GoodPractice/classroom/Redesigning – extracted November 2007.

Chapter 15

Teacher appraisal

Introduction

The education of students is becoming increasingly results-driven and as a result attention is focused on the quality of teachers and how they perform in teaching students. It seems that many stakeholders want to measure or appraise the quality of teaching which occurs in schools. According to Burnett and Meacham,

> [the stakeholders] range from governments who are keen to dispel beliefs concerning the decline in the quality of public instruction, school administrators wishing to derive maximum benefit from their staffing dollar, professional teaching bodies looking to enhance the professional status of their members, individual teachers desiring job security and promotion on merit, and parents wanting the best for their children, to the children themselves.
>
> (Burnett and Meacham 2002, p. 141)

As professionals, teachers are constantly monitoring their work and that of colleagues working at the same school. In some schools, site-based initiatives have involved more formal monitoring of teachers' contributions.

It is useful to distinguish between evaluations/appraisals that occur at several stages of a teacher's career (Kleinhenz *et al.*, 2002). They include the following:

- pre-service or initial teacher education phase – this appraisal involves a teacher gaining a tertiary qualification which will gain them acceptability as a teacher;
- first employment as a teacher – the appraisal of teachers occurs largely in the selection/interview process;
- induction – all teachers have to serve a probation period and usually formative and summative evaluations are carried out by the principal or senior staff;
- career progression – teachers are expected to go through regular performance appraisals.

Some basic terms

How persons define teacher appraisal will depend on their attitudes and values. Parents at local social events often swap war stories about 'good' and 'bad' teachers. They apparently have criteria for making these judgements and see appraisal as a means of getting rid of the 'bad' teachers who teach their children.

In private industry, and increasingly in the public service, 'performance appraisal' activities are commonly undertaken. These involve managers and staff in planning particular targets. Criteria are used to judge levels of performance of staff in achieving or working towards these targets. In these situations the targets are clearly defined and so the measurement of achievement or lack of achievement is usually easily prescribed. Wragg (1987) argues that an interpolation of 'performance appraisal' to teaching is very problematic because do we really know what effective teaching is and can we recognize it when we see it?

L. Bell (1988) argues that teachers attach different meanings to the purposes of staff appraisal, namely:

- to identify incompetent teachers;
- to improve pay and promotion;
- to provide external accountability;
- to improve teacher performance;
- to provide effective management of teachers;
- to provide professional development.

This wide-ranging listing of meanings by a UK educator needs to be contrasted with that provided by a US educator (Danielson, 2001) who contends that teacher appraisal (in the USA the term is typically 'teacher evaluation') has only one major purpose and that is quality assurance:

> As trustees of public funds who are responsible for educating a community's young people, educators in public schools must ensure that each classroom is in the care of a competent teacher. Most educators recognize that teaching is a complex activity and that a simple, brief observation of a teacher in the classroom is not enough. An evaluation system should recognize, cultivate and develop good teaching.
>
> (Danielson, 2001, p. 13)

The weeding out of incompetent teachers is of course a less than helpful reason for implementing teacher appraisals but it is cited regularly in education documents, and given great prominence in the media. For example, Tucker (2001), citing empirical research in the USA, states that 5–15 per cent of the 2.7 million teachers in public school classrooms perform at incompetent levels. She provides details of assistance plans that have been used in some public schools in the USA and notes that 'the remediation requires a substantial investment of effort by both the teacher and the administrator, but has the potential to yield substantial benefits for all concerned parties, especially students' (p. 55).

A more positive meaning is to link appraisal to improving pay and promotion. In many countries advanced teacher status positions are now available to teachers who can demonstrate that they have high-quality classroom skills. This approach to appraisal is promoted by Ingvarson and Chadbourne (1994) in terms of a career development model in Australia. Yet there have been difficulties in establishing criteria and operationalizing the concept of an Advanced Skills Teacher (AST).

For many interest groups, teacher appraisal is needed to provide accountability to a range of external parties, but especially to parents and employers. This point of view seems to indicate that there is considerable room for improvement within the teaching profession – there are deficits to be overcome. School councils could be appropriate groups to initiate these accountability measures. It is also argued that teacher appraisal schemes are a powerful way of motivating teachers to perform better. Again this appears to be based on a deficit model in which teachers need assistance in refining their strengths and overcoming their weaknesses. Another view is that teacher appraisal is needed because management in schools by principals, deputy principals and senior teachers relies on effective deployment of staff – they need to know more about the skills and competencies of individual teachers.

A less threatening view of teacher appraisal is to perceive it as a basis for professional development. Systematic assessment of each teacher's performance provides the information needed for designing appropriate staff development activities (Hannay and Seller, 1998). It provides for professional enhancement because it pinpoints areas where a teacher can obtain specific in-service or related assistance. Some would argue that this is the major meaning that should be attributable to teacher appraisal – it would increase job satisfaction and benefit the school as a whole (Darling-Hammond, 1998).

This preliminary analysis of meanings of teacher appraisal reveals that it is a very slippery term! Depending upon how the term is interpreted there is likely to be either opposition and rejection or support. The degree of support or opposition is also dependent upon the historical contexts, and these matters are explored in the next section.

Teacher appraisal developments

United Kingdom

In the United Kingdom, the Education Act of 1986 enabled local education authorities to consider teacher appraisal schemes for their respective schools.

In due course, various pilot schemes were introduced. According to Bennett (1992) the pilot schemes were influenced by two conflicting models: a control model and a staff development model. The control model had its antecedents in the 'great debate' era of the 1970s with the emphasis upon efficient and effective use of resources and parent-power, governor-power and national intervention. The staff development model can be traced to the James Report (James, 1972) and its emphasis upon the in-service needs of teachers, the prioritizing of these needs and the provision of appropriate resources to service them.

The directors of the pilot schemes, coordinated under the School Teacher Appraisal Pilot Study, eventually accepted the staff development model as the basis for their activities after some initial disagreements. Each of the pilot schemes trialled procedures involving teacher self-appraisals and designed targets to improve performance.

When the Education Regulations for School Teacher Appraisal were passed by Parliament in mid-1991, appraisal became a requirement for all teachers. The government declared that all teachers would be appraised by the end of 1995. Unfortunately, government priorities changed the staff development emphasis quite considerably and more of a control emphasis slipped into the regulations.

In 1998, the Green Paper *Teachers Meeting the Challenge of Change* was issued. The minister's aim was to strengthen school leadership and develop a strong culture of professional development, but the teaching profession was not consulted. A private consulting firm was used to devise standards for the threshold assessment (top of the incremental scale to gain a 10 per cent pay increase and a new extended pay scale) and produced observational checklists. According to Ingvarson (2002), 'the method used for assessing teacher performance at the threshold was almost breathtakingly crude' (p. 3). He argues that the UK system seemed to ignore the fact that the profession could have expertise in designing teaching standards and assessments.

As might be expected, teachers were generally not favourably disposed to these requirements (Wragg et al., 2003). For many teachers, appraisal is perceived as disconnected from their teaching. It only heightens their feelings of stress. Winter (2006) queries whether appointed appraisers will be capable of appraising across a variety of subjects.

There have been even further government controls introduced since the mid-1990s. The Office for Standards in Education (OFSTED) was initiated by the government as a replacement group of inspectors to those from Her Majesty's Inspectorate (HMI) to 'collect objective evidence about schools and to report on their failings' (Lawlor, 1993). According to Furlong (2002), OFSTED has developed rigorous forms of quality control, and inspection results are not published in the national press in the form of competitive 'league tables'.

Although the OFSTED inspection reports focus upon the overall achievements of individual schools, they can appraise the school principal quite rigorously about staff (even though individuals are not named). For example, the inspection report of Adderley Primary School, Birmingham, makes the following comments about the head teacher:

> The time expended in dealing with a mutual lack of confidence between the head teacher and governors, and between a significant minority of parents and the school, has deflected the focus of raising standards.
>
> (OFSTED, 2004, Inspection Report 266277, p. 6).

> Achievement in mathematics is poor. Pupil achievement, particularly that of boys and potentially higher attaining pupils, in English and science is unsatisfactory. The school does not set out to support gifted and talented pupils.
>
> (OFSTED, 2004, Inspection Report 266277, p. 6).

The election of the Blair government in 1997 brought with it a new goal of raising educational standards. The school inspectors (OFSTED) and the new bureaucracy (the Department of Education and Employment, DfEE) were gathered together in a new partnership to improve school management and leadership through school targets (Crump, 1998). A National Teacher Education Board was created and this was charged with bringing about workplace reform. The National College for School Leadership was well funded to provide leaderships for school heads, who were deemed to be the major catalysts for change. The government also established an Innovations Unit to stimulate new teaching ideas (Mackay, 2002).

Not surprisingly, work-related stress for teachers has increased dramatically (Brown *et al.*, 2002). The drive to raise standards and managerialism has caused major problems of stress for teachers and head teachers (McMahon, 2000). It appears that the government has concentrated predominantly on central management and incentives for producing higher student standards, with only limited interest in the professional development and needs of teachers.

USA

In the USA, teacher appraisal (termed teacher evaluation) has always been given a high priority but the schemes used have varied in emphasis over the decades. In keeping with the USA's penchant for testing, it is not surprising that the schemes have largely depended upon assessment instruments to measure teacher performance. Most states have introduced legislation requiring assessment of all beginning teachers and in some cases for principals, superintendents and continuing teachers. The assessment instruments tend to be standardized tests which either are low-inference (relatively objective counts of behaviours) ones such as direct instruction behaviours or high-inference (more subjective, professional judgements) ones dealing with descriptions of classroom behaviour (Porter *et al.*, 2000).

Teacher knowledge continues to be an important focus. Darling-Hammond (1997) argues that teacher knowledge and teacher expertise are significant influences on student learning. This was one of the major findings of the National Commission on Teaching and America's Future (1997). An interesting perspective on teacher knowledge by Heibert *et al.* (2002) places the emphasis upon practitioner knowledge – knowledge that is integrated and organized around problems of practice. In-service programmes on 'lesson study' approaches focus upon developing practitioner knowledge, building upon lesson study research in Japan (Fernandez *et al.*, 2003).

The other ongoing scheme, and one that has major support currently at all levels, is the focus upon teacher professional standards. According to Delandshere and Arens (2001), the professional standards for teachers approach parallels the movement towards developing curriculum standards for students. National organizations have been working together to 'strengthen the teaching profession and raise its standards – eventually enhancing the quality of student learning – by redesigning teacher licensing and accountability requirements for teacher education programs, and engaging teachers in ongoing professional development' (p. 548).

The standards-based professional learning system generated by the National Board for Professional Teaching Standards (NBPTS) has been extremely influential. It assesses teacher performance within the context of specific subjects at different levels of schooling:

> Teachers undertake two types of task. One asks them to prepare a portfolio with four entries: one based on documented contributions to the school and professional community. The other uses an examination format to assess subject-specific pedagogical knowledge over one half day.
>
> (Ingvarson, 2002, pp. 14–15)

Recent research studies support the validity of the NBPTS standards and methods for assessing teacher performance (for example Guskey, 2002). Strongly supportive accounts of NBPTS standards at specific schools are appearing in the literature (for example Howard and McColskey, 2001).

As noted by Ingvarson (2002), NBPTS certification is gaining in credibility and, as a consequence, governments and education authorities are creating a market for National Board-certified teachers. Forty-four states now recognize this award and provide tangible rewards such as salary increases. NBPTS has 'progressed slowly and steadily because it has worked on carrying out one core function well – to provide a national voluntary system to assess and certify teachers who reach high standards' Ingvarson (2002, p. 13).

Another influential scheme is the Interstate New Teacher Assessment Consortium (INTASC), the Praxis System developed by the Educational Testing Service. The Praxis System assesses subject-matter knowledge and generic teaching practices across subjects (Porter *et al.*, 2000).

Some teacher induction schemes, which appear to be very successful, have been developed by state licensing bodies in Connecticut and California. For example, the California Formative Assessment and Support System for Teachers (CFASST) provides an ongoing process of structured learning and thinking for teachers (Olebe *et al.*, 1999; Lucas, 1999). The teacher peer assistance and review (PAR) scheme was initiated in California in 1999 (Goldstein, 2004). Consulting teachers, or CTs, are identified for excellence and released from teaching duties for two or three years. Their role is to mentor teachers new to a district and intervene in appraising veteran teachers experiencing difficulty. In her study, Goldstein (2004), notes that teachers can evaluate teachers but that CTs preferred to work collaboratively with principals on teacher evaluation activities. CTs expressed concerns about difficulties in conducting evaluations and problems of programme ambiguity.

Despite these impressive developments, it should be noted that these schemes cannot address all the issues that confront teachers. The schemes focus on major aspects of what it means to be a knowledgeable and reflective practitioner, but other elements are omitted. For example, they do not appear to give attention to the 'teacher as activist, the skilled change agent with moral purpose, who will make a difference in the lives of students from all backgrounds' (Cochran-Smith, 2001a, 2001b).

Australia

In Australia, teacher appraisal is evolving on a number of fronts but is still embryonic in terms of major developments. There has been a quickening of the pace recently. Four of the largest teacher professional associations have entered into partnerships with universities to develop subject-specific sets of professional standards in English and literacy, mathematics and science. It should be noted that these standards appear to be modelled on those developed by the NBPTS in the USA; the standards are higher than those developed in the first wave of competencies and standards in the 1990s and they have been developed without input from employers or teachers' unions (Louden, 2000). It is highly likely that subject-based standards will be developed in quick succession by other subject associations.

National standards of teaching and teacher professional development are still evolving, despite numerous national meetings of educators (Ingvarson, 2002).

The Ministerial Council on Education, Employment, Training & Youth Affairs (MCEETYA) produced a consultation paper, 'National Framework for Standards for Teaching – A Consultation Paper', in 2003. This paper presented a number of possible options for a national institute and encouraged individuals and professional groups to submit reactions. The then Federal Minister for Education and Training, Brendon Nelson, appeared to be very keen to establish his own interpretation of a national institute. In a press statement in June 2004, the minister announced the formation of a National Institute for

Quality Teaching and School Leadership (NIQTSL), to be based in Canberra and to be headed by an interim chairman, Dr Gregor Ramsay, a very experienced educator and administrator. The four key functions of NIQTSL were listed as:

- professional standards development – it will facilitate the development and implementation of nationally agreed teaching and leadership standards;
- professional learning for school leaders and classroom teachers – it will facilitate and coordinate professional development courses;
- research and communication – it will initiate and draw on research that supports intellectual leadership;
- promotion of the profession – it will increase public awareness of the education profession.

It is too early to judge the effectiveness of NIQTSL. A number of professional associations have queried the composition of the interim board and interim council. NIQTSL will need to form partnerships with stakeholder organizations if it is to achieve its ambitious aims (Enabling Sciences Education Research Network, 2005).

If new methods of performance assessment for certification are developed nationally, it will be a powerful incentive for teachers to engage in the programmes. It is highly likely that employing authorities will give recognition (and financial rewards) to teachers who obtain the certification, as noted above with regard to US teachers gaining NBPTS awards.

Why do teacher appraisals?

From the outset, it is important to note that in everyday teaching teachers continually get informal and formal feedback about their actions. Teacher appraisal schemes are only part of this continual process of feedback, along with regular meetings, informal talks and staffroom and corridor conversations. Ingvarson, Meiers and Beavis (2005) assert that teacher appraisal should never become a substitute for frequent, informal feedback, nor should it be conducted in ways that cause a deterioration in professional relationships with other teachers.

Teacher appraisals enable balanced critiques of performance, which can include congratulations and recognition – a powerful motivator for teachers. As noted by Samuel (1987), 'indeed at times it can provide the opportunity for that measured congratulation that so many of us are too mealy-mouthed to express on the informal occasion' (p. 69). Teacher appraisals can produce a considerable amount of praise and can provide opportunities to celebrate good practice. Shulman, in an interview by Tell (2001), contends that many teachers in the USA preparing for NBPTS certification do so 'for the chance to demonstrate to themselves and to others that they are really, really good at what they do' (p. 10).

Another important reason is that teacher appraisal enables more detailed and, it is to be hoped, objective information to be made available to each teacher (Preiss, 1992). There are several elements of this point to be considered. Few would argue that in a busy day of teaching the teacher can never be aware of all the things that are happening. He or she will know a lot of what is happening, but not all. Research studies of teachers in action often provide surprising results for the teachers being observed. Teacher's self-descriptions can often be very different from the independently observed data.

Yet it must also be added that additional information obtained about teachers comes at a cost. In many cases fellow teachers at the school may be required to undertake the observations, thus creating yet another time-consuming burden. Also, observers have their own agenda about what is significant and what is not. Data about a teacher's behaviour are provided with an end always in mind – to encourage changes and progress toward particular, desired goals.

There is also the matter of curriculum planning and implementation. Curriculum planning done at the school level may appear to be very appropriate, but until it is implemented in the classroom and evaluated it is not possible to know what the outcomes will be. Appraisals of how curricula are used – either by individual teachers, or by the school as a whole – provide important feedback for future curriculum planning.

Table 15.1 Benefits and problems of teacher appraisal

Difficulties/Disadvantages	*Advantages and rewards*
Difficulties	Leads to the identification of clear aims and objectives
Suspicion	Improves relationships
Concern	Provides opportunity for honest communication, understanding, training and development
Lack of experience (in self-appraisal and appraising others)	Displays concern and commitment
Training may be required	Generates motivation
Opposition of significant groups	It is open and seen to be open
Disadvantages	Reduces subjectivity in assessment
Appraisal requires: time and commitment, especially from senior staff honesty from all involved the need for discipline	Provides permanent (and available) records
It can provoke conflict	Provides opportunity to praise
	Person being reviewed has an ownership in the process, which leads to clearer understanding of expectations, responsibilities and aspirations

Source: Based on L. Bell (1988)

Iwanicki (2001) argues that teacher appraisal (evaluation) should improve student learning in the classroom: 'In today's world we should not build professional employee appraisal systems to fire people. We should build systems to help them develop and increase the productivity of their organizations. In education, productivity means improved teaching and student learning' (p. 59).

The same can be said for general school planning. For a school to know whether it is achieving its goals requires systematic feedback, part of which is detailed information about teachers' contributions. There are time limitations regarding how frequently this information can be collected. A solution practised in many schools is for a smaller number of activities/functions to be evaluated each year.

The opportunity for professional development of teachers is a major reason for and a central focus of many of the appraisal schemes. The improvement of teaching is not just the arrival at a reasonable standard for the initial few years (probationary period) of teaching, but steady progress as a life-long process. The appraisal process can enable a teacher to become increasingly effective in his or her present role, to make better use of strengths, and provide further opportunities at a school or elsewhere in terms of career advancement. Professional development is also about dovetailing the professional needs of individual teachers with the needs of the school as a whole.

Ingvarson (2002) argues for elaborate forms of professional development for teachers but cautions that not all forms of appraisal are effective for professional development. In the United Kingdom, Haynes et al. (2001) surveyed English teachers who had prepared for the threshold promotion (97 per cent passed the threshold and were then placed on a new salary scale). Their research indicated that 98 per cent of the teachers reported that the experience had not had a positive effect on their practice, and in general had been detrimental to their morale.

Teaching portfolios

Shulman (1994) introduced the idea of using portfolios in teacher assessment in the early 1990s. He claims that a portfolio is a theoretical act – 'it is a broad metaphor that comes alive as you begin to formulate the theoretical orientation to teaching that is most valuable to you. Your theory of teaching will determine a reasonable portfolio entry' (p. 5).

Teaching portfolios have been promoted, especially in the USA, as a valuable method of appraising teachers at all levels from beginning teacher to master teacher (Lyons, 1999; Van Wagenen and Hibbard, 1998). Hurst et al. (1998) contend that professional teaching portfolios are especially useful for teachers because:

- they are reflective compendiums – representations of teachers' professional and personal lives;

- they are representations of teaching credentials and competencies – an organized collection of documents, letters, papers and photographs that lauds a teacher's personal and professional achievements in a compact, concrete way;
- they provide holistic views of teachers – they give teachers the opportunity to show not only their teaching strengths but also their heart and soul and passion for teaching;
- they provide documentation for strengthening interviews – it gives teachers applying for positions increased confidence and a competitive edge.

A teaching portfolio is likely to contain:

- carefully selected items about an appraisee's teaching and learning over a period of time;
- items that represent examples of best work;
- some examples of student work;
- reflective commentaries by the appraisee.

Painter (2001) makes the distinction between folios and portfolios. A teaching folio is just a collection of a teacher's artefacts. A portfolio must contain reflections about his or her teaching in terms of the standards or rubrics required. Portfolios must provide details of a teacher's intellectual and professional ideas – 'thoughtful reflection, not a colour printer, is the key to portfolio success' (Painter, 2001, p. 92).

Problems and issues

Experiences in the United Kingdom, USA and Australia indicate that a number of teachers are finding appraisals to be a valuable experience even though some were apprehensive about it initially – the first time for many teachers when they have been able to have a serious professional discussion about their work (McMahon, 1994; Glenbrook High School District, 2006). Case study accounts from various Australian states also provide confirmatory support for appraisals (e.g. Richards, 1994; Billing, 1994).

If appraisals are organized and planned just within a school, then a problem is finding the scarce resources required in terms of time and of money. As noted by L. Bell (1988), it is unrealistic to involve peers as appraisers and expect that they will do all their appraising outside normal working hours. Yet to free up teachers to be involved in interviews and class observations during the school day would require substantial payments for relief teachers.

Other problems relate to the need for the training of appraisers and the overcoming of suspicion and lack of trust by various interest groups. Some positive and negative elements of teacher appraisal are included in Table 15.1.

If teacher appraisals are organized through national organizations, such as the NBPTS in the USA, it is a voluntary decision by teachers and they make their own arrangements about when and where they will submit themselves to the certification process. Similar arrangements may be trialled in Australia under NIQTSL. It is highly likely that further trials will occur shortly in Australia using standards developed for English and literacy and mathematics and, in time, other subjects.

Concluding comments

There are various interpretations of teacher appraisal. For some it is 'a chimera, looming threateningly and foully over our shoulders; for others it is a fantasy that cannot come to pass; and for some it is a practical part of institutional autonomy and individual professionalism' (Clandinin, 1986, p. 3).

In this chapter the latter stance is taken. Given initiatives with teacher appraisals in the United Kingdom, the USA and Australia and the potential they have for improving schooling, it is extremely likely that teacher appraisals will become more widespread in the twenty-first century.

It is therefore of importance to all teachers to be aware of why appraisals are undertaken, who appraises and the methods commonly used. The practical examples included in this chapter should enable teachers at all levels to relate to important issues about teacher appraisals.

Reflections and issues

1 'Traditionally appraisal was what was done to teachers. The new approaches to teacher appraisal place teachers in more active and professional roles' (Danielson, 2001, p. 14). Is this what is really occurring? Discuss.
2 Smyth and Shacklock (1998) consider that teachers at a school should use collegial processes to appraise their own teaching rather than having experts undertake appraisal and thereby disempower teachers. He uses the term 'clinical supervision' to describe the face-to-face dialogue between classroom teachers. Take a stance for or against this argument.
3 There are numerous examples in industry where annual appraisals of staff are undertaken. Consider arguments for or against the assertion that education is an industry too and should use similar appraisal schemes.
4 Is it possible to develop a system of learning in the teaching profession that engages all teachers? Should it be developed at a local level or at a national level?
5 According to Wragg (1987), the major emphasis for teacher appraisals should be to improve the quality of teaching rather than increasing bureaucracy or power. Do you agree? Which methods of appraisal have the potential to improve the quality of teaching?

6 We should not forget that appraisal is about recognizing effort and achievement and praising the commitment of teachers. Bennett (1992) states that it 'must not be allowed to become a grand biennial ritual to be endured and ultimately ignored' (p. 129). Discuss.

7 Why is a national professional body needed in Australia? Is it appropriate and realistic for such a body to develop standards and responsibility for ensuring the system for assessing teacher performance against those standards is rigorous?

Web sources

Hot Issues: National Institute for Quality Teaching and School Leadership, http://www.aspa.asn.au/hotissue.htm – extracted 13 February 2007.

National Institute for Quality Teaching and School Leadership: Enabling Sciences Education Research Network, http://www.scs.une.edu.au/EnSE/national.html – extracted 13 February 2007.

Statutory Regulations, School Teacher Appraisal, England, http://www.opsi.gov.uk/si/si2000/20012855.htm – extracted 13 February 2007.

Teacher's Appraisal Doubts, http://news.bbc.co.uk/l/hi/education/635874.stm – extracted 13 February 2007.

Chadbourne, Putting Teachers in their Place, http://edoz.com.au/educationaustralia/news/wa.html – extracted 13 February 2007.

L. Ingvarson, M. Meiers and A Beavis (2005) 'Factors affecting the impact of professional development programs on teachers' knowledge, practice, student outcomes & efficacy'. *Education Policy Analysis Archives*, 13(10), http://epaa.asu.edu/epaa/v13n10/ – extracted 13 February 2007.

Teacher Appraisal, www.sbac.edu/∼profdc/Appraisal/teachers.htm – extracted 13 February 2007.

The Standing of Teachers and Teaching, https://det.nsw.ed.au/reviews/macqt/standa29.htm.

Teacher Performance Appraisal System, www.edu.gov.on.ca/eng/teacher/teachers.html – extracted 13 February 2007.

Part V

Collaborative involvement in curriculum

Chapter 16

Decision-makers, stakeholders and influences

Introduction

Schooling occurs as a result of decisions made by various individuals and groups, both professionals and lay-persons. To complicate matters, actions occur at different levels, especially national, state and local. It is of considerable value to analyse and understand the contributions of the various players.

Some basic terms

A classroom teacher's work is affected by many individuals and groups. Although various myths abound about the freedom of a teacher to do whatever he or she wishes in the privacy of 'behind the classroom door', this is not true in the twenty-first century – if in fact it ever was the case.

'Decision-makers' are those individuals or groups who, because of their professional status or position, are able to make specific decisions about what is to be taught, when, how and by whom. Obvious examples of decision-makers include education systems and their senior officers and school principals and senior teachers. But there are many others, including textbook writers, testing agencies, accreditation and certification agencies.

'Stakeholders' are individuals or groups of persons who have a right to comment on, and have input into, school programmes (Arends, 2000). In many cases they may have the authority to ensure that their inputs/directives are implemented, such as head office education directors or regional directors. Then again, they may have no official powers but rely upon their modes of persuasion, such as parent groups or newspaper editors.

'Influences' are individuals or groups who hold common interests and endeavour to persuade/convince authorities that certain changes should occur. They may be content to push a certain slogan/ideal or they may focus upon specific activities or processes that should occur in schools. Examples of such influences include various local interest/lobby groups representing environmental issues or specific religious beliefs.

There are obviously no clear demarcation lines between some forms of decision-makers, stakeholders and influence groups, as their degree of authority/control depends upon the eye of the beholder. Yet for the purpose of analysis it is useful to produce a tentative list of groups that might be considered under each of these headings.

Classification

So many different groups influence curriculum decision-makers in so many different ways that it is impossible to plot out with precision the various interactions and points of leverage they have at the various levels of educational systems (Fullan, 2001; Scott, 1999). However, it is possible to list some of the most influential groups and to describe in general ways how their influence works. Tables 16.1 and 16.2 list such groups, along with some tentative judgements about their levels of involvement and influence. The list includes both professional and non-professional organizations. Some of the groups listed ordinarily have benign motives, such as improving the quality of education in general. Other groups listed usually have narrower interests.

Decision-makers

Table 16.1 lists some individuals and groups ordinarily considered curriculum decision-makers. Their decisions may range from creating highly detailed and

Table 16.1   Decision-makers/stakeholders

Title and focus		Impact on schools
Politicians	Ministers of Education/ Secretary of State State/national	High
Superintendents	Superintendents, chief education officers, directors-general Region/state	High
State departments	State/LEAs	High
Assessment boards	State/national	High
Teacher unions	State/national	Medium/high
Parents and school councils/boards	School-focused	Medium/High
Principals/headmasters Teachers	School-focused School-focused	Medium/high
Students	School-focused	Low
Academics	Universities, TAFE, further education state/national	Medium/high
Employers	state/national	Medium

Table 16.2 Influences

	Examples	*Impact on schools*
Professional associations	National Association for the Teaching of English (NATE) (UK)	Medium (at secondary school level)
Textbook writers	Authors of major texts for primary/elementary and secondary students	Medium
National agencies	Office of Education (USA)	Low
Media	Editorials and feature articles in major daily newspapers; daily television news	Medium/high
Educational consultants	Specialists in reading instruction	High in individual schools
Lobby groups	Environmental groups	Low
The courts	Mandating instruction in a school district	High
Research and testing organizations	Literacy tests	Medium
Commercial sponsorship/contracting out	Sponsorship for a computer laboratory	Medium/high

individualized plans for specific classrooms to adopting externally created programmes for use throughout a school district or an entire state.

At the school level, teachers and principals are mainly concerned with decisions that are directly related to day-to-day teaching. Teachers tend to focus on the curricula of their own classrooms and the classrooms of other teachers with whom they work most closely. Principals tend to be more concerned with coordination within curricula or across grade levels (Ornstein and Hunkins, 1993; Wildy *et al.*, 2000). At the district level, superintendents are mainly concerned with decisions about general programmes. Usually they work closely with their school boards or school committees (ordinarily not educational professionals but groups of citizens charged by law with making many administrative decisions for their districts).

At the state (or sometimes even the federal) level, commissioners of education or officers of educational agencies make policy decisions about establishing or terminating total programmes, such as programmes for intellectually talented students.

Politicians

Ministers of Education/Secretaries of State at national and state levels have had, and continue to have, an enormous influence on curriculum, especially during the last few decades. In many cases, individual ministers have initiated major curriculum reforms single-handed, as a result of their position and extremely strong personalities – for example John Dawkins in Australia (Marsh, 1994), David Blunkett and his prime minister, Tony Blair, in the United Kingdom (Crump, 1998).

Marsh (1994) analysed Dawkins' efforts as Minister for Education in Australia in the 1980s – 'by using "crisis rhetoric" he steered state ministers into collaborative efforts to produce national statements and profiles in eight learning areas. His statements were largely economics-driven, coupled with assertions that education had failed' (p. 44). More recently, there is very strong evidence in Australia that federal ministers and their departments (for example, Department of Education, Science and Technology) are attempting to exert considerable central control. The federal ministers are pushing for compliance by requiring specific rules and requirements linked with funding and punitive threats if the states don't accept them.

Crump (1998) details the New Labour initiatives by the Blair government to drive skills improvement in schools by management and leadership targets, reinforced by national standards testing, the closure of failing schools and the sacking of teachers. Fullan and Earl (2002), as part of a team of consultants from the University of Toronto to monitor the implementation of National Literacy and Numeracy Strategies in the United Kingdom, conclude that the large-scale reform has been successful in raising literacy and numeracy standards, but they consider that the strong initiatives from the centre (top-down) now need to be followed by more local capacity-building and local networking.

It might be argued that the education budget is so large in most countries that it is only politicians who can provide direct levels of accountability to the general public to justify the expenditure. It is certainly the case that politicians have excluded the traditional senior educators and made many changes to the secret garden of curriculum (Lawton, 1980).

Superintendents/chief education officers/directors-general

Senior officers in charge of education systems have different titles in the USA, the United Kingdom and Australia, but they are typically responsible for a wide range of educational decisions, even though they delegate the authority in various ways and to varying degrees. Their personalities, modes of public relations and establishment of priorities are highly significant for the achievements of the education system.

From time to time a number of these senior officers have shown a major interest in curriculum and have been driving forces in establishing innovatory practices. For example, Bill Honig in California in the 1980s was instrumental in changing the nature of teaching and learning in that state by initiating frameworks and by aligning state-adopted textbooks and state tests to the frameworks (Ball *et al.*, 1994). In the United Kingdom, William Stubbs was an active exponent of local education authority responsibilities during his time as Director of the Inner London Education Authority (Stubbs, 1981).

State departments/local education authorities

Especially over the last two decades in the USA, state departments have greatly increased their influence over schooling. Standards-based approaches are currently being strongly supported. States have eagerly accepted these new standards because of purported gains in student academic levels, accountability for student outcomes, inclusion of all students in reform initiatives and flexibility to foster instructional change (Goertz, 2001). For example, 49 states have developed content standards and 48 states have state-wide assessments in subjects (Goertz, 2001).

In the United Kingdom, the implementation of the National Curriculum has brought about a diminution of the power and responsibilities of the local education authorities (LEAs). The largest LEA, the Inner London Education Authority, was quickly dismantled by the Conservative government. The provision for schools to opt out of their respective LEA and to operate as grant-maintained schools with direct funding from the central government has further weakened many LEAs (Whitty, 1995; Power and Whitty 1999).

Yet others such as Campbell and Murillo (2005) argue that LEAs, which they label as 'middle tier' between central government and schools, do have an important role in supporting and sustaining systemic education reform. They conclude that 'school-level reform alone will not necessarily bring about systemic improvements' (Campbell and Murillo, 2005, p. 82).

In Australia, state education systems, protected under the constitution as solely responsible for the delivery of education, have maintained their responsibilities and influence but economic rationalism has given enhanced emphasis to standards and efficiency. State-led reforms require schools to produce corporate plans and to be accountable for certain budget elements (Caldwell, 2000).

Assessment boards

Senior Secondary (Year 12) Examination Boards have a long tradition in the United Kingdom and Australia. They are responsible for developing examinations for matriculation entry into universities and, as a consequence, greatly influence the curriculum taught at senior secondary school levels. In Australia, such boards as the Board of Studies in New South Wales control the curriculum for all schooling levels K-12 but have a major impact on teaching in Years 11 and 12. In the United Kingdom, the Qualifications and Curriculum Authority and examination boards such as the Cambridge Examination Board produce syllabuses and examinations at GCSE and GCE (A levels).

Examination boards have traditionally been the preserve of university academics, but over recent decades there have been a considerable number of places allocated to senior secondary school teachers and, more recently, to vocational/further education personnel. As with other major stakeholders, examination boards are now forming alliances with other groups such as universities, research institutes and industry groups in their endeavours to undertake curriculum development projects, such as those associated with Standard Assessment Tasks (SATs) in the United Kingdom and profile reporting in Australia.

Teacher unions

In the United Kingdom and Australia, in particular, teacher unions have been a significant influence upon curriculum. Not unexpectedly, in times of rapid expansion of education, or periods of crisis in funding, teacher unions are especially active. Over recent decades there has been a disempowering of teacher unions, by design or by default.

According to Burrow and Martin (1998) the reason for the decline in union influence in Australia has been the open hostility by 'economic fundamentalist, right wing governments' (p. 98). They argue that the following tactics have been used:

- state governments have rescinded procedures whereby teachers automatically have payroll deductions for union dues and thereby have put strains on union cash flows;
- the removal of teacher unions from representative and consultative committees;
- the winding up of national bodies that had significant union representation (such as the Australian Teaching Council) or influence (such as the Schools Council);
- federal government financial support to other professional associations and especially principal associations;
- attacks on education standards in public schools, especially literacy and teacher standards.

Parents and school councils/boards

Parent influence on curriculum issues occurs most frequently through involvement on school boards/councils. In fact, school boards can be an ideal vehicle for parents and teachers to work together on curriculum decision-making. Yet school councils can never be the sole or even the most important facet of parent participation. They are just one means of trying to provide teacher–parent–student interaction in decision-making. In the everyday life of a school it is important that there are numerous opportunities for this joint decision-making to occur and that it is not restricted to the relatively few, formal meetings of a school council (Pettit, 1984).

Yet many parent groups are not well represented in decision-making at the school level. This is especially the case for parents of low socio-economic status and for parents in minority ethnic groups. These groups often need special encouragement and support before they are willing to become involved in decision-making (Maclure and Walker, 2000). Involvement on councils occurs most frequently among parents whose culture and lifestyle are closely aligned to the school's culture (Lee and Bowen, 2006).

School principals/heads

The position of school principal is certainly an exacting one to hold, as so many different groups and individuals have beliefs about what the school principal should do and should achieve (Lambert, 1998). Parents and community members expect a public-minded, highly principled person who is open to outside initiatives and who will communicate information regularly to them. Some of these expectations may conflict with those of the teachers, who expect their school principal to be an instructional leader and a supporter of curriculum initiatives and to be very visible and active around the school buildings. Students might have other expectations, including a sympathetic counsellor and the final arbiter on matters of justice, discipline and penalties, but, above all, an inspirational, charismatic figurehead.

State department officials and senior regional officers expect school principals to be thorough, reliable and efficient, to be capable of implementing and monitoring departmental policies, and not to be overly influenced by vocal minority groups. In total, these beliefs about the role of the school principal contain obvious conflicts and ambiguities. Even if it were possible to rationalize some of these conflicting points of view, it is doubtful whether single individuals could embody all the demanding characteristics. It seems that the public is setting unattainable goals and that only 'superstars' can achieve these standards (Copland, 2001).

Schools in the twenty-first century are being engulfed by multiple innovations and policy changes (Fullan *et al.*, 2004). Overload and fragmentation take their toll even on the superstar principals – their energy sources become so drained that they run on empty (Loader, 1998). Principals have the opportunity to make a number of decisions at school level. They are the critical change agents, even though their styles as leaders may vary, encompassing the bureaucratic, visionary, entrepreneurial or pedagogical (Sergiovanni, 1998; Hargreaves and Fink, 2000).

Southworth (2000) contends that, in the United Kingdom, principals are predominantly managerial. Woods (2000) concurs, pointing out that principals increasingly are subject to 'performativity', the expectation that they perform like enterprising, competitive entrepreneurs. Soder (1999) argues that 'school renewal' is now widely seen as secondary to 'school reform', with its emphasis on standards, high-stakes testing and immediate results.

Teachers

Teachers are involved in all the complexities associated with daily teaching and are responsible for a myriad of classroom decisions. They try to create order and stability in potentially chaotic surroundings. There are various interpretations about the level of decision-making that could be undertaken by classroom teachers and what actually occurs in practice. Guglielmi and Tatrow (1998) note the heightened job pressures on teachers and consequently their reduced interest in decision-making.

Smyth and Shacklock (1998) argue that there is now a widening gulf between manager-principals and teachers. Principals are so engrossed in financial management and meeting targets that teachers have to take on the role of pedagogical leaders, developing collaborative cultures and teamwork.

Fullan (1993) is more cautionary when he notes that teachers have the potential to be major decision-makers but it depends upon the extent to which they have been able to succeed with their inner learning (learning to cope with the immediate environment even if it is adverse) and with their outer learning (being able to work, learn and network with colleagues).

The emotions of teaching are also an issue taken up by Hargreaves (1998). Leadership by teachers in periods of rapid change is affected greatly by issues of emotion: 'Teaching is a form of emotional labour and teaching and learning involves emotional understanding' (Hargreaves, 1998, p. 319).

Recently, massive intensifications of teachers' workloads have occurred in many Western countries (Easthope and Easthope, 2000). McMahon (2000) identifies the drives to micro-manage schools and to raise standards as counter-productively placing new strains on how teachers use their time.

Beare (1998) suggests that in future teachers will deliver or apply specialist knowledge under contract – they will be one-person businesses. The traditional decision-making structures operating in schools will decline.

Students

Students are an important element in the learning environment and are the ultimate consumers. Various writers have been highlighting the role of students as key players in school reform and decision-making (Mitra, 2006; Leren, 2006; McNess, 2006). However, the concept of a student voice must gain legitimacy among powerful stakeholders in the school if this is to happen.

Students affect curriculum policy by mediating it – they come to classrooms with different backgrounds and as a result transform the taught curriculum in various ways (Schubert, 1986). Students can provide vision and be constructive participants in curriculum planning, so long as trusting and supportive environments are developed by teachers and administrators (Connect, 2007).

Although it might be assumed that student decision-making has the potential to occur in secondary schools there are many factors operating that inhibit student participation. Wilson (2002) cites some of these inhibiting factors as teachers' accountability mentality, management priorities for the school and an unwillingness to provide training for students for decision-making roles.

Smyth (2006) contends that administrators in education systems do not appreciate the crucial importance of relationships and the role that students can play in decision-making. According to Bryk and Schnaider (2002), 'the issue is rather one of deficit of political will and imagination to want to put relationship ties around the interests of students' (p. 6).

Academics

It has long been argued that academics are important decision-makers, especially at the secondary school level, as universities dictate the academic curriculum required of senior secondary school students. In many countries senior university academics are active participants on examination boards and do become involved in policy decisions about syllabus content and examinations. However, increasingly they are just one of the players on examination boards, as a result of the emerging roles being shaped by senior Technical and Further Education (TAFE) personnel and industry representatives.

Although key academics were consulted for specific tasks relating to national curriculum initiatives (for example P. Black on assessment in the United Kingdom and P. Fensham on science education in Australia), academics in general were largely bypassed in the 1980s and 1990s. Their influence occurred via post-hoc criticisms, such as Australian academics criticizing the Mathematics National Profile (Guttman, 1993; Ellerton and Clements, 1994) – 'the idea of wresting the control of school curricula from vested interests in universities, has been one of the underlying but relatively silent forces in the national curriculum movement' (p. 314).

In Australia over the last decade, under the chairmanship of Professor Stuart MacIntyre, academic members of the Civics Expert Group (MacIntyre et al., 2005) produced a strategic plan for developing citizenship education (Kennedy, 1997). The academics have been less influential since 1996, when new political priorities and government department plans for citizenship education (the Department of Education, Science and Training (DEST) and the Curriculum Corporation) caused some changes in direction and emphasis (Mellor et al., 2002).

Employers

Employer groups have been a relatively new but increasingly powerful player in the education stakes (Fullan, 2001). In many countries, award restructuring, skills training standards and economic instrumentalism ideology have led many employer groups to agitate for a greater voice in the curriculum of schools. Various vocational programmes, generic and core skills orientations and vocational awards have been implemented as a result of initiatives by these groups.

Economic arguments and rationalities are being used to justify changes to the secondary school curriculum (Poole, 1992). In the USA, Apple (1988) notes that schools must be brought more closely into line with policies that will 'reindustrialize' and 'rearm' America so that it will be more economically competitive.

Various writers support the emphasis upon vocation education and the need for schools to prepare students for the working world. Teachers do not have all the knowledge or the skills to prepare students effectively for the world of work (Price, 1991). It is likely that employer groups will continue to have a significant influence on curriculum, especially at the senior secondary school level.

Influences

Professional associations

Professional associations exercise their influence at national, state and local levels but especially at the national level. Their activities can include lobbying for or against political actions; publishing curriculum guidelines and producing scope and sequence charts; and establishing networks, workshops and conferences (Glatthorn, 1987).

In the USA various professional associations played a major role in the development of national standards, such as the National Council of Teachers of Mathematics and the National Council for the Social Studies. Professional associations have had mixed fortunes in the United Kingdom and Australia over recent decades. In the 1970s in the United Kingdom, professional associations such as the National Association for the Teaching of English (NATE) were very influential (Stenhouse, 1980), but their influence waned with the implementation of the National Curriculum. In Australia, professional associations were largely ignored in the development of national statements and profiles (Marsh, 1994) but subsequent intensive lobbying enabled national associations to play a role in developing teacher development materials for their respective learning-area profiles (Ellerton and Clements, 1994).

Textbook writers

Textbooks are a major learning source for many students. They can provide a core of important learning; up-to-date information; instruction on basic skills; and an introduction to or overview of particular topics. Good textbooks are often very popular with teachers because they bring together a massive amount of important material in one volume, thus saving the busy teacher considerable time.

Writers of popular textbooks can be extremely influential about what is taught and how it is taught. If teachers rely very heavily upon a textbook they are likely to accept the content structure and associated pedagogy put forward by a textbook author.

In countries where textbooks are selected by central committees or state committees, a selected few can dominate the market. In several states of the

USA, such as Texas and California, state textbook adoptions are a major activity and wield a significant influence on school education. It is interesting to note that alignment policies, especially in California, have required textbook publishers to ensure that their publications are congruent with state curriculum frameworks and state tests.

Some writers, such as Apple (1993) and Pinar *et al.* (1995), are concerned about the influence of textbooks:

> They are at once the results of political, economic and cultural activities, battles and compromises. They are conceived, designed and authored by real people with real interests. They are published with the political and economic constraints of markets, resources and power. And what texts mean and how they are used are fought over by communities with distinctly different commitments and by teachers and students as well.
>
> (Apple, 1993, p. 46)

The world wide web (www) is rapidly becoming a de facto textbook for many teachers and students. It has many advantages. It can provide data from a variety of sources all over the world and is available twenty-four hours a day. Most importantly, it is a cheaper means of accessing data than traditional sources and so is likely to become increasingly attractive for education systems.

National/federal agencies

In a number of countries national departments of education can have a major influence upon curriculum but there can be peaks and troughs. For example, in the USA the National Institute of Education/Department of Education oscillated between major and minor involvement in curriculum matters during the 1980s and 1990s due to different political priorities.

The election of the New Labour government in the United Kingdom in 1997 led to increased powers for national agencies with its emphases upon targets, national standards testing, and the Office for Standards in Education (OFSTED) inspections (Macpherson, 1998; Crump, 1998). The increase in national agency control was very evident in the policy paper 'Education and Skills: Investment for Reform' (Department for Education and Skills, 2002). The 'transformation' of secondary education focused upon the following centralist initiatives:

1   radical reform of school leadership;
2   radical reform of school structures;
3   radical reform of teaching and learning;
4   radical reform of partnerships beyond the classroom (Department for Education and Skills, 2002, p. 2).

The creation of the super-ministry the Department of Employment, Education and Training (DEET) in Australia in 1987 produced a major 'implementation arm' for federal ministers. Under the incumbent minister's direction, DEET established priorities consonant with political priorities and, in many cases, was able to provide substantial funding to ensure that specific and visible outcomes were achieved. The current national agency has been renamed the Department for Education, Science and Training.

Media

The media, through newspapers and television, have become increasingly influential over the last decade, due in no small measure to the fact that the topic of education is very newsworthy. Some daily newspapers provide regular education supplements, while all newspapers run major feature articles on specific issues from time to time.

The news media rarely deal fully with complex issues involved in education, yet the complexity is precisely what curriculum decision-makers must deal with if their decisions are to be soundly based. Often, therefore, news media create unrealistic expectations among the public about education, while at other times picking up and heightening unrealistic expectations that the public already holds. In either case, the news media indirectly exert influence on curriculum decision-makers because of what they have chosen to report about education and how they have chosen to report it. New sources of news via the Internet also include these biases (Futoran et al., 1995).

Educational consultants

Educational consultants are specialists who are involved in discussing current or potential problems of a class, department or school. In some cases they may be seconded teachers, located in regional or head offices of systems and available on call to assist classroom teachers. Other consultants may include university lecturers and management personnel external to the system. Consultants have the potential to be very influential for individual teachers or groups of teachers at particular schools because they can pass on a variety of professional skills relating to such areas as curriculum development, management, pastoral care.

Lobby groups

Lobby groups are always present in society but become very active and conspicuous when controversy arises over particular topics or policies. The media are always eager to publicize the actions of lobby groups because of their newsworthy nature. Kirst and Walker (1971) contend that there are two kinds of policy-making processes undertaken by lobby groups: normal policy-making and crisis policy-making. The day-to-day activities of lobby groups do not gain media attention but the crisis activities certainly do. Lobby groups can be very influential on school curriculum matters.

The courts

In a number of countries, but especially in the USA, court cases involving teachers, students and parents are becoming very common (Fischer *et al.*, 1995). In the USA court judges have made decisions about curriculum such as the mandating of specific tasks, methods and materials that schools must use (McNeil, 1985).

Research and testing organizations

Large research and testing organizations that are involved in developing and have responsibility for major educational tests have a major influence on curriculum. In the USA testing agencies such as the Educational Testing Service (ETS) have largely produced a 'national' curriculum (McNeil, 1985). Standardized tests for college admission have a major influence on what teachers present to students at the senior secondary school level. National standardized reading and mathematics tests greatly influence the content of the elementary (primary) school curriculum.

In the United Kingdom, the National Foundation for Educational Research (NFER) has played a similar role in the provision of testing and its association with the monitoring of student performance through the Assessment of Performance Unit (APU), set up in 1974. Yet, because standardized testing is far less an educational preoccupation in the United Kingdom, the NFER has had less influence on schools than the ETS.

The Australian Council of Educational Research has developed into a major influence upon curriculum through its research projects on schooling (for example King, 1998; McGaw *et al.*, 1992); its single-handed validation of national profiles in the eight learning areas (Marsh, 1994); its subsequent development of computer-aided teacher development packages for using the national profiles (Forster, 1994); and its leadership in sponsoring major curriculum seminars and conferences.

In addition, in many countries there are numerous research organizations that undertake public opinion surveys on educational topics (for example Gallup polls in the USA; Drake, 1991) and are successful in tendering for major government-sponsored contracts on specific educational issues (for example the Institute of Public Affairs; Nahan and Rutherford, 1993).

Commercial sponsorship/contracting out

In a period of privatization and corporate sponsorship, schools are becoming increasingly involved in sponsorship arrangements with private industry. To a certain extent, schools have always been involved in seeking sponsorship support from the local community – for example local firms advertising in the school magazine or paying for the printing of a programme for a school sporting event.

The opportunities and necessity for sponsorship have widened considerably. It is no longer a matter of gaining sponsorship to acquire resources or to supplement ongoing minor expenditure. For some schools it is rapidly becoming their life-blood. It is very evident that sponsors have the potential to greatly influence the curriculum of a school. Long-term sponsorships could be very helpful and produce a positive commitment from the staff and local community, so long as the integrity of the school and its goals are not compromised (Harty, 1990).

Concluding comments

The above listing of decision-makers, stakeholders and influences is derived from the assumption that spheres of influence are greatest at the school level or state/national level. This is, of course, a highly simplified account of what really happens.

Walker (1990) contends that a better understanding of stakeholders is obtained if consideration is given to the 'needs' and their potential areas of 'control'. For example, school principals need support from teachers and resources; their controls include subject offerings, school timetable, access to parents and community. A Secretary of Education (Federal Minister for Education) needs political support, compliance from states and districts and expertise; controls include federal budget, federal grants, authority of position.

The interactions among the many groups and individuals, arenas and decisions can become quite complex and produce unexpected results. New coalitions of groups keep on occurring. Success factors in one period and in a particular context do not necessarily provide success at other times and in other contexts.

Reflections and issues

1 Within your situation which agencies/groups appear to have the greatest influence on the school curriculum? Give reasons for your answer.
2 The dominant role of textbooks as a primary factor in the planning of the curriculum is further illustrated by the ways in which citizens and public agencies seek to control the choice of textbooks used. Discuss.
3 To what extent is it legitimate for politicians to make decisions about schooling? Are there other significant stakeholders? How can they co-exist? Give examples to support your argument.

4 Consider the impact of national/federal versus state initiatives in curriculum. Which have been the most significant for you in your situation? Explain.

5 Describe a recent alliance by two or more stakeholders associated with an innovatory curriculum or curriculum policy. Why do you think the alliance occurred? How successful has it been? Give reasons.

6 'School children are for sale to the highest bidder ... Today's corporations are slicker, more sophisticated in their marketing strategies than they were a decade ago. Intrusions into the classroom by business interests continue unabated' (Harty, 1990, p. 77). Have schools been exploited by these initiatives? Give examples that have occurred in your community. What checks and balances would you advocate?

7 How might greater harmony be developed between competing stakeholders on matters of curriculum? Choose two or more stakeholders and give examples to illustrate your argument.

8 'Much of the information the media offers about education comes from single troubled schools in large cities' (Drake, 1991, p. 57). Do the media provide a balanced picture of schooling? If not, what steps might be taken to provide a more balanced coverage?

Web sources

Ministerial Council on Education, Employment, Training and Youth Affairs (MCEE-TYA), http://www.mceetya.edu.au/mceetya/default.asp?id = 11318 – extracted November 2007.

Council of Australian Governments (COAG), http://www.coag.gov.au – extracted November 2007.

Students as Decision-Makers, http://www.soundout.org/decision-making.html – extracted November 2007.

Data Driven Decision Making, http://3d2know.org/ – extracted November 2007.

Parents the Final Decision Makers, http://www.ccrl.ca/index.php?id = 364 – extracted November 2007.

Chapter 17

Teachers as researchers

Action research and lesson study

Introduction

Esposito and Smith (2006) use the phrase 'from reluctant teacher to empowered teacher-researcher' in their paper to describe participants involved in
action research. Their phrase could also be used most appropriately to
describe the benefits of lesson study.

According to Calhoun (2002) action research is about seeking to understand
and acting on the best we know. As professionals, teachers want to grow – to
develop new insights, skills and practices (Elliott and Chan, 2002). Stigler and
Hiebert (1999) are equally positive about lesson study – they argue that teachers need to learn how to analyse practice – both other teachers' practice and
their own. This is the benefit of lesson study. Teachers from a single school
collaborate on planning single lessons, which are then observed and critically
reviewed (Watanabe, 2002).

Some basic terms

Stenhouse (1975) referred to action research as a self-reflexive process that is
systematic and public. Kemmis and McTaggart (1984) describe action research
'as a method for practitioners to live with the complexity of real experience,
while at the same time, striving for concrete improvement' (p. 6). Calhoun has
a wider definition indicative of her interest in school-wide and district-wide
action research:

> [action research] asks educators to study their practice and its content,
> explore the research base for ideas, compare what they find to their cur-
> rent practice, participate in training to support needed changes, and study
> the effects on themselves and their students and colleagues.
>
> (Calhoun, 2002, p. 18)

According to Wallace (1987), action research originated in the USA and its
name was coined by Collier in 1945. It can be traced to Lewin's (1948) studies

of the impact of change on community workers, originally referred to as action-training-research. Subsequently, other educators such as Corey (1953) used action research with groups of teachers to improve their schools through democratic means. Although action research was largely forgotten by educators in the 1960s, it was revived in the 1970s as a result of the efforts of Stenhouse (1973) and Elliott (1975) in the United Kingdom and Clark (1976) and Tikunoff *et al.* (1978) in the USA and Kemmis and McTaggart (1984) and Grundy (1982) in Australia.

This revival continued in the 1980s and 1990s and is still ongoing in the twenty-first century in the United Kingdom (Elliott, 1999; McKernan, 1998; McNiff *et al.*, 2003), the USA (Feldman *et al.*, 1999; Noffke, 1997; Calhoun, 2002), Canada (Clandinin, 1986; Hannay and Seller, 1998) and Australia (Brooker *et al.*, 2000; Kemmis, 2006).

Action research can be conducted entirely by individual teachers, by small groups of teachers, or by school-wide or district-wide groups. Lam (2005) and Calhoun (2002) note that action research over recent years has changed from individual, self-inquiry studies for teachers towards a more institutionalized formal practice for schools. Action research is now widely used with pre-service teacher education groups (Price, 2001; Esposito and Smith, 2006; El-Dib, 2007).

Frequently, 'external facilitators' are invited to enhance the processes. Bello (2006) noted that setting a collaborative action research project in motion can be very difficult for a school staff. External facilitators can help greatly with the initial negotiations and in supporting the change process (Warrican, 2006).

There is evidence that without ongoing support from facilitators, teachers find it difficult to sustain their action research. Calhoun (2002) argues that district-wide action research projects can benefit from multiple sources of data as an information source to guide practice. Adequate organizational support (for example externally run workshops, external technical assistance) and external knowledge bases can greatly assist action research teams.

Action research involves groups of teachers, or pre-service teachers, in systematically analysing educational problems of concern to them, planning programmes, enacting them, evaluating what they have done and then repeating the cycle if necessary. As such, action research is very much central to the approaches to curriculum planning and development taken by progressive educators throughout the twentieth century and currently. First, they identify a field of action. (The implementation of an innovative curriculum might fall within this field.) Next, they develop and then enact a specific plan. Throughout the steps of development and enactment the teachers continuously monitor what they are thinking and doing: observing, reflecting, discussing, learning and replanning. Eventually they evaluate what they have enacted in some kind of formal sense, using what they have discovered as the basis for revising plans and actions as they repeat the spiral (see Figure 17.1).

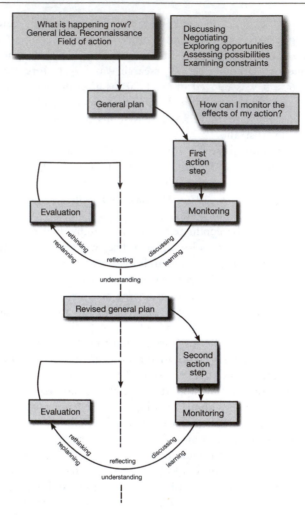

Figure 17.1 The action research spiral.

Making a start with action research

Kemmis and McTaggart (1984, pp. 18–19) suggest that participants in action research should commence by 'addressing questions' such as:

• What is happening now?
• In what sense is this problematic?
• What can I do about it?

And then go on to consider:

- How important is the issue to me?
- How important is it to my students?
- What opportunities are there to explore the area?
- What are the constraints of my situation?

To do action research, according to Kemmis and MacTaggart (1988), a person or group must undertake four fundamental processes or 'moments':

1 Develop a 'plan' of action to improve what is already happening: it must be forward looking; it must be strategic in that risks have to be taken.
2 'Act' to implement the plan: it is deliberate and controlled; it takes place in real time and encounters real constraints; it may involve some negotiations and compromises.
3 'Observe' the effects of action in the context in which it occurs: it is planned; it provides the basis for critical self-reflection; it must be open-minded.
4 'Reflect' on these effects as a basis for further planning and a succession of cycles: it recalls action; it comprehends the issues and circumstances; it judges whether the effects were desirable.

Although these fundamental processes are useful in describing likely phases of action, McKernan (1998) argues that teachers need additional assistance in selecting techniques for collecting data (see Box 17.1). For example, teachers can choose from a range of observational techniques (for example unstructured observation in a classroom by a teacher colleague) or non-observational techniques (for example getting students in a class to complete a questionnaire; McNiff *et al.*, 2003). Alternatively, a group of teachers might decide to get technical assistance from an external consultant in collecting appropriate data, especially product-centred data. A practical/collaborative approach might focus more upon process-oriented data.

Other complexities about action research

Action research cannot simply be characterized as following the basic steps of a spiral. There are additional points to consider. Feldman *et al.* (1999) contend that action research is located in a three-dimensional space, the three dimensions being purpose, theoretical orientation and types of reflection. This can be a useful way of seeing how purposes are linked to approaches and to the extent and depth of reflection undertaken.

Purposes dimension

There can be a variety of purposes for action research, including:

- professional purposes, including staff development;
- promoting school reform (Hursh, 1995);
- reforming teacher education and increasing the problem-solving skills of pre-service teachers (Price and Vallie, 2000);
- changing teaching practice (Burnaford *et al.*, 1996);
- personal purposes to better understand self and others (Noffke, 1997);
- political purposes – to critique the nature of teachers' work and workplaces (Noffke, 1997);
- to create social change (Carr and Kemmis, 1986).

As noted above there has been an increased use of action research for system-wide reform and in pre-service teacher education programmes.

Theoretical orientation dimension

Theoretical orientations in action research can also vary and there can be various combinations of the three types outlined below.

Technical

- directed by a person or persons with special expertise;
- the aim is to obtain more efficient practices as perceived by the directors;
- the activities are product-centred;
- operates within existing values and constraints.

Box 17.1: Techniques available to teachers

Observational

- unstructured observation in a classroom by a teacher colleague
- participant observation
- structured observation using checklists or rating scales by the teacher or a teacher colleague
- anecdotal records completed by the teacher or a teacher-colleague
- short case study accounts of a project or an event
- keeping a diary or journal
- photographs, videotape recording, audio recording

Non-observational

- attitude scales completed by students
- questionnaires completed by students
- interviews of selected students
- document analysis.

This orientation is towards control.

Practical/collaborative

- directed by the group;
- the aim is to develop new practices;
- the activities are process-oriented;
- personal wisdom is used to guide action.

This orientation is based upon consensus and is commonly cited in the literature as being most desirable (Bello, 2006; Esposito and Smith, 2006).

Emancipatory

- directed by the group;
- the aim is to develop new practices and/or change the constraints;
- involves a shared radical consciousness.

This orientation arises from a critical perspective. Various writers argue that postmodern stances are needed where knowledge in action research is treated as an object of speculative thinking (Elliott, 2002). Kemmis (2006), a strong supporter of this approach and an active writer in the 1980s, rues the limited use of this orientation in action research – 'it has not been the vehicle for educational critique we hoped it would be. Instead some [action research projects] may even have become a vehicle for domesticating students and teachers to conventional forms of schooling' (p. 459).

Kemmis (2006) gives further examples of action research projects which he considers are inadequate:

- those that aim only at improving techniques of teaching without examining wider questions;
- those that aim only at improving the efficiency of practices;
- those conducted solely to implement government policies;
- those that only consider the perspectives of some of the players;
- those that are conducted by people acting alone rather than in open communication.

Hooley (2005) supports an emancipatory approach, especially with indigenous groups in Australia, but considers that there is a huge struggle for legitimation of this approach. Tripp (1987) suggests that emancipatory action research is very rare because it can only occur in circumstances where a critical mass of radical participants can work together over a considerable period of time.

Type of reflection dimension

Reflection is a crucial element in action research but it is also likely to be inadequately developed in many teachers. Teachers need to develop skills to be able to interpret and understand what is happening when they do action research. Feldman *et al.*'s (1999) three types of reflection reveal a progression from individual reflection to much wider collaborative reflection, as listed below:

- individual, autobiographical reflection to examine the literal meaning of his or her stories;
- collaborative reflection – sharing personal theories;
- collaborative reflection with groups in a larger context/wider communities.

Van Manen (1977) has a similar sequence when he states that reflection can simply be applying knowledge to ascertain whether predetermined objectives at a higher level involve questioning, clarifying the objectives and the assumptions behind the teaching activities; or, at a higher level still, critically reflecting upon the larger context and considering wider moral and ethical questions. Ethical principles and practices for action research are also examined by Nolen and Putten (2007).

Capobianco and Feldman (2006) in a recent paper outline four conditions for quality collaborative research, namely:

- a community of practice in terms of a collective forum of teacher researchers who serve as critical friends;
- an epistemic community who want to create and construct knowledge about a topic;
- a thorough grounding in the nature of action research and to be able to adapt to personal, professional and political aspects that can arise;
- knowledge of appropriate research methods – knowing which methods to employ and which are most appropriate.

Limiting factors

According to Hannay and MacFarlane,

> Action research is perhaps the most demanding professional learning activity for a practitioner as it requires introspection which can challenge the individual's personal practice and beliefs. Participants engaged in action research need to have the personal confidence and system support to challenge their teaching and learning practice.
>
> (Hannay and MacFarlane, 1998, p. 36)

Carr and Kemmis (1986) identify problems of lack of autonomy and lack of emancipation as major limiting factors. However, Kemmis (2006) in a recent paper urges teacher-researchers to maintain a critical edge and to uncover 'unwelcome truths'. McKernan (1998) lists the major limiting factors as:

- lack of time to do action research;
- lack of resources;
- school organization (for example problems of timetable);
- lack of research skills and knowledge.

Impact of action research upon schools

A number of authors, such as Zeichner (1993), Cochran-Smith (1994) and Calhoun (2002), use terms such as 'overwhelming evidence', 'real power' and 'transformational qualities' when discussing action research. The many claimed advantages of action research can be summarized as follows:

1 Positive:
    - increased self-confidence for teachers;
    - feelings of empowerment;
    - greater school–staff collegiality;
    - greater willingness to experiment;
    - involved teaching practice and performance;
    - increased understanding of research processes;
    - increased practical knowledge;
    - increased understanding and reflection;
    - increased teacher autonomy.

Yet, there can be a variety of negative impacts due to barriers and impediments. These include the following:

2 Negative:
    - limited impact on school staff not directly involved;
    - limited impact because teachers are not allocated time or resources to engage in action research;
    - teachers are not free to make changes that they might feel are educationally worthwhile;
    - teachers are not skilled in examining and reflecting upon what is actually happening in classrooms – it takes considerable time to develop these skills;
    - difficulties can arise about areas of confidentiality such as who has control of materials gathered and who has access to them.

Lesson study

Lesson study is a very beneficial approach used by teachers who are interested in critically examining their classroom practice. The idea of 'lesson study' was derived from Chinese and Japanese teachers who conducted systematic and in-depth investigations into their own lessons (Matoba, Crawford Arani, 2001).

The use of lesson study has subsequently spread to many other countries, including the USA (Lewis *et al.*, 2006), Hong Kong (Lo *et al.*, 2005) and Singapore (Lee and Yanping, 2006).

Lesson study is premised on the idea that students will have a diverse range of ideas about a topic. Teachers will also have different ways of experiencing and understanding a topic. The processes involved in doing lesson study highlight ways of uncovering these differences and then producing lessons that are more viable. For example, the typical sequence is as follows:

1 A group of teachers decide to work as a team to analyse and produce better lessons for a subject/topic.
2 Students in a class are given a pre-test to find out critical elements of learning that are typically misunderstood or perceived differently.
3 The group of teachers collectively plan a lesson that they consider is more pedagogically sound and likely to be more effective with a greater number of students.
4 One teacher is selected to teach the lesson while other teachers observe.
5 The lesson is videotaped and/or other teachers make observational records.
6 The students in the class are given a post-test to ascertain their levels of understandings of the topic.
7 The total group of teachers review the lesson and make plans for revising it.
8 Another cycle begins. Several cycles may be completed before the teachers are satisfied with the lesson plans they have produced.

In a number of countries, lesson study teams have embarked enthusiastically on refining lesson plans for specific topics/subjects. It is proving to be an excellent form of professional development, both for inexperienced and experienced teachers.

A variation of lesson study developed in Hong Kong, termed 'learning study', provides a more rigorous theoretical basis for lesson study. Based upon a Theory of Variation developed by Marton and Booth (1997), it argues that teaching should be a conscious structuring act whereby the teacher actively constructs learning experiences for the students so that they can experience appropriate variations in the object of learning.

Lo (2006) and colleagues elaborated upon this theory of Variation and provided a three-phase conceptual framework. The three elements of their framework comprised the following:

• the object of learning;
• knowing as a way of seeing;
• building on three types of variation.

Object of learning

They maintained that there were three types of object of learning, namely the intended object of learning, the enacted object of learning and the lived object of learning. Lo (2006) notes that students do not always learn what is intended by the teacher: 'What is enacted by the teacher makes it possible for students to learn a particular object of learning, but what is lived by the students depends on how each individual student experiences the lesson' (p. 4).

Knowing as a way of seeing

Lo (2006) asserts that 'the range of ability of students in mainstream schools should not be so wide as to hamper them from learning what is normally expected of them' (p. 5). There are different ways of knowing and these depend on different ways of seeing the object of learning. Some aspects are critical to certain ways of understanding the object of learning, while others are not. Lo (2006) contends that 'when students do not learn it may not be due to their lack of ability but because they have not focused simultaneously on all the critical aspects and their relationships' (p. 5).

Variation

Lo and colleagues developed three aspects of variation which they considered important in learning study, namely:

- variation in terms of students understanding of what is to be taught – it is important to find out how all students recognize and address various learning issues; it is necessary to interview students before a lesson and to use a pre-test with them to diagnose possible learning difficulties;
- variation in the teachers' ways of dealing with particular topics – teachers need the opportunities to share ideas with others in the preparation meetings before doing research lessons;
- variation as a guiding principle of pedagogical design – 'Teachers should consciously make use of what has been learnt from the students and from their colleagues as inputs to decide on what aspects to focus, which aspects to vary simultaneously and which aspects to keep invariant or constant' (p. 6).

Over a period of three years, Lo (2006) and colleagues fine-tuned their approach to learning study. They were able to produce a sequence that seemed to work very well in developing a number of research lessons, namely:

1 Choosing and defining the object of learning. Is it worth learning? What kind of capabilities or new understanding do we want the student to develop? How does the learning of it link to the students' prior knowledge

and how does it fit into the curriculum? How does it relate to the students' life experience and how would the learning of it contribute to students' learning in future?

2   Identifying the critical aspects of the object of learning.
3   Identifying students' learning difficulties.
4   Learning from other teachers and researchers.
5   Formulating the lesson plan.
6   Teaching the research lesson.
7   Evaluating the research lesson.
8   Dissemination of information of the learning study.

Over the three-year period of the project a total of twenty-nine learning studies were carried out in the subjects of mathematics, Chinese language, general studies and English language in two project schools. The research data revealed that in twenty-four out of the twenty-seven learning studies the research lessons brought about a positive effect on the performance of the whole group.

Positive aspects of lesson study

The positive aspects are as follows:

- teachers can focus on specific elements of a lesson and advise practical alternatives;
- teachers learn from the students in trying to find out the nature of the potential difficulties;
- teachers work with other teachers and learn from them;
- teachers receive practical feedback on the level of success of specific lessons;
- students are likely to be more engaged and will achieve at higher levels.

Negative aspects of lesson study

There are also some negative aspects, namely:

- it is a very time-consuming process for teachers;
- not all teachers will be sufficiently motivated to work on the set phases;
- the focus is specifically on teacher-directed activities and there is little opportunity for student-initiated activities in a lesson.

Concluding comments

Although action research is complex and involves a number of tensions, there is considerable evidence from many countries that it is a successful vehicle for educational change. Over recent years it is also evident that lesson study encourages teachers to be researchers and to cater for individual differences in classrooms more successfully.

Reflections and issues

1   To what extent do you consider that school-based curriculum development (SBCD) has encouraged action research initiatives? If you have been involved recently in SBCD describe your experiences in this regard.

2   'Action research provides a way of working which links theory and practice into the one whole: ideas-in-action' (Kemmis and McTaggart, 1984, p. 5). From your experience does this happen? Give details.

3   Action research involves values and norms of behaviour. What are the rights and responsibilities of participants in action research? Can this cause unrealistic demands or expectations on the part of participants/ administrators?

4   'Emancipatory action research is essentially a political act – to change the consciousness of and constraints for those other than the immediate participants' (Tripp, 1987, p. 11). To what extent can action research transform practices, understandings and situations?

5   'One of the characteristics of action research is that it is research which people get on with and do quickly ... Academics are watchers of the world: teachers are actors in it. Teachers make decisions and search for "right" decisions' (Bassey, 1990, p. 161). Comment upon how action research differs from traditional academic research. What are its strengths and limitations compared with academic research?

6   'Action research stands or falls by its demonstrable relevance to the practical ethic of education, as well as whether it is reliable, valid and refutable as a methodology' (Adelman, 1989, p. 177). Have published studies demonstrated the relevance of action research? Is it difficult to prove the quality (reliability, validity) of action research? What solutions can you offer to this dilemma?

7   'Action research provides the necessary link between self-evaluation and professional development' (Winter, 1989, p. 10). Explain why reflection and self-evaluation are so important to action research. Should action research lead to actual changes in practice? If so, does this provide professional development for teachers?

8   'To place the teachers' classroom practice at the centre of the action for action researchers is to put the most exposed and problematic aspect of the teachers' world at the centre of scrutiny and negotiation' (Goodson, 1991, p. 141). Do you agree that it could be undesirable to start a collaborative mode of research from a study of classroom practice? Are teachers sensitive

to these studies? Are there advantages which outweigh the possibility of exposing teacher vulnerability?

9 The duty of action researchers is to uncover unwelcome or uncomfortable news about schooling (Kemmis, 2006). Can action research be used as a vehicle for educational critique? Give examples to support or refute this stance.

10 The tools that action researchers use to collect and analyse data are a crucial element (Wenbergren and Ronnerman, 2006). Describe some common tools that are used by action researchers and their relative usefulness.

11 Lesson study may be useful for individual teachers to improve their teaching skills but it has limited generalizability. Is this the case? What patterns can be generalized from lesson studies?

12 'Learning study encourages the teacher to take a research stance in teaching – instead of trying to apply theory to practice, theory and practice become one' (Lo *et al.*, 2005, p. 147). Is this what typically happens? What steps are necessary to support a research stance?

Web sources

Action Research, www.cudenver.edu/∼mryder/itc/act-res.html – retrieved 26 September 2007.

Action Research, www.scu.ed.au/schools/gcm/at/arhome.html/ – retrieved 26 September 2007.

Goshen College Action Research, http://www.goshen.edu/soan/soan96p.htm – retrieved 26 September 2007.

What Is Lesson Study? www.tc.edu/lessonstudy/lessonstudy.htm/ – retrieved 26 September 2007.

Lesson Study Group at Mills College, lessonresearch.net/ – retrieved 26 September 2007.

Lesson Study Project, www.uwlax.edu/sotl/ls/ – retrieved 26 September 2007.

Chapter 18

Parent–teacher participation

Introduction

There is widespread support among educators and the community for the notion that parents have a major role to play in education and in schooling in particular (Cavarretta, 1998). What is more difficult to get agreement upon is how to nurture a collaborative relationship between parents and teachers at a school site to enhance students' learning. There are various interpretations about activities that are perceived to be effective. Hayes and Chodkiewiez (2006) contend that the 'interface between schools and communities is a boundary that contains and excludes while affording limited views across it' (p. 3). Those positioned on opposite sides of this interface (teachers on one side and parents on the other) 'have limited opportunities for dialogue and for understanding each other' (p. 3).

Katyal and Evers (2007) provide a provocative comment when they state that '[t]he new reality of education is that schools are no longer the primary learning sites, at least for more senior students, and students view homes that are wired as the place where they learn in a meaningful manner' (p. 74). If this is the emerging pattern, then it will create different relationships between teachers and parents.

Some basic terms

The ways that parents work with schools can vary enormously. For many parents their role is of limited involvement via attendance at the following:

- parent–teacher nights;
- school sports days;
- fetes;
- tuck shops;
- working bees, in the USA;
- parents and citizens/parents and friends meetings;
- school council meetings.

McGilp and Michael (1994) sum up types of parental involvement in the following terms: 'as audience, spectators, fund raisers, aides, organizers, instructors, learners, policy makers, decision makers and advocates of school happenings' (p. 2).

As noted by Vick (1994), parents are usually on the sidelines when it comes to their children's education. 'Involvement' means very limited opportunities whereby parents undertake activities that have been designed and initiated by the school principal and staff. 'Participation' is to do with sharing or influencing decisions on policy matters and includes an active decision-making role in such areas as school policy, staffing and professional development of staff, budget, grounds and buildings, management of resources and the school curriculum. Participation can involve students too, especially at the secondary school.

Claims and counterclaims about parent participation

A major reason for parent participation in schools is a powerful pedagogical one: 'the closer the parent is to the education of the child, the greater the impact on child development and education achievement' (Fullan, 1991, p. 227). Of course this is a gross generalization and, although many educators support it, there have been a number of recent studies which have disputed it. For example, Mattingly, Prislin, McKenzie, Rodriguez and Kayzar (2002) analysed evaluations of forty-one parent involvement programs in the USA and they concluded that there was no 'substantial evidence to indicate a causal relationship' (p. 472). Domina's study (2005) noted that parental involvement did not independently improve children's learning but some involvement activities did prevent behavioural problems.

There are likely to be all kinds of variations related to the age and gender of students and cultural, ethnic and class differences.

Some claims in favour of parent participation include the following (see Box 18.1):

Box 18.1　Claims in favour of parent participation

- Parent participation will generally lead to improved student learning, intellectually, socially and emotionally.
- It increases the richness and variety of the school learning environment because of a wide range of skills that can be provided by parents.
- It increases the sense of identity for the local school community.
- It enables parents to understand education processes more fully and to support the goals of schooling.
- By increasing the number of interest groups involved in education it increases the likelihood that the interests of all students will be taken into account.

- Parents are also teachers and can and should support the teaching that goes on in classrooms. Parents have their own curriculum and teaching styles that are used in out-of-school learning situations (and in increasing numbers they are choosing home schooling; Finn, 1998). Hence there is a need for close collaboration between parents and teachers if children are to gain the full potential from their in-school and out-of-school learning experiences (Epstein and Salinas, 2004).
- Parents possess a variety of skills, talents and interests that can enrich the curriculum in so many ways beyond the capabilities of any one classroom teacher, no matter how talented he or she happens to be (Stevenson, 1998). Having a number of parents as active participants in a school will create a multiplier effect because of the energies, enthusiasm and motivation generated by these additional adults (Lee and Bowen, 2006).
- If parents become involved in schools they begin to understand the complexities of the teaching roles and structures. Too often parents are swayed by media accounts that frequently present derogatory accounts about schools, teachers and students (Dodd, 1998). If parents can experience at first hand the complicated issues that can arise in the school environment they are less likely to be influenced by superficial media accounts (see Table 18.1). As a specific example, research studies have demonstrated that when parents are employed as paid teacher-aides in a school, they have more positive attitudes about schooling and their children attending the same school develop better attitudes towards their work (Melaragno *et al.*, 1981).
- Parents have a democratic right and responsibility to further their children's education in whatever ways they can (Allen, 1990).

From time to time innovative attempts are made to provide for more democratic decision-making. For example, in the UK in 2005, a radical white paper outlined a plan by the British government to allow every primary and secondary school to become an independent entity run by 'trusts' of parents, businesses, faith groups and charities (ASCD, 2005). In the US a National Network of School Learning Communities was established in 1996. The network provides assistance to individual schools to customize and improve their programmes of family and community involvement (Epstein and Salinas, 2004).

Parent participation on school councils and in the general governance of a school contributes to student learning at that school. However, research evidence undertaken in the USA (Bowles, 1980) and the United Kingdom (Mortimer *et al.*, 1988) did not find any empirical support for this contention.

There are also a number of counter-claims about why parents should not participate actively in school decision-making (see Box 18.2), namely:

- Schools are dominated by middle-class norms. In schools where there is active participation by parents, these tend to be articulate, well-educated

Table 18.1 Continuum of parent participation

One-way information giving	Reporting progress	Special events	Sharing of ideas	Parent assistance at school in non-instruction	Parent assistance at school in instruction	Governance	Interaction partnerships
Notices sent home Posters	Home-school notebooks Call-in times Newsletters Telephone calls	Picnics Art shows Concerts Open days Tuckshops Working bees	Seminars Classroom observation days Informal discussions	Playground Assistance on excursions Liaison with local business Organizing sports days Preparing art material	Guest speakers Leaderson school camps Teaching various skills	Chairing subcommittees Members of school council	Specific parent-teacher working groups

Box 18.2: Claims against parent participation

- Many parents do not have the necessary problem-solving and communication skills to be effective participants.
- Many parents make conscious decisions not to participate and as a result a small number of articulate parents can monopolize the decision-making.
- School staff are sometimes reluctant or opposed to parent participation activities.
- Governments have not devolved professional authority to parents and the community – the rhetoric is stronger than the reality.
- Parents are being encouraged to be individual consumer-citizens and to see schooling as another product in the marketplace.

parents. Parents who cannot speak English, who have difficulty communicating well in groups, or who are poorly educated, are usually not represented (Cohn-Varas and Grose, 1998). That is, a significant number of parents are poorly equipped to be active participants in school decision-making (Power and Clark, 2000).

- Some parents from non-dominant groups may encounter psychological barriers to involvement at school – they lack confidence in their interactions with the education system (Reay, 1999).
- McGowan (2005) provides an interesting argument that the neo-liberal strategy by education authorities to have community run schools might appear to be liberal but it puts more pressure on parents to be responsible for a range of school-level decisions.
- It places additional burdens of time on the teachers. There is more likelihood that parents will be contacting teachers during outside school hours – teachers could be constantly on call to various demands, both trivial and important, and teacher exhaustion and 'burn-out' is a very real problem. It is small wonder that research studies indicate that only a minority of teachers in schools have goals and programmes for parent participation. For example, Rosenholtz's (1989) study showed that the majority of teachers were in 'stuck' schools rather than 'moving' schools. Teachers from 'stuck' schools held no goals for parent participation, while teachers in 'moving' schools 'focussed their efforts on involving parents with academic content, thereby bridging the learning chasm between home and school' (p. 152). In another study Becker (1981) surveyed 3,700 primary school teachers and 600 principals and concluded that 'very few appear to devote any systematic effort to making sure that parental involvement at home accomplishes particular learning goals in a particular way' (p. 22).
- Parents and community members should not be active participants because it leads to a reduction in the professional responsibilities of teachers.

- No teacher's school or work should be in any way controlled by the decisions of any non-professional or unpaid body or person, except with the teacher's concurrence. (NSW Teachers Federation, 1976, as reported in Hunt, 1981, p. 4)
- An Australian Council of Educational Research (ACER) survey of over 7,000 school stakeholders which culminated in the report 'Making Schools more Effective' (McGaw et al., 1992), revealed some opposition by school respondents to parent participation, namely: 'The principal concern was that inappropriate roles for lay people were being envisaged and pressed on schools and that this development undervalued the professional role and contribution of teachers' (p. 94).
- Parents are being increasingly perceived by governments to be 'consumer-citizens' (Woods, 1988). That is, parents operate largely as individual consumers in making decisions about schooling and schooling practices for their children. They rarely share school-related interests with other parents or lack the opportunity to do so. They do not constitute a monolithic group. Individualism and difference (in priorities, preference, philosophy) characterize the consumer-citizens (Woods, 1988, p. 328).

A continuum of parent participation

Various accounts in the educational literature refer to 'tapping parent power' and 'effective parent participation in schooling'. A number have been written by individual enthusiasts or vested interest groups and so their laudatory comments are not surprising (for example Morris, 1992; Gamage, 1992; Meadows, 1993; Scherer, 1998). To provide a balanced picture it is useful to distinguish between the different activities/roles that might be undertaken by parents and depict them on a continuum (Pomerantz et al., 2007) (see Table 18.1). The activities range from 'one way information giving' to 'interactive partnerships' and there are a myriad possible positions in between these two extremes of passive and active.

The examples listed in the second column of the continuum in Table 18.1 are simply 'reporting progress' to parents. Variations of this category can include parent–teacher conferences. These face-to-face meetings can be most satisfying to the parent and to the teacher, but few parents tend to take advantage of this opportunity because of their busy daily schedule or their reticence about appearing personally at the school (MacLure and Walker, 2000). Teachers will often complain that the parents they really need to meet to discuss urgent school problems do not come to parent–teacher conferences.

Home–school notebooks are another interesting variation whereby a parent and a teacher correspond with each other in a notebook that is sent regularly between the two participants. It requires, of course, a substantial commitment of time by both parties and a willingness to maintain a regular schedule. Yet it does have the potential for keeping contact between the teacher and parents and is a reasonably effective and time-saving alternative to face-to-face meetings.

In addition, teachers are likely to request that parents become involved in a number of learning activities with their children at home (e.g. giving reading assistance and listening to reading, home tutoring in other subjects). Research studies have demonstrated that teacher requests to parents for assistance are likely to be far more effective if individualized instructions and/or training are provided and if there are mechanisms for monitoring parents' and children's progress in the home instruction (Fullan, 1991; Finn, 1998).

Special events for parents are depicted in the third column of Table 18.1. These can take various forms, including parent evenings, open days, concerts and plays. Such events enable teachers to demonstrate certain special student skills (for example dance routines, art work), but they also provide an opportunity for teachers and parents to interact socially. Special occasions like these can enable a positive rapport to be developed between individual parents and a teacher.

Fund-raising activities have also been included under 'special events', although some parents might prefer to describe them as 'special chores'! Resources are always scarce in any school – funds are always needed to purchase additional library books or sporting equipment or microcomputers. Parents are usually very willing to be involved in fund-raising activities such as school fetes, jumble sales, cake stalls and managing a school canteen if they can see that the funds generated will provide additional resources that will benefit their children. However, it is very limited if this is the only contact that parents have with their school. Fortunately, the availability of national funds in the form of direct grants to schools rather than subsidy schemes has to some extent reduced the need for parent organizations to devote most of their energies to fund-raising.

Sharing of ideas, as indicated in the fourth column in Table 18.1, typically takes the form of informal discussions, special seminars and workshops (Gorman and Balter, 1997). The seminars, in particular, if held on the weekends or in the evenings, can be valuable occasions for parents and school staff to share ideas about school goals, values analysis, sex/AIDS education, mathematics skills, etc.

Parents can be involved in assisting school staff with a number of non-instructional activities. At the primary school level, in particular, parents are in considerable demand to assist as additional supervisors for excursions and visits. If handled sensitively by the school principals, developing a group of volunteer parents for these activities can establish strong links between them and their school. More and more, parents are being sought to assist school staff with a number of instructional activities (see Table 18.1). To a certain extent, changes in employment patterns and resultant early retirement and redundancy packages have enabled parents to become available and willing to take on some of these tasks (Halstead, 1994).

In the junior primary school, parents are often sought after to assist with reading and miming stories to small groups of children and also to assist with various art and craft activities. As noted by Comer (2005), it is important to give parent volunteers meaningful tasks that they are capable of accomplishing and to place them with compatible staff members. Parents possess a wide range of specialist skills that can be a welcome and varied addition to the school curriculum (Hoover-Dempsey *et al.*, 2005).

Governance activities by parents are in the penultimate column in Table 18.1. Many school councils/boards make major decisions about staffing, school building, resources and curriculum for their school. No outstandingly successful prototype for school councils has yet been found. Various combinations of membership, functions and legal status have been initiated, but these initial versions are often found to be unsuitable and different versions have replaced them.

Intended practices and actual outcomes

To date there have been few accounts in the literature about how parents operate within school communities. It is therefore not known what percentage of parent communities operate at the different points on the continuum depicted in Table 18.1. For example, there have been some accounts of successful governance by school councils (Gamage, 1993; Knight, 1995) but they are relatively few in number. Some parents maintain social networks with other parents, which can lead to very active participation at a local school (Sheldon, 2002).

It may be that only small numbers of parents are involved in the other categories listed in Table 18.1. Although governments establish structures for parent participation in schools by legislation there are enormous difficulties in bringing about a relocation of power and in many instances 'toothless tigers' have been established (Pettit, 1987).

The problem is multifaceted, and the blame does not lie solely with any one group. It is true that there are difficulties for parents, many of whom venture into the school environment with various anxieties, are considerably overwhelmed and are often poorly informed about typical school activities.

According to Power and Clark (2000), the problems that parents experience are not imaginary: 'Their sense of frustration, and often humiliation, of consultations with teachers is genuinely felt' (p. 44).

An area of major concern in Australia is Aboriginal parents and the extent to which their views and concerns are acted upon by school administrators. McInerney's (1989) study noted that Aboriginal parents (despite negative media portrayals) hold positive attitudes towards education. A typical Aboriginal response was '[w]ithout proper schooling our children have no future' (p. 47). Yet these parents were also concerned about negative consequences of attending school, such as the following:

- my child receives no praise or support from school;
- my child is ridiculed by others;
- even if my child does well at school he still can't get work.

McTaggart (1984) notes that '[p]arents' knowledge of what goes on in schools tends to be restricted to the treatment of educational problems given by the media ... The images are both incomplete and confrontationist' (p. 12).

For parents of lower socio-economic backgrounds, the problem is especially severe (Zady et al., 1998; Mutimer, 1999). They often perceive the school council to be an appendage of the principal, espousing traditional middle-class values. They often consider that the problems of their immediate neighbourhood are not translated into programmes at the school. These parents need special encouragement and support before they will become regular participants in the school community. Andrews (1985, p. 30) maintains that the typical response from such parents tends to be 'Every other time I've complained or spoken out too much, my kid has been picked on' or 'It doesn't affect my kid, she or he is doing OK'.

Teachers' language to the lay person can be almost incomprehensible. Not surprisingly, teachers receive new training in the academic disciplines and theory-building of various kinds and as a result of interaction with their peers establishes their educational jargon. This is particularly evident when teachers are asked to explain to parents why a child is not coping with a subject. In many cases, teachers use technical terms that lay persons simply cannot understand. MacLure and Walker (2000) contend that the discourse between teachers and parents is rather like the discourse between doctors and patients. The teacher is in control, chooses the topics of discussion and dominates the interaction.

Perhaps all stakeholder groups are to blame for building up their unique set of language modes, norms and expectations. Parents can certainly build up their barriers around their family life, interests and ambitions (Kenway et al., 1987). These barriers take a considerable amount of time and goodwill to break down. Boomer (1986) refers to this as a kind of '[e]ducational apartheid ... they develop their own special forms of protection; an array of the equivalent of moats, barricades, deflection and passwords' (Boomer, 1986, p. 1).

In the final analysis, it is likely that all stakeholders need skills training if they are to communicate effectively with each other. This is especially the case for parents and teachers.

Training needs

Parents

Although some parents, as a result of their schooling and professional activities, are highly articulate, enthusiastic and very capable of participating in school decision-making, there are many who are not (McGilp and Michael, 1994; Sheldon, 2002). The majority of parents do need assistance in such matters as knowledge of the educational system and interpersonal and communication skills (Zady et al., 1998).

Many parents do not have a clear idea of the education system in which their local school operates (Hughes and Greenhough, 1998). They need information about the various levels of the hierarchy and the respective powers and functions of head office, regions and individual school principals. In particular, parents need to know the kinds of activities that a principal and his or her staff can initiate and maintain at a local school level, and to have an awareness of the constraints and monitoring procedures used by head office officials.

Training needs for many parents are most evident in the areas of inter-personal and communication skills (MacLure and Walker, 2000). Experienced parent participants need to be able to break down the apathy of other parents and seek out their support by informal home visits, telephone calls and parent meetings. They have to be able to develop and demonstrate empathy for the needs of the apathetic or uninvolved parent and be able to devise ways of gradually wearing down that person's resistance. They have to be able to engage parents within the parent network (Barton et al., 2004).

Parent 'drop-in centres' are becoming more widespread in schools as principals realize that the provision of a meeting place for parents is a valuable strategy for getting them more involved in school activities. A drop-in centre can enable parents to interact socially and discuss various matters relating to their school community. In so doing, it may enable parents to increase their level of confidence and skills in communicating with other adults.

Special provision needs to be made to assist parents with language difficulties. Staff with second-language expertise can be used on home visits to encourage those parents to support school affairs (Colombo, 2004). Community liaison officers can also be used to good effect to maintain regular home visits to parents. Migrant adviser services are sometimes available to offer assistance. Information booklets about the school, printed in several languages, can also be a useful measure to attract the interest of parents of migrant families.

The building up of positive attitudes toward school participation among parents is a time-consuming process and requires the concentrated efforts of many participants, including teachers, liaison officers from various departments and experienced, supportive parents/friends (Griffith, 1997; Brandt, 1998).

As noted by Pomerantz, Moorman and Litwack (2007), these strategies in total can be summarized as being 'autonomy supportive rather than controlling, process rather than person focussed, characterised by positive rather than negative affect, and accompanied by positive rather than negative beliefs about children's potential' (p. 399).

Teachers

Training for many teachers revolves around learning about and demonstrating competence in planning and executing student lessons. Few pre-service courses focus upon the role of parents in the school community, especially in terms of techniques for communicating effectively with parents. As a result, some teachers tend to make minimal use of parent assistance or, in some instances, actively resist communicating with parents (Fullan, 1991).

According to Rich (1998), if parents were given the opportunity to rate their child's teacher, the rating might be very low indeed. She argues that many teachers would score low marks for the extent to which they know and care about the children and their willingness to communicate with parents. Bauch and Goldring (2000) contend that a school that has a caring atmosphere has the greatest influence on positive relationships between teachers and parents. Hiatt-Michael (2000) argues that beginning teachers need pre-service training modules in parent involvement.

Lasky (2000) asserts that emotionality is a major factor in teacher–parent relationships. She argues that emotions are not solely internal, personal phenomena but are also social in nature. Consequently, any training of teachers must focus upon the deep-seated emotions that can cause limited interactions between a teacher and parents.

School councils

School councils/boards are an important element of schooling. Although the composition and powers of school councils vary, the membership typically consists of the principal and representatives of the staff, parents, the community and students (in the case of secondary schools).

'Alternative schools' have a major commitment to a participative democratic process, and most of them operate some kind of school council. These alternative schools have typically very small enrolments and so it is feasible for all parents, teachers and students to meet regularly and make decisions jointly about all major school issues, including the curriculum, deployment of staff and the use of resources. For a number of years, many small parish schools operating within Catholic education systems have also maintained their own local boards of management, and these have had independent control over staff appointments, school buildings and finances (including the setting of school fees).

School councils have been established in many of the large government schools and there is some evidence that progress is being made. Gamage (1993) refers to successful examples in New South Wales. Knight (1995, p. 273) describes some successes in Victoria, despite problems occurring due to a current government priority to promote 'self-managed entrepreneurial schools' versus 'democratic control of school decision-making'.

In some cases school councils can be radically powerful and can bring about rapid change (Fullan, 1991). Gamage's (1993) studies revealed that 'councils have become effective and efficient organizations, and the principals are highly satisfied and totally committed to the collaborative form of governance adopted in terms of the school council system' (p. 102).

La Rocque and Coleman's (1989) study of school councils in British Columbia and Hatch's (1998) study of Alliance Schools in the USA conclude that school councils can make a difference. School council members can develop a clear sense of what they want to accomplish and engage in activities to bring about these ends (Johnson, 2003).

Harold (1997) describes the Boards of Trustees in New Zealand and notes that they have had a pivotal role in developing partnerships between teachers and parents. Each board consists of five elected parent representatives; an elected student representative (for schools with secondary students); the principal; and an elected staff representative. Clearly, this structure allows much wider powers of decision-making to be given directly to parents. Harold (1997) concludes that Boards of Trustees are operating successfully in the majority of schools.

However, as noted by Fullan (1991), how to increase or improve the effectiveness of school councils is an unstudied problem. There are still many unanswered issues and problems, and some of these are listed in Box 18.3.

Lutz (1980) questions whether school councils really practise democratic decision-making. He argues that school council participation by parents from a local school community is very limited and sporadic; that few council members are closely involved in decision-making; and that few issues are ever made public and widely debated. It is certainly evident that for large schools it is extremely difficult for school board members to represent more than a few of the community interests. Many of the disadvantaged community groups are never represented. Yet it might be argued that democracy means the freedom to participate or not to participate and that if individuals and groups feel strongly enough about an issue then they will participate vigorously.

Questions might also be raised about whether school councils actually reduce conflicts between various interest groups or heighten the conflicts still

Box 18.3   Problems and issues for school councils

1   Do councils have real power if their control over finances is limited?
2   Are school councils really able to practise democratic decision-making?
3   Is an adequate supply of dedicated and well-informed parents and community members available to fill school council positions?
4   Does the size of a school influence the effectiveness of school councils?
5   How can school council members understand and represent all sections of a local community if they tend to be better educated and more affluent than the majority of local citizens?
6   Will school councils ever be able to represent effectively such disadvantaged groups as migrants, the unskilled, the unemployed and low income earners?
7   Do school councils really provide a structure for school principal, teachers and parents to co-exist harmoniously?
8   Do school councils in the Australian context ever get complete control over decision-making?

more (see Table 18.2). For example, Knight (1995) highlights some of the conflicts between teacher and parent members. It is possible that parents' priorities (for example school discipline, and literacy and numeracy) are likely to be different from the priorities expressed by teachers (for example providing a caring atmosphere and building student self-esteem).

Finally, questions might also be raised about whether school councils operating an education system can ever anticipate becoming fully independent from head office policies and requirements. Recent accountability measures introduced into a number of education systems would seem to indicate that centralist requirements are increasing rather than decreasing.

Concluding comments

There are promising developments and opportunities for involving parents more effectively in classrooms and schools. However, there are many differences in outlook, priorities and values between teachers and parents and so, not unexpectedly, progress has not been as rapid as might have been expected.

Reflections and issues

1 Fullan (1991) argues that parent participation at the school and classroom level is a fundamental mission of an effective school. Present arguments for and against this statement.
2 Some school council members complain that they suffer from a lack of direction, the feeling of being a rubber stamp, and parent and staff apathy. How might some of these problems be resolved?
3 'Many parents and teachers are overloaded with their own work-related and personal concerns. They also may feel discomfort in each other's presence due to lack of mutual familiarity and to the absence of a mechanism for solving the problems that arise' (Fullan, 1991, pp. 249–50). Discuss this statement. What are some practical solutions to the problem?
4 Stevenson (1998) contends that parents want to: feel confident that their children will be happy; trust teachers; and share their insights about their children with the teacher. Have you experienced parents who share these goals? What steps can you take to bring about a more productive partnership with parents?
5 MacLure and Walker (2000) contend that many of the meetings between parents and teachers are ceremonial, where both parties enact ritual performances of interest and concern. In your experience, is this a realistic assessment? How can these meetings be used more successfully for both parties?
6 To what extent do you consider that computer technology (especially e-mail) enables teachers and parents to connect more successfully with each other?

7   Hughes and Greenhough (1998) argue that the knowledge bases of parents and teachers exhibit 'difference and diversity' rather than 'superiority and deficit'. If this is the case, how might this affect communications between teachers and parents?

8   'It is important that parent governors should be the choice of parents, people that parents feel they can approach with trust and confidence' (Edwards and Redfern, 1988, p. 109). Are there difficulties in getting representative governors? What are some possible solutions?

9   Parental involvement in schools not only improves teaching and learning: it can also transform families' lives (Comer, 2005). Explain situations when this might occur. What are some limiting factors?

10 Establishing true partnerships with parents entails educators acknowledging and validating parents' views and ultimately sharing power (Cooper and Christie, 2005). Discuss.

Web sources

School Improvement Series: Parent Involvement in Education, http://www.nwrel.org/scpd/sirs/3/cu6.html – accessed 27 September 2007.

Child Trends Data Bank: Parental Involvement in Schools, http://childtrendsdatabank.org.indicators/39ParentalInvolvementinSchools.cfm – accessed 27 September 2007.

About Parenting of K-6 Children, http://childparenting.about.com/cs/parentinvolvement/ – accessed 27 September 2007.

National Education Association, Parents and Community, http://www.nea.org/parents/index.html – accessed 27 September 2007.

National Coalition for Parent Involvement in Education, http://www.ncpie.org/ – accessed 27 September 2007.

Victorian Council of School Organizations, www.vicsu.org.au – accessed 27 September 2007.

Federation of Parents and Citizens' Associations of NSW, www.pandc.org.au/ab_who.asp – accessed 27 September 2007.

Curriculum ideology

Chapter 19

Curriculum theorizing

Introduction

Pinar *et al.* (1995) argue that the days of curriculum development and curriculum policy and planning are numbered. The bureaucratic approaches to curriculum planning as exemplified by users of the Tyler (1949) approach are stifling. Writing on alternative approaches in the 1970s and subsequently in numerous books and papers, Pinar *et al.* (1995) and Pinar (2004) argue that we must move from studies of curriculum development and theory to curriculum understanding. Theorizing by Pinar (1980), Grumet (1981), Giroux (1982) and Miller (1992) has moved on many diverse fronts. Klohr (1980) considered it to be 'gritty and ragged' in the 1980s, Wright, writing in 2000, considered it to be impossible to define – like 'trying to nail Jell-O to a wall'.

Yet in the first decade of the twenty-first century curriculum theorizing is needed more than ever. Pinar (2004) argues that curriculum theorizing must continue 'to engage in complicated conversations with our academic subjects, our students and ourselves' (p. 9).

What is curriculum theorizing?

It is 'to shift focus from the end product (the curriculum theory) to the process by which a theory is sought (the process of theorizing)' (Vallance, 1982, p. 8). Although theorizers are apparently involved in activities, the outcome of which is the completion of a theory, their real involvement is actually with the processes of arriving at such an outcome. Theorizing is thus a general process involving individuals in three distinct activities:

- being sensitive to emerging patterns in phenomena;
- attempting to identify common patterns and issues;
- relating patterns to one's own teaching context.

If theorizing is defined in this way, then it can and should be undertaken by all persons with an interest in curriculum, including teachers, academics and members of the community (Brady, 1984). Teachers in their daily work attempt to become increasingly sensitive to what is significant in their own classrooms and to establish some appropriate framework or orientation to guide what they do (Schubert, 1992). Academics, even though their primary motive may be to theorize in general rather than to guide teaching specifically, still interpret their experience with specific examples or episodes of teaching and attempt to identify patterns that may prove useful in orienting actions. In this way, the traditional dichotomy of theory–practice disappears since all now become practitioners who theorize about their teaching–learning experiences.

In Chapter 3 discussion focused upon curriculum models, including an analysis of the Tyler Model (1949) and Walker's Naturalistic Model (1971). These have been found to be most useful over the years to assist curriculum workers with the processes of curriculum planning, implementation and evaluation. Some of these models might be classed as *prescriptive* – frameworks for curriculum development that improve school practice (for example Tyler, 1949; Taba, 1962). Other models attempted to *describe* and identify how curriculum development actually takes place, especially in school settings (for example Walker, 1971; Schwab, 1969).

In this chapter the focus is not on these practical models or frameworks but on efforts to understand curriculum – interdisciplinary studies of educational experience (Pinar, 2004). These diverse forms of curriculum theorizing, which will be labelled generically as 'critical-exploratory theorizers', move in diverse directions. Reynolds and Webber (2004) suggest a metaphor of lines of flight – multiplicity thinking – 'the struggle is to keep on finding lines that disrupt and overturn' (p. 4).

Critical-exploratory theorizers

A number of curriculum scholars began to grapple with new and varied understandings of curriculum in the 1970s. Pinar was a driving force in these beginnings. In 1979 he founded the *Journal of Curriculum Theorizing* (now renamed *JCT: An Interdisciplinary Journal of Curriculum Studies*), which provided an important early outlet, especially for existential/psychoanalytic and phenomenological theorizers, and which has achieved worldwide recognition. In 1983 Van Manen founded another new journal, *Phenomenology and Pedagogy*. Also beginning in the 1970s, edited collections of papers (for example Pinar, 1974, 1975; Willis, 1978) started to appear, many of which provided new theoretical perspectives. Some of these publications were the product of annual conferences, the first being held at Rochester in 1973. These JCT conferences provided a meeting ground for curriculum theorizers to explore psychological, political and cultural dimensions of curriculum. Academics who were very active in this first wave of new theorizing included Macdonald (1971), Huebner (1975), Klohr (1980), Greene (1975) and Pinar (1974, 1975). Others quickly joined in, such as Grumet (1981), Pagano (1983) and Miller (1992).

According to Pinar *et al.* (1995), these early endeavours were undertaken to create an 'intellectual breakthrough' (p. 366). Academics had been stifled by the 1960s national curriculum reform movement, and in the 1970s 'the field shifted from preoccupation with the narrow proceduralism associated with the Tyler Rationale to theoretical understanding broadly conceived' (p. 366).

Pinar (1975) was one of the first to use the term 'reconceptualist' in the 1970s to describe new forms of theorizing that were then emerging. It is still frequently used today, especially to capture the sense of exploration, but its use has created some avoidable confusion. Initially, the term proved useful, for it seemed to suggest that whatever reconceptualists stood for was new – and probably better – than what had gone before, and reconceptualists certainly were united in their opposition to the rationalistic and scientific. However, as theorizers interested in reconceptualizing the field grew in number and in influence, it became increasingly important to clarify what they did – and did not – have in common. For instance, some theorizers used philosophical analysis and methods drawn from mainstream social science, while others used case studies, biography, psychoanalytical techniques and literacy theory. Perhaps the most successful effort to map the common characteristics of reconceptualists was undertaken by Klohr (1980), who identified nine foci of their efforts:

1 A holistic, organic view is taken of people and their relation to nature.
2 The individual becomes the chief agent in the construction of knowledge; that is, he or she is a culture creator as well as a culture bearer.
3 The curriculum theorists draw heavily on their own experiential base as method.
4 Curriculum theorizing recognizes as major resources the preconscious realms of experience.
5 The foundational roots of this theorizing lie in existential philosophy, phenomenology and radical psychoanalysis; they (reconceptualists) also draw from humanistic reconceptualizations of such cognate fields as sociology, anthropology and political science.
6 Personal liberty and the attainment of higher levels of consciousness become central values in the curriculum process.
7 Diversity and pluralism are characteristics both of the social ends and of the means proposed to attain these ends.
8 A reconceptualization of supporting political-social operations is basic.
9 New language forms are generated to translate fresh meanings, for example metaphors (Klohr, 1980, p. 3).

However, a close examination of Klohr's foci reveals that some are clearly not appropriate to all reconceptualists. For example, a focus on the 'preconscious realms of experience' applies to theorists such as Pinar and Grumet, who use psychoanalytical techniques in their theorizing, but it does not apply to Apple.

Conversely, a focus on a 'reconceptualization of supporting political-social operations' applies to Apple but far less to Pinar or Huebner.

Despite these difficulties with the term 'reconceptualist' (Wraga, 2002) and terms such as 'heightened consciousness' (Nixon, 1999), it is important to be aware of its history in carrying forward new forms of curriculum theorizing that emerged in the 1970s (see, for example, Pinar *et al.*, 1995; Pinar, 2003).

Whether the endeavours over the decades since the 1970s represent a shift in basic thinking about curriculum sufficiently profound to be considered a paradigm shift in Kuhnian terms (Kuhn, 1962) is debatable. Pinar *et al.* (1995; Pinar 2008) suggest that there has been such a shift and, along with Rogan and Luckowski (1990), that the work of reconceptualists represents a paradigmatic advancement over the Tyler rationale. Brown (1988) concludes that a first approximation to a paradigm shift has been underway and that the new generation of curriculum scholars, as they gain a firm foothold in universities, will begin to challenge the received wisdom of traditional points of view.

There is certainly nothing finished or final about reconceptualism, for ideas and methods are constantly evolving. Rather, a 'proliferation of schools' (Brown, 1988, p. 28) has developed, with considerable differences among them.

Social and cultural control, social reproduction and cultural reproduction

Proponents of these approaches are all concerned about the relationship between society or culture and schooling.

Early writers were sociologists, such as Young (1971) and Bernstein (1973), who focused on forms of power and social control. Other writers who theorized about the role of schools in society developed an approach known as social reproduction. For example, Althusser (1971) argues that schools are important because they reproduce the work skills and attitudes needed for social relations in the wider society. Bowles and Gintis (1976) claim that their economic analysis shows that social relationships in schools (for example relationships between administrators and teachers, teachers and students, and students and their work) directly correspond to hierarchical divisions of labour in society. Still other writers have broadened the focus from social reproduction to cultural reproduction. They identify and analyse the links among culture, class, domination and education. Such theorizers about cultural reproduction – as exemplified by Bourdieu and Passeron (1977), Giroux (1990, 1997, 2003) and Apple (1990) – often point out how schools have served to oppress groups disadvantaged by class, race and gender and how disadvantaged groups can work to change oppressive systems of education. Although these theorizers often write from a neo-Marxist perspective, their critiques have attacked the problems of society and schooling in a variety of ways. Giroux (1982) described traditional educational theorizing as 'dancing on the surface of reality ... ignoring not only the latent principles that shape the deep grammar of the existing social order, but also those principles underlying the genesis and nature of its own logic' (p. 1). Apple suggests a number of political questions that should be asked about the legitimacy of the knowledge included in a curriculum. For example: Why and how are particular aspects of a collective culture represented in schools as objective factual knowledge? How, concretely, may official knowledge represent the ideological configurations of the dominant interest in a society? How do schools legitimate these limited and partial standards of knowing as unquestioned truths (Apple, 1990, p. 7)?

There is no doubt that these curriculum theorizers have had a considerable impact on curriculum writings. They have alerted curriculum planners and developers to a number of ingrained problems in the usual – and usually unexamined – relationship between schools and the society in which they are embedded.

Literacy artist

Under this sub-category are scholars whose approach to curriculum theorizing can be exemplified by Eisner's approach to curriculum planning. In some ways this approach is similar to the deliberate approach of the descriptive theorizers already discussed. The main difference is that the deliberations of curriculum development committees usually lead towards public meanings and group decisions, whereas literacy artists are concerned with personal experience as well (Barone, 1982; Eisner, 1991, 1994, 2002; Eisner and Vallance, 1974). Indeed, all theorizers in this sub-category emphasize to one degree or another that learning is highly personal.

Essentially, members of this group see themselves, curriculum developers, teachers, students and virtually every other person as involved in an ongoing process of making meaning in their own lives and conveying meaning to others. This process centres on personal perception and choice. In it, the curriculum is considered a medium through which individuals learn how to deepen their understanding.

Existential and psychoanalytical

Writers who do existential and psychoanalytical theorizing begin with individual experience but point to the importance of how schooling influences experience. Schools represent nature (things that exist prior to human intervention, such as physical sites and space) and culture (things that are human creations, such as beliefs and objects), but the culture of schools tends to be taken for granted. Whenever people take culture for granted, they tend to become less aware – hence, less free. Therefore we need to attend especially to those parts of culture that are not compelled directly by nature and about which we can make decisions. In particular, the task is to transform schooling that constrains human freedom (Grumet, 1981; Miller, 1992, 2000; Pinar, 2000, 1980).

To be free, people need to be aware of how they as individuals experience the world around them and, thus, how their decisions about transforming the world are related to their decisions about how to define themselves as individual persons (Reynolds, 2003).

Macdonald (1981) goes about the task by considering the issue of human liberation and how this can be achieved through curriculum studies. According to Macdonald, each of us can become more liberated. He proposes a transcendental ideology of education under which curriculum decisions can be made (Macdonald, 1981, p. 143). That ideology centres on the individual person and on the question of how all potential for each person can be realized. Pinar (1980) uses the metaphor of an educational journey for each individual and suggests that autobiographical accounts are extremely useful for attending to, and reflecting on, lived experiences of the world. Each person must elucidate his or her journey and cultivate an awareness of his or her existential freedom. In Pinar's (1980) words: 'One experiences intellectual and biographic movement ... such a capacity to risk – intellectually biographically – is a capacity we are obligated to develop' (p. 11). The curriculum should foster this journey.

These theorizers thus value techniques that put individuals in touch with their own experience yet permit them to move on. Some theorizers (for example Grumet, 1981; Miller, 1992; Pinar, 1980; Reynolds, 2003) have published sensitive and insightful autobiographical accounts of their educational experience. Also, collections of autobiographical accounts by members of the curriculum field (Goodson, 1992; Willis and Schubert, 1991) have appeared. In fact, during the 1990s a growing number of insightful case studies and narratives that connect individual experience with the characteristics of schooling in increasingly sophisticated ways were written by these theorists, often using rich and evocative imagery and metaphors and thus fulfilling Van Manen's (1978) earlier description of their work as a synthesis of poetic and novelistic approaches.

Phenomenological theorizing

Willis (1979) uses the term 'phenomenology' to refer to the lived quality of the interior experience, or 'life world', of the individual and suggests that each individual holds a personal and peculiarly human consciousness about each concrete situation experienced. Each experience includes a fusing of affective, cognitive and physiological reactions to the situation. Phenomenology attempts to get at the experience itself, the curriculum each person lives. Both Willis (1991) and Van Manen (1980) cut through some of the highly technical language of phenomenological philosophers. For instance, Van Manen indicates that phenomenology is really asking one simple question: What is it like to have a certain experience – for example an educational experience? Although it is possible to express a feeling about an experience (for example 'I feel bored'), it is very difficult to describe in detail the particulars or components of such a feeling. According to Van Manen (1990), curriculum specialists such as Tyler somehow assume that it is possible to know about and describe learning experiences because they use phrases such as 'selecting, planning and organiz-ing learning experiences'. But this is false confidence, for we do not know what it is really like when a child has an experience or when he or she comes to understand something.

Van Manen (1990, 2000) uses phenomenological theorizing to question people about the root character of their experience. For instance, teachers can be asked: What is it like to be a teacher? In what ways is a teacher different from, say, a parent? He suggests that phenomenology helps people to reflect on their actual consciousness of situations rather than on public expressions of them. It is a means by which they get to know themselves and can be achieved only by examining concrete situations, such as teaching. Phenomenological theorizing is not about testing hypotheses but getting individuals to reflect thoughtfully about what they see, feel and believe; it involves teachers in con-stantly seeking out the essence of the experience of teaching.

Autobiographical/biographical theorizing

This approach to theorizing focuses on the centrality of personal experience in the curriculum. In 1972 Pinar first wrote about his interest in the auto-biographical method. Subsequently he formulated the term 'currere' to explain his emphasis. Currere refers to an existential experience of institutional struc-tures. The method of currere is a strategy for self-reflection that enables the individual to encounter experience more fully and more clearly, as if creating a highly personal autobiography (Pinar and Grumet, 1976).

In the mid-1990s, Pinar et al. (1995) contended that autobiographical/biographical theorizing had become a major area of scholarship. They distinguished three streams of scholarship:

- autobiography that focuses on such major concepts as currere, voice, place and imagination (as developed by Connelly and Clandinin, 1988; Grumet, 1976; Kincheloe and Pinar, 1991; Meath-Lang, 1999; Miller, 1992; and Pinar, 1974);
- feminist autobiography that focuses especially on community and the reclaiming of the self (as developed by Miller, 1992, 2000; Pagano, 1990; Britzman, 1992, 2002; and Luke, 1996);
- biography that focuses on the lives of teachers, using collaborative bio-graphy, autobiographical praxis and personal practical knowledge (as developed by Butt, 1983; Connelly and Clandinin, 1990; Goodson, 1981; and Schubert, 1991).

Clearly, autobiographical/biographical theorizing has proliferated since the early 1970s, as witnessed by new journals that have emerged and numerous research studies that have been funded. Pinar *et al.* (1995) stress that this kind of theorizing is not just about accumulating personal knowledge, but also using personal knowledge to transform both personal and social worlds.

Racial theorizing

Race is a 'complex, dynamic, and changing construct' (Pinar *et al.*, 1995, p. 316). Race has a powerful influence on schooling in general and the curriculum in particular, yet McCarthy (1988) contends that theorizing about race and racial inequality did not come into its own in curriculum until recent decades. Past neglect has been supplanted, however, by, theorizers such as Watkins (1993), McCarthy (1988, 2003), Villenas and Deyhle (1999), Pinar (2000) and Parker and Stovall (2004). Race can be a powerful, autonomous focal point for theorizers, yet it also intersects with other foci such as gender and postmodernism (De Cuir and Dixson, 2004).

Theorizing about race is likely to exert an increasingly powerful force on the direction of curriculum theorizing in general. Pinar *et al.* (1995) contend that 'any comprehensive theory of curriculum must include race and its concepts – such as multiculturalism, identity, marginality, and difference – as fundamental' (p. 310). Yet herein lies a problem.

Multiculturalism is not attractive to everyone. A number of writers, such as McCarthy (1988), Berlak (1999), Phillion (1999) and Richardson and Villenas (2000), argue that multiculturalism is a questionable solution to racial inequality in schooling since it does not deal directly with the underlying problem. Rather, in promoting pluralistic, culturally diverse curricula, it 'disarticulates elements of black radical demands for restructuring of school knowledge' (McCarthy *et al.*, 2003, p. 228).

Gender analysis and male identity

Feminist curriculum theorizers have been exploring the frontier of gender studies over a number of years. More recently issues associated with masculinities in schools have become publicized (Keddie and Mills, 2007). These issues are described in detail in Chapter 20.

Postmodern theorizing

Not only are there numerous interpretations of the term 'postmodern', but there are also distinctions that can be made between 'postmodernism' and 'postmodernity' and related terms such as 'poststructuralism', 'deconstruction', postcolonialism' and 'postindustrialism' (see Chapter 21).

Review of curriculum theorizing

Wright (2000) contends that we are surfing a third wave of cutting-edge curriculum theorizing: 'This latest group of academics is pushing the theoretical limits of curriculum theorizing, stressing inter/post-disciplinarity and complexifying the struggle for social justice in theory and in praxis' (pp. 9–10). He contends that the principal focal points for this latest wave of theorizing are race, class and gender. These are followed by multiculturalism, critical pedagogy, sexuality, sexual orientation, disability and cultural studies. He highlights in particular the recent theorizing about popular culture (Gough, 2000). The ideas and arguments of many of the academics listed above are compelling. Collectively, both their criticisms of the old and their explorations of the new contain many practical implications and applications for schools. However, hostile critics of these theorizers have disagreed on both counts.

On the count of compellingness, some critics have been put off by the enthusiasm and eloquence of these theorizers. For instance, the comprehensive volumes on curriculum theorizing and curriculum research by Pinar *et al.* (1995) and Pinar (2003) are classic examples of shared enthusiasm, and of rallying cries of celebration. Take, for example, the phrases 'a paradigm shift' and 'the future lies with the reconceptualist' in Pinar *et al.* (1995, p. 238). The *International Handbook of Curriculum Research* (Pinar, 2003) contains, for example, enthusiastic accounts of alternative theoretical approaches in Finland, Bildungstheroic in Netherlands and new and vigorous theoretical explorations in China, among thirty-eight chapters representing over thirty countries.

Milburn (2000) criticizes what he considers the partisan advocacy used by many of these theorizers and their simplification and exaggeration of the historical development of curriculum and their depiction of the contemporary scene. Tanner and Tanner (1981) suggest that many of these approaches to theorizing are 'remakes' of earlier theorizing and therefore their claims of a cataclysm are clearly overwrought. On the count of practicality, Milburn (2000) argues that these theorizers are overly concerned with presentism, and he questions the validity of the claim that their theorizing has produced a paradigm shift. Feinberg (1985) contends that although reconceptualist theorizers have produced exciting ideas, they have not yet produced practical ideas, since there is still no school implementing a reconceptualized curriculum.

Apple (2000), himself a critical-exploratory theorizer, insists on the importance of the 'gritty materialities' involved in making close connections between theoretical discourses and real transformations in educational practices, arguing that 'while the construction of new theories and utopian visions is important, it is equally crucial to base these theories and visions in an unromantic appraisal of the material and discursive terrain that now exists' (p. 229).

Kelly (2004) argues that we must strive to maintain the understandings we have achieved about theorizing. Further, he states that 'theorizing can't go very far in the absence of all real, practical reference' (p. 214).

Hlebowitsh (1999) offers the following challenge: 'To be the bearer of the field, the new curricularists have to have an answer. This means that they have to find a way to transcend their own proclivity toward criticism and protest, and frame a useful theory of conduct that could endure their own style of criticism' (p. 353).

Concluding comments

The examples of theorizing included here should be analysed in the light of history. They illustrate the divergent approaches that have been taken and continue to be developed by curriculum specialists. Some approaches have been more dominant at some times than others. In the last decade, approaches based on the analysis of social structures or personal experience became increasingly common. New classifications of theorizing continue to appear in the literature. These conceptions of curriculum add insights about diversity and directions in theorizing, but further studies of the effects of theorizing at the school level are needed.

What is needed more urgently, however, is increasing and continuing dialogue between theorizers at all levels, from teachers to academics, so that we can learn from our history and our diverse perspectives. Walker (1980) claimed that a 'rich confusion is the right state for curriculum writing' (p. 81). This may be so, but writing is only one of many ways to contribute to the dialogue about the richness of curriculum theorizing.

Reflections and issues

1 The use of technical/rational administrative solutions to complex social issues of equity and access in schools is wrong-headed, superficial and fundamentally flawed, according to Smyth and Shacklock (1998). Critically analyse this statement.

2 'Curriculum theorizing has been overtly politicized, it has been variously institutionalized ... queered, raced, gendered, aestheticized, psychoanalysed, moralized, modernized and postmodernized ... [so] that it presently demands a high degree of flexibility and tolerance from all involved' (Wright, 2000, p. 10). Consider the implications of this point of view for the future of curriculum theorizing and school practice.

3 'Over the past twenty years the American curriculum field has attempted "to take back" curriculum from the bureaucrats, to make the curriculum field itself a conversation, and in so doing, revitalize practice theoretically' (Pinar, 1999, p. 367). In light of this statement, consider the point of view you hold about the relationship between curriculum theorizing and school practice.

4 Until we know a particular value we hold, it holds us – we are not in
   possession of it; it affects our work and thinking although we are unaware
   of it. Reflect upon the major explicit and implicit values that have guided
   your teaching. How do they relate to the values implicit in the theories
   described in this chapter? Try to describe your current value orientation
   and its influence on how you now theorize about curriculum.

Web sources

Reconstructing Experience: Curriculum Theorizing in Experimental Education, http://
   cs.earlham.edu/∼wiki/Reconstructin_Experience:_Curriculum_Theori   ...   –
   extracted 18 October 2007.
Journal of Curriculum Theorizing – Home, www.jctbergamo.com/ – extracted 18
   October 2007.
The Question Concerning Curriculum Theory, www.uwstout.edu/soe/jaaacs/vol1/carlson.
   htm – extracted 18 October 2007.

Chapter 20

Gender, sexuality and the curriculum

Introduction

There are various terms used to describe the nature and impact of inequalities between the sexes at all levels of education. Robertson (1992) emphasizes the problems of androcentric or male-centred teaching, which involves seeing and valuing the world from a male point of view, and assuming that this is the universal experience. Schools try to achieve better sex equity by establishing teaching programmes that are purported to be gender-neutral.

The common use of such terms as 'homosexuality', 'heteronormativity', 'gay and lesbian young people' (Khayatt, 2006; Charlton, 2004) indicates the extent to which cultural awareness has changed. This in turn brings about further tensions for schools.

Feminist pedagogy

Kenway and Modra (1992) use the term 'feminist pedagogy' to describe not only the social theory and social movement aspects of feminists but its 'personal political practice', in its many forms. They cite a number of variations of feminism, including:

- liberal feminists: aspire to access and success and equality with males;
- socialist feminists: concerned about exploitative practices and their effects upon 'women as gendered and classed social beings';
- radical feminists: argue for a 'distinctively women's educational culture'.

The term 'pedagogy' refers to the processes of teaching and involves interactions between the teacher, learners, knowledge and milieu. Lusted (1986) considers that pedagogy includes what is taught, how it is taught and how it us learned, and wider issues of knowledge and learning. It is these wider social issues of pedagogy – the problematics in many of the accepted assumptions about pedagogy – that are of major concern to feminist academics and teachers.

Analysis of schooling in terms of feminist perspectives reveals that schools have been organized around different socially perceived roles and status for men and women. The dominant and enduring trend until the 1960s was for education to be male-oriented (Anyon, 1994; Shakeshaft *et al.*, 1991).

Since the 1970s various feminist theorizers have proposed curricula and school practices to assist teachers (Kenway and Willis, 1997; Datnow and Hubbbard, 2004; Sattler, 1997). Kenway *et al.* (1996) argue that typical schooling practices ignore the emotional dimensions of teaching and learning. Practices in which female students enjoy themselves and feel good about feminism encourage girls to 'become critical, informed, and skilled advocates for a better world' (p. 7).

Historical background

Schooling over the decades has been organized in terms of perceived roles and statuses of men and women in society. The dominant and enduring trend until the 1960s and 1970s was for education structures to be male-oriented.

The accounts of schooling in the nineteenth century in Western countries are strikingly similar about their male domination. Labaree's (1988) account of Central High School in Philadelphia, founded in 1838, indicates that its major purpose was to provide an academic curriculum for the children (mainly sons) of shopkeepers and master craftsmen in the district. It gave these proprietors' sons the 'cultural property' to ease into a middle-class existence. Clark (2005) examined twentieth-century Canadian history textbooks for their portrayals of women and concluded that even up to the 1980s the focus was on the exploits of white males – with females relegated to the role of 'nice little wife to make things pleasant' (p. 241). Sydney Girls' High School was an early school for girls, established in 1893 in Australia. According to Norman (1983), 'one has a sense of girls, hundreds of them, held back like a dam by a wall of super-ficiality and lack of education. With the opening of Sydney High the dam broke, and the first enrolment spilled out, followed by a flood of others' (p. 21). The subjects available over a period of three years which culminated in matriculation standard included:

- Latin;
- elementary mathematics;
- modern languages – French, German;
- English language and literature, elocution;
- history;
- physical science;
- drawing – freehand and perspective;
- music;
- cookery;
- needlework (Goodson and Marsh, 1996).

In keeping with earlier priorities that a girl's education should be fitting her for decorative wifehood, Norman (1983) asserts that 'cooking, music and drawing were on the curriculum partly as a sop to those who feared that higher education would make a girl unfeminine and unfit for her basic role of wife and mother' (p. 16).

In most Western countries by the beginning of the twentieth century co-educational and single-sex schools were operating. The teacher workforce was comprised mainly of female teachers who worked for lower wages than male teachers. Administrators of schools were almost entirely male. The curriculum was overwhelmingly male-centred – 'it represented the values and interests of white, Anglo-Saxon, Protestant, middle class males' (Tyack and Hansot, 1990, p. 5).

Pinar *et al.* (1995) refer to the various ways that gender differences were reinforced and that the male domination continued over the decades. For example, organized sports arose in schools due partly to a fear that boys were becoming feminized due to the few male role models at school (teachers). Organized sports glorified 'competition', and 'violence'. Girls were 'unable to find the same sense of glory and prestige in sports and were sidelined to the roles of spectators and cheerleaders' (p. 363).

Differentiation also occurred in terms of subject choices. Boys were directed into manual arts (woodwork, metalwork, technical drawing), while girls were required to attend home economics classes. Peer pressure and parental pressures also caused many girls to opt for subjects in a commercial programme, while boys did the 'hard' sciences and mathematics. However, it was not until the 1960s and 1970s that the feminist movement of liberation commenced. It appeared to occur at two levels:

- analyses and critiques of sexism and gender: stereotyping in schools;
- analyses and critiques of gender differences in society: including theoretical accounts of how they were produced and maintained.

These analyses have continued as various aspects of education have come under scrutiny by feminist critics; for some 'women's studies' is the solution, while other feminist groups have been concerned with reconceptualizing curriculum theory, ecological dimensions of feminist theory and knowledge, identity and popular culture, gender and postmodernism.

Feminist critiques of schooling

Early critiques of schooling in the 1960s and 1970s examined sex stereotyping and gender bias in content. The list of activities in Table 20.1 indicates some early endeavours to critique sex stereotyping. Other endeavours have focused upon ways of reforming the curriculum, especially in terms of reworking school knowledge and improving teaching practice.

Table 20.1 Some teaching activities to reduce sex stereotyping

1	Ask the students to describe their image of the 'typical' male and the 'typical' female. The students should then share their views with the rest of the class, the aim of the exercise being to make the students aware of sex-role stereotyping as an assumption, underpinning the socialization of males and females.
2	Students should be asked to complete the following activities: What do you feel it means to be male or female? Check off everything on the list in the box below that you feel applies to you.

Boys only

Because I am a boy, I would not:
- cook
- knit
- wash dishes
- help my mother around the house
- wear a dress in a play
- cry
- hit a girl
- wear jewellery
- babysit
- back out of a fight

Girls only

Because I am a girl, I would not:
- dress like a man in a play
- climb a tree
- wear a tie
- play football

- beat a boy at a sport or game
- try to join a boys' club or team
- kiss my mother
- get in a fist fight
- mow the lawn

3	Encourage the students to think carefully about their own actions and the extent to which they may be perpetuating gender-role stereotyping. For example, ask them to complete the following and to analyse their responses:

Book

Item	Girl	Boy	Girl or Boy
Lego			
Computer			
Ball			
Ice skates			
Train set			
Clothing			

In some countries national action plans were established, such as the National Policy and Action Plan for the Education of Girls in Australia 1993–97, which states that:

Curriculum reform requires a fundamental reworking of what knowledge is valued in the curriculum, how that knowledge is made available (for example, its placement on timetabling lines and competition with other subjects) and how it is taught.

Such curriculum reform should:

- consider where, how and why women's and girls' experiences, achievements and contributions have been excluded from the knowledge that is valued in society;
- provide both females and males with access to a wider range of knowledge, skills and ways of being. It should contain those areas of knowledge and living that are of particular significance to women and girls, to the same extent as it includes those areas that are of significance to men and boys;
- acknowledge the multiple perspectives that women have because of ethnicity, culture and class;
- students will be as knowledgeable about female as male contributions to society;
- there will be no difference by gender in the classroom interaction of students and teachers or in expectations for student success;
- there will be no sex bias in the content of courses taught or instructional materials used;
- there will be no sex stereotyping in the hidden curriculum of the school;
- unravel the ways through which social and institutional structures act to maintain the dominant position of men in society;
- explore system and personal models that fulfil expectations of social justice, and that are based on broad rather than narrow views of what it means to be female or male.

(Department of Employment, Education and Training, 1987)

These action plans and related policies were designed to reduce sexism and gender bias in schooling, yet it appears after a decade that differential outcomes from schooling still exist for girls in comparison with boys (Charlton, 2004).

Students

Stephens (1997) and Jobe (2003) both contend that the gendered life experience that students bring to the classroom will affect students' frame of reference. Shore (2001) puts the problem very succinctly: 'a girl in the process of her schooling, learns to layer the messages of a logo/androcentric culture over the insights born of her lived experience, muffling and silencing the still, small voice within' (p. 132).

Lundeberg (1997) argues that gender bias is often present in classrooms, even though it may be subtle and not immediately noticeable. Crowley et al.'s (1998) study concluded that not only in the classroom but in the home, parents are more likely to explain scientific matters to boys than to girls.

Sex-based harassment can be a disruptive factor in schools and can be promoted by particular subgroups and individuals and even by teacher expectations about typical and least typical boys and girls. For example, Abraham (1995) describes harassment that occurred in a secondary school between girls 'who mixed too much with the boys', the 'conscientious quiet' ones and the 'lads' and the 'gothic punks'.

Research studies have demonstrated that some forms of assessment seem to advantage males, for example multiple-choice tests (Allen, 1990). By contrast, females often achieve higher scores than males on essay tests. In pragmatic terms, multiple-choice tests are more commonly used by teachers because they are more convenient to set and mark, and so female students overall are at a disadvantage to their male counterparts. However, the assessment issue is complex because sex difference is just one of the factors – others include achievement variability across cultures and age levels and subject areas (Feingold, 1992). Then again, there are wider issues relating to assessment that may discriminate against girls, such as the test-taking behaviours of males versus females (O'Connor and Robotham, 1991).

Teachers

As noted by Smith (2004), 'not only do schools provide a gendered experience for students, they also provide a gendered experience for teachers' (p. 354). Milligan (1994) observes that gender is a powerful factor in the daily lives of teachers. She also concludes, using Australian Bureau of Statistics data, that women remain heavily underrepresented in school leadership and promotions positions. Khayatt (2006), referring to her teaching experiences in Canada, uses an anecdote to reflect upon her dealings with a male student in her class: 'I am the teacher with institutionalised authority and I am female. He is a student with little institutional authority and he is male. He has a certain social power and one way to play it out is to reduce me to a sexual subject' (p. 134).

Put simplistically, teachers have to either make decisions about continuing the status quo (and maintaining the inequalities and discrimination) or get involved in reforms. In practice, it is not so easy.

As an example of the complexities involved, Kenway et al. (1996) suggest that a number of female teachers try to bring about improved learning situations by assuming the needs of the 'normal girl' and making the erroneous assumption that 'all girls have similar needs, interests, pleasures and anxieties, that what oppresses one, oppresses all, and that what "empowers one" "empowers" all'.

The same authors (Kenway et al., 1996) point to the 'authoritarian' and 'therapeutic' approaches used by teachers to improve teaching practice and suggest that both approaches ignore the emotional dimensions of teaching and learning. Authoritarian attempts, to the point of dogmatism by female teachers, often alienate many students. However, therapeutic approaches where the focus is upon female students enjoying themselves and feeling good about feminism underplay the need for girls to 'become critical, informed and skilled advocates for a better world' (p. 7).

Hubbard and Datnow (2000) studied women teachers' involvement in school reforms. They concluded that reforms that were compatible with women teachers' beliefs about nurturing and caring were well supported and advocated by women teachers, which in turn facilitated the success of the reforms. It was also found that an overrepresentation of women teachers in a reform effort had the potential of causing negative political reactions.

Rusch and Marshall (2006) argue that school leaders can have a major impact on reducing or consolidating gender inequity. They deplore the under-representation of women in school administrative positions – as a consequence 'there is a perpetuation and reification of a predominantly white male perspective in school administration' (p. 230). Rusch and Marshall (2006) suggest that school administrators use a number of gender filters to silence ideas and people who might disrupt the privileges of dominance. Some of these filters include:

- anger with challengers – using cold stares and impatience;
- denial – gender blinkers proclaiming that they are always gender-neutral;
- posturing – appearing to give open support for equity.

Gender differences in society

In addition to critiques of schooling, radical feminists over recent decades have criticized the academic disciplines – the reality interpreted by males in higher education and compartmentalized into disciplines with claimed objectivity. Studies undertaken by feminist critics have noticed that:

- research methodology of these academic disciplines excluded/prevented certain kinds of information;
- areas of enquiry related to women were minimal;
- generalizations made about males and females were based on the study of males only;
- research studies often claimed objectivity but were highly value-laden;
- extant knowledge and modes of inquiry prevented the introduction of new ideas;
- women were devalued in all the disciplines;
- much of the research was based upon highly rational, technological assumptions (Pinar et al., 1995).

A result of these critiques, especially at the higher education level, has been for feminists to introduce 'feminist critiques and theories within their various disciplines and departments as well as starting separate women's studies programs' (Middleton, 1992, p. 18).

'Women's studies' programmes have attempted to redefine and reconstruct the academic disciplines. It might be argued that some programmes have been very optimistic, as revealed by the charter document of the National Women's Studies Association in the USA:

> Women's Studies, diverse as its components are, has at its best shared a vision of a world free not only from sexism but also from racism, class-bias, ageism, heterosexual bias – from all the ideologies and institutions that have consciously or unconsciously oppressed and exploited some for the advantage of others ... The uniqueness of Women's Studies has been its refusal to accept sterile divisions between academy and community, between intellect and passion, between the individual and society. Women's Studies ... is equipping women ... to transform [society].
>
> (National Women's Studies Association, 1977)

Klein (1986) considers that 'women's studies' curricula can be summarized as being:

- re-action and re-vision, as women confront the androcentric world-view;
- action and vision as women assess women's experience from within a gynocentric perspective;
- a combination of these approaches that fuses critique and new vision.

However, it is debatable whether fusion has occurred; rather a myriad of advocacy movements (Charlton, 2004; Rusch and Marshall, 2006). Pagano (1992) considers that 'the educational challenge in the foreseeable future will be to teach people to acknowledge and understand their own passions, their own advocacy positions, without being reduced to them' (p. 150).

These advocacy movements have included the following:

- Essentialism: male/female differences are innate. The unique feminine characteristics that emerge from women's biology enable them to appropriate many societal functions previously carried out by males and to do them better (Belensky et al., 1988).
- Social constructionists: gender is socially constructed by economic, cultural and political forces in society (Chodorow, 1978; Kenway and Longmead, 1998).
- Ecological feminist theory: the humankind–nature relationship (De Mocker, 1986).
- Political feminist theory: relationships between gender politics and democratic education (Arnot and Dillabough, 1999; Blackmore, 1998; Yates, 1998).
- Poststructuralist: an exploration of the contradictions and injustices in society – to promote feminist self-understanding and self-determination (Lather, 1998; Grumet and Stone, 2000).

Gender analysis and challenges to heteronormativity

Sears (1992a, 1992b, 1999) has been a major figure in highlighting homosexual issues and supporting the struggle for social justice for gays and lesbians. He uses the term 'queer' to signify 'those who have been defined or have chosen to define themselves as sexual outsiders' (Sears, 1999, p. 4). He defines teaching queerly as 'creating classrooms that challenge categorical thinking, promote interpersonal intelligence, and foster critical consciousness' (p. 5).

Sears (1999) contends that teaching queerly requires a re-examination of taken-for-granted assumptions about diversity, identities, childhood and prejudice. He elaborates upon this by offering five basic propositions, namely:

- Diversity is a human hallmark – despite the evidence, many educators, in terms of sexuality and gender, 'mold children into curriculum cookie-cutter identities' (Sears, 1999, p. 5) such as male/female; heterosexual/homosexual. 'This is a make-believe world of self and other' (p. 5).
- (Homo)Sexualities are constructed essences – sexual identity is constructed within a cultural context but the predisposition for sexual behaviour is biologically based.
- Homophobia and heterosexism are acquired – 'The belief in the superiority of heterosexuality … and the deep-seated hatred or fear of those who love the same gender (homophobia) are acquired early in life and serve a variety of functions' (p. 7).
- Childhood innocence is a fictive absolute – 'This is a veneer that we as adults impress onto children, enabling us to deny desire comfortably and to silence sexuality' (p. 9).
- Families are first – 'The concepts of family and parenthood have become 'unhinged' in this era of postmodernity' (Stacey, 1999).

Other theorizers within this group who also challenge heteronormativity include Leck (1999), Sumara and Davis (1999), Aitken (1999) and Pinar (1983, 2000). Leck (1999) contends that 'many of the consequences we see in the lives of racialized, gendered and sexualized minorities are the results of the dogmas that have disallowed teachers, parents and schools from participating in an open dialogue about children, sexuality and diversity' (p. 257). Sumara and Davis (1999) take an even stronger line in asserting that curriculum theorizers must interrupt heteronormative thinking. Their propositions for a queer curriculum theory include:

- the need to work toward a deeper understanding of the forms that curriculum can take so that sexuality is understood as a necessary companion to all knowing;
- the need to call into question the very existence of heterosexuality as a stable category and to examine the unruly heterosexual closet;

- the need to understand and interpret differences among persons rather than noting differences among categories of persons;
- the need to interrupt common beliefs of what constitutes experiences of desire, of pleasure and of sexuality (Sumara and Davis, 1999, p. 203).

Aitken's (1999) editorial in *Curriculum Inquiry* 29:2 captures the purposes of 'queer' curriculum theorists by his title 'Leaping Boundaries of Difference'. And they are doing it successfully. Aitken concentrates especially upon flawed premises of society such as a patriarchal notion of civil society and culturally sanctioned expressions of heterosexuality.

Pinar (1983, 1994, 1997, 2000) has also written extensively about homosexual issues within autobiographic frameworks. He warns that theorists must be aware of politically enforced heterosexuality, stating: 'as a feminist man it is clear to me I must confront my own manhood, understood of course not essentialistically, but historically, socially, racially, in terms of class and culture' (Pinar, 2000, p. 2).

Other theorists have been challenging heteronormativity, with a major emphasis on girls. Charlton (2004), an Australian academic, argues that 'with the displacement of girls from the educational agenda in Australia as a result of the "what about the boys?" discourse, spaces seldom exist to challenge anti-lesbianism and misogynist cultures in school in the same ways that they do in relation to homophobia and hegemonic masculinities' (p. 1). Khayatt (2006) takes a similar stance when she states that in North America, school sites practice hegemonic masculinity which disavows any deviation from heteronormativity.

Others have examined curriculum sources needed in schools to address lesbian/gay/bisexual/transgender topics. Capper *et al.* (2006) contend that social justice in schools is fraudulent if it does not fully address lesbian/gay/bisexual/transgender (LGBT) issues. They advocate the use of videos, panel discussions, and case presentation and analysis of LGBT matter. They also suggest that LGBT equity audits should be undertaken at the school level. Nixon (2006) argues that schools should seek to recruit more LGBT teachers. They can be role models and provide valuable pastoral support. They can also inspire necessary structural changes in schools (Rottmann, 2006; Martino and Kehler, 2006).

Concluding comments

The perspectives provided in this chapter highlight issues of power, oppression and inequalities. The severity of gender disadvantage can apply to both girls and boys (Gilbert and Gilbert, 1998; Keddie and Mills, 2007).

Disadvantage and discrimination often occurs due to different sexual preferences. As noted by Letts and Sears,

> much of the research on lesbian, gay, bisexual, transgender and queer youth has been testimonial to the fallout from oppression by

heterosexualized silences ... and that not enough has been done to speak of the risks and costs of extinction of unique and diverse individuals, and of certain cultural characteristics within our human symbioses.

(Letts and Sears, 1999, p. 260)

Reflections and issues

1 'Feminist pedagogy consists of a diversity of voices and practices and it exists in a wide variety of educational settings and modes' (Kenway and Modra, 1992, p. 25). Discuss.

2 In theorizing about feminist pedagogy we need to consider 'such concepts as pleasure, nurturance, pain, blame, shame, risk, investment, fantasy and positionality' (Kenway et al., 1996, p. 2). To what extent are feminist educators failing to attend to the subtleties of what girls think, feel, say and do in schools?

3 'If feminism cannot criticize itself, it cannot facilitate a multitude of emancipatory possibilities' (Miller, 1990, p. 10). To what extent has feminist theorizing been uncritical and oversimplified? Give examples of recent initiatives by feminists to overcome a failure to critically reflect upon their theory-building.

4 'A teacher's general ideology about sex roles is a major factor in determining their willingness to use non-sexist or anti-sexist curriculum materials' (Abraham, 1995, p. 133). Discuss.

5 'The time to make children aware of the ways they are limited, and the ways they limit themselves through gendered identities, is in the early childhood years' (Alloway, 1995, p. 26). What are some of the restrictions that can occur? Are there asymmetries in power relations at this level of schooling? How can teachers encourage children to contest inequitable gender relations?

6 'Feminist theorizing is clearly both the condition for a recognition of our unity across national boundaries but also the condition for recognizing our diversity, between nations and within nations' (Arnot, 1993, p. 2). Are there commonalities of women's experiences of schooling across different societies? Give examples to illustrate the commonalities and diversities.

7 'Homophobia and the vilification and violence it generates need to be seen as part of the construction of dominant masculinity' (Gilbert and Gilbert, 1998, p. 164). Discuss.

8 Is the major problem that modern societies have cemented our ideas of child development around behaviours that are assumed to be 'normal'? What understandings and actions regarding this problem can be taken by teachers?

9   As we study constructions of power, we can see the often defensive, reactionary and diverse responses of those who are in positions of power. Explain with reference to the treatment of boys with different sexual preferences.

10   'It is difficult to identify, recognise and address the experiences of heterosexism, anti-lesbianism and homophobia for young women ... the recognition and encouragement of certain kinds of masculinities perpetuates oppression of unrecognised and unencouraged versions' (Charlton, 2004, p. 19). Discuss.

Web sources

Welcome to the Center for Gender Equity, www.ucsf.edu/cge/- – accessed 27 September 2007.

Promoting Gender Equality United Nations Population Fund, www.unfpa.org/gender/ – accessed 27 September 2007.

Feminist Pedagogy, www.wlv.ac.uk/∼le1810/femped.htm/ – accessed 27 September 2007.

Using a Feminist Pedagogy as a Male Teacher, www.radicalpedagogy.icaap.org/content/issue2_2/Schacht.htm/ – accessed 27 September 2007.

Teaching About Homosexuality in Public Schools, www.religioustolearance.org/homteach.htm – accessed 27 September 2007.

Chapter 21

Postmodernism and the curriculum

Introduction

In education, especially over recent years, there has been massive bureaucratic standardization. Mainstream priorities by neo-liberal states have persisted with bureaucratic testing regimes and control over school operations (Waks, 2006). Various authors have argued that we should be on guard against those who have a narrow, positivist approach to education and who reject diverse epistemologies and methodologies in education (St Pierre, 2002; Waks, 2006)

The term 'postmodern' is used frequently – it has unleashed a wide range of divergences within education, especially against grand narratives of 'modernity' and modernist education. Jean-François Lyotard's (1984) widely used definition of postmodernism is very telling – 'I define postmodernism as incredulity toward metanarratives' (p. 3).

'Postmodern' has been interpreted in many ways but before it is analysed here it is necessary to examine what is being replaced – what is the 'modern' which is to be relegated to a previous era or replaced? Is postmodernism really *after* modernism? Is the notion of defining periods (as 'modern', 'postmodern') merely a rhetorical device – a means of comparing the present to something different (Newall, 2005)?

Some major terms

Modernity

According to Hargreaves (1995), 'modernity' is a social condition which was dominant in many countries up to the 1960s. Its characteristics included the following:

- a major emphasis upon rational, scientific methods and the use of technology to control nature;
- the division of production methods involving separation of family and work;

- the development of specialized, hierarchical bureaucracies to control decision-making;
- achievement of social progress by systematic development and rational applications;
- economic and social organizations focused upon capitalist production.

Modernity has had the potential to bring about progress. To a certain extent it has been successful – as witnessed by efficiency, productivity, prosperity in some quarters, creation of the welfare state, mass education (Weiss and Wesley, 2007). Yet there are also signs that modernity as a social condition has become exhausted and no longer relevant, in the following terms:

- economic markets have become saturated, profitability is declining; many Western economies are in fiscal crisis;
- bureaucracies are being blamed for inefficiencies and inflexible decision-making;
- there is a use of paradigms based on destructive reductionistic and mechanistic assumptions;
- education priorities are focused on control and domination.

With reference to many Western countries, especially the UK and the USA, bureaucratic standardization of modernity in education has accelerated. The National Curriculum introduced in the UK in the Education Act of 1988 now fills up almost the entire teaching time in state schools (Waks, 2006). In the USA the No Child Left Behind legislation of 2001 has ushered in standardized testing in reading and mathematics.

Of course, it may be the case that we are entering another phase of 'modernity'. Giddens (1990) uses the term 'high modernity' to describe a social condition where decisions and actions are more diffuse, radicalized and universalized than before. He argues that it is not sufficient to invent a new term such as 'postmodernism'; rather we should be examining the nature of modernity to understand the extension and intensification of conditions.

There is some evidence that more diverse approaches to education are now being used through multiple providers but their agendas still fall within a positivist approach (Waks, 2006).

Habermas (1970) argues that modernity offers considerable promise of integrating science, morality and art back into society through the use of reason. Yet many others argue that modernism is on the wane and must be replaced (Jencks, 1992; Griffin *et al.*, 1993; Slattery, 1995; St Pierre, 2002; Romer, 2003).

Postmodernism

Doll (1993a) contends that postmodernism, as characterized by open systems, indeterminacy, the discrediting of metanarratives and a focus on process, will bring about megaparadigmatic changes. McLaren and Farahmandpur (2000) argue that postmodernism has made impressive advances in helping educators map the hidden trajectories of power and peel away layers of ideological mystification.

Not only are there numerous interpretations of the term 'postmodern', but there are also distinctions which can be made between 'postmodernism' and 'postmodernity' and related terms such as 'poststructuralism', 'deconstruction', 'postcolonialism' and 'post-industrialism'.

Hargreaves (1995) uses the term 'postmodernity' to refer to a social condition – patterns of social, economic, political and cultural relations – whereas he perceives 'postmodernism' as a set of styles and practices such as intellectual discourse or cultural forms. Others, such as Slattery (1995), use the term 'postmodern' to refer to both social conditions and practices. This also appears to be the stance of other writers describing 'postmodern' in the following terms:

- as a diffuse sentiment rather than any set of common doctrines (Griffin *et al.*, 1993, p. vii);
- it is in continual growth and movement and thus no firm definitions are possible (Jencks, 1986, p. 9);
- it provides a space for forms of radical and emancipatory politics associated with new social movements and the bringing to the fore of issues of gender, race, ethnicity and sexuality (Ellsworth, 1997).

Atkinson cites some characteristic features of postmodernism, which she sums up as a 'release from certainties' (p. 6). Her list includes:

- resistance towards certainty and resolution;
- rejection of fixed notions of reality, knowledge or method;
- acceptance of complexity, of lack of clarity and of multiplicity;
- refusal to accept boundaries or hierarchies in ways of thinking (Atkinson, 2000, p. 7).

Houser (2005) lists the following characteristics:

- a rejection of the universal, structural and hierarchical in favour of an emphasis on difference, multiplicity and the context-specific nature of experience;
- a rejection that it is possible to know anything with certainty – including even the nature of ones own identity.

Not only are there numerous interpretations of the term 'postmodern', but there are theoretical approaches which are most commonly seen as postmodernist such as 'poststructuralism', 'deconstruction' and 'postcolonialism' (Beck, 1993).

Poststructuralism

Poststructuralist advocates criticize modernity by challenging a structuralist view of the world. For example, structuralists believe in invariant forms of knowledge and of society that give meaning to the world, whereas Foucault (1972) argues that attempts to establish such a system of homogeneous relationships – a network of causality – fail to take into account the underlying but changing social and political assumptions such systems are ultimately built on. Bourdieu and Passeron (1977) argues that structural models should be enriched and that there should be more emphasis on reflexivity. Structuralists identify systems to create meaning, whereas poststructuralists endeavour to dismantle systems to expose their variable and contingent nature (Slattery, 1995; Lye, 1997).

Deconstructionism

Deconstructionism is another postmodern theory involved in exposing the contradictions and fallacies embedded within modernity. The idea of deconstruction does not imply a tearing down; rather, it is simply being alert to contradictions and fallacies in Western thought and rationality, 'alert to the implications, to the historical sedimentation of the language we use' (Derrida, 1972, p. 73).

Deconstructionism involves demystifying a text to reveal internal arbitrary hierarchies and presuppositions (Weiss and Wesley, 2007). Rosenau's guidelines for deconstruction analysis make interesting reading:

- Find an exception to a generalization in a text and push it to the limit so that this generalization appears absurd. Use the exception to undermine the principle.
- Interpret the arguments in a text being deconstructed in their most extreme form.
- Deny the legitimacy of dichotomies because there are always a few exceptions (Rosenau, 1993, p. 21).

Lather (1991), in *Getting Smart: Feminist Research and Pedagogy with/in the Postmodern*, takes a deconstructivist stance. She argues that the modernist system of power, language and meaning has imploded and collapsed (p. 88) and that what is needed is knowledge constructed from self-understanding. In a recent publication Lather (2007) contends, using feminist research, that an emancipatory concept of language and power must emerge in education – self-understanding and self-determination are required.

Postcolonialism

Postcolonialism is a third and more specific variation of the postmodern that, according to Giroux (1992), challenges the ideological and material legacies of imperialism and colonialism.

Giroux's (1992) *Border Crossings: Cultural Workers and the Politics of Education* provides an account of the shifting borders that affect the different configurations of culture, power and knowledge. He uses the term 'border pedagogy' to signal a recognition of those margins (epistemological, political, cultural, social) that structure the language of history, power and difference. The term also signals the need for teachers to create learning situations so that students become border crossers – allowing them to write, speak and listen in a language in which meaning becomes multi-accentual and dispersed and resists permanent closure. Giroux states that

> border pedagogy necessitates combining the modernist emphasis on the capacity of individuals to use critical reason to address the issue of public life with a postmodernist concern with how we might experience agency in a world constituted in differences unsupported by transcendent phenomena or metaphysical guarantees. In that way, border pedagogy can reconstitute itself in terms that are both transformative and emancipatory.
>
> (Giroux, 1992, p. 29)

Postcolonial adherents challenge imperial centres of power and contest the dominant Eurocentric writing of politics, theory and history. Spivak (1985) argues that it is necessary to unlearn one's own privilege; the legacy of colonialism must be examined to make visible the various exclusions and repressions that permit specific forms of privilege to remain (for example privilege that benefits males, whiteness, heterosexuality and property holders).

Rizvi, Lingard and Lavia (2006) draw attention to the ways in which language works in the colonial formation of discursive and cultural practices. They note that 'conservative critics fear what they see as postcolonialism's attempts to undermine western culture itself' (p. 250). After the tragic events of 11 September 2001, 'postcolonialism' was cited in the US House of Representatives as essentially 'anti-American'.

Parkes (2006) theorizes a curriculum response to the development of a senior secondary history course in New South Wales. A central debate is over the representation of the colonization of Australia. Parkes (2006) argues that a full range of voices is needed in the telling of Australian history – the need to read history curriculum as postcolonial text.

Postmodernism and schooling

While different postmodernists may disagree on specific details of their critiques of the hidden political, social and cultural assumptions of the present, they (and related groups) collectively agree that schooling is far more complex and ambiguous than traditional curriculum writers describe it and, therefore, that modernist standardized curriculum packages are likely to be grossly inappropriate in the present, if they ever were appropriate. Thus, teachers need to enter into dialogue about the uncertainties, the concerns, the doubts and the questions that pervade teaching, including those that surround selecting and enacting curricula. The challenge is to transcend traditional, positivist approaches to curriculum development. According to Klages (2007), post-modernism is mainly concerned about 'disorder' (modernity is fundamentally about order) and so schooling needs to examine such 'disorders' as non-white, non-male, non-heterosexual, non-hygienic and non-rational.

Teachers need to create methods to develop and incorporate various post-modern discourses into their daily teaching. Examples of how this challenge can be met include the following:

- Teachers and students need to become engaged in telling their life stories, and especially to reflect upon ideas that appear to have been hidden or forgotten (Graham, 1991).
- Rorty (1990) refers to the 'moral self' as a network of beliefs, desires and emotions with nothing behind it – constantly reweaving itself. Rosenau (1993) suggest that the talking of life stories celebrates feelings and personal experiences and has an 'anti-rules' fashion of discourse.
- Curriculum experience in schools must be open to reflection, because from a postmodern standpoint everything requires recursive interpretation. Thus the official syllabuses and curriculum documents cannot be used in any passive way – as a teacher-proof curriculum (Mitchell, 1996; Beck, 1993).
- Through dialogue and debate, teachers and students must deconstruct norms and values about race and gender, especially those that perpetuate religious bigotry, political repression and cultural elitism (Parker, 1997).
- Teachers need to encourage students to undertake aesthetic reflections whereby they can gain some intrinsic coherence about the body, the spirit and the cosmos.
- Teachers need to promote holistic inquiry with their students in terms of the classroom environment, the natural environment and the inner envir-onment of students and teachers (Arends, 2000).
- Beck (1993) contends that we use a different form of inquiry – 'we are not seeking to uncover a pre-existing reality but are involved in an interactive process of knowledge creation' (p. 5). The knowledge arrived at can be ambiguous and unstable. It may be appropriate for specific local goals rather than grand narratives (Klages, 2007).
- 'Teachers and student will be encouraged to become ironic in reconciling the foundationless status of their beliefs and commitments – and the com-mitments of others – with the desire to create, develop and defend them' (Parker, 1997, p. 142).
- Teachers should encourage students to accomplish their learning in diverse ways using written, numerical, oral, visual, technological or dramatic media. Hierarchical distinctions of worth among different forms

of representation are eliminated. In a postmodern approach, the student's voice in the process of assessment is fundamental (Hargreaves *et al.*, 2001).

Just as the term 'reconceptualist', has many perspectives, so too does the term 'postmodern'. Postmodern theorizing is eclectic and takes many stances and directions. Slattery (1995) focuses upon eight different perspectives: it is worth remembering that postmodernism promotes eclecticism – there are no unified conceptions. His listing of perspectives includes the following:

- historical: ongoing reinterpretation; the primacy of subjective experience of history, interrelating events unified with time and space;
- aesthetic, qualitative: to prioritize the dramatic, artistic, non-rational, intuitive dimensions of the human person;
- social criticism: exposing contradictions and deconstructing notions of truth, language, knowledge and power in economic and political systems;
- cultural analysis: critiquing the negative impact of modern technology on the human psyche and the environment;
- a radical eclecticism: a discourse that accepts and criticizes, that constructs and deconstructs;
- cosmological dialogue: a search for personal and universal harmony;
- globally interdependent ecological perspective: the interrelated destruction of the ecosphere and the human psyche and how it can be halted;
- reconceptualizing and transcending the interlocking categories of race, gender and class: 'excavating the unconscious assumptions' (Miller, 1987).

Postmodernism and the curriculum

Curriculum is a central aspect of schooling. If it is accepted that schooling is currently in crisis (Pinar, 2004), then it is crucial for teachers to reflect deeply about the curriculum which is planned and implemented. A postmodern curriculum can address issues raised by uncertainty, challenges of change, difference and diversity. Some possible examples are included below.

Autobiographical reflection

Postmodern educators can no longer teach a subject in terms of facts, or a series of events to be memorized. What is needed is the following:

- for the teacher to continually tell his or her life story in terms of the subject: subjective reflections on what it has meant/what it could mean;
- for students to become engaged in telling their life stories about the subject;
- to encourage students to keep a journal during a particular course and to record their personal perspectives;

- to arrange classroom chairs in a circle to enable informal sharing by students of their personal perspectives;
- to reflect upon ideas that appear to have been hidden or forgotten: 'redeeming a lost sense of historical consciousness' (Graham, 1991, p. 13);
- to question linear descriptions and artificially contrived categories and to reflect upon events of the present and how they provide access to the future.

Collaborative interpretation

Postmodern educators need to engage in collaborative interpretation with their colleagues. The curriculum experience in schools must be open to reflection, because from a postmodern standpoint everything requires recursive interpretation. Thus, the official syllabuses and curriculum documents cannot be used in any passive way – as a teacher-proof curriculum. It requires:

- that teachers share ideas collaboratively with other teachers, and in so doing create a community of interpreters;
- that collaborative interpretation be viewed as a creative activity rather than a technical function;
- that teachers respect the interplay of individuals and expect infuriating and inciting experiences as well as rewarding ones – once teachers enter this hermeneutic circle they become involved in frank and candid interpretations, clarifications, deconstructions and challenges to all fields of study.

Multicultural debates

Postmodern teachers must depart from the notion of curriculum as being 'radically, gender and culturally neutral' (Slattery, 1995, p. 133). According to Hanley (2006), we must 'relinquish the mis-education of half-thoughts and distortions and embrace the dialectical shifting ambiguities of being if we are to approach the true potential of a multicultural people ready to shape an equitable society' (p. 54).

Through dialogue and debate between a teacher and students it is necessary to:

- shatter myths about race and gender, especially those that perpetuate religious bigotry, political repression and cultural elitism;
- encourage investigation of confrontational ideas outside a student's prior knowledge and experience in order to develop wide insights about self and society;
- use race and gender studies as vehicles to expose 'the impotence of traditional curriculum development in the face of the tragedies of contemporary global society' (Slattery, 1995, p. 136);
- deconstruct norms and values about race and gender through discussion and debate and through autobiographical accounts.

Aesthetic, integrated inquiry

Postmodern teachers need to encourage aesthetic reflections that help students to gain some intrinsic coherence about the body, the spirit and the cosmos. Houser (2005) suggests that the arts can help students become more critical and caring through the expression of feelings, emotions and relationships. Activities toward this end include:

• encouraging teachers and students to use multisensory phenomena and perceptions;
• encouraging a multiplicity of voices in making judgements;
• giving a higher priority to music, fine arts, drama, dance, poetry, speech, band (in the USA), painting and to use these sources to encourage interdisciplinary integrated inquiry.

Ecological sustainability and holistic inquiry

Postmodern educators realize the crisis of surviving due to ongoing destruction of both the ecosphere and forms of violence to the human psyche (Slattery, 1995). According to Sloan (1993), 'the world is collapsing under the impact of the homogenizing influences of the modern mindset and its attendant institutions [where] educational systems ... force children at an ever-earlier age into an adult culture already shot through with futility, greed and banality' (p. 1).

What is needed is the following:

• a holistic perspective to enable students and teachers to explore the dangers of environmental pollution and destruction and to search for alternatives;
• to give a higher priority to teaching activities that span the classroom and the outside community and to include field trips, guest speakers, nature studies and visits to museums;
• to focus upon, holistically, the classroom environment, the natural environment and the inner environment of teachers and students.

Critics of postmodernism

Postmodern theorizing is not without its critics. Barrow (1999) concludes 'that the label "postmodern" is simply too confused to be useful' (p. 419). Proponents of postmodernism postulate a theory that seeks to deny the coherence of theory – this is a central contradiction. Green (1994) contends that postmodernism 'has so far contributed little that is distinctive or theoretically fruitful and it seems unlikely that it will' (p. 73). 'Postmodernism taken to extremes, can only lead to moral nihilism, political apathy and the abandonment of the intellect to the chaos of the contingent' (p. 74). Behar-Horenstein

(2000) contends that the postmodern interpretation is short-sighted and 'represents a gross distortion of reality and a reductionist critique of the field' (p. 20).

According to Rosenau (1993) postmodernists can be divided into two broad camps, affirmatives and sceptics. The affirmative postmodernists such as Kincheloe (1993), Griffin et al. (1993) and Hargreaves (1995) deny claims of truth in modernist theory but consider that transformations are possible. Sceptical postmodernists such as Lather (1991), Giroux (1992) and Doll (1993a) consider that modernist theory conceals and distorts and that it is alienated and dissonant.

For example, Kincheloe (1993) is concerned about mapping the postmodern terrain historically and politically. He also constructs a philosophical and aesthetic theory of post-formal thinking. He perceives post-formal thinking as seeing relationships between ostensibly different things – making connections between logic and emotion – transcending simplistic notions of cause and effect. He attempts to create a middle ground by accepting progressive and democratic features of modernism but then moves to post-formal thinking 'as a new zone of cognition' (Slattery, 1995, p. 27).

Griffin et al.'s (1993) *Founders of Constructive Postmodern Philosophy* also takes a more moderate stance – some might consider it to be high modernist – by advocating an integration of the desirable features of pre-modern rural agrarian societies (for example family/tribal community values) and the desirable features of the modern societies (for example advances in healthcare) to construct a more balanced and ecologically sustainable global community. A new unity of scientific, ethical, aesthetic and religious perspectives is proposed to contribute to the construction of a world-view.

Hargreaves (1995) and Hargreaves et al. (2001) provide an analysis of the postmodern social condition and the challenges they pose for teachers. Hargreaves (1995) argues that 'while society moves into a post-industrial postmodern age, our schools and teachers continue to cling to crumbling edifices of bureaucracy and modernity' (p. x). He contends that it is the struggle between and within modernity and postmodernity that is the major challenge for teachers.

Although Hargreaves shares similar concerns about modernist priorities he is not so optimistic about postmodern developments when he states:

> Modernity has survived for centuries; its more recent forms for decades. It is not yet clear whether our generation will be witness to its complete demise, to the end of an epoch. Many facets of modernity clearly are in retreat or under review – standardisation, centralisation, mass production and mass consumption among them. Deeper continuing structures of power and control in society may not be eliminated so easily. They may, however, be changing their form: renovated and refurbished with postmodern facades of accessibility and diversity.
>
> (Hargreaves, 1995, p. 32)

Hargreaves *et al.* (2001) are concerned about change in postmodern society and that 'the worthy pursuit of continuous improvement can turn into an exhausting process of ceaseless change … If people are forever in a state of becoming, they never have the chance to be' (p. 123).

In summary, a number of criticisms have been advanced about post-modernism (Newall, 2005; Rosenau, 1993):

- although postmodernism focuses on irrational tendencies and appears to celebrate them, it still uses reason as a tool;
- its anti-theoretical position is essentially a theoretical stand;
- the postmodern prescription to focus on the marginal is itself an evaluative emphasis of precisely the sort that it otherwise attacks;
- postmodernism stresses intertextuality but often treats text in isolation;
- postmodernists contradict themselves by relinquishing truth claims in their own writings.

Concluding comments

Postmodernism provides opportunities for dialogue about the hidden political, social and cultural assumptions of present-day curriculum planning and schooling. Whilst not necessarily providing solutions to modernity issues, postmodern proponents provide mechanisms for challenging traditional, posi-tivist approaches to curriculum development. Yet there are numerous chal-lenges for postmodernists to resolve. For example, Schutz (2004) challenges postmodernists to develop a more 'nuanced dialogue about the relationships among oppression, resistance and privilege in education' (p. 21). Edwards (2006) concludes that the intellectual energy unleashed by postmodernists has ebbed – 'there are ripples and traces but they have not transformed the domi-nant discourse of education' (p. 26).

Reflections and issues

1 'The postmodern world is fast, compressed, complex and uncertain. Already it is presenting immense problems and challenges for our modernistic school systems and the teachers who work within them' (Hargreaves, 1995, p. 9). Discuss.
2 Teaching is more than well-formatted lesson plans with carefully crafted objectives and outcomes – this is a simplistic modernist/positive view of the world. Critique this statement from a postmodern stance.
3 'The postmodern curriculum, in all its kaleidoscopic perspectives, offers an opportunity for education to move beyond moribund modes of analysis to a new understanding of curriculum development' (Slattery, 1995, p. 257). Discuss.

4 To what extent have modern economies been beset by such massive chan- ges in economic, political and organizational life that postmodern alter- natives are inevitable? Examine some of these changes that have occurred and several postmodern alternatives.

5 Doll (1993b) suggests a new set of criteria for determining a quality postmodern curriculum. These criteria include 'richness' (multiple layers of interpretation to challenge the learner); 'recursion' (to revisit ideas, reflection); 'relations' (the more interconnections the better – non-linear explorations); 'rigour' (the process of moulding problems and perturbations into a coherent and dynamic unity). Comment on the potential of using these four 'R's in teach- ing. Do they constitute a new educational mindset and curriculum frame?

6 'Poststructuralism encourages ambiguity and multiplicity, opens up traditional boundaries and breaks out of frames' (Rhedding-Jones, 1995). What are the implications for classroom teachers? How might a diversity of meanings be addressed by the teacher? How does one acquire heightened awareness of wider discourses?

7 'In a postmodern curriculum there must be a sense of indecision and inde- terminacy to curriculum planning. The ends perceived are not so much ends as beginnings' (Doll, 1993a, p. 19). Explain how this transformation might occur. Would this bring about changes in the locus of power? Give exam- ples to illustrate your stance.

8 'The free-form processive dance of postmodernism is indeed preferable to the lock-step progressive control of modernity' (Slattery, 1995, p. 28). Explain and take a position that supports or refutes this statement.

9 According to Slattery (1995) we must move from 'curriculum development in the disciplines to the postmodern paradigm of understanding curriculum in various contexts – in this sense curriculum development becomes kalei- doscopic – it is always shifting perspectives and constantly reflecting new and liberating visions of learning and living' (p. 257). Discuss.

Web sources

S. Weiss and K. Wesley (2007) *Postmodernism and Its Critics*, http://www.as.ua.edu/ant/Faculty/murphy/436/pomo.htm – extracted 19 October 2007.

Paul Newall (2005) *Postmodernism*, http://www.galilean-libarary.org/int12.html – extracted 19 October 2007.

Clive Beck (2007) *Postmodernism, Pedagogy and Philosophy of Education*, http://ed.uiuc.edu/EPS/PES-yearbook/93_docs/BECK.HTM – extracted 19 October 2007.

Mary Klages (2007) *Postmodernism*, http://www.colorado.edu/English/courses/ENG-L2012Klages/pomo.html – extracted 19 October 2007.

Jacques Derrida (2007) *Structuralism/Poststructuralism*, http://www.colorado.edu/Eng-lish/coursesENGL2012Klages/1derrida.html – extracted 19 October 2007.

Themes in Theories of Colonialism and Postcolonialism, http://www.thecore.nus.edu.sg/post/poldiscourse/thesem/themes.html – extracted 19 October 2007.

Bibliography

Abedi, J. and Dietel, R. (2004) 'Challenges in the No Child Left Behind Act for English-language learners', *Phi Delta Kappan*, 85, 10 pp. 782–86.

Abraham, J. (1995) *Divide and School*, London: Falmer Press.

Adelaide Declaration Review Steering Committee (2007) *Federalist Paper 2: The future of schooling in Australia*. A report by the States and Territories, Department of Education, Victoria.

Adelman, C. (1989) 'The practical ethic takes priority over methodology', in Carr, W. (ed.), *Quality in Teaching*, London: Falmer Press.

AdvancEd (2007) *A guide to administering advanced surveys, advancing excellence in education worldwide*, Washington, DC: AdvancEd.

Ailwood, J. (2003) 'Governing early childhood through play', *Contemporary Issues in Early Childhood*, 4, 3, pp. 286–99.

Ainley, J., Fleming, M. and Rowe, K. (2002) 'Evaluating systemic school reform: Literacy advance in the early years', paper presented at the Annual Conference of the American Educational Research Association, New Orleans.

Ainscow, M., Booth, T. and Dyson, A. (2006) 'Inclusion and the standards agenda: negotiating policy pressures in England', *International Journal of Education*, 3, 6, pp. 295–308.

Aitken, J.A. (1999) 'Leaping boundaries of difference', *Curriculum Inquiry*, 29, 2, pp. 149–57.

Allen, S. (1990) 'The parent-teacher partnership in schooling', *Education Australia*, 8, 1, pp. 5–6.

Alloway, N. (1995) 'Eight's too late: Early childhood education and gender reform', *Unicorn*, 21, 4, pp. 19–27.

Allwright, D. (1990) *Autonomy in language pedagogy*, Stanford: CRILE Working Paper.

Althusser, L. (1971) 'Ideology and the ideological state apparatuses', in L. Althusser *Lenin and philosophy and other essays*, New York: Monthly Review Press.

Anderson, K.L. (2001) 'Voicing concern about noisy classrooms', *Educational Leadership*, 58, 7, pp. 77–87.

Anderson, L.W. and Sosniak, L.A. (1994) (eds), *Bloom's Taxonomy: A Forty-Year Retrospective, Ninety-Third Yearbook of the National Society for the Study of Education*, Chicago, IL: University of Chicago Press.

Anderson-Inman, L.A. and Horney, M. (1993) 'Profiles of hypertext readers: Results from the Electro Text Project', paper presented at the Annual Conference of the American Educational Research Association, Atlanta.

Andrews, G. (1985) *The Parent Action Manual*, Melbourne: Schools Community Interaction Trust.

Angus, M. (1995) 'Devolution of school governance in an Australian state school system: Third time lucky', in Carter, D.S.G. and O'Neill, M.H. (eds), *Case Studies in Educational Change: An International Perspective*, London: Falmer Press.

Anyon, J. (1994) 'The retreat of Marxism and socialist feminism: postmodern and poststructuralist theories', *Curriculum Inquiry*, 24, 2, pp. 115–34.

Apple, M.W. (1979) *Ideology and Curriculum*, London: Routledge and Kegan Paul.

—— (1986) *Teachers and texts*, New York: Routledge &Kegan Paul.

—— (1988) 'What reform talk does: Creating inequalities in education', *Educational Administration Quarterly*, 24, 3, pp. 272–81.

—— (1990) *Ideology and curriculum*, New York: Routledge.

—— (1993) *Official Knowledge*, New York: Routledge.

—— (2000) 'Can critical pedagogies interrupt rights policies?', *Educational Theory*, 50, 2, pp. 229–58.

Arends, R.I. (2006) *Learning to Teach*, 6th edn, Boston, MA: MA: McGraw Hill.

Ariav, T. (1988) 'Growth in teachers' curriculum knowledge through the process of curriculum analysis', paper presented at the Annual Meeting of the American Educational Research Association, New Orleans.

Armstrong, T. (1994) *Multiple intelligences in the classroom*, Alexandria, VA: ASCD.

—— (2007) 'The curriculum superhighway', *Educational Leadership*, 64, 8, pp. 16–21.

Arnot, M. (1993) 'Introduction', in Arnot, M. and Weiler, K. (eds), *Feminism and Social Justice in Education: International Perspectives*, London: Falmer Press.

Arnot, M. and Dillabough, J. (1999) 'Feminist politics and democratic values in education', *Curriculum Inquiry*, 29, 2, pp. 174–90.

Association for Supervision and Curriculum Development (ASCD) (2005) 'Parent involvement', Smart Brief, 27 October, ASCD.

—— (2006a) 'Illinois Standards Achievement Tests', ASCD Smart Brief, 18 March, Alexandria, VA: ASCD.

—— (2006b) 'Tutoring firms push ethical limits', 9 March, Alexandria, VA: ASCD.

Asp, E. (2000) '*Assessment in Education*: Where have we been? Where are we headed?', in Brandt, R.S. (ed.), *Education in a New Era*, Alexandria, VA: ASCD.

Atkinson, E. (2000) 'What can postmodern thinking do for educational research?', paper presented at the Annual Meeting of the American Educational Research Association, New Orleans.

Au, W. (2007) 'High-stakes testing and curricular control: a qualitative metasynthesis', *Educational Researcher*, 36, 5, pp. 258–67.

Ayers, W. (1993) *To Teach: The Journey of a Teacher*, New York: Teachers College Press.

Azzara, J. (2000) 'The heart of school leadership', *Educational Leadership*, 58, 4, pp. 62–68.

Back Pack Net Centre (2005) *Classroom of the Future*, http://www.backpack.com.sg/faq.html.

Bailey, D.B. and Palsha, S.A. (1992) 'Qualities of the stages of concern questionnaire and implications for educational innovations', *Journal of Educational Research*, 85, 4, pp. 226–32.

Baker, E.L. (2003) 'Reflections on technology-enhanced assessment', *Assessment in Education*, 10, 3, pp. 421–24.

——— (2007) 'Presidential address: The end(s) of testing', *Educational Researcher*, 36, 6, pp. 309–17.

Ball, D.L., Cohen, D.K., Petersen, P.L. and Wilson, S.M. (1994) 'Understanding state efforts to reform teaching and learning: Learning from teachers about learning to teach', paper presented at the Annual Conference of the American Educational Research Association, New Orleans.

Ball, S.J. (1994) *Education Reform*, Buckingham: Open University Press.

Barber, M. (2006) *Education reform lessons from England*, New York: Education Sector.

Barone, T. (1982) 'Insinuated theory from curriculum-in-use', *Theory into Practice*, 21, 1, pp. 38–43.

Barrow, R. (1999) 'The need for philosophical analysis in a postmodern era', *Interchange*, 30, 4, pp. 415–32.

Barry, K., King, L., Pitts-Hill, K. and Zehnder, S. (1998) 'An investigation into student use of a heuristic in a series of cooperative learning problem solving lessons', paper presented at the Annual Conference of the American Education Research Association, San Diego.

Barton, A.C., Drake, C., Perez, J., St Louis, K. and George, M. (2004) 'Ecologies of parental engagement in urban education', *Educational Researcher*, 33, 4, pp. 3–12.

Bass, B.M. and Avolio, B.J. (1994) *Improving Organisational Effectiveness Through Transformational Leadership*, Thousand Oaks, CA: Sage.

Bassey, M. (1990) 'Action research in action', in Dadds, M. and Lofthouse, B. (eds), *The Study of Primary Education, A Source Book, Vol. 4, Classroom and Teaching Studies*, London: Falmer Press.

Bauch, P.A. and Goldring, E.B. (2000) 'Teacher work context and parent involvement in urban high schools of choice', *Educational Research and Evaluation*, 6, 1, pp. 1–23.

Beane, J.A. (2001) *A middle school curriculum: from rhetoric to reality*, 3rd edn, Columbus, OH: National Middle School.

Beare, H. (1998) 'Who are the teachers of the future?', *IARTV Seminar Series*, August, No. 76, Melbourne: IARTV.

Beauchamp, G.A. (1981) *Curriculum Theory*, 4th edn, Itasca, IL: Peacock.

Beck, C. (1993) 'Postmodernism, pedagogy and philosophy in education', http://www.ed.uiuc.edu/EPS/PES-Yearbook/93_docs/BECK.HTM (extracted 19 October 2007).

Becker, H. (1981) 'Teacher practices of parent involvement at home: A statewide survey', paper presented at the Annual Meeting of the American Educational Research Association, Chicago.

Becker, H.J. (1998) 'Running to catch a moving train: schools and information technologies', *Theory into Practice*, 37, 1, pp. 20–30.

Behar-Horenstein, L. (2000) 'Can the modern view of curriculum be refined by postmodern criticism?', in Glanz, J. and Behar-Horenstein, L. (eds), *Paradigm Debates in Curriculum and Supervision*, Westport, CT: Bergin and Garvey.

Belensky, M., Clinchy, B., Goldberg, N. and Tarule, J. (1988) *Women's Ways of Knowing: The Development of Self, Voice and Mind*, New York: Basic Books.

Bell, G.H. (1988) 'Action inquiry', in Nias, J. and Groundwater-Smith, S. (eds), *The Enquiring Teacher: Supporting and Sustaining Teacher Research*, London: Falmer Press.

Bell, L. (1988) *Appraising Teachers in Schools*, London: Routledge.

Bell, P.A., Fisher, J.D. and Loomis, R.J. (1976) *Environmental Psychology*, Philadelphia, PA: W.B. Saunders.

Bello, E.E. (2006) 'Inviting a collaborative action research project: From choosing a school to planning the work on an issue', *Educational Action Research*, 14, 1, pp. 3–21.

Bennett, H. (1992) *Teacher Appraisal: Survival and Beyond*, London: Longman.

Bennett, N. and Anderson, L. (2005) 'School-LEA partnerships: recipe for success or chimera?', *Journal of Educational Change*, 6, 1, pp. 29–50.

Bennett, S.N. (1981) 'Time and space: Curriculum allocation and pupil involvement in British open-space schools', *The Elementary School Journal*, 82, 1, pp. 18–26.

Bennis, W.G., Benne, J. and Chin, K. (1976) *The Planning of Change*, New York: Holt, Rinehart and Winston.

Ben-Peretz, M. and Dor, B.Z. (1986) *Thirty years of school-based curriculum development: a case study*, Eric Ed 274096.

Berlak, A. (1999) 'Teaching and testimony: Witnessing and bearing witness to racisms in culturally diverse classrooms', *Curriculum Inquiry*, 29, 1, pp. 99–128.

Berman, P., McLaughlin, M.W. (1975) *Federal programs supporting educational change, Vol. 4: The findings in review*, Santa Monica, CA: Rand Corporation.

Bernstein, B.B. (1973) *Class, codes, and control: Vol. 1. Theoretical studies towards a sociology of language*, London: Routledge & Kegan Paul.

Betts, F. (1997) 'Scoreboards for schools', *Educational Leadership*, 55, 3, pp. 70–71.

Beyer, L.E. and Apple, M.W. (eds) (1998) *The curriculum: Problems, politics, and possibilities*, 2nd edn, Albany, NY: State University of New York Press.

Bigum, C. (1997) 'Teachers and computers: in control or being controlled?', *Australian Journal of Education*, 41, 3, pp. 247–62.

Billing, D. (1994) 'The development of appraisal in Tasmania', in Ingvarson, L. and Chadbourne, R. (eds), *Valuing Teachers' Work: New Directions in Teacher Appraisal*, Melbourne: ACER.

Binney, G. and Williams, C. (1995) *Leaning into the Future: Changing the Way People Change Organizations*, London: Brearley.

Bitter, G.G. and Pierson, M.E. (2005) *Using Technology in the Classroom*, 6th edn, Boston, MA: Pearson/Allyn & Bacon.

Black, P. (2001) 'Dreams, strategies and systems: Portraits of assessment, past, present and future', *Assessment in Education*, 8, 1, pp. 80–93.

Black, P. and Wiliam, D. (1998) *Inside the Black Box: Raising standards through classroom assessment*, London: King's College School of Education.

—— (2005) 'Lessons from around the world: How policies, politics and cultures constrain and afford assessment practices', *Curriculum Journal*, 16, 2, pp. 249–61.

Blackmore, J. (1988) *Assessment and Accountability*, Geelong: Deakin University Press.

—— (1998) 'Gender, restructuring the emotional economy of higher education', unpublished paper, Deakin University.

Bloom, B.S. (1956) 'Taxonomy of educational objectives: Cognitive domain', New York: David McKay.

Bloom, B.S., Engelhart, M.D., Frost, E.J., Hill, W.H. and Krathwohl, D.R. (1956) *Taxonomy of Educational Objectives, Handbook 1: Cognitive Domain*, New York: David McKay.

Blyth, A. (2002) 'Outcomes, standards and benchmarks', *Curriculum Perspectives*, 22, 3, pp. 13–22.

Bolin, F.S. and McConnell Falk, J. (1987) (eds), *Teacher renewal: Professional issues, personal choices*, New York: Teachers College Press.

Boomer, G. (1986) 'Long division: A consideration of participation, equality and brainpower in Australian education', paper presented at the ACSSO Annual Conference, Launceston.

Borman, G.D., Hewes, G.M., Overman, L.T. and Brown, S. (2003) 'Comprehensive school reform and achievement: a meta-analysis', *Review of Educational Research*, 73, 2, pp. 125–230.

Bottery, M. (2004) *The Challenges of Educational Leadership*, London: Paul Chapman.

Bottini, M. and Grossman, S. (2005) 'Centre-based teaching and children's learning', *Childhood Education*, 10, pp. 274–77.

Bourdieu, P. and Passeron, J. (1977) *Reproduction in education, society and culture*, London: Sage.

Bourke, S. (1994) 'Some responses to changes in Australian education', *Australian Educational Researcher*, 21, 1, pp. 1–18.

Bowles, D. (1980) *School community relations, community support, and student achievement: A summary of findings*, Madison, WI: University of Wisconsin.

Bowles, S. and Gintis, H. (1976) *Schooling in capitalist America*, New York: Basic Books.

Boyle, B. and Bragg, J. (2006) 'A curriculum without foundation', *British Educational Research Journal*, 32, 4, pp. 569–82.

Brady, L. (1996) 'Outcome-based education: A critique?', *The Curriculum Journal*, 7, 1, pp. 5–16.

Brady, L. and Kennedy, K. (2007) *Curriculum construction*, 3rd edn, Sydney: Pearson Prentice Hall.

Brady, P. (1984) 'Chasing ghosts out of the machine: A deconstruction of some curriculum theory'. *Curriculum Perspectives*, 4, 2, pp. 64–66.

Brandon, A., Carmichael, P. and Marshall, B. (2005) 'Learning about assessment for learning: A framework for discourse about classroom', *Teacher Development*, 9, 2, pp. 201–14.

Brandt, R. (1998) 'Listen first', *Educational Leadership*, 55, 8, pp. 25–30.

Brennan, R.T., Kim, J., Wenz-Gross, M. and Siperstein, G.N. (2001) 'The relative equitability of high-stakes testing versus teacher-assigned grades: An analysis of the Massachusetts Comprehensive Assessment System (MCAS)' *Harvard Educational Review*, 71, 2, pp. 173–12.

Britzman, D. (1992) 'The terrible problem of knowing thyself: Toward a poststructural account of teacher identity', *Journal of Curriculum Theorizing*, 8, 3, pp. 23–46.

—— (2002) 'The death of curriculum?', in W.E. Doll and N. Gough (eds), *Curriculum visions*, New York: Peter Lang.

Broadfoot, P. (1979) *Assessment, Schools and Society*, London: Methuen.

Brooker, R., Macpherson, I. and Aspland, T. (2000) 'Taking action research from the local to the global via an hermeneutic spiral', paper presented at the Annual Conference of the American Educational Research Association, New Orleans.

Brophy, J. (1981) 'Teacher praise: A functional analysis', *Review of Educational Research*, 51, 1, pp. 5–32.

Brown, M., Ralph, S. and Brember, I. (2002) 'Change-linked work-related stress in British teachers', *Research in Education*, 67, pp. 1–12.

Brown, T.M. (1988) 'How fields change: A critique of the "Kuhnian" view', in W.F. Pinar (ed.), *Contemporary curriculum discourses*, Scottsdale, AZ: Gorsuch Scarisbrick.

Brundrett, M. (2006) 'Evaluating the individual and combined impact of national leadership programmes in England: Perceptions and practices', *School Leadership and Management*, 26, 5, pp. 473–88.

Buckley, J. and Schneider, M. (2006) 'Are Charter School parents more satisfied with schools? Evidence from Washington, DC', *Peabody Journal of Education*, 81, 1, pp. 57–78.

Budin, H. (1999) 'The computer enters the classroom', *Teachers College Record*, 100, 3, pp. 656–70.

Burnaford, G., Fischer, J. and Hobson, D. (1996) *Teachers Doing Research: Practical Possibilities*, Mahwah, NJ: Lawrence Erlbaum.

Burnett, P.C. and Meacham, D. (2002) 'Measuring the quality of teaching in elementary school classrooms', *Asia-Pacific Journal of Teacher Education*, 30, 2, pp. 141–54.

Burns, C. and Myhill, D. (2004) 'Interactive or inactive? A consideration of the nature of interaction in whole class teaching', *Cambridge Journal of Education*, 34, 1, pp. 35–50.

Burrow, S. (1994) 'McDonalds in the classroom', in Deakin (ed.), *Centre for Education and Change, Schooling What Future?* Geelong, Deakin University.

Burrow, S. and Martin, R. (1998) 'Speaking up for public education workers – the Australian Education Union in hard times', in Reid, A. (ed.), *Going Public: Education Policy and Public Education in Australia*, Canberra: ACSA.

Butin, D.W. (2003) 'Of what use is it? Multiple conceptualisations of service learning within education', *Teachers College Record*, 105, 9, pp. 1674–92.

Butt, R. (1983) 'The elucidatory potential of autobiography and biography in understanding teachers' thoughts and actions', paper presented at the Bergamo Conference, Dayton, Ohio.

Cairns, L. (1992) 'Competency-based education: Nostradamus's Nostrum', *Journal of Teaching Practice*, 12, 1, pp. 1–31.

Caldwell, B. (2000a) 'Scenarios for leadership and abandonment in the transformation of schools', *School Effectiveness and School Improvement*, 11, 4, pp. 475–99.

—— (2002b) 'Policy priorities for the transformation of Australia's Schools', *Occasional Paper Series*, Paper No. 2, Australian College of Education, Canberra.

—— (2002b) 'Autonomy and self-management: Concepts and evidence', in Bush, T. and Bell, L. (eds), *The Principles and Practice of Educational Management*, London: Paul Chapman.

Caldwell, B.J. and Spinks, J.M. (1998) *Beyond the Self-managing School*, London: Falmer Press.

Caldwell, R. (1993) 'Paradox and uncertainty in the governance of education', in Beare, H. and Boyd, W.L. (eds), *Restructuring Schools*, London: Falmer Press.

Calfee, R. and Perfumo, P. (1996) (eds), *Writing Portfolios in the Classroom*, Mahwah, NJ: Lawrence Erlbaum.

Calhoun, E.F. (2002) 'Action research for school improvement', *Educational Leadership*, 59, 6, pp. 12–17.

Campbell, C. and Murillo, F.J. (2005) 'Big change question: do local central authorities make a difference in school reform?', *Journal of Educational Change*, 6, 1, pp. 77–89.

Campbell, E. (2006) 'Curricular and professional authority in schools', *Curriculum Inquiry*, 36, 2, pp. 111–18.

Campbell, L. (1997) 'How teachers interpret MI theory', *Educational Leadership*, 55, 1, pp. 14–19.

Campbell, R.J. (1993) (ed.), *Breadth and Balance in the Primary Curriculum*, London: Falmer Press.

Capobianco, B.M. and Feldman, A. (2006) 'Promoting quality for teacher action research: Lessons learned from science teachers' action research', *Educational Action Research*, 14, 4, pp. 497–512.

Capper, C.A., Alston, J., Gause, C.P., Koschoreck, J., Lopez, G., Lugg, C. and McKenzie, K. (2006) 'Integrating lesbian/gay/bisexual/transgender topics and their intersections with other areas of difference into the leadership preparation curriculum: Practical ideas and strategies', *Journal of School Leadership*, 16, 2, pp. 142–57.

Carless, D. (2004) 'Continuity and teacher-centred reform: Potential paradoxes in educational change', *Curriculum Perspectives*, 24,1, pp. 13–21.

—— (2007) 'Learning-oriented assessment: Conceptual bases and practical implications', *Innovations in Education and Teaching International*, 44, 1, 57–66.

Carr, M. (2001) *Assessment in Early Childhood Settings: Learning Stories*, London: Paul Chapman.

Carr, W. and Kemmis, S. (1986) *Becoming Critical: Education, Knowledge and Action Research*, London: Falmer Press.

Casas, F.R. and Meaghan, D.E. (2001) 'Renewing the debate over the use of standardised testing in the evaluation of learning and teaching', *Interchange*, 32, 2, pp. 147–81.

Cavarretta, J. (1998) 'Parents are a school's best friend, *Educational Leadership*, 55, 8, pp. 12–15.

Chapin, J.R. and Messick, R.G. (1999) *Elementary School Studies*, 2nd edn, New York: Longman.

Charlton, E. (2004) *Disrupting heteronormativity: What about the girls?*, Melbourne: Association for Research in Education.

Chase, C.I. (1999) *Contemporary Assessment for Educators*, New York: Longman.

Chatterji, M. (2002) 'Models and methods for examining standards-based reforms and accountability initiatives: Have the tools of inquiry answered pressing questions on improving schools?', *Review of Educational Research*, 72, 3, pp. 345–87.

Chen, H.L. and Chung, J. (2000) 'A study of the problems and coping strategies for school-based curriculum development', *Journal of Taiwan Normal University*, 47,1, pp. 1–57.

Chodorow, N. (1978) *The Reproduction of Mothering*, Berkeley, CA: University of California Press.

Christie, K. (2004) 'The state/federal cogs of change', *Phi Delta Kappan*, 85, 7, pp. 485–88.

Churchill, R. and Williamson, J. (1999) 'Traditional attitudes and contemporary experiences: Teachers and educational change', *Asia-Pacific Journal of Teacher Education and Development*, 2, 2, pp. 43–51.

Clandinin, J. (1986) *Classroom Practice: Teachers Images in Action*, London: Falmer Press.

Clark, A.F. (ed.) (1976) *Experimenting with Organisational Life: The Action Research Approach*, New York: Plenum Press.

Clark, D.L. and Guba, E.G. (1965) 'Potential change roles in education', paper presented at the Symposium of Innovation and Planning School Curricula, Airlie House, VA.

Clark, D.L. and Meloy, J.M. (1990) 'Recanting bureaucracy: A democratic structure for leadership in schools', in Lieberman, A. (ed.), *Schools as Collaborative Cultures: Creating the Future Now*, London: Falmer Press.

Clark, P. (2005) '"A nice little wife to make things pleasant": Portrayals of women in Canadian history textbooks approved in British Columbia', *McGill Journal of Education*, 40, 2, pp. 241–64.

Clarke, S. (1998) *Targeting Assessment in the Primary Classroom*, London: Hodder and Stoughton.

—— (2001) *Unlocking Formative Assessment*, London: Hodder & Stoughton.

Clough, E., Aspinwall, K. and Gibbs, B. (eds) (1989) *Learning to Change: An LEA School-focussed Initiative*, London: Falmer Press.

Cochran-Smith, M. (1994) 'The power of teacher research in teacher education', in Hollingsworth, S. and Sockett, H. (eds), *Teacher Research and Educational Reform*, Ninety-Third Yearbook of the National Society for the Study of Education, Chicago, IL: University of Chicago Press.

—— (2001a) 'The outcomes question in teacher education', *Teaching and Teacher Education*, 17, 1, pp. 527–46.

—— (2001b) 'Higher standards for prospective teachers: What's missing from the discourse?', *Journal of Teacher Education*, 52, 3, pp. 179–81.

Cocklin, B., Simpson, N. and Stacey, M. (1995) 'School planning to achieve student outcomes: processes of change in a secondary school', paper presented at the Annual Conference of the Australian Association for Research in Education, Hobart.

Coffey, J., Sato, M. and Thiebault, M. (2005) 'Classroom assessment: Up close – and personal', *Teacher Development*, 9, 2, pp. 169–84.

Cohen, D. (1974) *Some considerations in the development, implementation and evaluation of curricula, Technical Report 2*, Science Education Centre, University of Iowa.

Cohen, D.K. and Hill, H.C. (2001) *Learning policy: when state education reform works*, New Haven, CT: Yale University Press.

Cohen, L., Manion, L. and Morrison, K. (1998) *A Guide to Teaching Practice*, 6th edn, London: Routledge.

Cohn-Varas, B. and Grose, K. (1998) 'A partnership for literacy', *Educational Leadership*, 55, 8, pp. 45–48.

Collins, C. (1994a) 'Is the national curriculum profiles brief valid?', *Curriculum Perspectives*, 14, 1, pp. 45–48.

—— (1994b) *Curriculum and Pseudo-Science. Is the Australian National Curriculum Project Built on Credible Foundations?*, Canberra: ACSA.

Colombo, M.W. (2004) 'Family literacy nights – and other home-school connections', *Educational Leadership*, 61, 8, pp. 48–51.

Comer, J.P. (2005) 'The rewards of parent participation', *Educational Leadership*, 62, 6, pp. 38–43.

Connelly, F.M. (1978) 'How shall we publish case studies of curriculum development? An essay review of Reid and Walker's case studies in curriculum change', *Curriculum Inquiry*, 8, pp. 73–82.

Connelly, F.M. and Ben-Peretz, M. (1980) 'Teachers' roles in the using and doing of research and curriculum development', *Journal of Curriculum Studies*, 12, 2, pp. 13–19.

Connelly, F.M. and Clandinin, D.J. (1990) *Teachers as curriculum planners*, 2nd edn, New York: Teachers College Press.

Conservative Party (1987) *General Election Manifesto*, London: Conservative Central Office.

Cook-Sather, A. (2002) 'Authorising students' perspectives: toward trust, dialogue and change in education', *Educational Researcher*, 31, 4, pp. 3–14.

Coombs, P. (1985) *The World Crisis in Education: The View from the Eighties*, Oxford: Oxford University Press.

Cooper, C.W. and Christie, C.A. (2005) 'Evaluating parent empowerment: A look at the potential of social justice evaluation in education', *Teachers College Record*, 107, 10, pp. 2248–74.

Cooper, I. (1982) 'The maintenance of order and use of space in primary school buildings', *British Journal of Sociology of Education*, 3, 3, pp. 45–63.

Copland, M. (2001) 'The myth of the superprincipal, *Phi Delta Kappan*, 82, 7, pp. 528–33.

Corbett, H.D. and Rossman, J.B. (1989) 'Three paths to implementing change: A research note, *Curriculum Inquiry*, 19, 2, pp. 163–90.

Corey, S. (1953) *Action Research to Improve School Practices*, New York: Teachers College Press.

Cornbleth, C. (1990) *Curriculum in Context*, London: Falmer Press.

Coulby, D. (2000) *Beyond the National Curriculum*, London: Routledge/Falmer Press.

Council of Chief State School Officers (2007) *Interstate School Leaders Licensure Consortium: Standards for school leaders*, Washington, DC: Council of Chief State School Officers.

Cousins, J.B., Goh, S.C. and Clark, S. (2006) Data use leads to data valuing: evaluative inquiry for school decision making.

Cradler, J. and Bridgforth, E. (2004) 'Effective site level planning for technology integration,' www.wested.org/techplocy/planning.html.

Craig, C.J. (2006) 'Why is dissemination so difficult? The nature of teacher knowledge and the spread of curriculum reform', *American Educational Research Journal*, 43, 2, pp. 257–93.

Crandall, D.P. and associates (1983) *The study of dissemination efforts supporting school improvement*, Dessio Andover, MA: The Network.

Cromer, J.P. (2005) 'The rewards of parent participation', *Educational Leadership*, 62, 6, pp. 38–43.

Cronbach, L.J. (1986) *Essentials of psychological measurement*, New York: Harper & Row.

Crowley, K., Callanan, M., Tenebaum, H. and Allen, E. (1998) 'Evidence of early gender bias in informal science activity: A study of everyday parent–child explanation', unpublished paper, University of Pittsburgh.

Crowther, F., Hann, L., Mcmaster, J. and Ferguson, M. (2000) 'Leadership for successful school revitalisation: Lessons from recent Australian research', paper presented at the Annual Conference of the American Educational Research Association, New Orleans.

Cruickshank, D., Jenkins, D. and Metcalf, K. (2005) *The act of teaching*, 4th edn, Boston, MA: McGraw Hill.

Crump, S. (1998) 'New Labour, new conservatism?', paper presented at the Annual Conference of the American Educational Research Association, San Diego.

Cuban, L. (1988) 'Reforming again, again and again', *Educational Researcher*, 19, 1, pp. 3–13.

—— (1992) 'Curriculum stability and change', in Jackson, P.W. (ed.), *Handbook of Research on Curriculum*, New York: Macmillan.

Cullingford, C. (2006) 'Children's own vision of schooling', *Education* 3–13, 34, 3, pp. 211–21.

Cumming, J.J. and Maxwell, G.S. (2004) 'Assessment in Australian Schools: Current practices & trends', *Assessment in Education*, 13, 1, pp. 89–198.

Cunningham, G.K. (1998) *Assessment in the classroom*, London: Falmer.

Curriculum Development Centre (1977) *Social Education Materials Project (SEMP)*, Canberra: Curriculum Development Centre.

Dalin, P. and McLaughlin, M.W. (1975) 'Strategies for innovation in higher education', Educational Research Symposium on Strategies for Research and Development in Higher Education, Stockholm.

Danielson, C. (2001) 'New trends in teacher evaluation', *Educational Leadership*, 58, 5, pp. 12–15.

Daresh, J.C. (2006) 'Teaching and school leaders: Overdue or overload?', *Journal of Thought*, 41, 1, pp. 27–39.

Darling-Hammond, L. (1994) 'Performance-based assessment and educational equity', *Harvard Educational Review*, 64, 1, pp. 5–30.

—— (1997) *The Right to Learn: A Blueprint for Creating Schools that Work*, San Francisco, CA: Jossey-Bass.

—— (1998) 'Teacher learning that supports student learning', *Educational Leadership*, 55, 5, pp. 6–11.

Darling-Hammond, L. and Falk, B. (1997) 'Using standards and assessments to support student learning', *Phi Delta Kappan*, 79, 3, pp. 190–99.

Darling-Hammond, L., Ancess, J. and Falk, B. (1995) *Authentic Assessment in Action*, New York: Teachers College Press.

Datnow, A. (2000) 'Power and politics in the adoption of school reform models', *Educational Evaluation and Policy Analysis*, 22, 4, pp. 357–74.

Datnow, A. and Castellano, M. (2000) 'Teachers' responses to success for all: how beliefs, experiences and adaptations shape implementation', *American Educational Research Journal*, 37, 2, pp. 775–99.

Datnow, A. and Hubbard,L. (eds) (2004) *Doing gender in policy and practice: perspectives on single-sex and co-educational schooling*, New York: Routledge/Falmer.

Davies, B. and Hentschke, G. (2006) 'Public-private partnership in education: Insights from the field', *School Leadership and Management*, 26, 3, pp. 205–26.

Davies, J., Hallam, S. and Ireson, J. (2003) 'Ability groupings in the primary school: Issues arising from practice', *Research Papers in Education*, 18, 1, pp. 45–60.

Day, C. (1990) 'United Kingdom: managing curriculum development at Branston School and Community College', in C.J. Marsh, C. Day, L. Hannay and G. McCutcheon (eds), *Reconceptualising school-based curriculum development*, London: Falmer.

Day, C. and Roberts-Holmes, T. (1998) 'Beyond transformational leadership', *Educational Leadership*, 57, 7, pp. 56–59.

Day, C., Johnston, D. and Whitaker, P. (1985) *Managing Primary School*, London: Harper and Row.

De Castell, S. (2000) 'Literacies, technologies and the future of the library in the "information age"', *Journal of Curriculum Studies*, 32, 3, pp. 359–76.

De Cuir, J.T. and Dixson, A. (2004) '"So when it comes out, they aren't that surprised that it is there": Using critical race theory as a tool of analysis of race and racism in education', *Educational Researcher*, 33, 5, pp. 26–31.

De Mocker, S. (1986) *A Trail of Desire: Aspects of Relationship with Nature*, unpublished doctoral dissertation, University of Rochester.

De Vaney, A. (1998) 'Educational technology', *Theory into Practice*, 37, 1, pp. 2–3.

Delandshere, G. and Arens, S.A. (2001) 'Representations of teaching and standards-based reform: Are we closing the debate about teacher education?' *Teaching and Teacher Education*, 17, 1, pp. 547–66.

Department for Children, Schools and Families (2007) 'Personalised Learning', http://www.standards.dfes.gov.uk/personalisedlearning/ (extracted 9 October 2007).

Department for Education and Science (DFES) (2004) *Guidance on the mandatory requirement to hold the national professional qualifications for headship*, London: DFES.

Department for Education and Skills (2002) *Education and Skills: Investment for Reform*, London: HMSO.

Department of Education (2002) *Forming judgments about school performance: a resource for successful self-assessment*, Perth: Department of Education.

Department of Education and Early Childhood Development, Victoria (2005) *School Accountability and Improvement Framework*, Melbourne: DEECD.

—— (2007) *Value-added measures for school improvement*, paper 13, Melbourne: DEECD.

Department of Education, Science and Training (1993) *National policy for the education of girls in Australian schools*, Canberra: AGPS.

Department of Education and Training, Victoria (2005) *School self-evaluation overview*, Melbourne: DET.

Department of Education, Western Australia (2002a) *The School Accountability Framework*, Perth, Government Printer.

—— (2002b) *Forming Judgments About School Performance: A Resource For Successful Self-Assessment*, Perth, Department Of Education

Department of Employment, Education and Training (1987) *National policy for the education of girls in Australian schools*, Canberra: AGPS.

Derrida, J. (1972) 'Discussion: Structure, sign and play in the discourse of the human sciences', in Macksey, R. and Donato, E. (eds), *The Structuralist Controversy, Baltimore*, Johns Hopkins University Press.

Deschamp. P.A. (1983) 'Planning for teaching: A study of teachers' intentions in planning' unpublished doctoral thesis, Murdoch University.

Desimone, L. (2002) 'How can comprehensive school reform models be successfully implemented?', *Review of Educational Research*, 72, 3, pp. 433–80.

Dimmock, C. (1993) (ed.), *School-based Management and School Effectiveness*, London: Routledge.

Dinkelman, T. (2001) 'Service learning in student teaching: "What's social studies for?", *Theory and Research in Social Education*, 29, 4, pp. 617–39.

Dockrell, J.E. and Shield, B.M. (2006) 'Acoustical barriers in classrooms: The impact of noise on performance in the classroom', *British Educational Research Journal*, 32, 3, pp. 509–25.

Dodd, A.W. (1998) 'What can educators learn from parents who oppose curricular and classroom practices?', *Journal of Curriculum Studies*, 30, 4, pp. 461–78.

Doll, W.E. JR (1993a) *A Post-modern Perspective on Curriculum*, New York: Teachers College Press.

—— (1993b) 'Curriculum possibilities in a "post" future', *Journal of Curriculum and Supervision*, 8, 4, pp. 277–92.

Domina, T. (2005) 'Levelling the home advantage: assessing the effectiveness of parental involvement in elementary school', *Sociology of Education*, 78 (July), pp. 233–49.

Drake, C., Spillane, J.P. and Hufferd-Ackles, K. (2001) 'Stored identities: teacher learning and subject-matter context', *Journal of Curriculum Studies*, 33, 1, pp. 1–24.

Drake, N.M. (1991) 'What is needed most: School reform or media reform?', *Phi Delta Kappan*, 73, 1, p. 57.

Dryfoos, J. (2000) 'The mind–body building equation', *Educational Leadership*, 57, 6, pp. 14–17.

—— (2004) 'Evaluation of community schools: an early look', www.Community-schools.org/evaluation/evalbrieffinal.html.

Du Four, R. (2002) 'The learning-centred principal', *Educational Leadership*, 59, 8, pp. 12–15.

Duke, D.L., Tucker, P., Salmonowicz, M.L. and Levy, M. (2006) 'Challenges facing principals of low-performing schools?', *Educational Practice and Theory*, 28, 2, pp. 5–25.

Dunn, R., Beaudry, J.S. and Klavas, A. (1989) 'Survey of research on learning styles', *Educational Leadership*, 46, 6, pp. 50–58.

Earl, L.M. (2005) *Thinking about purpose in classroom assessment: Assessment for, as and of learning*, Canberra: ACSA.

Earley, P. and Weindling, D. (2006) 'Consultant leadership – a new role for head teachers?', *School Leadership and Management*, 26, 1, pp. 37–53.

Easthope, C. and Easthope, G. (2000) 'Intensification, extension and complexity of teachers' workload', *British Journal of Sociology of Education*, 21, 1, pp. 43–56.

Eckman, E.W. (2006) 'Co-principals: Characteristics of dual leadership teams', *Leadership and Policy in Schools*, 5, 2, pp. 89–107.

Education Commission of the States (1998) *Comprehensive school reform: Allocating federal funds*, Denver, CO: Education Commission of the States.

Edwards, B.W. (2006aEnvironmental design and educational performance', *Research in Education*, 76, 3, pp. 14–32.

Edwards, R. (2006bAll quiet on the postmodern front?', *Studies in Philosophy of Education*, 25, 1, pp. 273–78.

Edwards, V. and Redfern, A. (1988) *At Home and School: Parent Participation in Primary Education*, London: Routledge.

Egan, K. (2003) 'Testing what for what?', *Educational Leadership*, 61, 3, pp. 27–30.

Eisner, E. and Vallance, E. (1974) (eds), *Conflicting Conceptions of Curriculum*, Berkeley, CA: McCutchan.

Eisner, E.W. (1974) 'Instructional and expressive objectives: Their formulation and use in curriculum', AERA Monograph Series in Curriculum Evaluation, No. 3, in M. Golby (ed.), *Curriculum design*, London: Open University Press.

—— (1991) *The Enlightened Eye*, New York: Macmillan.

—— (1993) 'Reshaping *Assessment in Education*: Some criteria in search of practice', *Journal of Curriculum Studies*, 25, 3, pp. 219–33.

—— (1994) *The educational imagination: On the design and evaluation of school programs*, 3rd edn, New York: Macmillan.

—— (1997) 'The promise and perils of alternative forms of data representation', *Educational Researcher*, 26, 6, pp. 4–9.

—— (2002) *The arts and the creation of mind*, Boston, MA: Yale University Press.

Eisner, E.W. and Vallance, E. (1974) *Conflicting conceptions of curriculum*, Berkeley, CA: McCutchan.

El-Dib, M.A.B. (2007) 'Levels of reflection in action research: An overview and an assessment tool', *Teacher and Teacher Education*, 23, 1, pp. 24–35.

Elkins, T. and Elliott, J. (2004) 'Competition and control: the impact of government regulation on teaching and learning in English schools', *Research Papers in Education*, 19, 1, pp. 15–30.

Ellerton, N.F. and Clements, M.A. (1994) *The National Curriculum Debacle*, Perth: Meridian Press.

Elliott, J. (1975) 'Initiation into classroom discussion', in Elliott, J. and MacDonald, B. (eds), *People in Classrooms*, Norwich, Centre for Applied Research in Education, University of East Anglia.

—— (1991) 'Changing contexts for educational evaluation: The challenge for methodology', *Studies in Educational Evaluation*, 17, pp. 215–38.

—— (1999) *The Curriculum Experiment*, Milton Keynes: Open University Press.

—— (2002) 'Action research as the basis of a new professionalism for teachers in an age of globalisation', paper presented at the Beijing Normal University, August.

Elliott, J. and Chan, K.K. (2002) 'Curriculum Reform East & West: Global Trends and Local Contexts', unpublished paper, University of East Anglia,

Elliott, J. and Kushner, S. (2007) 'The need for a manifesto for educational programme evaluation', *Cambridge Journal of Education*, 37, 3, pp. 5–19.

Ellis, A.K. and Fouts, J.T. (1997) *Research on Educational Innovations, Eye on Education*, New Jersey, Princeton Junction.

Ellis, D. (2003) 'Storefront: A school in a shopping mall', *EQ Australia*, 3 (spring), pp. 38–39.

Ellsworth, E. (1997) *Teaching positions: difference, pedagogy and the power of address*, New York: Teachers College Press.

Elmore, R.F. (1988) 'Modes of restructured schools', unpublished paper, Michigan State University.

Emmer, E.T. and Gerwell, M.C. (1998) 'Teachers' views and uses of cooperative learning, paper presented at the Annual Conference of the American Educational Research Association, San Diego.

Emmer, E.T., Evertson, C. and Worsham, M. (2000) *Classroom Management for Secondary Teachers*, 5th edn, Boston, MA: Allyn and Bacon

Enabling Sciences Education Research Network (2005) 'National Institute for Quality Teaching and School Leadership', scs.une.edu.au/EnSE/national.html – retrieved 5 September 2008.

Epstein, J.L. and Salinas, K.C. (2004) 'Parenting with families and communities', *Educational Leadership*, 61, 8, pp. 12–19.

Eraut, M., Goad, L. and Smooth, G. (1975) *The Analysis of Curriculum Materials*, Brighton: University of Sussex.

Eriksen, A. and Wintermute, M. (1983) *Students, Structure, Spaces: Activities in the Built Environment*, ERIC Research in Education, Washington, DC: ED233796.

Esposito, J. and Smith, S. (2006) 'From reluctant teacher to empowered teacher-researcher: One educator's journey toward action research', *Teacher Education Quarterly*, 33, 3, pp. 45–59.

Evans, K. (1990) 'Messages conveyed by physical forms', in Lofthouse, B. (ed.), *The Study of Primary Education: A Source Book, Vol. 2, The Curriculum*. London: Falmer Press.

Farrar, E., Desanctis, J.E. and Cohen, D.K. (1979) *Views from below: implementation research in education*, Cambridge, MA: Huron Institute.

Farrell, J.P. (2001) 'Can we really change the forms of formal schooling? And would it make a difference if we did?', *Curriculum Inquiry*, 31, 4, pp. 389–94.

Feinberg, P.R. (1985) 'Four curriculum theorists: A critique in the light of Martin Buber's philosophy of education', *Journal of Curriculum Theorizing*, 6, 1, pp. 5–164.

Feingold, A. (1992) 'Sex differences in variability in intellectual abilities: A new look at an old controversy', *Review of Educational Research*, 62, 1, pp. 74–81.

Feldman, A., Rearick, M. and Weiss, T. (1999) 'Teacher development and action research: Findings from five years of action research in schools', paper presented at the Annual Conference of the American Educational Research Association, Montreal.

Fernandez, C., Chokski, S., Cannon, J. and Yoshida, M. (2003) 'Learning about lesson study in the United States', *New and Old Voices on Japanese Education*, Armonk, NY: M.E. Sharpe.

Ferrero, D.J. (2006) 'Having it all', *Educational Leadership*, 63, 8, pp. 8–15.

Field, T. (1980) 'Imaginative alternative use of learning spaces', in Poole, M. (ed.), *Creativity Across the Curriculum*, Sydney: George Allen and Unwin.

Finn, J.D. (1998) 'Parental engagement that makes a difference', *Educational Leadership*, 55, 8, pp. 20–24.

Finn, J.D., Gerber, S.B., Achilles, C.M. and Boyd-Zaharias, J. (2001) 'The enduring effects of small classes', *Teachers College Record*, 103, 1, pp. 145–83.

Firestone, W.A. and Martinez, M.C. (2007) 'Districts, teacher leaders and distributed leadership: Changing instructional practice', *Leadership and Policy in Schools*, 6, 3, pp. 3–29.

Fischer, L., Schimmel, D. and Kelly, C. (1995) *Teachers and the Law*, 4th edn, New York: Longman.

Fisher, D. and Frey, N. (2007) *Checking for Understanding*, Alexandria, VA: ASCD.

Fisher, D.L. and Fraser, B.J. (1981) 'Validity and use of the "My class inventory"', *Science Education*, 65, pp. 3–11.

Flinders, D.J. and Thornton, S.J. (2004) *The curriculum reader*, London: Routledge.

Ford, N. and Chen, S.Y. (2001) 'Matching/mismatching revisited: An empirical study of learning and teaching styles', *British Journal of Educational Technology*, 32, 1, pp. 5–22.

Ford, R.W. (2001) 'A virtual enrichment program for primary students living in outback areas', *Australian Journal of Educational Technology*, 17, 1, pp. 45–51.

Forster, M. (1994) 'DART: Assisting Teachers To Use The English Profile In Assessing And Reporting, in Warhust, J. (ed.), *Teaching and Learning, Implementing the Profiles*, Canberra: ACSA.

Foster, W. (1989) 'Toward a critical practice of leadership', in Smyth, J. (ed.), *Critical Perspectives of Educational Leadership*, London: Falmer Press.

Foucault, M. (1972) *The Archaeology of Knowledge and the Discourse on Language*, New York: Pantheon.

Francis, D. (2001) 'The challenge of involving students in the Evaluation Process', *Asia-Pacific Journal of Teacher Education*, 29, 2, pp. 13–37.

Franek, M. (2006) 'Foiling cyberbullies in the new Wild West', *Educational Leadership*, 63, 4, pp. 39–43.

Franklin, J. (2002) 'Assessing assessment: Are alternative methods making the grade?', ASCD *Curriculum Update*, Spring, 1–8.

—— (2004) 'How technology is transforming K-12 arts classes', *Curriculum Update*, Spring, 4–5.

Fraser, B.J. (1981) 'Australian research on classroom environment: State of the art', *Australian Journal of Education*, 25, pp. 31–42.

—— (1986) *Classroom Environment*, London: Croom Helm.

Fraser, B.J. and Walberg, H.J. (1991) (eds), *Educational Environments*, London: Pergamon Press.

Fraser, B.J., McRobbie, C.J. and Fisher, D.L. (1996) 'Development, validation and use of the personal and class forms of a new classroom environment instrument', paper presented at the Annual Conference of the American Educational Research Association, New York.

Freebody, P. and Muspratt, S. (2007) 'Beyond generic knowledge in pedagogy and disciplinarity: the case of science textbooks', *Pedagogies: An International Journal*, 2, 1, pp. 35–48.

Frid, S. (2001) 'Supporting primary students' on-line learning in a virtual enrichment program', *Research in Education*, 66, 1, pp. 9–27.

Froese-Germain, B. (2001) 'Broadening the discourse on student assessment: Response to Casas and Meaghan', *Interchange*, 32, 2, pp. 183–90.

Fuhrman, S.H. and Elmore, R.F. (eds) (2004) *Redesigning accountability systems for education*, New York: Teachers College Press.

Fullan, M. (1989) *Implementing Educational Change: What We Know*, Ottawa, Education and Employment Division, Population and Human Resources Department, World Bank.

—— (1993) *Change Forces*, London: Falmer Press.

—— (2001) *Leading in a Culture of Change*, San Francisco, CA: Jossey-Bass.

—— (2002) 'The change leader', *Educational Leadership*, 59, 8, pp. 16–21.

—— (2003) 'Implementing change at the building level', in W.A Owings and L.S. Kaplan (eds), *Best practices, best thinking and the emerging issues in school leadership*, Thousand Oaks, CA: Corwin.

—— (2008) 'Curriculum implementation and sustainability', in F.M Connelly (ed.), *The Sage handbook of curriculum and instruction*, Los Angeles: Sage.

Fullan, M. and Earl, L. (2002) 'United Kingdom National literacy and numeracy strategies', *Journal of Educational Change*, 3, pp. 1–5.

Fullan, M. and Hargreaves, A. (1991) *Working Together for Your School. Melbourne*, Australian Council for Educational Administration.

Fullan, M.G. (1982) *The Meaning of Educational Change*, New York: Teachers College Press.

—— (1988) *What's Worth Fighting for in the Principalship?*, Toronto, ON: Teachers Federation.

—— (1991) *The New Meaning of Educational Change*, London: Cassell.

—— (1999) *Change Forces: The Sequel*. London: Falmer Press.

—— (2000) 'The three stories of education reform', *Phi Delta Kappan*, 81, 8, pp. 581–84.

—— (2004) *Leadership and sustainability: system thinkers in action*, San Francisco, CA: Corwin Press.

Fullan, M.G. and Pomfret, A. (1977) 'Research on curriculum and instruction implementation', *Review of Educational Research*, 47, 2, pp. 335–97.

Fullan, M.G., Bennett, B. and Rolheiser-Bennett, C. (1989) 'Linking classroom and school improvement', paper presented at the Annual Meeting of the American Educational Research Association, San Francisco.

Fullan, M.G., Bertani, A. and Quinn, J. (2004) 'New lessons for district wide reform', *Educational Leadership*, 61, 7, pp. 42–46.

Fullan, M.G., Hill, P. and Crevola, C (2006) *Breakthrough*, London: Routledge.

Furlong, J. (2002) 'Ideology and reform in teacher education in England: Some reflections on Cochran-Smith & Fries', *Educational Researcher*, 31, 6, pp. 23–25.

Futoran, G.C., Schofield, J.W. and Eurich-Fulmer, R. (1995) 'The Internet as a K-12 educational resource: Emerging issues of information access and freedom', *Computers in Education*, 24, 3, pp. 229–36.

Galton, M. (2002) 'A national curriculum balance sheet', *Education Review*, 15, 2, pp. 15–25.

Galton, M., Gray, J. and Rudduck, J. (2003) *Impact of Transitions and Transfers on Pupil Progress*, London: Department for Education and Skills.

Gamage, D. (2005) 'School-based management leads to shared responsibility and quality in education', *Curriculum and Teaching*, 20, 1, pp. 61–77.

Gamage, D.T. (1992) 'School-centred educational reforms of the 1990s: An Australian case study', *Educational Management and Administration*, 20, 1, pp. 5–14.

—— (1993) 'A review of community participation in school governance: An emerging culture in Australian Education', *British Journal of Educational Studies*, 41, 2, pp. 134–63.

Gardner, C. and Williamson, J. (2005) 'The forgotten interstices of education policy: the good, the bad and ugly', in C. Harris and C.J. Marsh (eds), *Curriculum development in Australia*, Adelaide: Open Books.

Gardner, H. (1983) *Frames of Mind: The theory of multiple intelligences*, New York: Basic Books.

Gay, K. (1986) *Ergonomics*, Hillsdale, NJ: Enslow Publishers

Gibbs, D. and Krause, K.L. (2000) (eds), *Cyberlines*, Melbourne: James Nicholas.

Giddens, A. (1990) *The Consequences of Modernity*, Cambridge: Cambridge University Press.

Gilbert, R. and Gilbert, P. (1998) *Masculinity Goes to School*, Sydney: Allen and Unwin.

Gillies, R.M. and Ashman, A.F. (2003) *Cooperative learning: the social and intellectual outcomes of learning in groups*, London: Routledge.

Ginsberg, R. and Wimpelberg, R.K. (1987) 'Educational change by commission: attempting 'trickle down' reform', *Educational Evaluation and Policy analysis*, 9, 4, pp. 344–60.

Gipps, C. and Murphy, P. (1994) *A Fair Test?: Assessment, Achievement and Equity*, Buckingham: Open University Press.

Gipps, C., Mccallum, B. and Hargreaves, E. (2000) 'Classroom assessment and feedback strategies of "expert" elementary teachers', paper presented at the Annual Conference of the American Educational Research Association, New Orleans.

Giroux, H.A. (1982) 'Power and resistance in the new sociology of education: Beyond theories of social and cultural reproduction', *Curriculum Perspectives*, 2, 3, pp. 1–14.

—— (1990) 'Curriculum theory, textual authority, and the role of teachers as public intellectuals', *Journal of Curriculum and Supervision*, 5, 4, pp. 361–83.

—— (1992) *Border Crossings: Cultural Workers and the Politics of Education*, New York: Routledge.

—— (1997) *Pedagogy and the politics of hope: Theory, culture and schooling*, New York: Routledge.

—— (2003) 'Public pedagogy and the politics of resistance: Notes on a critical theory of educational struggle', *Educational Philosophy and Theory*, 35, 1, pp. 5–16.

Glanz, J. (2007) 'On vulnerability and transformative leadership: An imperative for leaders of supervision', *International Journal of Leadership in Education*, 10, 2, pp. 115–35.

Glatter, R. (2006) 'Leadership and organisation in education: Time for a re-orientation?', *School Leadership and Management*, 26, 1, pp. 69–83.

Glatthorn, A.A. (1987) *Curriculum Leadership*, Glenview, Scott, Foresman and Company.

Glatthorn, A.A. and Fontana, J. (2002) *Standards and Accountability: How Teachers See Them*, Washington, DC: National Education Association.

Glatthorn, A.A. and Jailall, J. (2000) 'Curriculum for the new millennium', in R.S. Brandt (ed.), *Education in a New Era*, Alexandria, VA: ASCD.

Glenbrook High School District (2006) *Teacher Performance Appraisal Program*, Glenbrook, CA: Glenbrook School District.

Glickman, C.D. (2003) 'Symbols and celebrations that sustain education', *Educational Leadership*, 60, 6, pp. 34–39.

Goddard, J.T. (2007) 'School leadership and equity: Results from an international comparative study', *School Leadership and Management*, 27, 1, pp. 1–5.

Goldring, E.B. (1993) 'Principals, parents and administrative superiors', *Educational Administration Quarterly*, 29, 1, pp. 93–117.

Goldsmith, L.T. and Mark, J. (1999) 'What is a standards-based mathematics curriculum?', *Educational Leadership*, 57, 3, pp. 40–45.

Goldstein, J. (2004) 'Making sense of distributed leadership: the case of peer assistance and review', *Educational Evaluation and Policy Analysis*, 26, 2, pp. 173–97.

Good, T.L. (2006) 'No Child Left Behind: introduction', *Elementary School Journal*, 106, 5, pp. 453–54.

Good, T. and Braden, J. (2000) 'Charter schools: Another reform failure or a worthwhile investment?', *Phi Delta Kappan*, 81, 10, pp. 745–50.

Goodlad, J. (1979) *Curriculum Inquiry: The Study of Curriculum Practice*, New York: McGraw-Hill.

Goodlad, J. and Su, Z. (1992) 'Organisation of the curriculum', in Jackson, P. (ed.), *Handbook of Research on Curriculum*, New York: Macmillan.

Goodlad, J.I. and Klein, M.F. (1970) *Behind the classroom door*, Worthington, OH: Jones.

Goodlad, J.I. and Richter, M.N. (1966) *The development of a conceptual system for dealing with problems of curriculum and instruction*, Los Angeles: Institute for Development of Educational Activities.

Goodson, I. F. (1991) 'Teachers' lives and educational research', in Goodson, I.F. and Walker, R. (eds), *Biography, Identity and Schooling: Episodes in Educational Research*, London: Falmer Press.

—— (1981) 'Life history and the study of schooling', *Interchange*, 11, 4, pp. 15–29.

—— (1983) *School subjects and curriculum change*, London: Croom Helm.

—— (1985) (ed.), *Social Histories of the Secondary Curriculum*, London: Falmer Press.

—— (1988) *The Making of Curriculum*, London: Falmer Press.

—— (1992) 'On curriculum form: Notes toward a theory of curriculum', *Sociology of Education*, 65, pp. 66–75.

—— (1994) *Studying Curriculum; Cases and Methods*, New York: Teachers College Press.

—— (2000) 'Social histories of educational change', *Journal of Educational Change*, 2, 1, pp. 2–15.

—— (2001) 'Social histories of educational change', *Journal of Educational Change*, 2, 1, pp. 1–31.

Goodson, I.F. and Marsh, C.J. (1996) *Studying School Subjects*, London: Falmer Press.

Gordon, L. and Whitty, G. (2000) 'Giving the "Hidden Hand" a helping hand: the rhetoric and reality of the neo-liberal education reform in England and New Zealand', paper presented at the Annual Meeting of the American Educational Research Association, New Orleans.

Gorman, J.C. and Balter, L. (1997) 'Culturally sensitive parent education: A critical review of quantitative research', *Review of Educational Research*, 67, 3, pp. 339–69.

Gough, N. (2000) 'Locating curriculum studies in the global village', *Journal of Curriculum Studies*, 32, 2, pp. 329–42.

Grace, G. (1995) *School leadership – beyond education management*, London: Falmer.

Graham, R.J. (1991) *Reading and Writing the Self: Autobiography in Education and the Curriculum*, New York: Teachers College Press.

Greatorex, J. and Malacova, E. (2006) 'Can different teaching strategies or methods of preparing pupils lead to greater improvement from GCSE to A level performance?', *Research Papers in Education*, 21, 3, pp. 255–94.

Green, A. (1994) 'Postmodernism and state education', *Journal of Education Policy*, 9, 1, pp. 67–83.

Green, B. (2003) 'Curriculum inquiry on Australia: Towards a local genealogy of the curriculum field', in W.F. Pinar (ed.), *International handbook of curriculum research*, Mahwah, NJ: Lawrence Erlbaum.

Greene, M. (1975) 'Curriculum and consciousness', in W. Pinar (ed.), *Curriculum theorizing: The reconceptualists*, Berkeley, CA: McCutchan.

Gresham, A., Hess, F., Maranto, R. and Milliman, S. (2000) 'Desert bloom: Arizona's free market in education', *Phi Delta Kappan*, 81, 10, pp. 751–57.

Griffin, D.R., Cobb, J.B., Ford, M.P., Gunter, P. and Ochs, P. (1993) *Founders of Constructive Postmodern Philosophy: Pierce, James, Bergson, Whitehead, and Hartshorne*, Albany, State University of New York Press.

Griffin, P. (1998) 'Outcomes and profiles: Changes in teachers' assessment practices', *Curriculum Perspectives*, 18, 1, pp. 9–19.

Griffith, J. (1997) 'Student and parent perceptions of school social environment: Are they group based?', *Elementary School Journal*, 98, 2, pp. 135–50.

Griffith, R. (2000) *National Curriculum: National Disaster*, London: Routledge/ Falmer Press.

Grobman, H. (1970) *Developmental curriculum projects: decision points and processes*, New York: Peacock.

Gronn, P. (2000) 'Distributed properties: A new architecture for leadership', paper presented at the Annual Conference of the American Educational Research Association, New Orleans.

Grumet, M. (1976) 'Existential and phenomenological foundations', in W. Pinar and M. Grumet (eds), *Toward a poor curriculum*, Dubuque, IA: Kendall/Hunt.

—— (1981) 'Restitution and reconstruction of educational experience, an autobiographical method for curriculum theory', in M. Lawn and L. Barton (eds), *Rethinking curriculum studies*, London: Croom Helm.

Grumet, M. and Stone, L. (2000) 'Feminism and curriculum: Getting our act together', *Journal of Curriculum Studies*, 32, 2, pp. 183–97.

Grundy, S. (1982) 'Three modes of action research', *Curriculum Perspectives*, 2, 3, pp. 23–34.

—— (1987) *Curriculum: Product or praxis*, London: Falmer.

—— (1994) 'The National Curriculum debate in Australia: Discordant discourses', *South Australian Educational Leader*, 5, 3, pp. 1–7.

—— (2005) 'Junctions and dysfunctions, collaborations and contestation, positions and opposition – the strange dynamics of curriculum construction', in C. Harris and C.J. Marsh (eds), *Curriculum development in Australia*, Adelaide: Open Books.

Guan, H.K. (2000) *The implementation of an innovative computer course in Singapore: Perception and practice, unpublished doctoral dissertation*, University of Western Australia.

Guglielmi, R.S. and Tatrow, K. (1998) 'Occupational stress, burnout and health in teachers: A methodological and theoretical analysis', *Review of Educational Research*, 68, 1, pp. 61–99.

Guilfoyle, C. (2006) 'NCLB: is there a life beyond testing?', *Educational Leadership*, 64, 3, pp. 8–13.

Guskey, T. (2002) 'Does it make a difference? Evaluating professional development', *Educational Leadership*, 59, 6, pp. 45–51.

Guslsy, T.R. (2003) 'How classroom assessments improve learning', *Educational Leadership*, 60, 5, pp. 6–11.

Guttman, T. (1993) 'Petition to the Victorian Minister for Education regarding the mathematics national profile', May, University of Melbourne.

Habermas, J. (1970) *Knowledge and Human Interests*, Boston, MA: Beacon.

Hall, G.E. and Loucks, S.F. (1978) 'Innovation configurations: Analysing the adaptations of innovations', *Procedures for Adopting Educational Innovations Program*, Austin, University of Texas, Research and Development Centre for Teacher Education.

Hall, G.E., George, A.A. and Rutherford, W.L. (1979) *Measuring Stages of Concern About the Innovation: A Manual for Use of the SoC questionnaire*, 2nd edn, Austin, University of Texas, Research and Development Centre for Teacher Education.

Halstead, J.M. (1994) (ed.), *Parental Choice and Education*, London: Kogan Page.

Haney, W. and Madaus, G. (1989) 'Searching for alternatives to standardized tests: Whys, whats, and whithers', *Phi Delta Kappan*, 70, 9, pp. 683–87.

Hanley, M.S. (2006) 'Education: Transmission and transformation', *Journal of Thought*, 41, 3, pp. 51–55.

Hannan, B. (1992) 'National Curriculum: A system perspective', *Unicorn*, 18, 3, pp. 28–31.

Hannay, L. (1990) 'Canada: school-based curriculum deliberation', in C.J. Marsh, C. Day, L. Hannay and G. McCutcheon (eds), *Reconceptualising school-based curriculum development*, London: Falmer.

Hannay, L.M. and Macfarlane, N. (1998) 'Implementing action research: The influence of context and professional development processes', paper presented at the Annual Conference of the American Educational Research Association, San Diego.

Hannay, L.M. and Seller, W. (1998) 'Action research as performance assessment', paper presented at the Annual Conference of the American Educational Research Association, San Diego.

Hannay, L.M., Ross, J.A. and Brydges, B. (1997) 'The complexity of secondary school curricular change: the reculturing/restructuring shuffle', paper presented at the Annual Meeting of the American Educational Research Association, Chicago.

Hansen, J.M. (1989) 'Outcome-based education: A smarter way to assess student learning', *Clearing House*, 63, 4, pp. 172–74.

Hansford, G. (2000) 'Asynchronous and synchronous forms of instruction', Australian *Journal of Educational Technology*, 16, 2, pp. 38–53.

Hardy, T. (1990) 'Curriculum frameworks in the ACT: The case of could, should or must?' *Curriculum Perspectives*, 10, 4, pp. 1–8.

Hargreaves, A. (1995) *Changing Teachers, Changing Times*, London: Cassell.

—— (1997) 'Culture of teaching and educational change', in Fullan, M. (ed.), *The Challenge of School Change*, Arlington Heights, IL: Skylight Press.

—— (1998) 'The emotional politics of teaching and teacher development with implications for Educational Leadership', *International Journal of Leadership in Education*, 1, 4, pp. 315–36.

Hargreaves, A. and Fink, D. (2000) 'The three dimensions of reform', *Educational Leadership*, 57, 7, pp. 30–34.

Hargreaves, A., Earl, L. and Schmidt, M. (2002) 'Perspectives in alternative assessment reform', *American Educational Reform Journal*, 39, 1, pp. 69–95.

Hargreaves, A., Earl, L., Moore, S. and Manning, S. (2001) *Learning to Change*, San Francisco, CA: Jossey-Bass.

Hargreaves, D. (1994) *The Mosaic of Learning*, London: Demos.

Hargreaves, E. (2005) 'Assessment for learning? Thinking outside the (black) box', *Cambridge Journal of Education*, 35, 2, pp. 213–24.

Harlen, W. (1994) *Evaluating curriculum materials, SCRE Spotlights*, Edinburgh: Scottish Council for Research in Education.

Harlen, W. and Crick, R.D. (2003) 'Testing & motivation for learning', *Assessment in Education*, 10, 2, pp. 169–206.

Harold, B. (1997) 'Negotiating partnerships between the home and school: A New Zealand perspective', paper presented at the Biennial Conference of the Australian Curriculum Studies Association, Perth.

Harris, C. (2005) 'The key learning area movement: A force for pedagogical change or a façade for continued conservatism', in C. Harris and C.J. Marsh (eds), *Curriculum developments in Australia: Promising initiatives, impasses and dead-ends*, Adelaide: Open Book.

Harris, C. and Marsh, C.J. (2007) 'SOSE curriculum structure: Where to now?', paper presented at the Biennial Conference of the Australian Curriculum Studies Association, Melbourne: July.

Harris, C. and Marsh, C.J. (eds) (2005) *Curriculum development in Australia*, Adelaide: Open Books.

Harris, D. and Bell, C. (1990) *Evaluating and Assessing for Learning*, London: Kogan Page.

Harty, S. (1990) 'US corporations: Still pitching after all these years', *Educational Leadership*, 47, 4, pp. 77–78.

Hatch, T. (1998) 'How community action contributes to achievement', *Educational Leadership*, 55, 8, pp. 16–19.

—— (2000) 'What does it take to break the mold? Rhetoric and reality in new American schools', *Teachers College Record*, 102, 3, pp. 561–89.

Hatt, B. (2007) 'Most kids to be in private schools in next 30 years', *West Australian*, 30 July, p. 5.

Hayes, D. (2006) *Primary education: The Key Concepts*, London: Routledge.

Hayes, D. and Chodkiewicz, A. (2006) 'School-community links: Supporting learning in the middle years', *Research Papers in Education*, 21, 1, pp. 3–18.

Haynes, G.S., Wragg, E.C., Wragg, C.M. and Chamberlin, R.P. (2001) 'Threshold assessment: The experiences and views of teachers', paper presented at the Annual Conference of the British Educational Research Association, Leeds.

Hebert, E.A. (1998) 'Lessons learned about student portfolios', *Phi Delta Kappan*, 79, 8, pp. 583–85.

Heck, R.H. and Crislip, M. (2001) 'Direct and indirect writing assessments: Examining issues of equity and utility', *Educational Evaluation and Policy Analysis*, 23, 3, pp. 275–92.

Helsby, G. and Saunders, M. (1993) 'Taylorism, Tylerism, and performance indicators: Defending the indefensible', *Educational Studies*, 19, 1, pp. 55–77.

Hendrey, G.D., Heinrich, P., Lyon, P., Barratt,A., Simpson, J., Hyde, S., Gonsalkorale, S. Hyde, M. and Mgaieth, S. (2005) 'Helping students understand their learning styles. Effects on study self-efficacy, preference for group work and group climate', *Educational Psychology*, 25, 4, pp. 395–407.

Herman, J.L. and Winters, L. (1994) 'Synthesis of research: Portfolio research: A slim collection', *Educational Leadership*, 52, 2, pp. 48–55.

Herr, K. and Arms, E. (2004) 'Accountability and single sex schooling: a collision of reform agendas', *Educational Evaluation and Policy Analysis*, 26, 4, 78–95.

Hess, F.M. (2003) 'The case for being mean', *Educational Leadership*, 61, 3, pp. 22–26.

—— (2004) 'The political challenge of charter school regulation', *Phi Delta Kappan*, 85, 7, pp. 508–13.

Hewitt, B. (2001) 'I quit', *Guardian Education*, 9 January, pp. 2–3.

Hiatt, B. (2006) 'New OBE hits trouble over uni-entry marks', *West Australian*, 13 September, p. 5.

Hiatt-Michael, D. (2000) 'Parent involvement as a component of teacher education programs in California', paper presented at the Annual Conference of the American Educational Research Association, New Orleans.

Hirsch, E.D. (2004) 'Classroom research and cargo cults', *Policy Review Online*, http://www.policyreview.org/OCT2/hirsch.html.

Hirst, P.H. (1967) 'The logical and physiological aspects of teaching a subject', in Peters, R. (ed.), *The Concept of Education*, London: Routledge and Kegan Paul.

—— (1974) *Knowledge and the Curriculum*, London: Routledge and Kegan Paul.

Hlebowitsh, P.S. (1992) 'Amid behavioral and behavioristic objectives: Reappraising appraisals of the Tyler rationale', *Journal of Curriculum Studies*, 24, 6, pp. 533–47.

—— (1993) *Radical Curriculum Theory Reconsidered*. New York: Teachers College Press.

—— (1999) 'The burdens of the new curricularist', *Curriculum Inquiry*, 23, 3, pp. 343–53.

Hooley, N. (2005) 'Participatory action research and the struggle for legitimation', *Australian Educational Researcher*, 32, 1, pp. 67–82.

Hoover-Dempsey, K.V., Walker, J., Sandler, H.M., Whetsel, D., Green, C., Wilkins, A. S. and Closson, K. (2005) 'Why do parents become involved? Research findings and implications', *Elementary School Journal*, 106, 2, pp. 105–25.

Hopkins, B.D. and Higham, R. (2007) 'System leadership: Mapping the landscape', *School Leadership and Management*, 27, 2, pp. 147–66.

Hopmann, S. and Kunzli, T. (1997) 'Close our schools! Against current trends in policy making, educational theory and curriculum studies', *Journal of Curriculum Studies*, 29, 3, pp. 259–66.

Hord, S.M. and Huling-Austin, L. (1987) 'Curriculum implementation: How to know if it's there (or not there)', *Journal of Rural and Small Schools*, 1, 3, pp. 23–26.

House, E.R. (1979) 'Technology versus craft: A ten-year perspective on innovation', *Journal of Curriculum Studies*, 11, 1, pp. 1–16.

—— (1996) 'A framework for appraising educational reforms', *Educational Researcher*, 25, 7, pp. 6–14.

Houser, N.O. (2005) 'Art, aesthetics and equity education: A postmodern investigation', *Curriculum and Teaching*, 20, 1, pp. 41–60.

Howard, B.B. and Mccolskey, W.H. (2001) 'Evaluating experienced teachers', *Educational Leadership*, 58, 5, pp. 48–51.

Howes, A., Booth, T., Dyson, A. and Frankham, J. (2005) 'Teacher learning and the development of inclusive practices and policies: framing and context', *Research Papers in Education*, 20, 2, pp. 133–48.

Hoxby, C. (2004) 'Political jurisdictions in heterogenous communities', *Journal of Political Economy*, 112, 2, pp. 47–59.

Hubbard, L. and Datnow, A. (2000) 'A gendered look at educational reform', *Gender and Education*, 12, 1, pp. 115–29.

Huberman, M. (1980) 'Finding and using recipes for busy kitchens: a situational analysis of knowledge using schools', paper prepared for the Programme on Research in Education Practice, National Institute of Education, Washington, DC.

—— (1993) *The Lives of Teachers*, New York: Teachers College Press.

Huebner, D. (1975) 'Curricular language and classroom meanings', in W. Pinar (ed.), *Curriculum theorizing: The reconceptualists*, Berkeley, CA: McCutchan.

Huerta, L., Gonzalez, M.F. and d'Entremont, C. (2006) 'Cyber and home school Charter Schools: adopting policy to new forms of public schooling', *Peabody Journal of Education*, 81, 1, pp. 103–39.

Hughes, M. and Greenhough, P. (1998) 'Parents' and teachers' knowledge bases and instructional strategies', paper presented at the Annual Conference of the American Educational Research Association, San Diego.

Hughes, P.W. (1990) 'A national curriculum: Promise or warning?', Occasional Paper No. 14, Canberra: Australian College of Education.

Hunt, G. (1981) *The Curriculum and the Community*, Occasional Paper No. 5, Canberra: Curriculum Development Centres.

Hursh, D. (1995) 'Developing discourses and structures to support action research for educational reform', in Noffke, S. and Stevenson, R. (eds), *Educational Action Research: Becoming Practically Critical*, New York: Teachers College Press.

Ingall, A. (2005) 'The GTCE Teacher Learning Academy – a personal view', *Education Review*, 18, 2, pp. 27–33.

Ingersoll, R.M. (2007) 'Short on power, long on responsibility', *School Leadership*, 65, 1, pp. 20–25.

Ingvarson, L. (2002) 'Building a learning profession', Paper No. 1, *Commissioned Research Series*, Canberra: Australian College of Educators.

—— (2004) 'Tracking change in teaching practices: levels of use of new teaching and assessment approaches', paper presented at the Annual Conference of the Australian Association for Research in Education, Melbourne.

Ingvarson, L. and Chadbourne, R. (1994) (eds), *Valuing Teachers' Work: New Directions in Teacher Appraisal*, Melbourne: ACER.

Ingvarson, L., Meiers, M. and Beavis, A. (2005) 'Factors affecting the impact of professional development programs on teachers' knowledge, practice, student outcomes and efficacy', *Education Policy Analysis Archives*, 13, 10, pp. 1–5.

Ingvarson. L., Anderson, M., Gronn, P. and Jackson, A. (2006) *Standards for school leadership*, Melbourne: Teaching Australia.

Iwanicki, E.F. (2001) 'Focusing teacher evaluations on student learning', *Educational Leadership*, 58, 5, pp. 57–59.

Jackson, P. (ed.) (1992) *Handbook of research on curriculum*, New York: Macmillan.

James, E.J.F. (Chairperson) (1972) *Teacher Education and Training*, London: HMSO.

James, M. and Pedder, D. (2006) 'Beyond method: Assessment & learning practices and values', *Curriculum Journal*, 17, 2, pp. 109–38.

Jansen, T. and Van Der Vegt, R. (1991) 'On lasting innovation in schools: Beyond institutionalism', *Journal of Educational Policy*, 6, 1, pp. 33–46.

Jencks, C. (1986) *What is Post-modernism?*, New York: St Martin's Press.

Jencks, C. (ed.) (1992) *The Post-modern Reader*, New York: St Martin's Press.

Jobe, D.A. (2003) 'Helping girls succeed', *Educational Leadership*, 60, 4, pp. 64–67.

Johnson, J. (2003) 'What does the public say about accountability?', *Educational Leadership*, 61, 3, pp. 36–41.

Johnson, M., Jr (1967) 'Definitions and models in curriculum theory', *Educational Theory*, 17, pp. 127–40.

Jolliffe, W. (2006) 'The National Literacy Strategy: missing a crucial link? A comparative study of the National Literacy Strategy and Success for all', *Journal of Research in Education*, 34, 1, pp. 37–48.

Jones, B.D. (2002) 'Recommendations for implementing internet inquiry projects', *Journal of Educational Technology Systems*, 30, 3, pp. 271–91.

Jones, K. (2004) 'A balanced school accountability model: and alternative to high-stakes testing', *Phi Delta Kappan*, 85, 8, pp. 584–91.

Joseph, P.B., Mikel, E. and Windschiti, M. (2002) 'Reculturing curriculum: The struggle for curriculum leadership', paper presented at the Annual Meeting of the American Educational Research Association, Chicago.

Joyce, B. and Weil, M. (1986) *Models of Teaching*, 3rd edn, Englewood Cliffs, NJ: Prentice-Hall.

Joyner, E.T., Ben-Ave, M. and Comer, J.P. (2004) *Dynamic instructional leadership to support student learning and development*, San Francisco, CA: Corwin Press.

Juang, Y.R., Liu, T.C. and Chan, T.W. (2005) 'The web-based performance support system for enhanced school based curriculum development', Proceedings of the Fifth IEEEE International Conference on Advanced Learning Technologies, Taipeh.

Judson, G. (2006) 'Curriculum spaces: Situating educational research, theory and practice', *Journal of Educational Thought*, 40, 3, pp. 229–45.

Jupe, J. and Milne, T. (2005) 'Impact of the specialist schools programme on the teaching profession', *Education Review*, 18, 2, pp. 49–57.

Jury, T.W. (2004) 'Online versus traditional classes: the difference is that they are different', *Journal of Instruction Delivery Systems*, 18, 2, pp. 20–23.

Karlsson, J. (2007) 'Australian voices confront the education-for-boys backlash and normative discourse in education', *Pedagogy, Culture & Society*, 15, 1, pp. 129–33.

Katyal, K.R. and Evers, C.W. (2007) 'Parents – partners or clients? A reconceptualisation of home-school interactions', *Teaching Education*, 18, 1, pp. 61–76.

Keddie, A. and Mills, M. (2007) *Teaching boys: Developing classroom practices that work*, Sydney: Allen and Unwin.

Kelly, A.V. (2004) *The curriculum: Theory and practice*, 5th edn, London: Sage.

Kemmis, S. (2006) 'Participatory action research and the public sphere', *Educational Action Research*, 14, 4, pp. 459–76.

Kemmis, S. and McTaggart, R. (1984) *The Action Research Planner*, Geelong: Deakin University Press.

—— (1988) *The Action Research Planner*, 3rd edn, Geelong: Deakin University Press.

Kennedy, K. (1997) (ed.), *Citizenship Education and the Modern State*, London: Falmer Press.

Kennedy, K.J. (1995) 'An analysis of the policy contexts of recent curriculum reform efforts in Australia, Great Britain and the United States', in Carter, D.S.G. and

O'Neill, M.H. (eds), *International Perspectives on Educational Reform and Policy Implementation*, London: Falmer Press.

—— (2005) *Changing schools for changing times*, Hong Kong: Chinese University Press.

—— (2007) 'Barriers to innovative school practice: A Socio-cultural framework for understanding assessment practices in Asia', paper presented at the Redesigning Pedagogy – Culture, Understanding and Practice Conference, Singapore, 28 May.

Kenway, J. and Longmead, D. (1998) 'Fast capitalism, fast feminism and some fast food for thought', paper presented at the Annual Conference of the American Educational Research Association, San Diego.

Kenway, J. and Modra, H. (1992) 'Feminist pedagogy and emancipatory possibilities', in Luke, C. and Gore, J. (eds), *Feminisms and Critical Pedagogy*, New York: Routledge.

Kenway, J. and Willis, S. (1997) *Answering Back: Girls, Boys and Feminism in Schools*, Sydney: Allen and Unwin.

Kenway, J., Alderson, A. and Grundy, S. (1987) *A Process Approach to Community Participation in Schooling: The Hamilton Project*, Perth, Murdoch University.

Kenway, J., Blackmore, J. and Willis, S. (1996) 'Beyond feminist authoritarianism and therapy in the curriculum?', *Curriculum Perspectives*, 16, 1, pp. 1–12.

Kerr, D. (1989) 'Principles underlying the dissemination implementation of curriculum', paper presented at the Annual Cuuriculum Corporation Conference, Canberra.

—— (2006) 'Key developments in national curriculum work', paper presented at the Australian Curriculum Studies Association Invitational Symposium, Melbourne: August.

Khayatt, D. (2006) 'What's to fear: Calling homophobia into question', *McGill Journal of Education*, 41, 2, pp. 133–43.

Killen, R. (2007) 'Outcomes-based education: Principles and possibilities', http://www.ace/.org.au/affiliates/nsw/conference01/ts_1.html (extracted 9 October 2007).

Kincheloe, J. and Pinar, W. (eds) (1991) *Curriculum as social psychoanalysis: The significance of place*, Albany, NY: State University of New York Press.

Kincheloe, J.L. (1993) *Toward a Critical Politics of Teacher Thinking: Mapping the Postmodern*, Westport, Bergin and Garvey.

King, J.F. (1998) 'Assessment at the chalkface', paper presented at the 24th International Congress of Applied Psychology, San Francisco.

King, R. (2007) 'Deadening and saccharine curricula', John Howard, Prime Minister, reported in the West Australian, 9 February 2007, p. 6.

Kirst, M.W. (1993) 'Strengths and weaknesses of American education', *Phi Delta Kappan*, 74, 8, pp. 613–18.

Kirst, M.W. and Walker, D.F. (1971) 'An analysis of curriculum policy making', *Review of Educational Research*, 41, 5, pp. 486–95.

Klages, M. (2007) 'Postmodernism', http://www.colorado.edu/English/courses/ENG-L2012Klages/pomo.html (extracted 19 October 2007).

Klein, R. (1986) *The dynamics of women's studies: An exploratory study of its international ideas and practices in higher education*, unpublished doctoral thesis, University of London: Institute of Education.

Kleinhenz, E., Ingvarson, L. and Chadbourne, R. (2002) 'A discussion of teacher evaluation policies and practices in Australian states and their relation to quality teaching and learning', paper presented at the Annual Conference of the Australian Association for Research in Education, Sydney.

Klenowski, V. (2002) *Developing portfolios for learning & assessment: Processes & principles*, London: Routledge Falmer.

Kliebard, H.M. (1970) 'Reappraisal: the Tyler rationale', *School Review*, pp. 259–79.

—— (1977) 'Curriculum theory: Give me a "for instance"', *Curriculum Inquiry*, 6, 4, pp. 257–68.

Klohr, P. (1980) 'The curriculum theory field: Gritty and ragged', *Curriculum Perspectives*, 1, 1, pp. 1–8.

Knight, T. (1995) 'Parents, the community and school governance', in Evers, C. and Chapman, J. (eds), *Educational Administration: An Australian Perspective*, Sydney: Allen and Unwin.

Konza, D., Grainger, J. and Bradshaw, K. (2001) *Classroom Management: A Survival Guide*, Sydney: Social Science Press.

Kopriva, R. (1999) 'A conceptual framework for valid and comparable measurement', paper presented at the Annual Conference of the American Educational Research Association, Montreal.

Kridel, C. and Bullough, R.V. (2007) *Stories of the Eight-year Study*, New York: SUNY Press.

Kuhn, T. (1962) *The structure of scientific revolutions*, Chicago, IL: University of Chicago Press.

Kulm, G. and Grier, L. (1998) *Project 2061 – Mathematics Curriculum Materials Analysis Scheme – reliability study*, Washington, DC: American Association for the Advancement of Science.

La Rocque, L. and Coleman, P. (1989) 'Quality control: School accountability and district ethos', in Holmes, M., Leithwood, K. and Musella, D. (eds), *Educational Policy for Effective Schools*, Toronto, OISE Press.

Labaree, D. (1988) *The Making of an American High School: The Credentials Market and the Central High School of Philadelphia 1838–1939*, New Haven, CT: Yale University Press.

Lachat, M., Williams, M. and Smith, S. (2006) 'Making sense of all your data', *Principal Leadership*, 6, 2, pp. 16–21.

Lam, B.H. (2005) 'Action researching on an Action Research Tutorial Series for Curriculum Leaders in Primary Schools', unpublished paper, Hong Kong Institute of Education

Lambert, L. (1998) *Building Leadership Capacity in Schools*, Alexandria, VA: ASCD.

Landauer, T.K., Laham, D. and Foltz, P. (2003) 'Automatic essay assessment', *Assessment in Education*, 10, 3, pp. 295–307.

Liam, B.H. (2005) 'Action researching on an action research tutorial series for curriculum leaders in primary schools', unpublished paper, Hong Kong Institute of Education.

Lasky, S. (2000) 'The cultural and emotional politics of teacher-parent interactions', *Teaching and Teacher Education*, 16, 843–60.

Lather, P. (1991) *Getting Smart: Feminist Research and Pedagogy With/in the Postmodern*. London: Routledge.

—— (1998) 'Against empathy, voice and authenticity', paper presented at the Annual Conference of the American Educational Research Association, San Diego.

—— (2007) *Getting lost: Feminist efforts toward a double(d) science*, New York: SUNY Press.

Law, F. (2002) *Curriculum reform in Hong Kong*, address by F. Law, Permanent Secretary for Education and Manpower Law, Hong Kong: Education and Manpower Bureau.

Lawlor, S. (1993) *Inspecting the school inspectors*, London: Centre for Policy Studies, University of London.

Lawn, M. and Barton, L. (eds) (1981) *Rethinking curriculum studies*, London: Croom Helm.

Lawton, D. (1980) *The Politics of the School Curriculum*, London: Routledge and Kegan Paul.

—— (1993) *Curriculum Studies and Education Planning*, London: Hodder and Stoughton.

Lea, O. and Fradd, S.H. (1998) 'Science for all, including students from non-English-language backgrounds', *Educational Researcher*, 27, 4, pp. 12–21.

Leck, G.M. (1999) 'Afterword', in Letts, W.J. and Sears, J.T. (eds), *Queering Elementary Education*, Lanham, MD: Rowman and Littlefield.

Lee, C. and Wiliam, D. (2005) 'Studying changes in the practice of two teachers developing assessment for learning', *Teacher Development*, 9, 2, pp. 265–83.

Lee, C.K. and Yanping, F. (2006) 'Lesson study and the power of continuous improvement – Theorizing in light of a Singapore case', paper presented at the 2nd Annual Conference on Learning Study, Hong Kong.

Lee, J.S. and Bowen, N.K. (2006) 'Parent involvement, cultural capital and the achievement gap among elementary school children', *American Educational Research Journal*, 43, 2, pp. 193–216.

Lee, V.E., Smith, J.B. and Cioci, M. (1993) 'Teachers and principals: Gender-related perceptions of leadership and power in secondary schools', *Educational Evaluation and Policy Analysis*, 15, 2, pp. 153–80.

Leithwood, K. and Menzies, D. (1999) 'A century's quest to understand school leadership', in Murphy, J. and Seashore Louis, K. (eds), *Handbook of Educational Leadership and Change*, Chicago, IL: Macmillan.

Leithwood, K.A. (1981) 'Managing the implementation of curriculum innovations', *Knowledge: Creation, Diffusion, Utilization*, 2, 3, pp. 341–60.

Leithwood, K.A., Tomlinson, D. and Genge, M. (1996) 'Transformational school leadership', in Leithwood, K., Chapman, J., Corson, D., Hallinger, P. and Hart, A. (eds), *International Handbook of Educational Leadership and Administration*, Dordrecht, The Netherlands: Kluwer.

Leren, T.H. (2006) 'The importance of student voice', *International Journal of Leadership in Education*, 9, 4, pp. 363–67.

Letts, W.J. and Sears, J.T. (1999) (eds), *Queering Elementary Education*, Boulder, CO: Rowman and Littlefield.

Levin, H.M. (1998) 'Educational performance standards and the economy', *Educational Researcher*, 27, 4, pp. 4–11.

Lewin, K. (1948) *Resolving Social Conflicts*, New York: Harper and Row.

Lewis, C., Perry, R. and Murata A. (2006) 'How should research contribute to instructional improvement: The case of lesson study', *Educational Researcher*, 35, 3, pp. 3–14.

Lieble, J.A. (1980) 'Guideline recommendations for the design of training facilities', *NSPI Journal*, 19, pp. 21–30.

Lifter, M. and Adams, M.E. (1997) *Integrating Technology into the Curriculum*, Melbourne: Hawker Brownlow.

Liu, M. and Reed, W.M. (1994) 'The relationship between the learning strategies and learning styles in a hypermedia environment', *Computers in Human Behaviour*, 10, 4, 419–34.

Lo, M.L. (2006) 'Learning study – the Hong Kong version of lesson study: Development, impact and challenges', unpublished paper, Hong Kong Institute of Education.

Lo, M.L., Pong, W.Y. and Pakey, M.P. (2005) *For each and everyone: catering for learning studies*, Hong Kong: Hong Kong University Press.

Loader, D. (1998) *The Inner Principal*, London: Falmer Press.

—— (1999) 'Redefining "Public" in Education', *Curriculum Perspectives*, 19, 1, pp. 53–57.

Loi, D. and Dillon, P. (2006) 'Adaptive educational environments as creative spaces', *Cambridge Journal of Education*, 36, 3, pp. 363–81.

Longstreet, W.S. and Shane, H.G. (1993) *Curriculum for a New Millennium*, Boston, MA: Allyn and Bacon.

Lortie, D. (1975) *Schoolteacher*, Chicago, IL: University of Chicago Press.

Loucks, S.F. and Crandall, D.P. (1982) *The Practice Profile: An All-purpose Tool for Program Communication, Staff Development, Evaluation and Improvement*, Andover, MA, The Network.

Louden, W. (2000) 'Standards for standards: The development of Australian professional standards for teaching', *Australian Journal of Education*, 44, 2, pp. 118–34.

Louden, W. and Wildy, H. (1997) 'Short shrift to long lists: An alternative approach to the development of performance standards for school principals', paper presented at the Annual Conference of the American Educational Research Association, Chicago.

Loyd, B.H. and Loyd, D.E. (1997) 'Kindergarten through grade 12 standards: A philosophy of grading', in Phye, G.D. (ed.), *Handbook of Classroom Assessment*, San Diego, Academic Press.

Lucas, C.A. (1999) 'Developing competent practitioners', *Educational Leadership*, 56, 8, pp. 45–48.

Lucas, S. and Valentine, J. (2002) 'Transformational leadership: Principals, leadership teams, and school culture', paper presented at the Annual Meeting of the American Educational Research Association, Chicago.

Luke, C. (ed.) (1996) *Feminisms and pedagogies of everyday life*, Albany, NY: State University of New York Press.

Lundeberg, M. (1997) 'You guys are overreacting: Teaching prospective teachers about subtle gender bias', *Journal of Teacher Education*, 48, 1, pp. 55–61.

Lusi, S.F. (1997) *The role of state departments of education in complex school reform*, New York: Teachers College Press.

Lusted, D. (1986) 'Why pedagogy?', *Screen*, 27, 5, pp. 2–14.

Lutz, F.W. (1980) 'Local school board decision-making: A political-anthropological analysis', *Education and Urban Society*, 12, 4, pp. 17–29.

Lye, J. (1997) 'Some post-structural assumptions', http://www.brocku.ca/english/courses/4F70/poststruct.html (extracted 19 October 2007).

Lyons, N. (1999) 'How portfolios can shape emerging practice', *Educational Leadership*, 56, 8, pp. 63–66.

Lyotard, J.F. (1984) *The postmodern condition: A report on knowledge*, Manchester: Manchester University Press.

MacDonald, B. and Walker, R. (1976) *Changing the curriculum*, London: Open Books.

Macdonald, J.B. (1971) *Curriculum development in relation to social and intellectual systems, seventieth yearbook of the National Society for the Study of Education*, Chicago: University of Chicago.

—— (1981) 'Curriculum, consciousness and social change', *Journal of Curriculum Theorizing*, 3, 1, pp. 143–53.

Mackay, T. (2002) 'Challenges in perspective: Transforming secondary education, the view from the UK', paper presented at the Invitational Curriculum Policy Seminar, Hong Kong.

Macklin, P. (2004) 'School-based curriculum development: does it work', *IARTV Seminar Series*, 132, pp. 1–15.

Maclure, M. and Walker, B.M. (2000) 'Disenchanted evenings. The social organization of talk in parent–teacher consultations in UK secondary schools', *British Journal of Sociology of Education*, 21, 1, pp. 18–22.

Macpherson, I. (1998) 'Creating space for the voices of significant stakeholders in curriculum leadership', paper presented at the Annual Conference of the American Educational Research Association, San Diego.

Mager, R.F. (1984) *Preparing Instructional Objectives*, 3rd edn, Belmont, CA: Lake Publishers.

Male, T. (1998) 'The impact of national culture on school leadership in England', paper presented at the Annual Conference of the American Educational Research Association, San Diego.

Mann, L. (1997) 'The learning environment', ASCD Education Update, September, 3–6.

Mansvelder-Longayroux, D., Beijaard, D. and Verloop, N. (2007) 'The portfolios as a tool for stimulating reflection by student teachers', *Teaching and Teacher Education*, 23, 2, pp. 47–62.

Marsh, C.J. (1994) *Producing a national curriculum*, Sydney: Allen & Unwin.

—— (1997) *Key Concepts for Understanding Curriculum*, London: Falmer Press.

—— (2006) 'A critique of curriculum models', unpublished paper, Curtin University, Perth.

—— (2007) *Analysis of curriculum models*, Singapore: Ministry of Education.

—— (2008) *Becoming a teacher*, 4th edn, Sydney: Pearson Education Australia.

Marsh, C.J. and Stafford, K. (1988) *Curriculum: Alternative approaches on-going issues*, Sydney: McGraw Hill.

Marsh, C.J. and Willis, G. (2007) *Curriculum: alternative approaches, ongoing issues*, 4th edn, Columbus, OH: Pearson Merrill Prentice Hall.

Marsh, C.J., Day, C., Hannay, L. and McCutcheon, G. (eds) (1990) *Reconceptualising school-based curriculum development*, London: Falmer.

Marshall, B. and Drummond, M.J. (2006) 'How teachers engage with assessment for learning: Lessons from the classroom', *Research Paper in Education*, 21, 2, pp. 133–49.

Martino, W. and Kehler, M. (2006) 'Male teachers and the "boy problem": An issue of recuperative masculinity politics', *McGill Journal of Education*, 41, 2, pp. 113–23.

Martino, W. and Pallotta-Chierolli (2005) *Being normal is the only way to be: boys and girls' perspectives on school*, Sydney: University of NSW Press.

Marton, F. and Booth, S. (1997) *Learning and awareness*, Mahwah, NJ: Lawrence Erlbaum.

Marx, R.W. and Harris, C.J. (2006) 'No child left behind and science education: opportunities, challenges, and risks', *Elementary School Journal*, 106, 5, pp. 467–77.

Marzano, R.J. and Kendall, J.S. (1996) *A Comprehensive Guide to Designing Standards-based Districts, Schools and Classrooms*, Alexandria, VA: ASCD.

Marzano, R.J., Waters, T. and McNulty, B.A. (2005) *School leadership that works: from research to results*, Alexandria, VA: ASCD.

Matheison, S. (1991) 'Implementing curricular change through state-mandated testing: Ethical issues', *Journal of Curriculum and Supervision*, 6, 3, pp. 201–12.

Matoba, M., Crawford, K.A. and Aranni, R.S. (2001) (eds), *Lesson study: International perspective on policy and practice*, Beijing: Educational Science Publishing House.

Matthews, J., Trimble, S. and Gay, A. (2007) 'But what to do with the data?', *Principal Leadership*, 7, 9, pp. 31–33.

Mattingly, D., Prislin, R., McKenzie, T., Rodriquez, J. and Kayzar, B. (2002) 'Evaluating evaluations: The case of parent involvement program', *Review of Educational Research*, 72, 4, pp. 549–76.

McCarthy, C. (1988) 'Rethinking liberal and radical perspectives on racial inequality in schooling: Making the case for nonsynchrony', *Harvard Educational Review*, 58, 3, pp. 265–79.

McCarthy, C., Giardina, M.D., Harewood, S.J. and Park, J.K. (2003) 'Contesting culture: Identity and curriculum dilemmas in the age of globalisation, postcolonialism and multiplicity', *Harvard Educational Review*, 73, 3, pp. 449–66.

McCaslin, M. (2006) 'Student motivational dynamics in the era of school reform', *Elementary School Journal*, 106, 5, pp. 479–90.

McChesney, J. and Hertling, E. (2000) 'The path to comprehensive school reform', *Educational Leadership*, 57, 7, pp. 10–15.

McCulloch, G. (1998) 'The National Curriculum and the cultural politics of secondary schools in England and Wales', paper presented at the Annual Conference of the American Educational Research Association, San Diego.

McDonald, B. and Boud, D. (2003) 'The impact of self-assessment training on performance in external examinations', *Assessment in Education*, 10, 2, pp. 209–20.

McFarlane, A. (2003) 'Assessment for the digital age', *Assessment in Education*, 10, pp. 261–66.

McGaw, B., Piper, K., Banks, D. and Evans, B. (1992) *Making Schools More Effective*, Melbourne: ACER.

McGehee, J.J. and Griffith, L.K. (2001) 'Large-scale assessments combined with curriculum alignment: Agents of change', *Theory into Practice*, 40, 2, pp. 22–31.

McGilp, J. and Michael, M. (1994) *The Home–School Connection*, Armadale, NSW, Eleanor Curtain Publishing.

McGowan, W.S. (2005) '"Flexibility", community and making parents responsible', *Educational Philosophy and Theory*, 37, 6, pp. 891–903.

Mcinerney, D.M. (1989) 'Urban Aboriginal parents' views on education: A comparative analysis', *Journal of Intercultural Studies*, 10, 2, pp. 43–65.

McInnis, J.R. and Devlin, M. (2002) *Assessing Learning in Australian Universities*, Canberra: Centre for the Study of Higher Education, AUTC.

McIntyre, D., Pedder, D. and Rudduck, J. (2005) 'Pupil voice: comfortable and uncomfortable learnings for teachers', *Research Papers in Education*, 20, 2, pp. 149–68.

McKernan, J. (1998) *Curriculum action research*, London: Kogan Page.

McLaren, P. and Farahmandpur, R. (2000) 'Reconsidering Marx in post-Marxist times: A requiem for postmodernism', *Educational Researcher*, 29, 3, pp. 25–33.

McLaughan, M. (2001) 'Community counts', *Educational Leadership*, 58, 7, pp. 14–18.

McLaughlin, M.W. (1987) 'Learning from experience: Lessons from policy implementation', *Educational Evaluation and Policy Analysis*, 9, 2, pp. 171–78.

McLaughlin, M.W. and Shepard, L.A. (1995) *Improving Education Through Standards-based Reform*, Stanford, CA, National Academy of Education.

McMahon, A. (1994) 'Teacher appraisal in England and Wales', in Ingvarson, L. and Chadbourne, R. (eds), *Valuing Teachers' Work: New Directions in Teacher Appraisal*, Melbourne: ACER.

—— (2000) 'Managing teacher stress to enhance pupil learning', paper presented at the Annual Conference of the American Educational Research Association, New Orleans.

McMillan, J., Myran, S. and Workman, D. (2002) 'Elementary teachers' classroom assessment and grading practices, *Journal of Educational Research*, 95, 4, pp. 203–13.

McNeil, J.D. (1985) *Curriculum: A Comprehensive Introduction*, 3rd edn, Boston, MA: Little Brown.

—— (2003) *Curriculum: the teachers initiative*, 3rd edn, Columbus, OH: Merrill Prentice Hall.

Mcneil, L. (1988) 'Contradictions of control. Part 2: Teachers, students, and curriculum', *Phi Delta Kappan*, 69, 10, pp. 729–34.

McNess, E. (2006) 'Nous écouter, nous soutenir, nous apprehender: a comparative study of puplis' perceptions of the pedagogic process', *Comparative Education*, 42, 4, pp. 517–32.

McNiff, J., Lomax, P. and Whitehead, J. (2003) *You and your action research project*, 2nd edn, London: Routledge Falmer.

McTaggart, R. (1984) 'Action research and parent participation: Contradictions, concerns and consequences', *Curriculum Perspectives*, 4, 2, pp. 7–14.

McTighe, J. (1997) 'What happens between assessments?', *Educational Leadership*, 54, 4, pp. 6–13.

McTighe, J. and Wiggins, G. (2004) *Understanding by design: Professional development workbook*, Alexandria, VA: ASCD.

—— (2007) *Schooling by design: Mission, action and achievement*, Alexandria, VA: ASCD.

Meadmore, D. (2001) 'Uniformly testing diversity? National testing examined', *Asia–Pacific Journal of Teacher Education*, 29, 1, pp. 19–30.

Meadows, B.J. (1993) 'Through the eyes of parents', *Educational Leadership*, 51, 2, pp. 31–34.

Means, B. (2000) 'Technology in America's Schools: Before and after Y2K', in Brandt, R.S. (ed.), *Education in a New Era*, Alexandria, VA, ASCD.

Means, R. (2001) 'Technology use in tomorrow's schools', *Educational Leadership*, 58, 4, pp. 57–61.

Meath-Lang, B. (1999) 'Teachers responding to the voice of others', paper presented at the Bergamo Conference on Curriculum Practice, Dayton, Ohio.

Medina, J. and Riconscente, M.M. (2006) 'Accounting for quality', *Journal of Education*, 186, 3, pp. 3–9.

Meir, D. (1998) 'Authenticity and educational change', in Hargreaves, A. *et al.* (eds), *International Handbook of Educational Change*, Dordrecht, The Netherlands, Kluwer.

Melaragno, R., Lyons, M. and Sparks, M. (1981) *Parents and Federal Education Programs, Vol. 6, Parental Involvement in Title 1 Projects*, Santa Monica, CA: Systems Development Corporation.

Mellor, S., Kennedy, K. and Greenwood, L. (2002) *Citizenship and Democracy: Students' Knowledge and Beliefs: Australian Fourteen Year Olds and the IEA Civic Education Study*, Melbourne: Australian Council for Educational Research.

Melton, J. (2004) 'Online course presentation: program issues to consider', *Journal of Instruction Delivery Systems*, 18, 3, pp. 17–19.

Middleton, S. (1992) 'Developing a radical pedagogy: Autobiography of a New Zealand sociologist of women's education', in Goodson, I.F. (ed.), *Studying Teachers' Lives*, London: Routledge.

Milburn, G. (2000) 'Understanding curriculum', *Journal of Curriculum Studies*, 32, 3, pp. 445–52.

Miliband, D. (2004) Press release, 18 March, by the Minister of State for School Standards, United Kingdom.

Miller, J.L. (1987) 'Women as teacher/researchers: Gaining a sense of ourselves', *Teacher Education Quarterly*, 14, 2, pp. 52–58.

—— (1990) *Creating Spaces and Finding Voices: Teachers Collaborating for Empowerment*, Albany, NY: State University of New York Press.

—— (1992) 'Shifting the boundaries: Teachers challenge contemporary curriculum thought', *Theory into Practice*, 31, 3, pp. 245–51.

—— (2000) 'What is left in the field: A curriculum memoir', *Journal of Curriculum Studies*, 32, 2, 253–66.

Milligan, S. (1994) *Women in the Teaching Profession*, Canberra: AGPS.

Miner, B. (2007) 'Can NCLB be left behind?', *Rethinking Schools*, spring, pp. 28–31.

Ministerial Council on Education, Employment and Training Task Force (MCEETYA) (2003) *Development of a National Standards framework for the teaching profession*, Canberra: MCEETYA

Mislevy, R.J. (2002) 'The roles of technology in the assessment argument', paper presented at the Annual Conference of the American Educational Research Association, New Orleans.

Mitchell, J.A. (1996) *Teacher work, practices and places*, unpublished doctoral dissertation, University of Melbourne.

Mitra, D. (2006) 'Student voice from the inside and outside: the positioning of challengers', *International Journal of Leadership*, 9, 4, pp. 315–28.

Molnar, A. (2000) 'Zap me! Linking schoolhouse and marketplace in a seamless web', *Phi Delta Kappan*, 81, 8, pp. 601–3.

Monke, L.W. (2006) 'The overdominance of computers', *Educational Leadership*, 63, 4, pp. 2–23.

Moore, A. (2006) *Classroom Teaching Sills*, 7th edn, Boston, MA: McGraw Hill.

Moore, K.D. (2001) *Classroom Teaching Skills*, 5th edn, Boston, MA: McGraw-Hill.

Moos, R.H. and Trickett, E. (1974) *Classroom Environment Scale Manual*, Palo Alto, CA: Consulting Psychologist Press.

Morell, J.A. (2005) 'Why are there unintended consequences of program action, and what are the implications for doing evaluation?', *American Journal of Evaluation*, 26, 4, pp. 443–63.

Morris, W. (1992) 'Parents and school governance', paper presented at the Annual Conference of the Western Australian Primary Principals' Association, Perth.

Mortimer, P., Sammons, P., Stoll, L., Lewis, D. and Ecob, R. (1988) *School Matters: The Junior Years*, London: Open Books.

Moss, P. and Godinho, S (2007) 'Reforming curriculum and assessment practices: implications for educating teachers in the A to E economy', *Curriculum Perspectives*, 27, 3, pp. 35–48.

Munns, G. and Woodward, H. (2006) 'Student engagement and student self-assessment: The REAL framework', *Assessment in Education*, 13, 2, pp. 193–213.

Murphy, D. and Rosenberg, B. (1998) 'Recent research shows major benefits of small class size', *Educational Issues Policy Brief 3*, Washington, DC: American Federation of Teachers.

Murphy, J. and Rodi, M. (2000) 'Principal evaluation: A review', paper presented at the Annual Meeting of the American Educational Research Association, New Orleans.

Mutimer, A. (1999) 'From home to school', *EQ Australia*, 2, Winter, 9–10.

Myhill, D. (2006) 'Talk, talk, talk: teaching and learning in whole class discourse', *Research Papers in Education*, 21, 1, pp. 19–41.

Nahan, M. and Rutherford, T. (1993) *Reform and Recovery*, Perth, Institute of Public Affairs.

National College for School Leadership (2005) *Adding value to school leadership and management*, London: National College for School Leadership.

National Commission on Excellence in Education (1983) *A Nation at Risk: The Imperative for Educational Reform*, Washington, DC: Government Printing Office.

National Commission on teaching and America's Future (1997) *What Matters Most: Teaching for America's Future*, Woodbridge, VA: NCTAF.

National Science Resources Centre (1999) 'Learning science by doing science', www.nsrconline.org, extracted 5 September 2008.

Nave, B., Miech, E. and Mosteller, F. (2000) 'A lapse in standards', *Phi Delta Kappan*, 82, 2, pp. 128–32.

Neill, M. (2007) 'Overhauling NCLB', *Rethinking Schools*, spring, pp. 32–34.

Nelson, J.L., Palonsky, S.B. and McCarthy, M.R. (2004) 'Inclusion and mainstreaming: special or common education', in J.L. Nelson, S.B. Palonsky and M.R. McCarthy (eds), *Critical issues in education: dialogues and dialectics*, Boston: McGraw Hill.

Nevo, D. (2001) 'School evaluation: internal or external?', *Studies in Educational Evaluation*, 27, 1, pp. 95–106.

Newall, P. (2005) Postmodernism, http://www.galilean_library.org/int12.html (extracted 15 October 2007).

Newton, P.E. (2003) 'The defensibility of national curriculum assessment in England', *Research Papers in Education*, 18, 2, pp. 137–40.

Nixon, D. (2006) 'In praise of diversity: Why schools should seek gay and lesbian teachers, and why it's still difficult', *Forum*, 48, 3, pp. 275–85.

Nixon, G.M. (1999) 'Whatever happened to "heightened consciousness!"', *Journal of Curriculum Studies*, 31, 6, pp. 625–34.

Noddings, N. (1986) 'Fidelity in teaching, teacher education and research for teaching', *Harvard Educational Review*, 56, 4, pp. 496–510.

—— (2000) 'Care and coercion in school reform', paper presented at the Annual Meeting of the American Educational Research Association.

—— (2006) 'Educational leaders as caring teachers', *School Leadership and Management*, 26, 4, pp. 339–45.

Noffke, S.F. (1997) *International action research*, London: Routledge.

Nolen, A.L. and Putten, J.V. (2007) 'Action research in education: Addressing gaps in ethical principles and practices', *Educational Researcher*, 36, 7, pp. 104–407.

Norman, L. (1983) *The Brown and Yellow: Sydney Girls' High School 1883–1983*, Melbourne: Oxford University Press.

Norton, P. and Wiburg, K.M. (2003) *Teaching with Technology*, 2nd edn, Belmont, CA: Thomson/Wadsworth.

NSW Teachers Federation (1976) *ATF charter*, Sydney: NSW Teachers Federation.

O'Connor, C. and Robotham, M. (1991) *Towards Equity in the Queensland Core Skills Test*, Brisbane, BSSS.

O'Donnell, B. (2000) 'Prospects for the profession of teaching in Australia in the new millennium', *Unicorn*, 24, 1, pp. 13–21.

O'Neil, J. (2000) 'Fads and fireflies: the difficulty of sustaining change', *Educational Leadership*, 57, 7, pp. 6–9.

OFSTED (1997) *Inspection quality audits for registered inspectors and contractors*, London: OFSTED.

—— (2004) *Inspection Report of Adderley Primary School*, Inspection Report 266277, London: OFSTED.

—— (2007) *School poll helping UK schools with SEF*, London: OFSTED.

Olebe, M., Jackson, A. and Danielson, C. (1999) 'Investing in beginning teachers: The California model', *Educational Leadership*, 56, 8, pp. 41–44.

Oliva, P.F. (2004) *Developing the Curriculum*, 6th edn, New York: Longman.

Olson, J. (1989) 'The persistence of technical rationality', in Milburn, G., Goodson, I.F. and Clark, R.J. (eds), *Re-interpreting Curriculum Research: Images and Arguments*, London: Falmer Press.

Orland-Barak, L. (2005) 'Portfolios as evidence of reflective practice: What remains "untold"', *Educational Research*, 47, 1, pp. 25–44.

Orlich, D.C., Harder, R.J., Callahan, R.C. and Gibson, H.W. (1998) *Teaching Strategies*, 5th edn, Boston, MA: Houghton Mifflin.

Ornstein, A.C. and Hunkins, F.P. (2004) Curriculum: *Foundations, Principles and Issues*, 4th edn, Boston: Allyn and Bacon.

Orpwood, W.F. (1985) 'The reflective deliberation: A case study of curriculum policy making', *Journal of Curriculum Studies*, 17, 1, pp. 293–304.

Osborn, M. and McNess, E. (2002) 'Teachers, creativity and the curriculum: a cross-cultural perspective', *Education Review*, 15, 2, pp. 28–34.

Pagano, J.A. (1983) 'Moral fictions', paper presented at the Annual Meeting of the American Educational Research Association, Montreal.

—— (1990) *Exiles and communities: Teaching in the patriarchal wilderness*, Albany, NY: State University of New York Press.

—— (1992) 'Women and education: In what ways does gender affect the educational process?', in Kincheloe, J. and Steinberg, S. (eds), *Thirteen Questions*, New York: Lang.

Paige, R. (2006) 'No child left behind: the ongoing movement for Public Education reform', *Harvard Educational Review*, 76, 4, pp. 461–73.

Painter, B. (2001) 'Using teaching portfolios', *Educational Leadership*, 58, 5, pp. 31–34.

Paris, S.G. and Ayres, L.R. (1994) *Becoming reflective students and teachers with portfolios and authentic assessment*, Washington, DC: American Psychological Association.

Parker, L. and Stovall, D. (2004) 'Actions following words: critical race theory connects to critical pedagogy', *Educational Philosophy and Theory*, 36, 2, pp. 169–82.

Parker, S. (1997) *Reflective Teaching in the Postmodern World*, Buckingham: Open University Press.

Parkes, R.J. (2006) 'School history as postcolonial text: The on-going struggle for histories in the New South Wales Curriculum', paper presented at the Second World Curriculum Conference, Tampere, Finland, May.

Passow, A.H. (1988) 'Whither (or wither)? School reform?', *Educational Administration Quarterly*, 24, 3, pp. 246–56.

Paton, G. (2007) 'Taxpayers foot bill for class sizes of just 18 in Scotland', *Times Educational Supplement*, 15 May, p. 2.

Payne, D.A. (2003) *Applied Educational Assessment*, 2nd edn, Belmont, CA: Wadsworth/Thomson.

Peddie, R. (1995) 'Culture and economic change: The New Zealand school curriculum', in Carter, D. and O'Neill, M. (eds), *Case Studies in Educational Change: An International Perspective*, London: Falmer, pp. 146–56.

Pedulla, J.J. (2003) 'State-mandated testing: What do teachers think?', *Educational Leadership*, 61, 3, pp. 42–49.

Pettit, D. (1984) 'Governing in an equal partnership: The move to school councils', *Education News*, 18, 8, pp. 75–88.

—— (1987) *Schooling at a crossroad, Parent Participation in Victorian Schools*, Melbourne: Ministry of Education.

Phillion, J. (1999) 'Narrative and formalistic approaches to the study of multiculturalism', *Curriculum Inquiry*, 29, 1, pp. 129–48.

Phillips, D.C. (1995) 'The good, the bad and the ugly. The many faces of constructivism, *Educational Researcher*, 24, 7, pp. 5–12.

Pinar, W.F. (1972) 'Working from within', *Educational Leadership*, 29, 4, pp. 329–31.

Pinar, W.F. (ed.) (1974) *Heightened consciousness, cultural revolution, and curriculum theory*, Berkeley, CA: McCutchan.

—— (1975) *Curriculum theorizing: the reconceptualists*, Berkeley, CA: McCutchan.

Pinar, W.F. (1978) 'Notes on the curriculum field', *Educational Researcher*, 7, 8, pp. 5–11.

—— (1980) 'The voyage out: Curriculum as the relationship between the knower and the known', *Journal of Curriculum Theorizing*, 2, 1, pp. 7–11.

—— (1983) 'Curriculum as gender text: Notes on reproduction, resistance, and male-made relations', *Journal of Curriculum Theorizing*, 5, 1, pp. 26–52.

—— (1994) *Autobiography, Politics and Sexuality: Essays in Curriculum Theory*, 1972–92, New York: Peter Lang.

—— (1997) 'Regimes of reason and male narrative voice', in Gierney, W.G. and Lincoln, Y.S. (eds), *Representation and the Text: Reframing the Narrative Voice*, Albany, State University of New York Press.

—— (1999) 'Not burdens – breakthroughs', *Curriculum Inquiry*, 23, 3, pp. 365–67.

—— (2000) 'Strange fruit: Race, sex and an autobiographics of alternity', paper presented at the Annual Meeting of the American Educational Research Association, New Orleans.

—— (2004) *What is curriculum theory?*, Mahwah, NJ: Lawrence Erlbaum.

—— (2008) 'Curriculum theory since 1950: Crisis, reconceptualization internationalization', in F.M. Connolly (ed.), *The Sage Handbook of curriculum and instruction*, Los Angeles, CA: Sage.

—— (ed.) (2003) *International handbook of curriculum research*, Mahwah, NJ: Lawrence Erlbaum.

Pinar, W.F. and Grumet, M. (1976) *Toward a poor curriculum*, Dubuque, IA: Kendall/Hunt.

Pinar, W.F., Reynolds, W.M., Slattery, P. and Taubman, P.M. (1995) *Understanding curriculum*, New York: Lang.

Piper, K. (1976) *Evaluation and the Social Sciences*, Canberra: AGPS.

Plitt, B. (2004) 'Teacher dilemmas in a time of standards and testing', *Phi Delta Kappan*, 85, 10, pp. 745–49.

Pomerantz, E.M., Moorman, E.A. and Litwack, S.D. (2007) 'The how, whom and why of parents' involvement in children's academic lives', *Review of Educational Research*, 77, 3, pp. 373–410.

Poole, C.H. (2004) 'Plagiarism and the online student: what is happening and what can be done?', *Journal of Instruction Delivery Systems*, 18, 2, pp. 11–14.

Poole, M. (1992) (ed.), *Education and Work*, Melbourne: ACER.

Popham, W.J. (1995) *Classroom Assessment: What Teachers Need to Know*, Boston, MA: Allyn and Bacon.

Poppleton, P. (2000) 'Receptiveness and resistance to education change. Experiences of English teachers in the 1990s', paper presented at the Annual Conference of the American Educational Research Association, New Orleans.

Portelli, J.P. (1987) 'On defining curriculum', *Journal of Curriculum and Supervision*, 2, 4, pp. 354–67.

Porter, A.C. (1993) 'School delivery standards', *Educational Researcher*, 22, 5, pp. 24–30.

Porter, A.C., Youngs, P. and Odden, A. (2000) 'Advances in teacher assessments and their uses', in Richardson, V. (ed.), *Handbook of Research on Teaching*, 4th edn, Chicago, IL: McNally.

Porter, P. (1994) 'Women and Leadership in Education', *Occasional Paper No. 23*, Canberra: Australian College of Education.

Posner, G.F. (1982) 'A cognitive science conception of curriculum and instruction', *Journal of Curriculum Studies*, 14, 4, pp. 343–51.

—— (1998) 'Models of curriculum planning', in L.E. Beyer and M.W. Apple (eds), *The curriculum: Problems, politics, and possibilities*, Albany, NY: State University of New York Press.

Postman, N. and Weingartner, C. (1987) *Teaching as a Subversive Activity*, New York: Dell.

Power, S. and Clark, A. (2000) 'The right to know: Parents, school reports and parents' evenings', *Research Papers in Education*, 15, 1, pp. 25–48.

Power, S. and Whitty, G. (1999) 'New Labours' education policy: first second or third way?', *Journal of Education Policy*, 14, 5, pp. 535–46.

Prawat, R.S. (2000) 'The two faces of Deweyan pragmatism: Inductionism versus social constructivism', *Teachers College Record*, 102, 4, pp. 805–40.

Preiss, A. (1992) 'Teacher appraisal', *EQ Education Quarterly*, May, 5, pp. 4–8.

Presseisen, B.Z. (1989) *Unlearned Lessons: Current and Past Reforms for School Improvement*, London: Falmer Press.

Price, B. (1991) *School Industry Links*, Melbourne: ACER.

Price, J.N. (2001) 'Action research, pedagogy and change', *Journal of Curriculum Studies*, 33 1, pp. 43–74.

Price, J.N. and Vallie, L. (2000) 'Becoming agents of change: Cases from preservice teacher education', paper presented at the Annual Meeting of the American Educational Research Association, New Orleans.

Priestley, M. and Sime, D. (2005) 'Formative assessment for all: A whole-school approach to pedagogic change', *Curriculum Journal*, 16, 4, pp. 475–92.

Pryor, J. and Torrance, H. (1996) 'Teacher–pupil interaction in formative assessment: Assessing the work or protecting the child?', *Curriculum Journal*, 7, 2, pp. 205–26.

Qualifications & Curriculum Authority (2007) http://www.qca.org.uk/14–19/11–16-schools/110_112.htm (extracted 9 October 2007).

Quellmalz, E.S. and Kozma, R. (2003) 'Designing assessments of learning with technology', *Assessment in Education*, 10, 3, 391–408.

Raikes, N. and Harding, R. (2003) 'The Horseless Carriage Stage: Replacing conventional measures', *Assessment in Education*, 10, 3, pp. 267–77.

Ramsay, P., Harold, B. Hill, D., Lang, C. and Yates, R. (1995) *Final report of the SBCD project*, Hamilton: University of Waikato.

Rapaport, W.J. and Kibby, M.W. (2003) 'Contextual vocabulary acquisition: From algorithm to curriculum', *KIMAS*, 1–3 October, pp. 306–11.

Ray, H. (1992) *Summary of Mainstream Amplification Resource Room Study (MARRS) Adoption Data Validated in 1992*, Norris City, IL, Wabash and Ohio Special Education District.

Reay, D. (1999) 'Linguistic capital and home-school relationships: Mothers' interactions with their children's primary school teachers', *Acta Sociological*, 42, pp. 159–68.

Rees, N.S. and Johnson, K. (2000) 'A lesson in smaller class sizes', *Heritage Views* 2000 (Online). Available: www.heritage.org/views/2000/ed053000.html.

Reichman, J. and Healey, W. (1993) 'Learning disabilities and conductive hearing loss involving otitis media', *Journal of Learning Disabilities*, 16, pp. 272–78.

Reid, A. (1992) '"Accountability" and education: The great profile debate', *Curriculum Perspectives*, 12, 1, pp. 55–56.

—— (2005) 'The politics of national curriculum collaboration: how can Australia move beyond the railway gauge metaphor', in C. Harris and C.J. Marsh (eds), *Curriculum development in Australia*, Adelaide: Open Books.

—— (2007) 'Curriculum, capabilities and nation building', *EQ Australia*, spring, pp. 8–9.

Reid, W.A. (1993) 'Does Schwab improve on Tyler? A response to Jackson', *Journal of Curriculum Studies*, 25, 6, pp. 499–510.

—— (1999a) *Curriculum as Institution and Practice*, Mahwah, NJ: Lawrence Erlbaum.

—— (1999b) 'The voice of the practical: Schwab as correspondent', *Journal of Curriculum Studies*, 31, 4, pp. 385–97.

—— (2000) 'Why globalisation may cause fundamental curriculum change: A theoretical framework', paper presented at the Annual Meeting of the American Educational Research Association, New Orleans.

Resnick, L. and Tucker, M. (1992) *The New Standards Project*, Pittsburgh, PA: University of Pittsburgh Press.

Resnick, L.B. and Klopfer, L.E. (1989) (eds), *Toward the thinking curriculum: Current cognitive research*, Alexandria, VA: ASCD.

Reynolds, W.M. (2003) *Curriculum: A river runs through it*, New York: Peter Lang.

Reynolds, W.M. and Webber, J.A. (eds) (2004) *Expanding curriculum theory: Dis/positions and lines of flight*, Mahwah, NJ: Lawrence Erlbaum.

Rhedding-Jones, J. (1995) 'What do you do after you've met poststructuralism?', *Journal of Curriculum Studies*, 27, 5, pp. 479–500.

Rhodes, C. and Brundrett, M. (2006) 'The identification, development, succession and retention of leadership talent in contextually different primary schools: A case study located within the English West Midlands', *School Leadership and Management*, 26, 3, pp. 269–87.

Ribbins, P. (1992) *Delivering the National Curriculum: Subjects for Secondary Schooling*, London: Longman.

Rich, D. (1998) 'What parents want from teachers', *Educational Leadership*, 55, 8, pp. 37–39.

Richards, R. (1994) 'Teacher review in the Australian Capital Territory', in Ingvarson, L. and Chadbourne, R. (eds), *Valuing Teachers' Work: New Directions in Teacher Appraisal*, Melbourne: ACER.

Richardson, T. and Villenas, S. (2000) 'Other encounters: Dances with whiteness in multicultural education', *Educational Theory*, 50, 2, pp. 255–73.

Ridgway, J. and McCusker, S. (2003) 'Using computers to assess new educational goals', *Assessment in Education*, 10, 3, pp. 309–28.

Riley, K. and Macbeath, J. (2000) 'Quality assurance "Effectiveness " indicators & support systems: Putting self-evaluation in place', www1.worldbank.org/education/ est/resources/Training&presentations/SelfEvaluation – retrieved 4 September 2008.

Ritchie, S.M., Tobin, K., Wolff-Michael, R. and Carambo, C. (2007) 'Transforming an academy through the enactment of collective curriculum leadership', *Journal of Curriculum Studies*, 39, 2, pp. 151–75.

Rizvi, F., Lingard, B. and Lavia, J. (2006) 'Postcolonialism and education: Negotiating a contested terrain', Pedagogy, *Culture and Society*, 14, 3, pp. 249–62.

Robertson, H.J. (1992) 'Teacher development and gender equity', in Hargreaves, A. and Fullan, M.G. (eds), *Understanding Teacher Development*, New York: Teachers College Press.

Rogan, J. and Luckowski, J. (1990) 'Curriculum tests: The portrayal of the field, Part 1', *Journal of Curriculum Studies*, 22, 1, pp. 17–39.

Rogers, E.M. (1983) *Diffusion of Innovations*, 3rd edn, New York: Free Press.

Rogers, G. and Badham, L. (1992) *Evaluation in Schools*, London: Routledge.

Roitman, D.B. and Mayer, J.P. (1982) 'Fidelity and re-invention in the implementation of innovations', paper presented at the Annual Meeting of the American Psychological Association, Washington, DC.

Romer, T.A. (2003) 'Learning and assessment in postmodern education', *Education Theory*, 53, 3, pp. 313–27.

Rorty, R. (1990) 'The dangers of over-philosphication, reply to Arcilla and Nicholson', Educational Theory, 40, 1, pp. 43–47.

Rosenau, F.S. (1973) *Tactics for the Educational Change Agent*, San Francisco, CA: Far West Laboratory.

—— (1993) 'Factors for the educational change agent', San Francisco, CA: Far West Laboratory.

Rosenfeld, A. (1999) 'Natural light lets students work better', *The Weekend Australian*, 23 October, p.16.

Rosenholtz, S. (1989) *Teacher's Workplace: The Social Organisation of Schools*, New York: Longman.

Rosenholtz, S.J. (1991) *Teacher's Workplace: The Social Organization of Schools*, New York: Teachers College Press.

Ross, A. (2000) 'Curriculum studies and critique', London: Falmer.

Ross, R.P. (1982) 'The design of educational environment: An expression of individual differences or evidence of the "press toward synomorphy?"', paper presented at the Annual Meeting of the American Educational Research Association, New York.

Rossi, P.H. and Freeman, H.E. (1993) *Evaluation: A Systematic Approach*, San Francisco, CA: Sage.

Rothstein, R., Wilder, T. and Jacobsen, R. (2007) 'Balance in the balance', *Educational Leadership*, 64, 8, pp. 8–15.

Rottmann, C. (2006) 'Querying *Educational Leadership* from the inside out', *International Journal of Leadership in Educational*, 9, 1, pp. 1–20.

Rudduck, J. and Hopkins, D. (eds) (1985) *Research as a basis for teaching*, London: Heinemann Educational Books.

Rudduck, J. and Kelly, P. (1976) *The dissemination of curriculum development*, Windsor: National Foundation for Educational Research.

Rusch, E.A. and Marshall, C. (2006) 'Gender filters and leadership: Plotting a course to equity', *International Journal of Leadership in Education*, 9, 3, pp. 229–50.

Russell, G. and Bradley, G. (1996) 'Computer anxiety and student teachers: Antecedent and intervention', *Asia–Pacific Journal of Teacher Education*, 24, 3, pp. 245–57.

Russell, M., Goldberg, A. and O'Connor, K. (2003) 'Computer-based testing and validity: A look back into the future', *Assessment in Education*, 10, 3, pp. 279–93.

Rutherford, D. and Jackson, L. (2006) 'Setting up school partnerships: some insights from Birmingham's Collegiate Academies', *School Leadership and Management*, 26, 5, pp. 437–51.

Ryan, J. (2006) 'Inclusive leadership and social justice for schools', *Leadership and Policy in Schools*, 5, 1, pp. 3–17.

Ryan, K. and Cooper, J. (2006) *Those who can, teach*, 9th edn, Boston, MA: Houghton Mifflin.

Sabar, N. (1983) 'Towards school-based curriculum development: training school curriculum coordinators', *Journal of Curriculum Studies*, 15, 4, pp. 15–28.

Salvia, J. and Ysseldyke, J.E. (1998) *Assessment*, 7th edn, Boston, MA: Houghton Mifflin.

Samuel, G. (1987) 'An establish appraisal scheme', in Bunnell, S. (ed.), *Teacher Appraisal in Practice*, London: Heinemann.

Sandholtz, J.H., Ogawa, R.T. and Scribner, S.P. (2002) 'A standard gap: the unintended consequences of local standards for assessment, curriculum and instruction', paper presented at the Annual Meeting of the American Educational Research Association, New Orleans.

Santrock, J.W. (1976) 'Affect and facilitative self-control: Influence of ecological setting, cognition and social agent', *Journal of Educational Psychology*, 68, 5, pp. 529–35.

Sarason, S.B. (1990) *The Predictable Failure of Educational Reform*, San Francisco, CA: Jossey-Bass.

Sattler, C.L. (1997) *Talking about a revolution: the politics and practice of feminist teaching*, Cresskill, NJ: Hampton Press.

Saylor, J.G., Alexander, W.M. and Lewis, A.J. (1981) *Curriculum Planning for Better Teaching and Learning*, 4th edn, New York: Holt, Rinehart and Winston.

Scherer, M. (1998) 'The shelter of each other: A conversation with Mary Papper', *Educational Leadership*, 55, 8, pp. 6–11.

Schiller, K.S. and Muller, C. (2000) 'External examinations and accountability: Educational expectations and high school graduation', *American Journal of Education*, 108, February, pp. 73–77.

Schmidt, W.H., Valverde, G.A., Houang, R.T., Wiley, D.E., Wolfe, R.G. and Bianchi, L.J. (1996) 'Studying the intended, implemented and attained curriculum: Strategies for measurement and analysis in large-scale international research', paper presented at the annual meeting of the American Educational Research Association, New York.

Schmoker, M. and Marzano, R.J. (1999) 'Realizing the promise of standards-based education', *Educational Leadership*, 56, 6, pp. 17–21.

Schofield, J.W. and Davidson, A.L. (2000) 'Internet use and teacher change', paper presented at the Annual Meeting of the American Education Research Association, New Orleans.

Schon, D.A. (1983) *The reflective practitioner*, New York: Basic Books.

—— (1987) *Educating the Reflective Practitioner*, San Francisco, CA: Jossey-Bass.

Schubert, W.H. (1986) *Curriculum: Perspective, Paradigm, and Possibility*, New York: Macmillan.

—— (1991) 'Teacher lore: A basis for understanding praxis', in C. Witherall and N. Noddings (eds), *Stories lives tell: Narrative and dialogue in education*, New York: Teachers College Press.

—— (1992) 'Practitioners influence curriculum theory: Autobiographical reflections', *Theory into Practice*, 31, 3, pp. 236–44.

Schubert, W.H., Schubert, A.L., Thomas, T.P. and Waroll, W.M. (2002) *Curriculum Books: The first hundred years*, 2nd edn, New York: Peter Lang.

Schutz, A. (2004) 'Rethinking domination and resistance: Challenging postmodernism', *Educational Researcher*, 33, 1, pp. 15–23.

Schwab, J.J. (1950) 'Criteria for the evaluation of achievement tests: From the point of view of the subject-matter specialist', in *Proceedings of the Educational Testing Service Invitational Conference on Testing Problems*, Princeton, NJ: Educational Testing Service.

—— (1969) 'The practical: A language for curriculum', *School Review*, 78, 1, pp. 1–23.

—— (1970) *The Practical: A Language for Curriculum*, Washington, DC: National Education Association.

Schwartz, G. (1996) 'The rhetoric of cyberspace and the real curriculum', *Journal of Curriculum and Supervision*, 9, 4, pp. 326–28.

Scott, G. (1999) *Change Matters*. Sydney: Allen and Unwin.

Scriven, M. (1967) 'The methodology of evaluation', in R. Tyler, R. Gagné and M. Scriven (eds), *Perspectives on Curriculum Evaluation*, AERA Monograph, Chicago, IL: Rand McNally.

Sears, J. (1992b) 'The second wave of curriculum theorizing: Labyrinths, orthodoxies and other legacies of the glass bead game', *Theory into Practice*, 31, 3, pp. 210–18.

—— (1999) 'Teaching queerly: Some elementary propositions', in Letts, W. J. and Sears, J.T. (eds), *Queering Elementary Education*, Lanham, MD: Rowman and Littlefield.

Sears, J. (ed.) (1992) 'Sexuality and the curriculum', New York: Teachers College Press.

Seashore Louis, K. (2007) *Leadership for change and school reform: international perspectives*, London: Routledge.

Segall, A. (2003) 'Teachers' perceptions of the impact of state-mandated standardized testing: the Michigan Educational Assessment Program (MEAP) as a case study of consequences' *Theory and Research in Social Education*, 31,3, pp. 287–325

Seitsinger, A.M. (2005) 'Service-learning and standards-based instruction in middle schools', *Journal of Educational Research*, 99, 1, pp. 19–30.

Seller, W. (2005) 'Schools and school districts in educational reform: examining the space in-between', *Journal of Educational Change*, 6, 1, pp. 1–5.

Sergiovanni, D.T.J. (1998) 'Leadership as pedagogy, capital development and school effectiveness', *International Journal of Leadership in Education*, 1, 1, pp. 37–46.

Shakeshaft, C., Nowell, I. and Perry, A. (1991) 'Gender and supervision', *Theory into Practice*, 30, 2, pp. 134–39.

Shanmugaratnam, T. (2006) 'Opening address', *Work Plan Seminar*, Singapore, September.

Sheldon, S.B. (2002) 'Parents' social networks and beliefs as predictors of parent invol-vement', *The Elementary School Journal*, 102, 4, pp. 301–22.

Shore, Z.L. (2001) 'Girls learning, women teaching: Dancing to different drummers', *Education Studies*, 31, 2, pp. 132–45.

Shulman, L. (1994) 'Portfolios in historical perspective', paper presented at the Portfolio Conference, Cambridge, MA: Radcliffe College.

Simkins, M., Cole, K., Tavalin, F. and Mwans, B. (2002) *Increasing Student Learning through Multimedia Projects*, Alexandria, VA: ASCD.

Simmons, W. and Resnick, L. (1993) 'Assessment as the catalyst of school reform', *Educational Leadership*, 50, 5, pp. 11–15.

Simons, H. (1987) *Getting to Know Schools in a Democracy: The Politics and Process of Evaluation*, London: Falmer Press.

Simpson, G.W. (1990) 'Keeping it alive: Elements of school culture that sustain inno-vation', *Educational Leadership*, 47, 8, pp. 34–37.

Sirotnik, K.A. and Kimball, K. (1999) 'Standards for standards-based accountability systems', *Phi Delta Kappan*, 81, 3, pp. 209–15.

Sizer, T. (1989) 'Diverse practice, shared ideas: The essential school', in Walberg, H. and Lane, J.J. (eds), *Organising for Learning: Toward the 21st Century*, Reston, VA: National Association of Secondary School Principals.

—— (1992) *Horace's School*, New York: Houghton Mifflin.

Skilbeck, M. (1976) 'School-based curriculum development', in J. Walton and J. Welton (eds), *Rational curriculum planning: Four case studies*, London: Ward Lock.

—— (1990) *School-based curriculum development*, London: Paul Chapman.

Slack, N. and Norwich, B. (2007) 'Evaluating the reliability and validity of a learning styles inventory: a classroom-based study', *Educational Research*, 49, 1, pp. 51–63.

Slater, B. (1968) 'Effects of noise on pupil performance', *Journal of Educational Psy-chology*, 59, 3, pp. 87–94.

Slattery, P. (1995) 'Curriculum development in the postmodern era', New York: Garland.

Slavin, R.E. (1999) *Success for All: how replicable reform models can save America's schools*, Baltimore, MD: Johns Hopkins University.

—— (2001) 'Putting the school back in school reform', *Educational Leadership*, 58, 4, pp. 22–27.

Slavin, R.E. and Madden, N.A. (2001) (eds), *One million children: success for all*, Mahwah, NJ: Lawrence Erlbaum.

Sloan, D. (1993) *Insight-imagination: The Recovery of Thought in the Modern World*, New York: Teachers College Press.

Smith, D. and Lovat, T.J. (2003) *Curriculum: Action on Reflection*, 4th edn, Sydney: Social Science Press.

Smith, J. (2004) 'Gender and schooling', in Marsh, C. (ed.), *Teaching Studies of Society and Environment*, 4th edn, Sydney: Pearson.

Smyth, J. (1994) (ed.) *A Socially Critical View of the Self-managing School*, London: Falmer Press.

—— (2006) 'The politics of reform of teachers' work and the consequences for schools: some implications for teacher education', *Asia-Pacific Journal of Teacher Education*, 34, 3, pp. 301–19.

Smyth, J. (ed.) (1989) *Critical perspectives of Educational Leadership*, London: Falmer Press.

Smyth, J. and Shacklock, G. (1998) *Remaking Teaching: Ideology, Policy and Practice*, London: Routledge.

Soder, R. (1999) 'When words find their meaning: Renewal versus reform', *Phi Delta Kappan*, 80, 8, pp. 568–70.

Soltis, J.F. (1978) *An Introduction to the Analysis of Educational Concepts*, Reading, MA: Addison-Wesley.

Southworth, G. (2000) 'School leadership in English schools at the close of the twentieth century: Puzzles, problems and cultural insights', paper presented at the Annual Conference of the American Educational Research Association, New Orleans.

Southworth, G. and Doughty, J. (2006) 'A fine British blend', *Educational Leadership*, 63, 8, pp. 51–55.

Spady, W. (1993) *Outcome-based Education*, Workshop Report No. 5, Canberra: ACSA.

Spillane, J.P. (1999) 'External reform initiatives and teachers' efforts to reconstruct their practice', *Journal of Curriculum Studies*, 31, 2, pp. 143–76.

Spillane, J.P., Halverson, R. and Diamond, J.B. (2004) 'Towards a theory of leadership practice: A distributed perspective', *Journal of Curriculum Studies*, 36, 1, pp. 3–34.

Spillane, J.P., Reiser, B. and Reimer, T. (2002) 'Policy implementation and cognition: Reframing and refocusing implementation research', *Review of Educational Research*, 72, 3, pp. 387–432.

Spivak, G.C. (1985) 'Strategies of vigilance', *Block*, 10, 9, pp. 12–17.

St Pierre, E.A. (2002) '"Science" Rejects Postmodernism', *Educational Researcher*, 31, 8, pp. 25–27.

Stacey, J. (1999) 'Gay and lesbian families are here', in Coontz, S. (ed.), *American Families: A Multicultural Reader*, New York: Routledge.

Starratt, R.J. (1993) *The Drama of Leadership*, London: Falmer Press.

Stengel, B. (1997) '"Academic discipline" and "school subject": Contestable curricular concepts', *Journal of Curriculum Studies*, 29, 5, pp. 585–602.

Stenhouse, L. (1973) 'The Humanities Curriculum Project', in Butcher, H. and Pont, H. (eds), *Educational Research in Britain*, Vol. 3, London: University of London Press.

—— (1975) *An introduction to curriculum research and development*, London: Heinemann Educational.

—— (1980) (ed.) *Curriculum Research and Development*, London: Heinemann.

Stephens, M. (1997) 'Negotiating the curriculum: The discursive embodiment of gender', paper presented at the Biennial Conference of the Australian Curriculum Studies Association, Sydney.

Stevenson, C. (1998) *Teaching Ten to Fourteen Year Olds*, 2nd edn, New York: Longman.

Stigler, J. and Hiebert, J. (1999) *The teaching gap: Best ideas from the world's teacher for improving education in the classroom*, New York: The Free Press.

Stoll, L. and Fink, D. (1996) *Changing our schools*, London: Open University Press.

Stubbs, B. (1981) 'Pressures on the school curriculum', *Curriculum*, 2, 1, pp. 15–20.

Sukhnandan, L., Lee, B. and Kelleher, S. (2000) *An investigation into gender differences and achievement: Phase 2 school and classroom strategies*, Slough: Slough National Foundation for Educational Research.

Sulla, N. (1998) 'Maximising the effectiveness of external consultants in the educational reform agenda', paper presented at the Annual Conference of the American Educational Research Association, San Diego.

Sumara, D. and Davis, B. (1999) 'Interrupting heteronormativity: Toward a queer curriculum theory', *Curriculum Inquiry*, 29, 2, pp. 191–206.

Swaffield, S. and Macbeath, J. (2005) 'School self-evaluation and the role of the critical friend', *Cambridge Journal of Education*, 35, 2 pp. 239–52.

Swan, W.W. (1998) 'Local school system implementation of state policy actions for educational reform', paper presented at the Annual Meeting of the American Educational Research Association, San Diego.

Swanson, C.B. and Stevenson, D.L. (2002) 'Standards-based reform in practice: Evidence on state policy and classroom instruction from the NAEP State Assessments', *Educational Evaluation and Policy Analysis*, 24, 1, pp. 1–28.

Taba, H. (1962) *Curriculum development: Theory and practice*, New York: Harcourt, Brace, & World.

Tanner, D. and Tanner, L. (1981) 'Emancipation from research: The reconceptualists' prescription', *Educational Researcher* 8, 6, pp. 8–12.

Taras, M. (2005) 'Assessment – summative and formative – some theoretical reflections', *British Journal of Educational Studies*, 53, 4, pp. 466–78.

Teaching and Learning Research Programme (2007) http://www.tlp.org/ (extracted 9 October 2007).

Teaching Australia (2007) *National standards drafting group invitation*, Melbourne: Teaching Australia.

Tell, C. (2001) 'Appreciating good teaching: A conversation with Lee Shulman', *Educational Leadership*, 58, 5, pp. 6–11.

Tessmer, M. and Richey, R.C. (1997) 'The role of context in learning and instructional design', *Educational Technology, Research and Development*, 45, 2, pp. 85–116.

Thiessen, D. (2006) 'Student knowledge, engagement, and voice in educational reform', *Curriculum Inquiry*, 36, 4, pp. 345–58.

Thompson, S. (2001) 'The authentic standards movement and its evil twin, *Phi Delta Kappan*, 85, 5, pp. 358–62.

Thomson, P. and Gunter, H. (2006) 'From "consulting pupils" to "pupils as researchers": a situated case narrative', *British Educational Research Journal*, 32, 6, pp. 839–56.

Thornton, P. (2001) Is it time to review Review?', *The Practising Administrator*, 23, 3, pp. 11–15.

Tikunoff, W.J., Ward, B.A. and Stacey, F. (1978) 'Toward an ecology based curriculum: Professional growth through participatory research and development', in American Association of Teacher Educators (eds), *Breakaway to Multidimensional Approaches: Integrating Curriculum Development and In-Service Education*, Washington, DC: American Association of Teacher Educators.

Tillman, L.C., Brown, K., Campbell Jones, F. and Gonzalez, M. (2006) 'Transformative leadership for social justice: Concluding thoughts', *Journal of School Leadership*, 16 (March), pp. 207–9.

Titman, W. (1997) 'Special places, special people: The hidden curriculum of school grounds', Set 1, 1–4, Winchester, United Kingdom. Research paper, Educational Research Unit, University of Winchester.

Tobias, S. and Duchastel, P. (1974) 'Behavioural objectives, sequence and anxiety in CAI', *Instructional Science*, 3, 2, pp. 232–42.

Tomlinson, C.A. and Germundson, A. (2007) 'Teaching as jazz', *Educational Leadership*, 64, 8, pp. 27–31.

Tomlinson, C.A. (1999) *The differentiated classroom*, Alexandria, VA: ASCD.

—— (2002) 'Invitations to learn', *Educational Leadership*, 60, 1, pp. 6–11.

—— (2005) *How to differentiate instruction in mixed classes*, Alexandria, VA: ASCD.

Tomlinson, C.A. and Kalbfleisch, M.L. (1998) 'Teach me, teach my brain', *Educational Leadership*, 56, 3, pp. 53–55.

Toombs, W.E. and Tierney, W.G. (1993) 'Curriculum definitions and reference points', *Journal of Curriculum and Supervision*, 8, 3, pp. 175–95.

Torrance, H. and Pryor, J. (1995) 'Making sense of "formative assessment": Investigating the integration of assessment with teaching and learning', paper presented at the Annual Meeting of the American Educational Research Association, San Francisco.

Townsend, T. (1999) 'Public and private schools – new priorities and practices?', *Curriculum Perspectives*, 99, 1, pp. 58–64.

Trepanier-Steet, M.L., Mcnair, S. and Donegan, M.M. (2001) 'The views of teachers on assessment: A comparison of lower and upper elementary teachers', *Journal of Research in Childhood Education*, 15, 2, pp. 234–41.

Tripp, D.H. (1987) 'Action research and professional development', in Hughes, P. (ed.), *Better Teachers for Better Schools*, Melbourne: Australian College of Education.

Tucker, M.S. and Godding, J.B. (1998) *Standards for our schools*, San Francisco, CA: Jossey-Bass.

Tucker, P. (2001) 'Helping struggling teachers', *Educational Leadership*, 58, 5, pp. 52–56.

Tunstall, P. and Gipps, C. (1996) '"How does your teacher help you to make your work better?" Children's understanding of formative assessment', *The Curriculum Journal*, 7, 2, pp. 185–203.

Twomey, S. (2005) 'Contingent conditions of change: An exploration of feminist theatre practice', *Alberta Journal of Educational Research*, 51, 4, pp. 354–67.

Tyack, D. and Cuban, L. (1995) *Tinkering towards utopia: a century of public reform*, Cambridge, MA: Harvard University Press.

Tyack, D. and Hansot, E. (1990) *Learning Together: A History of Coeducation in American Schools*, New Haven, CT: Yale University Press.

Tyler, R.W. (1949) *Basic principles of curriculum and instruction*, Chicago, IL: University of Chicago Press.

United States Environmental Protection Agency (2006) 'Healthy school environments', http://www.epa.gov/schools/ (extracted 25 April 2006).

US Department of Education (2002) *Elementary and secondary education: No Child Left Behind Act*, Washington, DC: US Department of Education.

US Environmental protection Agency (2006) *Air pollution and cardio-vascular disease*, Washington, DC: EPA.

Vallance, E. (1982) 'The practical uses of curriculum theory', *Theory into Practice*, 21, 1, pp. 4–10.

—— (1986) 'A second look at conflicting conceptions of curriculum', *Theory into Practice*, 25, 1, pp. 24–30.

Van Den Berg, R. (1993) 'The concerns-based adoption model in the Netherlands, Flanders, and the United Kingdom: State of the art and perspective', *Studies in Educational Evaluation*, 19, pp. 51–63.

—— (2002) 'Teachers' meanings regarding educational practice', *Review of Educational Research*, 72, 4, pp. 577–626.

Van Dervegt, S. and Vandenberghe, H. (1992) 'Schools implementing a central reform policy: Findings from two national educational contexts', paper presented at the Annual Meeting of the American Educational Research Association, San Francisco.

Van Manen, M. (1977) 'Linking ways of knowing with ways of being practical', *Curriculum Inquiry*, 6, 3, pp. 205–28.

—— (1978) 'Reconceptualist curriculum thought: A review of recent literature', *Curriculum Inquiry*, 8, 4, pp. 365–74.

—— (1980) 'Pedagogical theorizing', paper presented at the Annual Meeting of the American Educational Research Association, Boston.

—— (1990) *Researching lived experience*, Albany, NY: State University of New York Press.

—— (2000) 'Moral language and pedagogical experience', *Journal of Curriculum Studies*, 32, 2, pp. 315–27.

Vandenberghe, R. (1983) 'Studying change in the primary and secondary schools of Belgium and the Netherlands', paper presented at the Annual Meeting of the American Educational Research Association, Montreal.

Vanhoof, J. and Van Petegem, P. (2007) 'Matching internal and external evaluation in an era of accountability and school development: lessons from a Flemish perspective', *Studies in Educational Evaluation*, 33, 2, pp. 101–19.

Vanterpool, M. (1990) 'Innovations aren't for everyone', *Principal*, 69, 4, pp. 38–43.

Varnham, S. (2001) 'Conduct unbecoming: the dilemma of a school's responsibility in respect of teacher misconduct towards pupils', *Education and the Law*, 13, 2, pp. 109–23.

Vaughan, W. (2002) 'Professional development and the adoption and implementation of new innovations: Do teacher concerns matter?', *International Electronic Journal for Leadership in Learning*, 6, 5, pp. 1–24.

Vick, M. (1994) 'Parents, schools and democracy', *Education Australia*, 28, pp. 11–13.

Vidovich, L. (2004) 'Re-activating democracy in curriculum policies and practices in globalising new times', *Curriculum Perspectives*, 24, 3, pp. 61–68.

Villenas, S. and Deyhle, D. (1999) 'Critical race theory and ethnographics challenging the stereotypes: Latino families, schooling, resilience and resistance', *Curriculum Inquiry*, 29, 4, pp. 416–43.

Vine, K., Brown, T. and Clark, G. (2000) 'Which way for information technology in our schools?', *The School Principal's Handbook Series*, pp. 5–8.

Visscher, A.J. (2001) 'Public school performance indicators: Problems and recommendations', *Studies in Educational Evaluation*, 27, pp. 199–214.

Von Glaserfield, T. (1995) *Radical Constructivism: A Way of Knowing and Learning*, London: Falmer Press.

Waks, L.J. (2006) 'Globalization, state transformation and educational re-structuring: Why postmodern diversity will prevail over standardization', *Studies in Philosophy of Education*, 25, 2, pp. 403–24.

Walker, D.F. (1971) 'A naturalistic model of curriculum development', *School Review*, 80, 1, pp. 51–65.

—— (1980) 'A barnstorming tour of writing on curriculum', in Foshay, A.W. (ed.), *Considered Action for Curriculum Development*, Washington, DC: Association for Supervision and Curriculum Development.

—— (1990) *Fundamentals of Curriculum*, New York: Harcourt Brace Jovanovich.

—— (2003) *Fundamentals of Curriculum*, 2nd edn, Mahwah, NJ: Lawrence Erlbaum.

Walker, D.F. and Soltis, J. (2004) *Thinking about curriculum: Curriculum and aims*, New York: Teachers College Press.

Walker, J. (1994) *Competency-based Teacher Education: Implications for Quality in Higher Education*, II. Canberra, Higher Education Research Conference.

Walker, R. and Kushner, S. (1991) 'Theorizing a curriculum', in Goodson, I.F. and Walker, R. (eds), *Biography, Identity and Schooling: Episodes in Educational Research*, London: Falmer Press.

Wallace, M. (1987) 'A historical review of action research: Some implications for the education of teachers in their managerial role', *Journal of Education for Teaching*, 13, 2, pp. 97–116.

Wallace, M. and Hoyle, E. (2005) 'Towards effective management of a reformed teaching profession', paper presented at the Fourth Seminar of the Economic and Social Research Council (ESRC), Kings College, London.

Warrican, S.J. (2006) 'Action research: a viable option for effecting change', *Journal of Curriculum Studies*, 38, 1, pp. 1–14.

Watanabe, T. (2002) 'Learning from Japanese lesson study', *Educational Leadership*, 59, 6, pp. 36–39.

Watkins, W.H. (1993) 'Black curriculum orientations: A preliminary inquiry', *Curriculum Inquiry*, 63, 3, pp. 321–38.

Watt, M. (2000) 'The National Education Agenda, 1916–99: Its impact on curriculum reform in the states and territories', *Curriculum Perspectives*, 20, 3, pp. 25–38.

Watt, M.G. (1998) 'National curriculum collaboration: The state of reform in the states and territories', *Curriculum Perspectives*, 18, 1, pp. 21–34.

Webb, R. and Vulliamy, G. (2006) *Roles and responsibilities in the primary school: changing demands, changing practices*, Buckingham: Open University Press.

Webb, R., Vulliamy, G., Sarga, A. and Hamalainen, S. (2006) 'Globalization and leadership and management: A comparative analysis of primary schools in England and Finland', *Research Papers in Education*, 21, 4, pp. 407–32.

Weinstein, C.S. and Weinstein, N.D. (1979) 'Noise and reading performance in an open space school', *Journal of Educational Research*, 72, 4, pp. 210–13.

Weiss, S. and Wesley, K. (2007) 'Postmodernism and its critics', http://www.as.ua.edu/ant/Faculty/murphy/436/pomo.htm (extracted 19 October 2007).

Wells, A.S. (1999) 'Charter school reform in California: Does it meet expectations?', *Phi Delta Kappan*, 80, 4, pp. 305–12.

Wells, A.S., Lopez, A., Scott, J. and Holme, J.J. (1999) 'Charter schools as postmodern paradox: Rethinking social stratifications in an age of deregulated choice', *Harvard Educational Review*, 69, 2, pp. 172–90.

Wells, J.G. and Anderson, D.K. (1997) 'Learners in a telecommunication course: Adoption, diffusion, and stages of concern', *Journal of Research on Computing in Education*, 30, 1, pp. 83–105.

Wenbergren, A. and Ronnerman, K. (2006) 'The relation between tools used in action research and the zone of proximal development', *Educational Action Research*, 14, 4, pp. 547–68.

Westbury, I. (2000) 'Why globalization will not cause fundamental curriculum change', paper presented at the Annual Meeting of the American Educational Research Association, New Orleans.

—— (2007) 'Making curricula: why do states make curricula, and how?', in F.M. Connelley, M.F. He and J. Phillion (eds), *Handbook of curriculum and instruction*, Thousand Oaks, CA: Sage.

—— (2008) 'Making curricula: Why do states make curricula and how?', in F.M. Connolly (ed.), *The Sage handbook of curriculum and instruction*, Los Angeles, CA: Sage.

Whitehead, A.N. (1929) *The aims of education*, New York: Macmillan.

Whitty, G. (1994) 'Deprofessionalising Teaching?', Occasional Paper No. 22, Canberra: Australian College of Education.

—— (1995) 'School-based management and a National Curriculum: Sensible compromise or dangerous cocktail?', paper presented at the Annual Conference of the American Educational Research Association, San Francisco.

Wideen, M.F. (1994) *The Struggle for Change*, London: Falmer Press.

Wiegand, P. and Rayner, M. (eds) (1989) *Curriculum Progress 5–16: School Subjects and the National Curriculum Debate*, London: Falmer Press.

Wiggins, G. (1998) *Educative Assessment*, San Francisco, CA: Jossey-Bass.

Wiggins, G. and McTighe, J. (1998) *Understanding by Design*, Alexandria, VA: ASCD.

Wilcox, B. (1992) *Time-Constrained Evaluation*, London: Routledge.

Wildy, H., Louden, W. and Robertson, J. (2000) 'Using case studies for school principal performance standards: Australian and New Zealand experiences', paper presented at the Annual Meeting of the American Educational Research Association, New Orleans.

Wiliam, D. (2003) 'National curriculum assessment: How to make it better', *Research Papers in Education*, 18, 2, pp. 129–36.

Williams, M. (2000) 'Connecting teachers to the Dot. Com world', *EQ 2*, Winter, 9–11.

Williams, R. (2001) 'Automated essay grading: An evaluation of four conceptual models', unpublished paper, Perth, Curtin University.

Willingham, W.W. and Cole, N.S. (1997) *Gender and Fair Assessment*, Mahwah, NJ: Lawrence Erlbaum.

Willis, G. (1979) 'Phenomenological methodologies in curriculum', *Journal of Curriculum Theorizing*, 1, 1, pp. 65–79.

—— (1981) 'A reconceptualist perspective on curriculum theorizing', *Journal of Curriculum Theorizing*, 3, 1, pp. 185–92.

Willis, G. (ed.) (1978) *Qualitative evaluation: Concepts and cases in curriculum criticism*, Berkeley, CA: McCutchan.

Willis, G. and Schubert, W.H. (eds) (1991) *Reflections from the heart of educational inquiry: Understanding Curriculum and Teaching through the arts*, Albany, NY: State University of New York Press.

Willis, S. (1991) 'A national statement on mathematics for Australian schools: Some background', unpublished paper, Canberra.

Willis, S. and Kissane, B. (1997) *Achieving Outcome-Based Education*, Canberra: ACSA.

Willmott, G. (1994) 'National collaborative curriculum development: Statements and profiles and senior secondary education', *Curriculum Perspectives*, 14, 1, pp. 52–56.

Wilson, B. (2002) 'Curriculum – is less more?', paper presented at the Curriculum Corporation Conference, Canberra.

—— (2006) 'A national and international perspective', address given at the Australian Curriculum Studies Association Invitational Symposium, Melbourne: August.

Winter, B. (2006) 'Teachers' appraisal doubt', *BBC Homepage*, 1–10.

Winter, R. (1989) *Learning from Experience: Principles and Practice in Action Research*, London: Falmer Press.

Wise, A.E. (2000) 'Creating a high quality teaching force', *Educational Leadership*, 58, 4, pp. 18–21.

Withers, G. and McCurry, D. (1990) 'Student participation in assessment in a cooperative climate', in Low, B. and Withers, G. (eds), *Developments in School and Public Assessment*, Melbourne: ACER.

Witkin, H.A., Moore, C.A., Goodenough, D.R. and Cox, P.W. (1977) 'Fielddependent and field-independent cognitive styles and their ed implications', *Review of Educational Research*, 47, pp. 1–64.

Wohlstetter, P., Van Kirk, A.N., Robertson, P.J. and Mohrman, S. (1997) *Organising for successful school-based management*, Eric Ed 413655.

Woods, A. (2007) 'What's wrong with benchmarks? Answering the wrong questions with the wrong answers', *Curriculum Perspectives*, 27, 3, pp. 1–10.

Woods, P. (1988) 'A strategic view of parent participation', *Journal of Education Policy*, 3, 4, pp. 323–34.

Woods, P.A. (2000) 'Redefining professionality and leadership: Reflexive responses to competitive and regulatory pressures', paper presented at the Annual Conference of the American Educational Research Association, New Orleans.

Woods, P.A., Woods, G. and Gunter, H. (2007) 'Academy schools and entrepreneurialism in education', *Journal of Education Policy*, 22, 2, pp. 237–59.

Wood, R. (1991) *Assessment and Testing*, New York: Cambridge University Press.

Worthen, B.R. and Sanders, J.R. (2003) *Educational evaluation: theory and practice*, Worthington, OH: Jones.

Wraga, W.G. (2002) 'Recovering curriculum practice: Continuing the conversation', *Educational Researcher*, 31, 6, pp. 17–19.

Wragg, E.C. (1987) *Teacher Appraisal: A Practical Guide*, London: Macmillan.

Wragg, T., Haynes, G., Chamberlin, R. and Wragg, C. (2003) 'Performance-related pay: the views and experiences of 1,000 primary and secondary head teachers', *Research Papers in Education*, 18, 1, pp. 3–24.

Wright, H.K. (2000) 'Nailing Jell-O to the wall: Pinpointing aspects of state-of-the-art curriculum theorizing', *Educational Researcher*, 29, 5, pp. 4–13.

Wroe, A. and Halsall, R. (2001) 'School self-evaluation: Measurement and reflection in the school improvement process', *Research in Education*, 65, 5, pp. 41–52.

Yates, L. (1998) 'Feminism's fandar go with the state revisited', paper presented at the Annual Conference of the American Educational Research Association, San Diego.

Yeh, S.S. (2001) 'Tests worth teaching to: Constructing state-mandated tests that emphasize critical thinking', *Educational Researcher*, 30, 9, pp. 12–17.

—— (2006) 'High-stakes testing: Can rapid assessment reduce the pressure?' *Teachers College Record*, 108, 4, pp. 621–61.

Young, M.F.D. (ed.) (1971) *Knowledge and Control*, London: Collier Macmillan.

Younger, M.R. and Warrington, M. (2006) 'Would Harry and Hermione have done better in single-sex classes? A review of single-sex teaching in coeducational secondary schools in the United Kingdom', *American Educational Research Journal*, 43, 4, pp. 579–620.

Yu, H., Leithwood, K. and Jantzi, D. (2002) 'The effects of transformational leadership on teachers' commitment to change in Hong Kong', *Journal of Educational Administration*, 40, 4, pp. 368–89.

Zady, M., Portes, P., Delcastillo, K. and Dunham, R. (1998) 'When low SES parents cannot assist their children', paper presented at the Annual Conference of the American Educational Research Association, San Diego.

Zaltman, G., Florio, D.H. and Sikorski, L.A. (1977) *Dynamic Educational Change*, New York: Free Press.

Zandvliet, D.B. and Fraser, B.J. (2005) 'Physical and psychosocial environments associated with networked classrooms', *Learning Environments Research*, 8, 3, pp. 1–17.

Zeichner, K.M. (1993) 'Action research: Personal renewal and social reconstruction', *Educational Action Research*, 1, pp. 199–219.

Zemylas, M. (2007) 'The power and politics of emotions in teaching', *International Journal of Research and Method in Education*, 3, 4, pp. 62–75.

Index

NB. Numbers in bold type indicate a figure or table.